Normative Readings of the Belt and Road Initiative

Wenhua Shan • Kimmo Nuotio • Kangle Zhang
Editors

Normative Readings of the Belt and Road Initiative

Road to New Paradigms

Springer

Editors
Wenhua Shan
School of Law
Xi'an Jiaotong University
Xi'an, China

Kimmo Nuotio
Faculty of Law
University of Helsinki
Helsinki, Finland

Kangle Zhang
Faculty of Law
University of Helsinki
Helsinki, Finland

ISBN 978-3-030-08601-5 ISBN 978-3-319-78018-4 (eBook)
https://doi.org/10.1007/978-3-319-78018-4

Printed on acid-free paper

This Springer imprint is published by the registered company Springer International Publishing AG part of Springer Nature.
The registered company address is: Gewerbestrasse 11, 6330 Cham, Switzerland

Contents

List of Contributors

Daniele Brombal Department of Asian and North African Studies, University Ca' Foscari Venice, Venice, Italy

Chi He Peking University Law School, Beijing, China

Desheng Hu Law School, Silk Road Institute for International and Comparative Law, Xi'an Jiaotong University, Xi'an, P.R. China

Xueyue Hu Department of Geography and Environment, London School of Economics and Political Science, London, UK

Nicholas Morris Faculty of Law, University of New South Wales, Sydney, NSW, Australia

The Martin School, Oxford, UK

China Executive Leadership Academy, Pudong, P.R. China

Kimmo Nuotio University of Helsinki, Helsinki, Finland

Jun Ou Law School, Xi'an Jiaotong University, Xi'an, P.R. China

Wenhua Shan School of Law, Xi'an Jiaotong University, Xi'an, China

Anastas Vangeli Polish Academy of Sciences, Warsaw, Poland

Guilherme Vasconcelos Vilaça The Erik Castrén Institute of International Law and Human Rights – Helsinki University, Helsinki, Finland

The Collaborative Innovation Centre for Silk Road Economic Belt Studies (CIC-SREBS), Xi'an Jiaotong University, Xi'an, P.R. China

Yongping Xiao International Law Institute, Wuhan University, Wuhan, Hubei Province, P.R. China

Collaborative Innovation Center of Judicial Civilization, China University of Political Science and Law, Wuhan, Hubei Province, P.R. China

Meng Yu Collaborative Innovation Center of Judicial Civilization, China University of Political Science and Law, Beijing, P.R. China

Tommi Yu Legal & Risk Control Department, Country Garden Group, Shunde, P.R. China

Kangle Zhang The Erik Castrén Institute of International Law and Human Rights, University of Helsinki, Helsinki, Finland

Shu Zhang Deakin Law School, Deakin University, Burwood, VIC, Australia

Introduction

Wenhua Shan

One of the most dramatic changes the world has been witnessing in recent years is the growing willingness of China taking initiative and practicing leadership on global stage. A most visible demonstration of such a change is the speech delivered by President Xi Jinping in 2017 at the Davos World Economic Forum, in which he robustly defended open trade and global cooperation,[1] against the populist backlash that has reverberated around the world in the past years. Xi's remarks highlighted China's potential impact on world development and its changing role in the international system. Indeed, after over 30 years of economic growth averaging about 10%, China has become the second largest economy and is emerging as a major power in search of meaning and purpose of its own in this world of rapid change and grave uncertainty.

Such is also clearly reflected in the 19th CPC Congress Report, the most important policy paper of China setting out the mission and action plan for the country in the years and decades to come. In the report, President Xi announced that China committed herself to forge "a new form of international relations featuring mutual respect, fairness, justice, and win-win cooperation" and to build "a community with a shared future for mankind (CSFM)" and "an open, inclusive, clean, and beautiful world that enjoys lasting peace, universal security, and common prosperity".[2] Clearly China is no longer shy or hesitant to talk about or to take a leading role in world affairs.

The central plank to the construction of China's vision of a new world or the CSFM, is the Belt and Road Initiative (BRI). The initiative comprises a continental belt the "Silk Road Economic Belt" and a maritime road the "21th Century Maritime

[1]Xi (2017a).

[2]Xi (2017b).

W. Shan (✉)
School of Law, Xi'an Jiaotong University, Xi'an, China
e-mail: shan@xjtu.edu.cn

W. Shan et al. (eds.), *Normative Readings of the Belt and Road Initiative*,
https://doi.org/10.1007/978-3-319-78018-4_1

Silk Road", named after two speeches by President Xi in 2013 successively in Kazakhstan[3] and Indonesia.[4] The initiative is sometimes translated as the "One Belt and One Road (OBOR)" initiative before the now official English translation BRI was adopted. In March 2015, the Chinese Government published the "Vision and Action Plan" for the BRI, outlining the concept of the initiative and the work plan for its construction.[5] In May 2017, President Xi hosted the first Belt and Road Forum of International Cooperation, which was attended by over 1500 representatives from all over the world including 29 heads of states.[6] Late 2017, the BRI was expectedly highlighted in the 19th CPC Congress Report: "China will actively promote international cooperation through the Belt and Road Initiative. In doing so, we hope to achieve policy, infrastructure, trade, financial, and people-to-people connectivity and thus build a new platform for international cooperation to create new drivers of shared development."[7]

The significance of the BRI therefore cannot be overestimated. It is the first time that China has published a major initiative for international cooperation and has taken great efforts to implement it. Given Chinese Government's tremendous overall capacity and firm commitment thereto and the tremendous demand of investment particularly in infrastructure sectors along the BR countries, the BRI is bound to leave a significant and lasting mark on China and the rest of the world, economically and otherwise. To many, it is a sign that China has changed the emphasis from the former to the latter half of the "[K]eeping a low profile, but trying to make a difference when appropriate" (Tao Guang Yang Hui, You SuoZuo Wei) diplomatic policy, which has been adhered to by the Chinese Government since Deng Xiaoping's era.

Unsurprisingly the BRI has attracted extensive attention worldwide, with numerous policy briefing and studies on the Initiative in general, its geopolitical and economic drivers, its impact on regional and global cooperation, and ways to make use of it to enhance local and regional development in particular. Understandably, it has also met with suspicion and criticism for the lack of detailed explanations from the Chinese side, particularly at earlier stages. The Vision and Action Plan helped by enlisting a series of cooperation priorities, but those priorities are described in a general and abstract terms without more detailed schedules of their implementation. Indeed, the BRI project has been described as informal, cooperative and loosely structured, leaving the international community struggling to appreciate its substance and to evaluate its potential impact.

In an effort to "decode" the BRI and its social legal implications, an International Conference on "Road to New Paradigms: Impact of China's Silk Road Initiative in China, Central Asia and the EU" was held on 9–10 May 2016 at Helsinki, Finland.

---

[3]Witte (2013).

[4]Wu (2013).

[5]Vision And Actions On Jointly Building Silk Road Economic Belt And 21st-Century Maritime Silk Road (2015).

[6]For extensive details of the forum, visit: http://beltandroadforum.org/english/index.html (accessed 30 January 2018).

[7]Xi (2017b).

The conference was jointly organised by Faculty of Law, Aleksanteri Institute, Faculty of Social Science, of University of Helsinki, and School of Law of Xi'an Jiaotong University, in collaboration with The New Silk Road Law Schools Alliance, an alliance jointly established by the two law schools in 2015 at Xi'an, together with 19 other leading law schools from different continents of the world.[8] The conference went beyond the goal of economic development strongly underlined in the Initiative and focused on important but unexplored issues such as mobility, national identity or cultural, constitutional and legal developments of Silk Road cooperation. The conference brought together some of the finest scholars in the field from more than 10 countries across the silk road and 29 different institutions/organizations to share their perspectives on the Initiative and to debate on its legal and social implications.[9]

As a most important outcome originated from the conference, this volume provides normative readings combined with legal analyses of the Initiative and the role of China in global legal order, making it a unique contribution to the field of BRI studies. We are deeply indebted to all the authors for their contributions and committment to the book. Special thanks must go to Ms. Suvi Kurki-Suonio for her assistance in editing the volume: this volume would not have come in shape without her great support. We are also grateful to Springer for taking this book on board.

The volume contains ten chapters which can be divided into two sections: The first four chapters offering more general readings of the BRI, whilst the other six chapters focusing on some of the most important specific issues such as finance, investment and their social and environmental implications, as well as the role of the judiciary and lawyers in the course of the BRI construction.

Among the general reading chapters, *Vilaça* (chapter 'Strengthening the Cultural and Normative Foundations of the Belt and Road Initiative: The Colombo Plan, Yan Xuetong and Chinese Ancient Thought') refers to traditional Chinese thinking for China to develop the philosophy and values of the BRI, and to exercise a distinctive style of normative leadership. Vilaça puts BRI into a historical context by comparing it with the Colombo Plan. The historical context and lessons from the Colombo Plan, together with the sources in Chinese thinking and philosophy, as Vilaça argues, provide answers to critiques of the Initiative, and contribute to building a more sustainable normative vision of the initiative. In chapter 'Developing a Sustainable

[8]Based on the "Silk Road Spirit", the alliance aims to become a leading international platform for the promotion of international collaboration on legal education and research, to contribute to the enhancement of the rule of law. The alliance was originally formed with 10 law schools from Mainland, 2 from China's Hong Kong and Taiwan, and 8 foreign law schools, including the Law School of Singapore National University, the Law School of University of New South Wales, Australia, the Law School of University of Helsinki, Finland, the Law School of Delhi University, India, the Law School of People's Friendship University, Russia, the Law School of FGV University, Brazil, the Law School of Seoul National University, South Korea and the Law School of National University, Kyrgyzstan. It now consists of 23 members from 14 countries and regions, with its most recent annual conference held in Wuhan, China in November 2017. For further details, see Ma (2015) and Wuhan University Law School (2017).

[9]Neffe (2016).

Legal System for the Belt and Road Initiative', *Morris* highlights the role of the Law, including in bilateral and multilateral trading arrangements, to ensure that relationships between market players and stakeholders are as fair and transparent as possible, through mechanisms that influence norms and hold those who behave in untrustworthy ways to account. He suggests that understanding and taking into account differences both of legal and regulatory systems, and of local culture, is important in the development of a harmonized legal and regulatory system to underpin the Initiative. In chapter 'The Normative Foundations of the Belt and Road Initiative: Shared Destiny, Sovereignty, State-led Economics, Connectivity and Flexibility', *Vangeli* analyzes the normative sources of the BRI found in China's own developmental model and its new foreign policy, and explores the six core normative principles of the BRI: shared destiny, sovereignty, state-led economic cooperation, new regionalism, and the flexible, experimental and exception-ridden practice. It discusses the potential pathways of diffusion of these normative principles along the BR countries and regions and points out that a successful diffusion of these principles would further facilitate the process of diversification of political and economic models of development. Based on the Chinese conception of world order which is ingrained in the old philosophical concept "Tian-xia" (All-Under-Heaven), *He* (chapter 'The Belt and Road Initiative as Global Public Good: Implications for International Law') proposes a new perspective to revive the public facet of international law to genuinely meet the Global Public Good (GPG) expectation of the BRI. It considers that a Chinese perspective of international law includes not only rules but also moral maxims that set a high moral standard for the rules. For the BRI, how to harmonize competing national interests and integrate them within the common interests, is a paradox to be solved.

On the specific issues, *Kangle Zhang* (chapter 'A Tale of Ending Poverty: The New Financial Institutions and China's Global Strategy') argues that "end poverty" is the common-ground between various BRI players including the sovereign nations, new and established financial institutions. The moral endowment and indeterminacy of the term enables WB, AIIB and other institutions to engage with the BRI for the purpose of its own agendas, but also covers up the story of the struggle of the member countries of the new institutions for strategic advantages in multilateral lending and global economic governance, and conceals the political objectives and effects of particular countries within the new institutions. In deploying the term and furthering the global strategy, BRI infrastructure financing might increase uncertainty and risks in the global financial system. *Brombal* (chapter 'Planning for a Sustainable Belt and Road Initiative (BRI): An Appraisal of the Asian Infrastructure Investment Bank (AIIB) Environmental and Social Safeguards') seeks to appraise the rationale, scope, legitimacy, and decision-making implications of environmental and social policies applicable to BRI projects, taking AIIB as a case representative of current progress and challenges ahead. It finds that AIIB's environmental and social safeguards may constitute a tool to promote social inclusion and environmental protection within BRI projects. Their effectiveness, however, depends on the Bank's political commitment towards sustainability and its capacity to foster institutional change in client countries. *Shu Zhang* (chapter 'Developing China's

Investor-State Arbitration Clause: Discussions in the Context of the "Belt and Road" Initiative') reviews investor-state arbitration (ISA) clauses in international investment agreements (IIAs) between China and the BR countries and identifies divergence and flexibility, as well as some degree of policy convergence in a few most recent IIAs. It argues for a more adaptable Model ISA clause and a more consistent approach to ISA clause drafting and evaluates the possible negotiation arenas in which China may pursue its new generation of ISA clauses. *Hu, Ou* and *Hu* (chapter 'On the Environmental Responsibility of Chinese Enterprises for Their FDIs in Countries Within the Belt and Road Initiative') analyzes the environmental responsibilities of Chinese enterprises investing in other BR countries. It proposes that Chinese enterprises should, on the basis of the just and reasonable settlement of environmental disputes, clarify the environmental standards, identify the legitimacy and rationality of governmental regulations, review the objective environmental consequence(s), and determine the doctrine of liability fixation to be applied. Chinese enterprises should also adjust their development principles, perform due diligence and prudence, and utilize multiple dispute resolution mechanisms.

The two last but certainly not least chapters relate to legal services relevant to BRI activities. *Xiao* and *Yu* (chapter 'Some Suggestions for Improving the International Credibility of the Chinese Judiciary: A Focus on the BRI') assesses the Supreme People's Court Opinions on People's Court's Provision of Judicial Service and Safeguards for the BRI in July 2015. They argue that the Opinions must be improved to meet the needs of the BRI by promoting a judicial ideology featuring equal protection, win-win cooperation, opening up, and efficiency. They recommend improving the judicial system through various measures, including fully guaranteeing foreigners' litigation rights, properly narrowing the ambit of exclusive jurisdiction, and properly settling parallel proceedings. Also they propose innovating judicial methods, such as actively applying *forum non conveniens*, actively confirming the existence of reciprocity, accurately applying international treaties and customs, and fully utilizing guiding cases, as well as promoting an inclusive judicial culture and a diversified resolution mechanism and ascertaining and correctly applying foreign law. Utilizing survey method, *Yu* (chapter 'China's "Belt and Road Initiative": What's in it for Law Firms and Lawyers?') offers new insights into the expectations within the legal services industry in PRC, and the peculiarities stretching lawyers beyond their traditional roles. Addressing short-term and long-term expectations of lawyers, and approaches utilized by law firms to authentically connect with potential clients, it offers further understanding into practice areas of current and future demand, and law firms' outreach activities and strategies. It concludes that the synergy between legal services industry and practitioners on the one side, and government institutions, policies and support on the other, will be the key condition for solidifying and materializing short to medium, and longer-term expectations in connection with the BRI.

This collection of papers have exhibited the depth and richness of the normative readings and legal analyses of the BRI, as well as the changing role of China in the global legal order. At the time the book is ready to go for print, the Chinese Government has decided that multiple mechanisms of dispute resolution should be explored and established to facilitate the BRI implementation. As a result, the Supreme

People's Court is contemplating to set up two new specialised "International Commercial Courts" at Xi'an and Shenzhen to serve the needs for the settlement of disputes arising out of the construction of the new continental and maritime silk roads, respectively.[10] It is beyond doubt that law will play a significant role in the development of the BRI, even though it might take time for this role to be fully realized. What is more important, however, is to make sure that as the BRI construction carries on, sensible laws and mechanisms are to be designed and developed impacting on the BR countries and the world in positive ways, as the CSFM rhetoric promises. Here lies a mission of legal scholars and practitioners, along and beyond the BR countries. This book represents a first attempt of the legal community taking up this mission and challenge and there should certainly be more such endeavors to come. The "Road to New Paradigms" might not be a short journey, but with joint efforts hopefully it will be one that leads to a better and brighter world!

References

ChinaDaily. (2017). SPC working towards commercial courts in Xi'an, posted at the SPC Official website: http://english.court.gov.cn/2017-10/25/content_33734581.htm

He, J., & Geng, Z. (2018). Creating International Commercial Courts, Judicially Safeguarding the Belt and Road Construction. http://www.rmfz.org.cn/mobile/21-0-120183-1.html

Ma, L. (2015, December 11). Chinese and foreign law schools launch New Silk Road alliance. *China Daily*. Retrieved January 31, 2018, from http://www.chinadaily.com.cn/china/2015-12/11/content_22693518.htm

Neffe, A. (2016, November 5). The New Silk Road Law Schools Alliance's Research Seminar was held in Helsinki. Retrieved January 31, 2018, from http://blogs.helsinki.fi/chinalawcenter/1851/

Vision And Actions On Jointly Building Silk Road Economic Belt And 21st-Century Maritime Silk Road. (2015, March). The National Development and Reform Commission, Ministry of Foreign Affairs, and Ministry of Commerce of the People's Republic of China, with State Council authorization. Retrieved January 31, 2018, from http://www.xinhuanet.com/english/china/2015-03/28/c_134105858.htm

Witte, M. (2013, September 11). Xi Jinping calls for regional cooperation via New Silk Road. *Astana Times*. Retrieved January 31, 2018, from https://astanatimes.com/2013/09/xi-jinping-calls-for-regional-cooperation-via-new-silk-road/

Wu Han University Law School. (2017). The School of Law successfully held the "New Silk Road Law School Alliance Annual Meeting 2017 & International Conference on Legal Education Reform". Retrieved January 31, 2018, from http://fxy.whu.edu.cn/en/show.aspx?info_lb=766&flag=766&info_id=2817

Wu, J. (2013, October 3). Xi in call for building of new 'maritime silk road'. *China Daily*. Retrieved January 31, 2018, from http://usa.chinadaily.com.cn/china/2013-10/04/content_17008940.htm

Xi, J. (2017a, January 17). *Jointly shoulder responsibility of our times, promote global growth*. Keynote Speech at the Opening Session of the World Economic Forum Annual Meeting 2017, Davos, 17 January 2017. Retrieved January 31, 2018, from http://www.xinhuanet.com/english/2017-01/18/c_135991271.htm

Xi, J. (2017b). *Secure a decisive victory in building a moderately prosperous society in all respects and strive for the great success of socialism with Chinese characteristics for a new era*. Delivered at the 19th National Congress of the Communist Party of China, Beijing, October 18, 2017. Retrieved January 31, 2018, from http://www.chinadaily.com.cn/china/19thcpcnationalcongress/2017-11/04/content_34115212.htm

[10]ChinaDaily (2017); See also He and Geng (2018).

Strengthening the Cultural and Normative Foundations of the Belt and Road Initiative: The Colombo Plan, Yan Xuetong and Chinese Ancient Thought

Guilherme Vasconcelos Vilaça

1 China's Belt and Road Initiative: Dream?

1.1 Motivation and Structure

On March 2016, I came across the following piece of news: "Drama 'Dream of Maritime Silk Road' performed in Malaysia".[1] In another journalistic piece, "Chinese Dance Drama to Boost Belt and Road Initiative in ASEAN", the show, also performed at the UNESCO headquarters in Paris, is described as:

> highlight[ing] a prosperous Quanzhou port and friendship forged among people along the Maritime Silk Road when they seek common prosperity and happiness, with cultural elements from China and other Maritime Silk Road countries.[2]

Since I had been working on the Silk Road Economic Belt for some time, this news brought it home to me that I should probe into the *dream* of China's "One Belt, One Road" (OBOR) also labelled "Belt and Road Initiative" (BRI):[3] What is China's dream and why should the rest of the world bother?

---

[1]Available at http://news.xinhuanet.com/english/photo/2016-03/30/c_135236689_2.htm.

[2]Lin Hao, "Chinese Dance Drama to Boost Belt and Road Initiative in ASEAN," Xinhua, 2016-03-30, available at http://news.xinhuanet.com/english/2016-03/30/c_135235907.htm.

[3]Throughout the chapter, I will use BRI and OBOR interchangeably to refer to the current agenda first named Silk Road Economic Belt.

G. Vasconcelos Vilaça (✉)
The Erik Castrén Institute of International Law and Human Rights, Helsinki University, Helsinki, Finland

The Collaborative Innovation Centre for Silk Road Economic Belt Studies (CIC-SREBS), Xi'an Jiaotong University, Xi'an, People's Republic of China
e-mail: Guilherme.vasconcelos@eui.eu

W. Shan et al. (eds.), *Normative Readings of the Belt and Road Initiative*,
https://doi.org/10.1007/978-3-319-78018-4_2

The Silk Road Forum hosted in May 2017 in Beijing, provided great impulse to communicate globally the agenda by seating country delegations across the world together with top representatives of international organizations such as the IMF, the WB and the UN. Reactions to the summit and China's vision are mixed with Europe, Oceania and South America being interested in trade and investment opportunities while the US and India (to name the most explicit) voiced concerns regarding the hidden hegemonic nature of the plan.[4]

I believe that this new Chinese agenda constitutes a needed international vision. In times of deep and longstanding economic and financial crisis (not to mention all the humanitarian disasters happening across the globe), China has decided to commit substantial resources to reactivate the image of the old Silk Road connecting East and West sponsoring infrastructure construction (but not only) along the way. More than the resources, however, what I deem visionary is the *dream*, the call for an international program of cooperation and reciprocal engagement in times dictated by the likely American inward-turn and the widespread disbelief in the European project. To put it simply, *I prefer a world in which the Belt and Road Initiative exists, to one in which it doesn't*. But my easy endorsement of the Chinese plan ends here as throughout the chapter I argue that either cultural and normative contents are added to the *economic* BRI's vision and practice or the latter risks betraying the announced ideals and being perceived as a form of neo-colonialism or imperialism. In other words, I argue that China should change the way in which it is communicating culturally and normatively about its plan.

I proceed as follows. First, I describe the main features of the Belt and Road Initiative highlighting the gap between the cultural root metaphor and the almost exclusively economic focus both in practice and academic commentary. Then, I identify a set of concerns which offer instrumental incentives for China to articulate better its normative vision. This leads to the main claim the chapter puts forward, i.e. China ought to develop the cultural dimension of the BRI and create a more robust philosophical discourse about its values. I propose to do so by arguing both in practical-historical terms, i.e. China ought to engage in *two-way* cultural exchange by treasuring past experiences; and in theoretical fashion, i.e. China should elaborate on the type of normative leadership the BRI expresses and the values of Chinese foreign policy because the former may be seen as an example of world leadership. I pursue the practical-historical argument by revisiting the Colombo Plan, an historical example of economic, cultural and educational concerted action between Southeast Asian and, at first, Commonwealth countries. In particular, I think China (and all of us) can and should learn from the missed opportunity this plan embodies in terms of

---

[4]These last two countries have not attended officially the summit. For a summary of the different reactions to China's BRI, see Ben Blanchard and Wong Sue-Lin, "China's New Silk Road Promises Trade And Riches, With President Xi At Helm", Reuters Business News, May 15 2017, available at http://www.reuters.com/article/us-china-silkroad-protectionism-idUSKCN18B0B5 and Anna Bruce-Lockhart, "China's $900 Billion New Silk Road. What You Need To Know", World Economic Forum, 26 June 2017, available at https://www.weforum.org/agenda/2017/06/china-new-silk-road-explainer/.

genuine, *two-way*, cultural exchange that is now advanced in Australia's New Colombo Plan. To put it differently, history shows that there are historical precedents for what China is putting forward offering some lessons to be learned to avoid repeating past mistakes. As for the theoretical argument, I argue that there is awareness within Chinese-authored writing on the moral poverty of its international relations agenda and the need to overcome it. I focus chiefly on the work of Yan Xuetong proposing that China should strive for "humane authority". In turn, this requires a moral vision and vocabulary which he finds in pre-Qin philosophy.

The two ways of communicating China's BRI proposed here can also be seen more broadly as contributing to suggest avenues through which China can better pursue its new role as an emerging superpower dealing with global issues while being forced to operate in the existing world—largely made by others—of international norms and organizations.

All in all, this chapter aims to take advantage of the momentum created by China's initiative to renew efforts to think of a different style of doing and thinking about international relations. In addition to recovering the importance of looking at historical grand projects of cooperation, the chapter adds to the now emerging debate on virtue ethics in international relations. It does so by bringing to the table Chinese voices on international relations promoting a more inclusive approach to academic discourse. Because the author chosen, Yan Xuetong, bases his work on ancient Chinese thought, this chapter also contributes to the ongoing reevaluation of the still predominant (outside Sinology departments) Kantian[5] and Hegelian[6] received views denying any interest, or even existence, to classical Chinese philosophy.[7]

In choosing the research path sketched above I downgrade two alternative approaches, one overly managerial and one overly idealistic.

Contrary to what one often reads and hears in conferences and talks about the OBOR, I think we should go beyond purely *managerial* solutions directed at strengthening dispute resolution mechanisms and international investment laws so as to protect better Chinese interests.[8] Proposals suggest improved new BITs between China and the relevant countries as well as the development of OBOR-

---

[5]See Ching (1978), p. 169 reporting Kant's famous sayings "Philosophy is not to be found in the whole Orient ... a concept of virtue and morality never entered the heads of the Chinese."

[6]On Confucius, for instance, Hegel (2013), p. 240 wrote "He is for the most part a moral educator. He was a moralist as such, not actually a philosopher; for in his case we do not find theory that occupies itself in thought as such."

[7]The question "Is Chinese philosophy real philosophy (in the Western sense)?" is too big to approach here starting with the fact that the Chinese word "philosophy" only appeared in the nineteenth century and was introduced by a Japanese. The leading view answering in the positive argues that "Chinese thinkers were interested primarily in *practical* rather than *theoretical* questions." See Slingerland (2003), p. 3.

[8]For instance, at the Xi'an Jiaotong University—School of Law's Silk Road Institute of International and Comparative Law 10th International Symposium Xi'an 1 November 2016, the mentioned conference "Road to New Paradigms: Impact of China's Silk Road Initiative in China, Central Asia and the EU" held in Helsinki and in a 2017 special issue of the *Transnational Dispute Management* journal.

specific forms of dispute resolution. While it is legitimate that China safeguards its interests (while inducing compliance within the OBOR), such a line of action does nothing to promote cultural exchange and understanding among peoples as the OBOR initiative also advocates.

Another option could have been to deepen the philosophical content of the BRI and infuse the latter with a Chinese cosmopolitan philosophical ideal which could then be defended rationally and not only historically, i.e. by appealing to the glorious past of the Silk Road. I also set aside such an approach and do not discuss, for instance, Zhao Tingyang's work arguing that China's concept of *tianxia*, or all-under heaven, could provide a cosmopolitan political philosophy for the world, peoples and institutions.[9] To my mind, Zhao's thesis offers little argument on how to develop the necessary institutional framework to fulfil the prescribed normative vision. I believe that the same can be said roughly about two decades of debates on global ethics and cosmopolitanism following an *ideal theory* approach[10] (which has also failed to overcome moral disagreement in the face of moral pluralism).[11] Therefore, I do not pursue such a strategy here. Far from relying on theory only, this chapter builds on the historical and practical experiences of the Colombo Plans to support an overall argument for China's normative vision.

1.2 Methodological Approach

Before proceeding, it is important to clarify the following point.[12] Throughout the chapter, I claim that China ought to engage the "Other" genuinely and articulate more clearly a normative vision for its interaction with the world. Furthermore, I claim that China would benefit from doing so.

First and foremost, China will benefit from an *instrumental* point of view since I offer several reasons as to why China both needs the Belt and Road Initiative and at the same time may be jeopardizing its sustainability. This is not a purely moral egoistic position, but rather a consequentialist one, as I believe that China's project is beneficial for the world given the troubled times we face. Moral consequentialism, would then justify two-way cultural exchanges, as discussed in the chapter, between

[9]See Zhao (2006, 2009). For analysis and critique, see Callahan (2008). Importantly, Callahan points out that the global order set up by *tianxia* promotes conversion of difference and not simple co-existence and harmony between different ideals.

[10]For a guide to the literature on the distinction between ideal and non-ideal theory, see Valentini (2012).

[11]For a similar argument (with sources) voiced against global political and legal projects, see Vilaça (2015).

[12]I thank Walter Rech and Goncalo Vilaça for pushing me to spell out this tension lurking throughout the chapter.

more and less developed countries even if these would probably fail to be cost/benefit sound from a self-interest standpoint.[13]

Second, can my suggestions also be justified on deontological grounds, i.e. irrespective of the effects produced and carried out with the right motivation? Am I also defending such a justification? This is a thorny question as I employ a highly charged normative term: "genuine" as in genuine cultural exchange. I believe that China ought to pursue a normative and cultural policy that recognizes equal dignity to the different peoples and countries along the BRI on the moral grounds that all countries with their cultures and populations deserve *qua* human products our equal cultural attention. In other words, their worth cannot be captured if understood only as beings with economic potential. However, I operate this cosmopolitan attitude not at the level of values and principles (which would lead us to the affirmation and need to defend substantive universal values) but at the level of concrete policies. This entails, for instance, that China cannot adopt a unilateral cultural approach spreading its culture and language and conducting its business along the different target countries *without reciprocating* the cultural openness it is demanding from the "Other". Thus, it ought to send its own nationals to live and learn from such countries' traditions and languages.

Notice, however, that such principled positions can always be read and justified from a narrow instrumental standpoint, i.e. as being beneficial or detrimental to China.

For instance, it could be said that China would benefit from morally labelling its own position before others do it for herself. Alternatively, one could say that it is inevitable that China engages in more explicit normative construction as the fulfillment of the Belt and Road Initiative, the one road between East and West, raises important public law type of questions. For example, normatively charged discussions on immigration and visa policies, labor laws and product safety standards cannot be dodged in the future. Or even, it could be defended that we cannot escape normative questions or create normative expectations due to the nature of social life. The latter, furthermore, relies on the medium of language which displays a pervasive evaluative vocabulary.[14]

On the other extreme, one could claim, as the critics of Yan Xuetong's turn to ancient Chinese philosophy I discuss do, that his entire project aims at instrumentally embellishing China's rise to expand its power. Finally, it could still be argued that moralizing China's engagement with the "Other" may be unwelcoming because (1) not needed (countries may be dissatisfied but will continue to deal with China because of economic necessity provided that some basic standards of fairness are observed); and, (2) merely trapping China in a position in which it would have to justify future breaches of the normative expectations created.

Ultimately, the pragmatic ethical stance I adopt allows me to accept as unproblematic mixed moral reasons when justifying a specific policy or course of

[13]The work of Yan Xuetong I discuss also resorts to a principled argument grounded on Chinese tradition and its distinction between *de facto* and legitimate authority, for China's endorsement of a moral style of normative leadership.

[14]This is the guiding vision of Frost (2009).

action. As American Pragmatism has shown, it is due to the predominance of ideal thinking in moral theory that we feel constrained to choose a specific ethical tradition even before we define a given moral situation.[15] Such an ideal-theory approach prevents learning from the (always constructed) facts of the situation locking us into falsely and simplistically thinking that we have to be *either* instrumentalists *or* deontologists (until recently virtue ethics was neglected). Sending us thus looking for either self-interest or altruism; not both.[16]

2 The Belt and Road Initiative

The Silk Road Economic Belt was presented by President Xi Jinping in 2013 in a speech at Nazarbayev University in Astana, Kazakhstan. It is an international relations design that wishes to re-activate the old Silk Road(s)—land and maritime—building a single "road" between East and West, from North to South creating a corridor spanning Asia, Africa and Europe.[17] The original discourse urged the promotion, within the "One Belt, One Road" of "policy consultation", "transport facilitation", "unimpeded trade", "monetary circulation" and "understanding between our peoples".[18] These goals were reaffirmed and articulated in greater detail later in 2015 in the official document "Vision and Actions on Jointly Building Silk Road Economic Belt and 21st-Century Maritime Silk Road".[19] The same logic was kept, with the document presenting a win-win program based on finance and trade and the idea that the latter promotes peace and development in a world of civilizational diversity. This new document, however, added a more explicit focus on "connectivity", explicitly positioned China by creating a historical link between the Silk Road Economic Belt and the "weak recovery of the global economy" as well as it announced the universal vocation of the plan.[20] The emphasis on economic aspects was preserved, though, since only one priority, among five, targets culture.

[15]For a concise statement of pragmatism applied to international relations, see Kratochwil (2001).

[16]Within instrumentalism we should distinguish between moral egoism and consequentialism since the former is not, from an ethical theory standpoint a moral, i.e. other-regarding, position. In the text, I use instrumentalism because whenever we discuss foreign policy authors tend to assume that instrumentalism stands for self-interest and is opposed simply to altruism. With such simplification consequentialism is thrown overboard with the obvious discursive effects of caricaturing moral analysis.

[17]For a comprehensive assessment, see Johnson (2016).

[18]I refer to the discourse as it appears in Xi (2014), pp. 315–319.

[19]Available at http://www.fmprc.gov.cn/mfa_eng/zxxx_662805/t1249618.shtml. This was a joint statement by the National Development and Reform Commission, Ministry of Foreign Affairs, and Ministry of Commerce of the People's Republic of China, with State Council authorization.

[20]"The Initiative is open for cooperation. It covers, but is not limited to, the area of the ancient Silk Road. *It is open to all countries*, and international and regional organizations for engagement, so that the results of the concerted efforts will benefit wider areas. The Initiative is harmonious and inclusive." *Ibidem*, emphasis added.

Concretely, promoting "understanding between our peoples" became "enhance people-to-people and cultural exchanges".

Despite all the cultural and metaphorical rhetoric recovering the image of the grand Silk Road as standing for exploration, cultural and religious exchanges as well as Xi Jinping's parallel agenda for civilizational diversity and mutual learning,[21] a quick glance over the many news on the BRI shows an unabashed practical focus on economic aspects and the managerial language of figures, stats and logistics. We hear of more than 60 participating countries comprising around 63% of the world's population, China's willingness to invest around $900 billion in countries along the Belt (mostly in Central Asia), estimated economic effects in the range of $21 trillion not to mention the bilateral agreements for the construction of rail and road infrastructure in Central Asian and African countries, agreements for free-circulation of goods, currencies and capital as well as the conclusion of the first direct train routes and lines between China and European countries such as Germany that promise unprecedented levels of circulation of commodities. Culture remains residual in the project and, as we shall see in detail later, consists chiefly of China's unilaterally spreading its language, culture and the BRI through a variety of media *putting in place a problematic view of the new Silk Road as a one-way road from China to the rest of the world.*

This economic focus also fits China's distinctive discourse about globalization which, after being rejected,[22] is now welcomed but only in its economic dimensions.[23] As Yu Keping has argued,[24] while Chinese authors now accept that globalization does not necessarily mean Westernization or Capitalism they still see the cultural and political discourse in globalization as a threat to the "___with Chinese characteristics" model.[25] At the same time, recent Chinese international practice embodies an acceptance of participating in economic globalization by means of its role in creating some regional institutions, e.g. the Asian Infrastructure Investment Bank and the New Development Bank which includes the Contingent Reserve Arrangement. Thus, to my mind, we could see the BRI as providing the much sought-after answer as to *how* should China engage globalization.

---

[21]Xi Jinping, speech at UNESCO, March 2014, available at http://www.fmprc.gov.cn/mfa_eng/wjdt_665385/zyjh_665391/t1142560.shtml.

[22]See Yu (2004).

[23]That globalization is a Western-origin economic phenomenon cannot be seen as a natural narrative. For instance, the historian Lynn Hunt (2014) documents different narratives of non-Western cultural globalization such as those associated to ostrich plume trade (among other commodities) or to ethnic groups such as Armenian merchants that brought coffee shops to Europe, first London and then Paris. It goes without saying that whereas this still appears to be a narrative of economic globalization, such circulation of commodities was in fact intrinsically cultural having been responsible for deep changes in taste and lifestyle.

[24]Yu (2004). Even though Yu does not mention it, this shift parallels the sudden domestic turn to accept the role of markets (and law) as *necessary* for development whereas they were seen earlier as instruments of bourgeois oppression of the proletariat. On this shift, see Yu (1989).

[25]The label "with Chinese characteristics" was deployed originally by Deng Xiaoping to describe Chinese *socialism* but is now used to speak of Chinese conceptions of *democracy* and *rule of law* among others. For useful background, see Zhang (2010) and Boer (2014).

Academic commentary has also been focusing on material, hard, aspects of the BRI privileging the study of China's contribution to a new institutional (economic) order, one that respects countries' differences and starts with regions (Asia) and alternative geopolitical formations (BRICS) rather than the world and existing international institutions often perceived as an expression of US and/or broader Western interests.[26] Some authors emphasize, side-by-side with the obvious opportunities for international cooperation, security concerns behind the plan highlighting the presentation of China's new neighborhood policy as well as the attempt to curb internal terrorism in Xinjiang.[27] While other works zoom in on the new neighborhood policy from the point of view of China's attempt to prevent US action in the former's surrounding countries.[28]

And yet, it appears that *this* dream, as just described, does not and cannot trigger stares of surprise and fascination (most likely with the wild, exotic and the unknown) as those in the faces of the actors in the news with which I opened this chapter.[29] It doesn't particularly bring to life either the rich cultural transformations and exchanges that the ancient Silk Road witnessed and fostered limiting the appeal of the root metaphor.[30] Indeed the latter applies only if we reduce human hopes and visions to some sort of Futurism-alike praise of material factors: train tracks, speed and technology.[31] Marinetti's "Holiness of wheels and rails".[32]

To be sure, the Futurism-analogy is certainly both illegitimate and revealing. Illegitimate because Futurism presented a clear moral vision which upheld the debunking of tradition and the apology of originality, violence and youth (we couldn't be further away from China's professed respect of traditions, civilizational diversity and peace). Illegitimate too because Futurism was not premised on economic aspects. But *revealing*, because it helps to see that there is no clear oneiric component in what is branded as a dream: the "One Belt, One Road". In other words, China would appear to be in the business of selling dreams. Both literally and in its opposed urban meaning when one is not being serious about what is promising.

---

[26]See Ren (2016) and Liu (2016).

[27]See Wang (2016) and Pan (2014).

[28]Wang (2016), p. 458.

[29]Dream here, as in China's Dream, should best be seen as a clear normative goal that mobilizes social and psychological utopian energies and wraps social life as a constitution, a normative horizon. It evokes more the Australian Aboriginal communities' dream than the modern Freudian derivation into psychological interpretation of dreams as revealing unfulfilled desires.

[30]For a full description of this point, see Lostal and Vilaça (2015), pp. 2–4.

[31]There are of course advantages behind technological change and speed. Enough to recall that during the sixteenth century, Matteo Ricci—a man that embodied in many ways a bridge between East and West—was used to wait 7 years for replies to his letters sent from China to Rome. Spence (1985), p. 66 tells of Ricci's growing despair with the discovery he was often writing to people that had died without him knowing. Much earlier, if one believes the diaries of Marco Polo, we are told that Marco's uncle and father, Niccolo and Maffeo, took 15 years in their first roundtrip between Venice and Kublai Khan's kingdom. See Polo (2003), p. 10.

[32]Marinetti (2008), p. 58.

3 The Lack of Moral Vision in the OBOR as a Problem

3.1 General Concerns

More seriously though, the assumption of this chapter is that the lack of elaboration of cultural and normative aspects in the BRI may have deleterious effects for its sustainability and long-term success. This is for several reasons.

First, as Bai Tongdong wrote recently "China is rising, but both Chinese and non-Chinese are wondering what message this rise offers. What do the Chinese want from the world? What can they give the world?"[33] The BRI can probably be seen as an extension of the vision delivered by Hu Jintao "Harmonious World"[34] as well as the more recent "Asian Community of Shared Destiny".[35] Together with the new institutional impetus, all these mark a major shift in Chinese foreign policy and participation in international relations. Used to the dictates of realpolitik and economic mantras such as "there are no free lunches", China's plea for win-win cooperation and massive investments of capital as being *neutral* raises, understandably, many eyebrows. A vision of happiness is always *someone's* vision of happiness as highlighted by the reply of the reluctant and somber Japanese envoy Matsuki to Padre Velasco in Shusaku Endo's novel *The Samurai:*

> The happiness you padres preach is poison to Japan. That has been very clear to me since we arrived in Nueva España. This country would have lived in peace if the Spanish ships had not come. Your version of happiness has disrupted this country.[36]

Second, and compounding the first point, even if the normative and practical contours of the Silk Road Economic Belt are still blurred, it is quite clear that the latter—especially when put together with the establishment of new regional international organizations such as the New Development Bank—signals a turn on China's foreign policy towards reshaping the existing world order.[37] Here, we should recall that since the foundation of the People's Republic of China,[38] its attitude to international law and international order has been described as ranging

[33]Bai (2012), p. 1.

[34]For the original discourse, see Hu (2005). For an analysis, see Masuda (2009).

[35]Liu (2014).

[36]Endo (1997), p. 113.

[37]For an analysis of China's institution making activity and the nature of its contribution to global governance, see Vilaça (2017).

[38]China's famously reported indifference to foreigners is evoked by Jonathan Spence (1985), p. 122 through an historical episode. Asked to comment on a painting of Matteo Ricci's audience (in absentia) with the Emperor Wanli, the latter said, "They are huihui", referring to both Ricci, a Jesuit, and the Muslim courtiers in oblivion, as Spence remarks, to "[t]he huge and cosmic battle that lay at the heart of European history..." (huihui was an expression used to name foreigners in Ming and Qing dynasties albeit it originally identified China's Muslims only).

from total denial and rejection to the five principles of co-existence which emphasize sovereignty and non-intervention.[39] More recently, commentators, have noticed China's move towards taking an active stance in international law and behaving as a morally responsible actor.[40]

Third, the shift just portrayed is paralleled in China's move from a target country of FDI to a massive outward foreign investor especially in the sectors of banking, utilities, insurance as well as construction of infra-structure (most notably in Africa). However, Chinese foreign investment is often regarded with mixed feelings due to China's so-called "state capitalism" which covers its investments with the suspicion they are made to create positions of power which the Chinese government could exercise when deemed desirable to advance its geopolitical interests.[41]

Fourth, China has been changing domestically too and at voracious speed in the last decades and these shifts have been destabilizing its very own nature.[42] The OBOR seems to be but the last example in the road of a distinctive project: a Chinese form of socialism.[43] After 30 years of material development (actually those prophetically identified from the outset as required to attain a reasonably well-off society),[44] different challenges, though, are triggering, to my mind, a need for the Chinese government to appeal for broader intellectual, or let us say it, "spiritual", resources. Along these lines, it should be noticed the (opposing?) domestic public agendas of resuscitating Confucianism and Marxism with the creation of thematic research centers with large endowments.

3.2 *Two Specific Charges*

One would expect that against the background of such changes, a clarification of the international goals could help to appease some of the international fears given the opacity of China in general. But even more directly, the absence of a clear cultural message in the BRI can harm the prospects of a sustainable and long-lasting successful OBOR in two ways. Tackling them shall be the focus of the next pages.

---

[39]For general accounts of China's foreign policy and its evolution towards increasing participation and responsibilities, see Kent (2006, 2013) and Lanteigne (2009).

[40]Evaluating whether China is a responsible state, see Foot (2013).

[41]The failed CNOOC's bid for UNOCAL was probably the earliest case of Chinese FDI to trigger alarms in the so-called developed world. For details of the case, see Casselman (2007), p. 161ff. For details on CPC's influence on Chinese companies, see McGregor (2012).

[42]Wang (2005), p. 275 wrote "Thus, almost every generalization about China – that it is a communist-led socialist society as before, that at its core it is a society of traditionally centralized power, that it has virtually become capitalist, that it is a fully-fledged consumer society, or even that it is already postmodern – can be supported with examples, as can its opposite." For an account of the main intellectual debates and participants, political alternatives and social and cultural events, see Hui (2005).

[43]For a description of the concept, see Zhang (2010).

[44]Zheng (2005), p. 76.

3.2.1 Neo-Colonialism

The first problem lies with the fact that China's new grand vision is dangerously close to being interpreted as promoting a new iteration of neo-colonialism.[45] Especially now that China's economy is slowing down and constantly subject to demanding challenges. After all, so far, China's BRI initiatives are mostly bilateral agreements with poorer countries in Africa and especially Central Asia granting it access to cheap energy sources and fresh markets where to dump its excess production of goods as well as its excess productive capacity in terms of infrastructure and heavy industry. This was recognized explicitly by Xiao Ren commenting on the OBOR:

> It is not true that China is simply altruistic. At present, the overall Chinese economy is undergoing a restructuring process. As its economy slows down and evolves, the country needs to find new markets for its capital goods. Better transport links will make nearby countries more attractive as suppliers to Chinese manufacturers and as consumers of Chinese-made goods. The new financial institutions also enable China to diversify foreign-exchange reserves still predominantly invested in US Treasury bonds. China will also extend its international influence by supporting the various projects through financial aid.[46]

As in Western powers' heyday, China—a protectionist country until it acquired enough power—is now invoking the principles of free-trade (and free-currency) and comparative advantage to say that trade makes everyone better off and is a sound foundation for peace. This echoes the words of the economist Bradford DeLong about pre-World War I economies which

> had managed to avoid the problems of overproduction, insufficient consumption and consequent financial crises, deep depressions and worker immiserization through imperialism: *maintaining employment at home by force-flooding the rest of the world with exports.*[47]

At play here, it is not only China's shift in attitude now that it needs to keep feeding its huge economic growth[48] and has the money to do so, but also its (apparent) repeating of historical behavior that was already much criticized due to the fact that trade has created structural dependencies and crushed local industries and economic activities. And crucially, a behavior condemned by China long ago.

> As Zhou Enlai put it at the first conference of Afro-Asian countries held in Bandung in 1955, the various delegations should put aside differences and band together on the 'common ground' of overturning the 'sufferings and calamities of colonialism'.[49]

Furthermore, in today's normative environment which increasingly denounces the growing inequality in the world, it is hard to justify naive claims that trade makes

---

[45]Recall that already in 2006, Hu Jintao's speech triggered charges of neo-colonial behavior from China. As Johnson recalls, Hu Jintao himself also criticized the foreign action of domestic Chinese actors for raising suspicions of neo-colonial behavior which would be particularly damaging and insulting for China due to its alignment with non-developed countries. See Johnson (2016), p. 17.

[46]Ren (2016), p. 440.

[47]DeLong (2004), p. 32, emphasis added.

[48]Johnson (2016), p. V, adds the opportunity for indebted companies to access new funds as well as to use the Silk Road to test their capacity to become global competitors.

[49]Foot (2013), p. 25, footnote omitted.

everyone better off and that should be the end of conversation.[50] The point is that the assumption that a win-win economic plan allowing for civilizational diversity is ethically and politically neutral is clearly unwarranted. Despite China's recent "charm offensive"[51] conducted globally through dialogue linking trade, peace and prosperity, the OBOR is no natural, self-justified, output. Violent outbursts and political movements against Chinese workers in different African countries highlight just that.[52]

Ultimately, the BRI may cut *against* the international system Western-led *convergence* towards shared values such as rights, democracy, responsibility to protect and the rule of law. Here, the re-discovery of Leibniz's love for China in Western academia as expressing and embodying the maxim "harmony as maximization of order and diversity"[53] fully fits the OBOR. By the same token, the institutional competition China is triggering with new regional designs also introduces regionalism and geographies that may not sit well with the existing order. Thus, unless China clarifies the normative vision behind its grand initiative, it risks having it interpreted by others in purely instrumental (self-interest) terms; a project on the surface for the world which would however have as its main catalyst the needs of contemporary China. And, lest we forget, such an agenda could go against China's favorite position as the champion of the Southern developing countries in the North/South divide with the OBOR presenting just a new facet of China's growing assertive and international "system-reforming approach" and behavior.[54]

3.2.2 Resentment and Volatile Political Support of the Initiative

Authors also have been pointing out how the style of Chinese investment and participation in economic life in African and Central Asian countries does not really give these countries "much" while leading them to open their markets, liberalize currencies and so on.[55] In turn this has triggered deep resentment and opposition against Chinese migrants and workers as well as investment deals with China.

---

[50]Even within mainstream economics as shown by Rodrik (2011).

[51]For this concept, see Lanteigne (2009), p. 12.

[52]Reporting episodes on Zambia, Ethiopia and Nigeria, see Mohan and Tan-Mullins (2009), p. 600. Though, see Sautman and Yan (2009) arguing that African views on China are not nearly as negative as Western media has it (and blaming anecdotal evidence for such a view).

[53]Perkins in Nijman (2016), p. 10. Leibniz saw the Emperor Kangxi as an example of a sage king that ruled following his proposed virtues and universal law.

[54]The expression "system-reforming approach" is taken from Kent (2013), p. 140.

[55]For example, a recent work establishes that in Kazakhstan there is a deep cleavage between elites and popular perceptions of China and the Silk Road Economic Belt. The authors also examine the different attitudes towards China-Kazakhstan relations present in Kazakhstani national vs private media. The results show that general population and private media (especially Kazakh language-based) are quite critical of China and rely heavily on stereotypes and forms of sinophobia. See Burkhanov and Chen (2016). See also Chu et al. (2014).

Popular unrest has inclusively led to the suspension of different land, energy and infrastructure deals with China.[56]

On the other hand, such a stance also creates problems with the political leadership of partner countries especially in cases in which there is political transition and the new leaders revise official views on Chinese investments capitalizing on resentment against China's exclusive economic focus. Recently, the Financial Times starred an article showing how political transition now labelled what first were heralded as great deals with a reliable partner as "selling out" the country to China while subjecting the latter to tremendously high level of credit risks.[57] Several Chinese deals in Sri Lanka were also reviewed due to lack of transparency.[58] Obviously, this threatens the Chinese vision and actions because it puts into question the solvency of Chinese investments.[59]

The bottom line is that the last two main points jeopardize the stability of the whole endeavor as well as the efficacy of China's "charm offensive". Furthermore, they also seem to point to the difficulties inherent in fulfilling the BRI key priority "people-to-people bonds" given China's somehow poor record on what concerns cultural exchanges and cultural diplomacy. What can and should China do about it?

4 Promoting a Two-Way Cultural BRI: The Colombo and the New Colombo Plans

4.1 China's Cultural Diplomacy

As pointed out, China's 5th priority, the only non-economic one of the "Vision and Actions" program, is the people-to-people bonds

[56]For Myanmar, see Adam Pasick, 'China's Cancelled Burma Railway Is Its Latest Derailment in Southeast Asia,' *Quartz* (July 25 2014) available at http://qz.com/240436/chinas-cancelled-burma-railway-is-its-latest-derailment-in-southeast-asia/. For Kazakhstan see Keith Johnson, 'China's New Silk Road Into Europe Is About More Than Money,' Foreign Policy, June 1 2016, available at http://foreignpolicy.com/2016/06/01/chinas-new-silk-road-into-europe-is-about-more-than-money/.

[57]Highlighting Venezuela, Ecuador, Zimbabwe, Myanmar, Sri Lanka, Argentina, Russia and Ukraine, see James Kynge and Gabriel Wildau, 'China: With Friends Like These: Beijing Has Lent Billions to Spread Its Influence, but as Defaults Loom Its Approach Is Shifting,' Financial Times, 18 March 2015, available at https://www.ft.com/content/2bb4028a-cbf0-11e4-aeb5-00144feab7de#axzz3UjntSr6oInboxx.

[58]See Shihar Aneez, 'Sri Lanka Intensifies Scrutiny of Chinese Projects' (2015) available at http://www.reuters.com/article/us-srilanka-projects-china-idUSKBN0MU16A20150403.

[59]In a recent talk, 'Is the One Belt One Road Initiative a New BIT to China's BIT Law Regime?' delivered at the Xi'an Jiaotong University—School of Law's Silk Road Institute of International and Comparative Law 10th International Symposium Xi'an 1 November 2016, Professor Wei Shen made this point by using the political stability index (I suppose for lack of specification he is referring to the *Worldwide Governance Indicators* developed by the World Bank) to show that the vast majority of OBOR countries represent extremely risky investment for China.

> provid[ing] the public support for implementing the Initiative. We should carry forward the spirit of friendly cooperation of the Silk Road by promoting extensive cultural and academic exchanges, personnel exchanges and cooperation, media cooperation, youth and women exchanges and volunteer services, so as to win public support for deepening bilateral and multilateral cooperation.

I have hinted at the fact that China has eschewed cultural actions from its OBOR initiatives but it is perhaps time to requalify the statement. As a matter of fact, China has engaged in ample cultural diffusion within and outside the Silk Road. For instance, and in addition to the drama show with which I opened the chapter, one could think of the production of a cartoon series and a multi-episode series documentary both on the history of the Silk Road as well as different cultural festivals in China, Central Asia and in South East Asia. Or the recent motion picture *Dragon Blade* starring John Cusack, Adrien Brody and Jackie Chan with the latter being the wise captain, Huo An, of the Silk Road Protection Squad, who tells the Roman General, Lucius, "You train kill people. We train save people".[60]

Furthermore, the Government of China has been sponsoring rather lavishly academic conferences, think tanks, research and university networks discussing and propagating the idea. For example, Xi'an Jiaotong University has launched the University Alliance of the Silk Road (UANSR) and the New Silk Road Alliance of Law Schools as well as started the think tank Collaborative Innovation Centre for Silk Road Economic Belt Studies. Funding for conferences includes both a plethora of domestic and international meetings.[61]

And these Silk Road-specific initiatives must be piled up on top of the spread of Mandarin-language education through an ever-expanding network of Confucius Institutes,[62] China's openness and financial support to foreign students learning a number of subjects (including Mandarin) in the mainland through government and city scholarships as well as special bilateral agreements providing scholarships for country-specific students in particular those coming from Africa and Central Asia.

---

[60]This sentence is produced in the context of a fight between Huo An and Lucius interrupted by the former due to an impending sandstorm suggesting the Chinese force could host the Roman army behind the castle walls and later help them fight the "evil" Roman Tiberius. I mention this here because, as we shall see, there is a line of inquiry that views China's promotion of some of its classical philosophy and virtues as being purely instrumental. In this context, the movie *Dragon Blade* easily fits the bill by portraying China as the "good guys" providing and ensuring justice and friendship along the Silk Road.

[61]In addition to the conference mentioned on footnote 60, I was involved in the organization of a recent event "Road to New Paradigms: Impact of China's Silk Road Initiative in China, Central Asia and the EU" held jointly by different institutions of XJTU and Helsinki University taking place in Helsinki, May 9–10 2016.

[62]For an analysis of China's recent efforts on international education through the creation of Confucius Institute(s) and China's participation in United Nations Educational Programs, see Li (2012) also highlighting China's contribution towards building schools in developing countries as well as offering scholarships without, arguably, wishing to exercise political influence. But see the recent article (Yuan et al. 2016) suggesting that the impact of Confucius Institutes in China's global interests has not been positive.

Yet, despite China's efforts, to my mind, there is something off about its cultural initiatives. In order to see what, I suggest we take a look at another historical cooperation design: The Colombo Plan. By analyzing how Australia is reinterpreting and refashioning the old Colombo Plan we can learn from what it deems to be a missed opportunity for *genuine cultural exchange* and one which we can fruitfully use to think ahead regarding the OBOR. In that regard, I will briefly introduce the original Colombo Plan focusing on Australian perceptions. Then, I present the New Colombo Plan and the reasons that led to such refashioning. I highlight what can be learned in terms of the relationship between education and soft power.[63]

4.2 *No, It Is Not the Marshal Plan. It Is the Colombo Plan!*

The BRI was promptly compared to the 1948 US-led Marshall Plan.[64] The Chinese government and press has rejected such a comparison from the outset mostly due to its ideological Western liberal connotations (in less charitable terms, its crusade against communism) whereas the OBOR is arguably universal.[65] While I think this statement is unfair as different accounts show how the Marshall Plan was open to liberal and socialist (it was rejected by the Soviet Union and Soviet countries), small and large countries alike[66]; I think this is also an unwise comment as the Marshall Plan is probably "one of the few positive metaphors in circulation in the gloomy circuits of world affairs."[67] Especially, because irrespective of what we may think of the plan, it clearly stands with the BRI as a needed example of resolute action in a depressing (albeit for different reasons) international economic and social context.

In any case, I want to recall and focus on the Colombo Plan[68] which evokes an atmosphere of voyage due to its origin—the Sri-Lankan city of Colombo—its lack of present day currency and the totally unrelated coincidence of being named similarly to one of history's greatest explorers.

The Colombo Plan, a nearly forgotten but significant venture,[69] was set up in 1950 in the form of 6-year plans by the Commonwealth Foreign Ministers and

[63]For an introduction to the concept applied to China, see Hunter (2009).

[64]For the inspiration of the plan, see Alfred Marshall's words in Spahn (2004), 191.

[65]Some of the data reported in the first sections of the present chapter cast doubts on whether the OBOR's is not actually advancing a path towards liberalization to help economies in transition. On the conditions attached to US aid—"free play for market forces"—see DeLong (2004).

[66]See the volume Agnew and Entrikin (2004b).

[67]Agnew and Entrikin (2004a), p. 18.

[68]For an introduction, see Cohen (1951) and Ward (1951). For an early reaction to the program's first decade, see Bryant (1961).

[69]Younger generations of participating donor countries have never heard of it.

considered by Daniel Oakman the "world's longest running bilateral aid program".[70] The forgetfulness of the plan has probably something to do with its low-profile. While it is true that there was an opening exhibition, one cannot compare it with the propaganda apparatus deployed to foster the OBOR.[71] Just recently for instance, Chinese silk worms on board of China's *Tiangong II* space mission have spun "Silk Road".[72] The monitoring of the execution of the program is also being advertised in style with the publication of the results of the ranking of 64 countries on a China-created index of contribution towards the OBOR goals.[73] Russia, Kazakhstan and Thailand occupy the first three positions (in this order) and the first two were lauded as having been "extremely cooperative" with the initiative.

The Colombo Plan founding countries were Australia, Canada, Ceylon, India, New Zealand, Pakistan and the United Kingdom (including Malaya and British Borneo) though it now comprises 27 countries. The plan was set up to improve the living conditions of South East Asian countries and its first eight million sterling pounds were destined to improve agriculture, infrastructure and technical assistance (education and training) to lift those countries from poverty. There was a clear political goal: given the widespread misery in South East Asia[74] and the perceived relationship between misery and road to communism, the donor countries conceived the plan as an attempt to thwart the spread and rise of communism in the region.[75]

The priorities were agriculture, transport and communication as well as fuel, energy and mining. However, 20% of the plan's budget was devoted to investments on social capital including housing, health and education leading for instance to thousands of students going to the donor countries to study and acquire solid training

---

[70]See Oakman (2004), p. 3.

[71]For some details on the activities and products devised to spread the Colombo Plan, see Lowe (2010).

[72]http://www.chinadaily.com.cn/china/2016-10/27/content_27189979.htm.

[73]http://www.chinadaily.com.cn/china/2016-10/29/content_27211979.htm. The index analyses five areas of cooperation "policy communication, connectivity, trade, finance and public support" and was based on "300 billion pieces of information".

[74]This is a key distinguishing element behind the Colombo Plan as it was devised to lift an entire region out of poverty fact which is confirmed by looking at the projects sponsored by capital aid. The OBOR aims to increase social well-being but the purpose is more to develop markets in Central Asia and connect better existing ones rather than avowedly fight poverty. Explicitly highlighting the poor diets and caloric intake in most target countries at the time and the subsequent focus on developing farming, dairy and sugar industries, see from the perspective of New Zealand, Gorrie (1959).

[75]In 1961, the donor countries were Australia, New Zealand, the United Kingdom, U.S.A. and Japan and the target countries were Burma, Cambodia, Ceylon, India, Indonesia, Laos, Federation of Malaya, Nepal, North Borneo, Pakistan, Philippines, Sarawak, Singapore, Thailand and Vietnam.

in different disciplines. For example, until 1961 some "23,000 students trained under the Technical Assistance scheme".[76]

Money was not poured into the countries directly but the latter had to present projects which specifics and nature were then decided through bilateral funding agreements with the donors.[77] As in the BRI, there is no central and external determination of domestic policy at least not *de jure*, though, *de facto*, it is unquestionable that negotiations are hardly free and untainted by power asymmetries.[78] Also as in the OBOR, the Colombo plan was supported by an international development bank, the International Bank for Reconstruction and Development.[79] It is worth saying too that as in the other plans, commentators praised the gesture of international cooperation even if the impact would prove to be limited.[80]

4.3 *Australia's Soft Regionalism and the Colombo(s) Plan(s)*

In the case of Australia, the first 10 years of funding for training and education purposes were described as follows:

> The Colombo Plan training programme is the stimulus which is bringing so many private Asian students to Australia. In June, 1952, there were 2,307 private Asian students in this country. By June, 1960, this number had grown to 7,918. ... Australia has provided 3,184 training awards up to the end of 1960. During 1961 over 900 students will be here studying under the Colombo Plan. Australia has trained 480 engineers, 346 specialists in education, 314 in public administration, 222 in nursing, 176 in agriculture and 208 in medicine and health; in addition, training has been given to students in many other fields (such as accountancy, science, etc. Australia has also given 2,107 awards under a correspondence scholarship scheme. This has produced results beyond the mere numbers of trainees. Malaya has now established a correspondence scheme of its own, for which key personnel have been trained in Australia under the Colombo Plan. Australian experts have served overseas at the request of Asian Governments in the last ten years.[81]

---

[76]Bryant (1961), p. 10.

[77]For early figures and a description of some of the investments, see Guiducci (1952).

[78]The same basically applies to the Marshall Plan though the latter instituted a much more multilateral approach especially on the target countries' side which were forced to agree among themselves upon a project and then submit it to the US Congress.

[79]The OBOR is supported by the AIIB and the New Development Bank.

[80]Bryant (1961), p. 15.

[81]*Idem*, p. 10.

And by the 1970s when the program was restructured, Australia had already trained and provided education to around 40,000 South East Asians.[82] The hosting of Colombo plan students in Australia (together with other private students) is defined by different authors as embodying a form of *Australia's soft regionalism*,[83] a gesture to signal Australia's openness towards Asia.[84] At the same time, it was also seen as an opportunity to educate the "Other", i.e. the Asians, about them (the Australians) and thus to train and hopefully create Western-minded elites which then would return home and act accordingly. This cultural focus is important as the plan was considered, among one of the countries at least, to have "potential in generating personal relationships between Asians and Australians" and it was absolutely central to introduce Asia "into Australian consciousness".[85]

Recent work on the Colombo Plan as Australia's and New Zealand's "soft regionalism" highlights the role of the Colombo plan in generating "cultural diplomacy" but speaks of different fates regarding the cultural impact of the plan abroad and domestically. David Lowe's research argues that while it is difficult to say that Australia and New Zealand managed to communicate strongly a cultural message outside of the elites of the target countries, the same is not true for what the Colombo Plan has managed to do within the borders of donor countries. As such, David Lowe writes that "[i]n the late 1960s ... departments in both countries were remarking how, in the public mind, every Asian student on the street was assumed to be a Colombo Plan student".[86]

It is easy to see though, that we are essentially speaking about a *one-way form of cultural communication* since it is Asians who are told about Australia, its history and cultural specificity. In other words, everything is about *the donor country telling the target country and its population* about itself through books, radio programs and magazines[87] in addition to having students learning the language of the host country as well as their culture during their training or program of studies. But whereas awareness of things-Asian (and people) was achieved, together with publicity of the country; the opposite is not true. Little have Australians learned about Asia, its cultures, languages, knowledges and lifestyles. That is, the Colombo plan largely failed to generate *two-way cultural exchange* among the participating countries and populations.

This is my point of contention for China as I believe that given the already existing resentment towards Chinese investment, work and business ethics in target

---

[82]Weigold (2013), p. 16.

[83]*Ibidem.*

[84]Megarrity (2007), p. 89 demonstrates that "during much of the 1950s and 1960s, the Australian government saw Colombo Plan scholarships as the central means of providing publicity for Australia's positive new relationship with Asia in the post-war period...".

[85]Oakman (2004), p. 4. As a byproduct, the Colombo Plan helped Australia to move forward on its racial "White Policy". See also Megarrity (2007).

[86]Lowe (2010), p. 16.

[87]*Idem*, p. 10.

countries' populations; China would certainly benefit from taking seriously the shortcomings of cultural exchange within the Colombo Plan and it can draw inspiration from Australia which has explicitly recognized and addressed such cultural shortcomings.

As Auriol Weigold reports, the New Colombo Plan outline was advanced by the Coalition Government's Foreign Policy plan and the new cultural policy is reflected in two of the 25 objectives to be achieved by 2025 sketched in the Australian Labor Government's White Paper *Australia in the Asian Century's Implementation Plan* released in April 2013: "Australia will have deeper and broader people-to-people links with Asian nations ...', and 'Australia will have stronger, deeper and broader cultural links with Asian nations'."[88]

But for Weigold having meaningful and deep knowledge of the "Other", the Asians, requires shifting from *one-track* to a *two-way* vision of cultural exchange.[89] The New Colombo Plan Scholarship and Mobility programs achieve just that by offering conditions to Australian undergraduate students aged 18–28 and to Australian universities to sponsor "semester-based or short-term study, internships, mentorships, practicums and research in 38 host locations across the Indo-Pacific region."[90]

In turn, for Auriol Weigold, this change requires motivating the youth much more directly than was done so far.[91] She proposed that funded student-exchange and degree programs and internships to be undertaken by Australian students in South East Asia, require adequate Asian and South East Asian language-training to be provided in Australia.[92] In fact, already early on, in 1961, G.M. Bryant noted, the depth and quality of Australia's contribution to the Colombo Plan was curtailed due to insufficient linguistic knowledge and training:

> ... the principal recipients have been those where it is comparatively easy to find students and workers with an adequate knowledge of English. In Cambodia and Laos, it is difficult to find students with sufficient knowledge of English to be able to gain any benefit from coming to an English-speaking country. Similarly, it is difficult to find experts able to impart their skills in these countries. *The failure of Australia's education systems to develop any Asian language training is now preventing Australia from being a fully effective contributor to the technical development of our Northern neighbours.*[93]

What is more as Weigold wisely adds, this enhanced exotic languages training requires a matching School's Policy and indeed the Coalition program boasted teaching of the main languages of the region by 2015 by rapidly raising the numbers

---

[88]Weigold (2013), p. 13. Notice the unequivocal textual resemblance between these statements and China's BRI "people-to-people bonds".

[89]*Idem*, p. 14.

[90]Taken from the official website available at http://dfat.gov.au/people-to-people/new-colombo-plan/mobility-program/Pages/mobility-program.aspx.

[91]Weigold (2013), p. 14.

[92]*Idem*, p. 15.

[93]Bryant (1961), p. 12, emphasis added.

of those teaching such languages either by reconverting them into teaching diplomas, mobilizing available existing resources and ensuring high-quality university language education.[94] It should be mentioned that both prongs of the New Colombo Plan mentioned above support the learning of one of the host country's official or widely spoken language, though this learning is to take place in the host location.

The lessons for China of this short example are three I believe.

First, the shift in attitude from the Colombo Plan to the New Colombo Plan reflects a healthy acceptance that the once target country can become an inspiring source of knowledge and example and thus we should be open to motivate national populations to go and learn from them and hopefully return enriched and better-prepared culturally speaking. Of course, this shift in Australian policy is not naive and just culture-friendly driven. Asia has become the engine of the world's growth and thus it is only logical that politicians believe that *now* Australian citizens have good reasons to learn from Asia and go back as enlightened elites. In any case, I believe that China has much to gain in terms of cultural diplomacy and soft power if it communicates to the OBOR countries that it is open to have its citizens be exposed to what the OBOR nations have to offer well beyond economic goods, currencies and energy sources. Recent evidence on the results of China's growing engagement with African countries[95] (including at the educational level),[96] highlights exactly this one-sidedness of the learning process with Africans being led to learn Mandarin and to study or train in China[97] while concomitantly Chinese migrants in Africa showing low levels of integration in local life in part due to poor language skills (which are not emphasized or provided by China either; it is important to stress this as much of the migration to Africa took, and still takes, place within a governmental framework and thus one should identify the responsibilities of the said government in framing the style of migration it wishes to pursue).[98] More importantly, this has led to the politicization of China's investment and migration by African leaders accusing China of "new imperialism"[99] and African business organizations and trade unions

[94]Weigold (2013), p. 15.

[95]For a comprehensive survey of the literature on China-Africa relations up to 2015, see Asongu and Ssozi (2015).

[96]It goes without saying that there is no unified African attitude or voice on China and Chinese migration.

[97]For Cameroon, see Nordtveit (2011). For Kenya, and highlighting how growing interest of Kenyan citizens in learning Mandarin and study or train in China is connected to China's economic presence in Kenya, see King (2010).

[98]Mohan and Tan-Mullins (2009), p. 597. See also Asongu and Ssozi (2015), p. 21ff.

[99]For sources, see Mohan and Tan-Mullins (2009), p. 589.

publicly denouncing the model of Chinese development (based on low labor standards and unfair competition) and "China's role in national economies."[100]

Second, the Australian shift and Weigold's remarks remind us that while China has a generous cultural-diplomacy policy of funding scholarships for foreign students to come to China it should focus too on sending its students outwards. China would gain from sending its own students and young professionals (in the context of internships) even to countries which are not perhaps the most developed in the world. Only by expanding its cultural interest beyond the most prestigious American, British and other Western powerhouse university traditions can China signal genuine interest outside established logics of immediate economic gain. To be open to send Chinese students abroad to less rich countries, to study less-known and popular or useful languages and knowledge (*savoirs*) is an idea worth keeping in mind in the context of China's expansion of academic cooperation as evidenced by the already mentioned Silk Road University and Law School Alliances. China would probably be the first country in the world (with superpower ambitions) doing it but that would be just right for a country *which claims to exert a different style of normative leadership in and for the world*. This idea may be hard to sell but given that China wishes to build a sustainable OBOR and generate "people-to-people bonds" then both goals marry well in a form of deep two-way engagement with the citizens and peoples of all OBOR countries. Once again, the Australian New Colombo Plan could serve as a model since the list of the 38 host locations together with the prohibition of sending more than 15 recipients to any single country, readily conveys the impression that cultural openness rather than immediate economic benefit is the goal.[101]

Third, as Weigold's article makes clear, such a change in policy requires clear institutional articulation and vision since it needs the deployment of a considerable teaching force in language-training. This is particularly important in China, I submit, due to its traditional focus in encouraging its students to study "useful" languages only and inclusively, as of recently, even reducing the weight of English in the *Gaokao* exam (with plans to remove it altogether) as well as postponing the teaching of English in elementary school.[102]

[100] *Idem*, p. 600. See also Asongu and Ssozi (2015), p. 22ff highlighting the need for deep thinking about the actual benefits of Chinese investment in Africa for the latter if we are to see a sustainable model of development to emerge in the area; rather than one that is often said to jeopardize local economies.

[101] The full list includes Bangladesh, Bhutan, Brunei Darussalam, Cambodia, China, Cook Islands, Federated States of Micronesia, Fiji, Hong Kong SAR, India, Indonesia, Japan, Kiribati, Laos, Malaysia, Maldives, Marshall Islands, Mongolia, Myanmar, Nauru, Nepal, Niue, Pakistan, Palau, Papua New Guinea, Philippines, Republic of Korea, Samoa, Singapore, Solomon Islands, Sri Lanka, Taiwan, Thailand, Timor-Leste, Tonga, Tuvalu, Vanuatu and Vietnam.

[102] For a survey of the causes behind this shift which include Chinese identity and culture preservation concerns, see Zhao (2016).

5 Normative Leadership in International Relations

I have just proposed one practical avenue for China to improve its image in the countries along the OBOR thereby reinforcing the prospects of a sustainable Belt and Road Initiative. The reader could, however, think that such a plea for China to engage genuinely with the Other along the OBOR is plainly too idealistic and typical of Western minds wishing to encumbering China's rise with exceptional normative responsibilities. After all, despite potential 'neo-colonialism" charges or beliefs about the impossibility of a purely neutral OBOR (enough looking at the choice of the privileged target-countries), one could argue that money talks and thus there is nothing wrong in China proceeding with its initiative as it is. Even if at the cost of not dissipating widespread fears about the nature of its rise and the role of the BRI and regional institutional frenzy in the latter.

I would like to argue, in this section, that there are important voices in China that ask for a clear articulation of China's moral vision behind its foreign policy and the OBOR. Thus, the argument I have built so far is no foreigner's folly. Moreover, some of these voices propose that China puts forwards a new style of normative leadership leading by moral example rather than hard power. Thus, I suggest we look at Yan Xuetong's recent turn to pre-Qin philosophy in order to devise a moral style of international leadership. Yan is certainly not the only author looking back to ancient Chinese philosophy but he offers both the most comprehensive account (in English) and a middle-ground level of analysis.[103] He also sides with my complaints against China's obsession with economic factors and argues that if China wants to be seen as a responsible power and to exercise a distinctive style of leadership,[104] it has to overcome its narrow focus on economic interests.

In the following sub-sections, I first introduce the thought of Yan Xuetong helping to show he is promoting a moral view of international leadership and how this plea joins forces with the "virtue ethics turn" in international relations and international law. Then, I present and afterwards discuss a number of criticisms of Yan's work which raise suspicions about the desirability (for the rest of the world) to strengthen China's public diplomacy via the articulation of a moral vision. My goals are twofold. On the one hand, I want to establish that there is a Chinese discourse that can be mobilized to help shaping the BRI into a more full-fledged cultural and moral agenda. On the other hand, I wish to show that while it is important that China builds a clearer moral vision, we should evaluate it immersed in its context and based on its institutional implications.

[103]Another presentation of Chinese political philosophy partially dealing with international relations and arguing for China to lead by moral example is Bai (2012). In addition, it is worth mentioning his remark that "Chinese" was originally indicated by characters that meant "civilized people" and not any racial distinction making Chinese thinking truly universal. Bai also suggests we should turn to ancient Chinese philosophy to help deal with some contemporary problems arguing that ancient Chinese philosophy is properly "modern". This is because it was *already* concerned with (1) providing a new social glue for shifting territories with large populations; and, (2) discussing legitimacy standards of the ruler.

[104]Yan (2011), pp. 65–66.

5.1 *Yan Xuetong's Vision*

With the OBOR and the new regionalist institutional design I have traced in the paper, China is undoubtedly raising its game at the international level. It does so according to a traditional Chinese idea according to which the responsibilities of each state should depend on each country's power and capabilities.[105] The OBOR is a direct expression of this thought with China assuming its responsibilities due to its increasing power. But these initiatives reveal a deeper stance on the international system confirming that China is a now a player that wants to *write* the rules of the game and not just follow existing ones.

Yan Xuetong, a worldwide famous International Relations scholar typically associated to neo-realism (a school of thought within International Relations which emphasizes material factors such as military capabilities and wealth),[106] believes that China can become or will become the next superpower of the world. From this starting point, he argues though that China ought to pursue this state of affairs not by becoming a *hegemon* (like the United States) but by exercising *moral* or *humane authority*, i.e. being all-under-heaven or *tianxia*. He argues that after Hu Jintao's promising "Harmonious World", China retrogressed by suggesting that "economic construction" should guide foreign affairs. And he is barely alone. Xu Jin also writes:

> ... when China's GDP has already attained a considerably high standard, the Chinese government should be all the more concerned about what kind of political ideal and model of social development should be created. This is not only to build a firm foundation for China's own rapid progress but, even more, to exert sufficient attraction to transcend the political ideals and social system of the West.[107]

The basic idea is that hegemonic authority still lacks a *legitimate basis* as it cannot ensure a beneficial effect *for the system as a whole*.[108] Yan grounds such a claim in ancient Chinese philosophy or pre-Qin thinking (a label which typically includes Confucian, Daoist, Mohist and Legalist authors together with the Guanzi and The Stratagems of the Warring States).[109]

For Yan, a hegemon is a superpower that acts with double standards deploying a strict instrumental ethical stance. That is, it upholds existing norms whenever that is in his interests and when it deals with friends but it breaches those norms whenever it deals with enemies or that breach can promote its national interest. A humane authority instead always acts morally promoting moral norms in all circumstances,

[105] See Zhang and Austin (2013) and Foot (2013).

[106] For a complete presentation of Yan Xuetong's credentials, see Cunningham-Cross (2014).

[107] Xu (2011), p. 179.

[108] Yan (2011), p. 65.

[109] For a complete panorama of ancient Chinese thought, see Schwartz (1985) and Fung (1983).

leading by moral example.[110] Yan grounds the difference between these two forms of authority in some ancient Chinese philosophy which emphasizes that benevolent authority ought to be moral and not simply backed by power and force, though it can't do away with them either.[111] A humane authority also has the duty to create new moral norms.[112] Yan summarizes it in an intervention for Theory Talk:

> Simply stated: being humane means having more friends and having a good political system that can mobilize both domestic and international support. Authority means, first of all, having huge material power and secondly, undertaking more international responsibility. If a state is not capable of using these resources, it means it has no power."[113]

How is this moral authority to be achieved and what does it translate into? Pre-Qin philosophers emphasized the quality of the political leadership of the state. Rather than postulating a grand-ethical vision for the world, ancient Chinese authors wrote that it is the quality of leaders and the quality of their appointed staffs that dictate the moral superiority and the exercise of good government.[114] For instance, in recalling a short passage, "an intelligent king and worthy prime-minister", from the classical text *The Stratagems of the Warring States*, Yan goes on to say

> The notion of the intelligent prince stresses the importance of the leadership of the ruler, whereas that of the worthy prime minister stresses the importance of the collective leadership of the policy makers.[115]

Thus, it is no wonder that Yan Xuetong extracts two practical suggestions from such a normative framework under the heading: "employ the best!".[116] First, China ought to choose its political staff based on merit alone (and not nationality) thus opening up the Government to foreigners and allowing them to climb hierarchically. Second, China should distinguish *technical expertise* from *leadership skills* and ought to employ people possessing the latter; a thought that is consentaneous with pre-Qin thinkers who often emphasized political leadership over technical expertise. It is interesting to note that the focus on recruitment and the morality of leaders or elite officials parallels a

---

[110]Yan (2011), p. 49 discusses Xunzi's view putting it like this "Xunzi thinks that both royal and hegemonic authority need the twin forces of power and morality, but that human authority relies more on morality and hegemonic authority more on power."

[111]Yan (2011), pp. 211–212.

[112]Creutzfeldt (2012).

[113]*Idem*, p. 2.

[114]Domestically, increasing importance is now paid to the quality of the training of the cadres of the Chinese Communist Party. See for example, Xi Jinping's speech "Train and Select Good Officials" (Xi 2014).

[115]Yan (2011), p. 117.

[116]*Idem*, p. 67.

recent turn in international relations[117] and international law[118] literatures towards virtue ethics and how international organizations' reputation and success largely depend on the exercise of leadership and virtues by their highest officials.

Pre-Qin philosophy is also deployed to put forward a theory about the stability of the international system which would be positively related to the morality of leaders and their political offices.[119] In turn, this moral authority will, arguably, lead to the emergence of a new, superior, world order. As two commentators aptly put:

> The most important aspect of the story Yan tells through his interpretation of pre-Qin thought is the pre-Qin belief that a *wang* state was beneficial not just for its own people but for the health of the whole interstate system.[120]

Furthermore, Yan notes, the label "morally superior power" cannot be proclaimed but *has to be ascribed* by the existing subjects and actors in the system.[121] This last comment makes it clear why such an agenda fits my line of argument as I have repeatedly stressed that China needs to change its cultural communication in order to *draw in* the partner countries along the OBOR in a durable and sustainable way. It can neither rely on economic interests nor on unilateral affirmation of it cultural superiority alone. Put shortly, Yan Xuetong's message[122] is:"[f]or China to become a true kingship state, therefore, its strategic goal must be to present to the world a better social role model."[123]

As argued before, in a period in which China is increasingly pointed at as offering a way out of Western Liberal Modernization it would be highly detrimental, because self-defeating, to its own aspirations to insist on a purely economic agenda.[124] Furthermore, while Yan Xuetong recognizes the need for China to improve its image diplomatically and for this to occur it needs to move beyond a pure economic agenda, his emphasis on moral authority and normative leadership is rather contentless. But in the previous sections we have provided some indications as to where to go. It should not just be about respecting international norms or asserting with Mencius that "the Benevolent has no enemies"; but to engage genuinely with the "Other" especially when you are turning into a superpower.

---

[117]Gaskarth (2012). The author explicitly connects the recruitment of International Criminal Court officials with the possession of certain virtuous character traits which, he argues, are necessary for the fulfilment of the international organization mission.

[118]Klabbers (2011).

[119]Yan (2011), p. 64ff. He gives Clinton and George W. Bush as examples elaborating how with Clinton's stress on multilateralism and respect for international norms, the international system was much more stable than with George W. Bush's unilateralism.

[120]Cunningham-Cross and Callahan (2011), p. 357.

[121]See Yan (2011), p. 65.

[122]See also from a pre-Qin (Mencian) perspective, Xu (2011), p. 179 "Hence, if China wants [to] become a humane authority, it should establish itself as a model polity for the world."

[123]Cunningham-Cross and Callahan (2011), p. 370.

[124]To avoid entering superficial debates on whether China is capitalist or socialist, I recommend consulting Arrighi (2008), where the author suggests, following a rereading of Adam Smith, that we should distinguish between capitalist and non-capitalist market-based development.

5.2 *Critiques to Yan's Pre-Qin Philosophy Turn: Chinese Hierarchical Supremacy Not Moral and Cultural Pluralism*

Is Yan's proposal a panacea? Not really as we shall see. Furthermore, his agenda was openly criticized in a number of articles by Linsay Cunningham-Cross, both alone and writing with William Callahan.[125]

Undeniably, there are obvious methodological shortcomings in Yan Xuetong's approach to pre-Qin philosophy. For instance, it is too stretched to speak of "pre-Qin philosophy teachings" as a unified concept since as Yan himself admits, for instance, Laozi would be against an agenda for international relations or active promotion of a normative vision. Enough to revisit the end of the famous chapter 80 of the Laozi

> Although your neighboring states are within eyesight
> And the sounds of their dogs and cocks are within earshot,
> Your people will grow old and die without having anything to do with them.[126]

A more important critique perhaps is that these authors accuse Yan Xuetong of turning to culture and traditional Chinese thought in order to *promote China's global domination* rather than contributing to a more pluralistic world. They do so by placing Yan's turn to ancient Chinese thought within the full scope and contents of his work which emphasizes power, security, individual state sovereignty and national interest. Thus, the authors argue, ancient Chinese thought and the moral authority that is spoken of ought to be read as a mere instrumental component of domestic and international power build-up.[127]

Cunningham-Cross and Callahan also caution strongly against the "new universal" Yan Xuetong's vision presupposes. According to them, Yan provides a reductive and dichotomous reading of history in which powers are either bad/hegemons (*ba*) or good/humane authorities (*wang*) offering a teleological model which, in its application, is tainted by the fact that the US are always *ba* and China always *wang*.[128] As they write:

> Yan, however, takes for granted the moral goodness of China's rise and seeks to help policy-makers universalize these largely unexamined values. Hence these public intellectuals are

---

[125]See Cunningham-Cross (2014).

[126]See Ames and Hall (2003), p. 202. Thus, an initiative such as the OBOR would just trigger more problems in the future. Likewise, Daoist teachings are explicitly against employing virtuous persons as they would create further distinctions which only produces conflicts. This "cherry-picking" critique is developed in greater detail by Cunningham-Cross and Callahan (2011).

[127]See Cunningham-Cross (2014), p. 39.

[128]Cunningham-Cross and Callahan (2011), p. 366ff. Quite coherently, they also call attention to the non-neutral editorial decision of translating *wang* by "humane" rather than "kingly" way which downgrades the unipolar and hierarchical nature of Yan's model for the world system.

addressing quite different publics: special interests (Liu), human interest (Xu), and national interest (Yan).[129]

Thus, having moral norms and moral authority would only deepen the powers and influence of the world leader and would simply amount to cover up the replacement of one hegemonic authority and normative vision for another equally non-pluralistic.[130] This conclusion needs to be taken seriously as it would jeopardize the deployment of Yan's theses in favor of a richer Chinese moral vision for international relations. It is true that Yan's proposals can easily be read in the instrumental way just sketched. After all, he relies on power and supports the rise of China. Indeed, Yan's writings could represent but one more iteration of Gloria Davies's famous argument according to which, in their research, Chinese scholars must follow the moral imperative of worrying about China and contributing to solving China's problems.[131] And yet, I don't think the objections raised by the authors are unsurmountable. Let us see why starting with an additional critique against Yan's project.

5.3 Displacing the Critiques: Non-Ideal Theory, no Cosmopolitanism, Institutional and Moral Competition

When for instance, Yan advocates for the establishment of norms as an example of moral authority, one ought to recall that for Xunzi, the ancient Chinese author he deploys, these norms are norms about *hierarchical and social divisions*. This is because, for Xunzi, social hierarchies are *necessary* to prevent social conflict by determining clearly the role and status of each individual and in turn defining what he/she is entitled to; hence curbing human nature's drive to desire endless things (the source of social disharmony). After all, without classes or ranks, the unrestrained desires of individual beings would clash endlessly as there would be no limits as to what they could desire.[132] Thus, "establishing norms" as moral behavior is to create classes and introduce hierarchy in world relations.

But this doesn't enable the conclusion that the hierarchically superior groups have no duties towards society and/or the least privileged ones. In fact, in the Confucian tradition, it is up to *li* (rites) to both create events where all social groups can meet (irrespective of distinctions) and uphold the different distinctions by imposing stricter obligations to more privileged groups.

---

[129] *Ibidem.*

[130] This charge against the potential for a harmonizing force imposing a hierarchy in the world, was also the central critique made to Zhao Tingyang's *tianxia*-based political philosophy by Callahan (2008).

[131] See Davies (2009).

[132] See the discussion in Yan (2011), p. 104ff. For more details, see chapter nine "The Rule of a True King" in Hutton (2014), pp. 68–82.

One can read Confucius, Xunzi or Mencius (within the classics) but I think that the best way of seeing how rites are designed to balance privileges and duties and thus ensure social harmony by avoiding that lower groups resent the privileged ones and that the latter simply disconnect from the former, is to read one of the four Chinese classical novels: *The Story of the Stone*. It tells the rise and fall of the *Jia* family partially due to unrestrained spending and *incuria* but also due to the different burdens and obligations *a rich family* is tied to *and cannot refuse.*[133] A contemporary example of this type of positive integrative social function of hierarchy[134] is Yan's example of how international sovereign equality does not amount to equity and thus to achieve equity we may have to forego perfect equality among states at the level of norms. For example, he discusses how China accepted an unequal norm with ASEAN (applying zero tariffs in agricultural trade) before ASEAN countries had to. In contrast, Japan has insisted on equal tariffs and thus relations with ASEAN have developed more slowly.[135]

This type of reasoning could help to justify the proposal I made in previous sections according to which China ought to engage genuinely with the "Other" by for instance engaging in two-way cultural and educational exchanges. Even if this involves sending students and young professionals to countries where a typical cost/benefit analysis would highly disapprove doing so. The point is that following Yan's line of argument, China's moral vision behind the OBOR and its growing status in the world would demand from it exemplary moral behavior as well as creating new moral norms. These would be necessary to counterbalance the growing power of China and the factual inequalities and hierarchies that come associated to this status which any critical eye finds in the array of contracting and negotiations around and along the OBOR. The only difference is that reliance on Yan's proposal (and Xunzi) here would make it *explicit* rather than hidden behind a neutral technocratic win-win and poetic civilizational diversity discourse.

In other words, I believe that behind the critiques of Cunningham-Cross and Callahan may lie an *undiscussed preference* for ideal as opposed to non-ideal theorizing and analysis in ethical discourse. For instance, a pragmatist evaluation of international affairs would emphasize that more than cosmopolitan universal and abstract principles (such as for instance R2P which the authors do not discuss), the real challenge lies in determining who has which responsibilities allocated on the basis of which principles. Therefore, the factual inequality of states in terms of capabilities would necessarily have to be considered in the definition of the duties to be shouldered by each state.

Furthermore, it seems to me that in claiming that Yan is actually promoting the superiority of Chinese values and not a truly morally pluralistic stance, Linsay Cunningham-Cross and William Callahan write from the typical Western perspective

[133]For a modern take on rites along the lines just described applied to different issues, see Bell (2008).

[134]Arguing that international order is hierarchical, not anarchical, see Lake (2009).

[135]Yan (2011), p. 104ff.

of rejecting competition between different moral visions every time the latter are not to the West's liking. This is quite clear for example when Cunningham-Cross and Callahan compliment other Chinese thinkers which are said to go beyond what is good for the Chinese people by considering what can be good for the people of the world.

> While Liu seeks to rebalance (economic) wealth and (military) power, Xu thinks that the real choice is between promoting 'wealth and power' or 'civilization'. He chooses 'civilization'; but unlike historicists who look to the exceptionalism of China's ancient values, Xu looks to the future. He argues that China needs to pursue the global mainstream universal values of liberal democracy, human rights and social justice.[136]

But it turns out that Cunningham-Cross and Callahan end up applauding the author, Xu, who promotes *global mainstream values such as "liberal democracy, human rights and social justice"*. It is hard to just do away with the feeling that at stake is a pure preference for authors who endorse Western global values. A preference for which any moral vision that does not converge towards the existing axiological model is a dangerous moral vision or one that should have no place in our discourses. I think otherwise and since ethical theorizing has been unable to ground foundational arguments for universal moral visions and there is little hope that such a task can be achieved any time soon,[137] I believe that a pluralistic moral world needs competing and clashing moral visions and not just the incumbent one, i.e. "ours" as of Western (or a cosmopolitan one with our values).[138]

I should hasten to add that I find it very difficult—not to say impossible—to conceive of any moral vision that is not, by definition, totalizing. Even the liberal moral imaginary promotes a specific understanding of the Good, one in which, for instance, it is not proper to blast liberal values or impose another version of the Good[139] that does not follow the liberal canons, e.g. first and foremost, human rights.[140]

Furthermore, because the background and default position is not a blank state but a Western moral and institutional vision with a specific superpower (albeit arguably in a declining route), the promotion of Chinese values and the action of Chinese-led regional institutions such as the already mentioned AIIB and New Development Bank together with older ones such as the Shanghai Cooperation Organization will

---

[136]Cunningham-Cross and Callahan (2011), p. 365.

[137]On the difficulty of making ethical arguments after postmodernism taking Badiou's work as an example, see Vilaça (2014).

[138]Arguing that the Legalist classic, Han Feizi, was probably the first text where it was asserted that pluralism of thought is inevitable and interpreted to give rise to unsolvable disagreement, see Bai (2012), p. 132. Han Feizi famously overcame the problem by proposing a political philosophy which "eradicated" all critical voices.

[139]I am quite critical of Badiou's conceptual work on ethics, but his diagnosis, on how "democratic materialism" in Western liberal societies prevents radical politics positing alternative visions of the Good (by labeling them totalitarian) thereby making Evil primary in ethics, is spot on. See Badiou (2013), pp. 1–9.

[140]Which however are not equally enforced. Hirschl (2007) argues that the triumphal spread of new constitutionalism hides a powerful ideological bias. Despite their constitutional status social rights remain poorly enforced (unlike liberal rights) and thus the new constitutionalism in practice, and paradoxically, has probably reinforced the liberal vision.

not conquer the world overnight. That is, an institutional clash between different sets of values and political visions must take place in and over time through a myriad of channels. And we should keep in mind that it's not only China that wishes to shape international law according to its values. For instance, pluralist writers may well have to come to terms with the coming into operation of the International Islamic Court of Justice created by the Organization of the Islamic conference.[141]

While Yan Xuetong fabricates a tradition that is not univocal (even if he admits it throughout his main book on the topic) and reduces international relations history to a binary logic, I still believe that his (based on Ancient Chinese thought) ideas are worth discussing *qua* ideas and that his vision can help push forward a more explicit moral grounding of the OBOR initiative. Pulling the different threads together, I believe that the gap between his work and some of the criticism voiced by Linsay Cunningham-Cross and William Callahan lies in that these authors seem to rely on a non-agonistic vision of politics. Such a consensual view of politics, as Chantal Mouffe has analyzed, replaces politics with *morals* and thus helps to establish the illusion that we can rationally solve political questions by moral fiat.[142] If it is true that Yan's reading of history as superpowers being hegemons or human authorities is premised on a simplistic moral code; his critics commit the same mistake by denying the institutional, political and moral context in which the rise of China is taking place. And they incur this error by replacing *political* engagement and disagreement with the view that China's *moral* vision is not morally desirable because it is not pluralist enough.

6 Conclusion

The reader could ask why I have criticized China's outlook *a propos* the lack of culture in the OBOR but not in the case of a potential promotion of a hierarchical vision of the world. I still see a difference between the appeal for China's genuine engagement with the "Other" and a critique of China's moral vision that is too unipolar. I believe that the OBOR is a plan with potential at a time the world needs some sort of impulse but I think that its success and sustainability depend on China changing the way in which it is perceived by many other countries and their populations. I suggested that this could be achieved by means of its cultural policy reversing the one-way or economic-oriented outlook deployed so far. Thus, I called for reorienting the cultural stance of China within existing commitments by evoking the historical, but still living, Colombo Plan for its "soft power" effect and the missing opportunities made patent in Australia's New Colombo Plan.

[141]For details on this court and more generally on the challenges of Islamic jurisprudence to existing international law, see Prost (2012), p. 115ff.

[142]Mouffe (2005).

I brought in Yan Xuetong's work because he also argues that China needs to do better diplomatically. Cunningham-Cross and Callahan claim that Yan's appeal hides purely instrumental and nationalistic goals, a sort of moral egoism and thus are afraid the turn to Chinese ancient thought only enacts and simultaneously legitimates China's rise to becoming a superpower that is necessarily good. Precisely because there is little explicit moral vision, I find this more an attack on Yan's lack of engagement with Western values and arguable instrumentalist thinking—as pointed out above—than a critique of specific values in his normative proposal. In doing so however, I believe that the authors are eschewing the way in which Yan Xuetong communicates with the recent virtue ethics turn in normative international relations and international law and the power of some ideas from Chinese traditional thinkers. When we disagree on values and fail to devise procedures to overcome such disagreement, one of the open ways of still trying to improve the quality of our institutions and policies may well be a focus on the moral cultivation and virtues of leaders and their apparatuses together with institutional competition. In this respect, albeit Yan's proposal is mostly directed at Chinese institutions, it can easily be translated into the international sphere not to mention the indirect contribution that better Chinese officials and leadership produce.

Of course, this does not dissolve the ethical problem as the debate then moves to the problem of knowing and applying the virtues in concrete contexts as well as that of knowing whether moral cultivation indeed leads to better choices. But due to this non-ideal world we live in, the complexity of moral inquiry and evaluation as well as the challenges of human life, I believe we have more to gain from open and transparent competition of ideas, moral visions and institutional plateaus than from cosmopolitan ideal formulations that fail to recognize agonistic politics and tend to suffocate politics with morals.

Acknowledgements I gratefully acknowledge the support of China Postdoctoral Science Foundation grant no. 2016M592767. A version of this chapter was presented at the conference "Road to New Paradigms: Impact of China's Silk Road Initiative in China, Central Asia and the EU" held jointly by different institutions of XJTU and Helsinki University taking place in Helsinki, May 9–10 2016. I thank the participants for their comments. The chapter benefited greatly from Gabriele Escoffier, Walter Rech, Goncalo Vilaça, Su Bian and three referees' detailed comments and feedback. All errors remain mine.

References

Agnew, J., & Entrikin, J. N. (2004a). Introduction: The Marshall Plan as model and metaphor. In J. Agnewa & J. N. Entrikin (Eds.), *The Marshall Plan today: Model and metaphor* (pp. 1–22). London: Routledge.

Agnew, J., & Entrikin, J. N. (Eds.). (2004b). *The Marshall Plan today: Model and metaphor*. London: Routledge.

Ames, R. T., & Hall, D. L. (Trans.) (2003). *Daodejing "making this life significant": A philosophical translation*. New York: Ballantine Books.

Arrighi, G. (2008). *Adam smith in Beijing: Lineages of the twenty-first century*. London: Verso.

Asongu, S., & Ssozi, J. (2015). *Sino-African Relations: Some solutions and strategies to the policy syndromes* (MPRA Paper No 67851). Retrieved from: https://mpra.ub.uni-muenchen.de/67851/1/MPRA_paper_67851.pdf

Badiou, A. (2013). *Logics of worlds (Logiques des Mondes).* (A. Toscano, Trans.). London: Bloomsbury.

Bai, T. (2012). *China: The political philosophy of the middle kingdom*. New York: Zed Books.

Bell, D. (2008). *China's new confucianism: Politics and everyday life in a changing society*. Princeton, NJ: Princeton University Press.

Boer, R. (2014). Socialist democracy with Chinese characteristics. *Crisis and Critique, 1*(1), 47–65.

Bryant, G. M. (1961). The Colombo plan: A decade of co-operation. *The Australian Quarterly, 33*(2), 7–17.

Burkhanov, A., & Chen, Y.-W. (2016). Kazakh perspective on China, the Chinese, and Chinese migration. *Ethnic and Racial Studies, 39*(12), 2129–2148.

Callahan, W. A. (2008). Chinese visions of world order: Post-hegemonic or a new hegemony? *International Studies Review, 10*, 749–761.

Casselman, J. W. (2007). China's latest 'Threat' to the United States: The failed Cnooc-Unocal merger and its implications for Exonflorio and Cfius. *Indiana International & Comparative Law Review, 17*(1), 155–186.

Ching, J. (1978). Chinese ethics and Kant. *Philosophy East and West, 28*(2), 161–172.

Chu, Y.-H., Kang, L., & Huang, M.-H. (2014). How east Asians view the rise of China. *Journal of Contemporary China, 24*(93), 398–420.

Cohen, J. B. (1951). The Colombo plan for cooperative economic development. *Middle East Journal, 5*(1), 94–100.

Creutzfeldt, B. (2012, November 28). *Yan Xuetong on Chinese Realism, the Tsinghua School of International Relations, and the Impossibility of Harmony* (Theory Talk #51). Retrieved from: at http://www.theory-talks.org/2012/11/theory-talk-51.html

Cunningham-Cross, L. (2014). A realist never changes his spots: A critical analysis of Yan Xuetong's turn to culture in Chinese international relations. In N. Horesh & E. Kavalski (Eds.), *Asian thought on China's changing international relations* (pp. 34–53). Basingstoke: Palgrave MacMillan.

Cunningham-Cross, L., & Callahan, W. A. (2011). Ancient Chinese power, modern Chinese thought. *The Chinese Journal of International Politics, 4*, 349–374.

Davies, G. (2009). *Worrying about China: The language of Chinese critical inquiry*. Cambridge, MA: Harvard University Press.

DeLong, J. B. (2004). Post-world war II western European exceptionalism: The economic dimension. In J. Agnew & J. N. Entrikin (Eds.), *The Marshall plan today: Model and metaphor* (pp. 25–57). London: Routledge.

Endo, S. (1997). *The Samurai* (V. C. Gessel, Trans.). New York: New Directions.

Foot, R. (2013). Chinese power and the idea of a responsible power. In Y. Zhang & G. Austin (Eds.), *Power and responsibility in Chinese foreign policy* (pp. 21–47). Canberra: ANU Press.

Frost, M. (2009). *Global ethics: Anarchy, freedom and international relations*. Oxon: Routledge.

Fung, Y.-L. (1983). *A history of Chinese philosophy. Vol. I: The period of the philosophers* (D. Bodde, Trans.). Princeton, NJ: Princeton University Press.

Gaskarth, J. (2012). The virtues in international society. *European Journal of International Relations, 18*(3), 431–453.

Gorrie, A. M. (1959). The Colombo plan. *New Zealand Geographer, 15*(1), 99–100.

Guiducci, U. (1952). Developments of the "Colombo plan" and possibilities for Euro-Asian collaboration. *East and West, 3*(2), 76–80.

Hegel, G. W. F. (2013). *Lectures on the philosophy of world history: Vol 1. Manuscripts of the introduction and the lectures of 1822–3* (R. F. Brown & P. C. Hodgson, Trans.). Oxford: Clarendon Press.

Hirschl, R. (2007). *Towards Juristocracy: The origins and consequences of the new constitutionalism*. Cambridge, MA: Harvard University Press.

Hu, J. (2005). *Build towards a harmonious world of lasting peace and common prosperity*. Retrieved from: http://www.un.org/webcast/summit2005/statements15/china050915eng.pdf
Hui, W. (2005). The new criticism. In C. Wang (Ed.), *One China, many paths* (pp. 55–86). London: Verso.
Hunt, L. (2014). *Writing history in the global era*. New York: W. W. Norton & Company.
Hunter, A. (2009). Soft power: China on the global stage. *Chinese Journal of International Politics, 2*, 373–398.
Hutton, E. L. (Trans.) (2014). Xunzi: The complete text. Princeton, NJ: Princeton University Press.
Johnson, C. K. (2016). *President Xi Jinping's 'Belt and Road' initiative: A practical assessment of the Chinese Communist Party's roadmap for China's global resurgence*. Washington, DC: Center for Strategic and International Studies.
Kent, A. (2006). Compliance v cooperation: China and international law. *Australian International Law Journal, 13*, 19–32.
Kent, A. (2013). China's participation in international organisations. In Y. Zhang & G. Austin (Eds.), *Power and responsibility in Chinese foreign policy* (pp. 132–166). Canberra: ANU E Press.
King, K. (2010). China's cooperation in education and training with Kenya: A different model? *International Journal of Educational Development, 30*(5), 488–496.
Klabbers, J. (2011). Controlling international organizations: A virtue ethics approach. *International Organizations Law Review, 8*(2), 285–289.
Kratochwil, F. (2001). International law as an approach to international ethics: A plea for a jurisprudential diagnostics. In J.-M. Coicaud & D. Warner (Eds.), *Ethics and international affairs: Extent and limits* (pp. 14–41). New York: United Nations University Press.
Lake, D. A. (2009). *Hierarchy in international relations*. London: Cornell University Press.
Lanteigne, M. (2009). *Chinese foreign policy: An introduction*. London: Routledge.
Li, S. X. (2012). China's international education initiatives and view of its role in global governance. *Frontiers of Education in China, 7*(1), 103–123.
Liu, M. (2016). BRICS development: A long way to a powerful economic club and new international organization. *The Pacific Review, 29*(3), 443–453.
Liu, Z. (2014). *Laying the foundations of peace and stability for an Asian Community of Shared Destiny*. Retrieved from: http://www.fmprc.gov.cn/mfa_eng/wjbxw/t1213622.shtml
Lostal, M., & Vilaça, G. V. (2015). The Bamiyazation of cultural heritage and the Silk Road economic Belt: Challenges and opportunities for China. *The Chinese Journal of Comparative Law, 3*(2), 1–19.
Lowe, D. (2010). *The Colombo Plan and 'Soft' Regionalism in the Asia-Pacific: Australian and New Zealand Cultural Diplomacy in the 1950s and 1960s*. The Alfred Deakin Research Institute Working Papers. Retrieved from: http://dro.deakin.edu.au/eserv/DU:30051862/lowe-colomboplan-2010.pdf
Marinetti, F. T. (2008). The new religion-morality of speed. In H. Rosa & W. E. Scheuerman (Eds.), *High-speed society: Social acceleration, power, and modernity* (pp. 57–59). University Park, PA: The Pennsylvania State University Press.
Masuda, M. (2009). China's search for a new foreign policy frontier: Concept and practice of "harmonious world". In M. Lida (Ed.), *China's shift: Global strategy of the rising power* (pp. 57–79). Tokyo: National Institute for Defense Studies.
McGregor, R. (2012). *The party: The secret world of China's communist rulers* (Rev. ed.). London: Penguin Books.
Megarrity, L. (2007). Regional goodwill, sensibly priced: Commonwealth policies towards Colombo plan scholars and private overseas students, 1945–1972. *Australian Historical Studies, 38*(129), 88–105.
Mohan, G., & Tan-Mullins, M. (2009). Chinese migrants in Africa as new agents of development? An analytical framework. *European Journal of Development Research, 21*(4), 588–605.
Mouffe, C. (2005). *On the political*. New York: Routledge.

Nijman, J. E. (2016). A universal rule of law for a pluralist world order: Leibniz's universal jurisprudence and his praise of the Chinese ruler. *ACIL Research Paper,* 2016-16.
Nordtveit, B. H. (2011). An emerging donor in education and development: A case study of China in Cameroon. *International Journal of Educational Development, 31*(2), 99–108.
Oakman, D. (2004). *Facing Asia: A history of the Colombo plan.* Canberra: Pandanus Books.
Pan, Z. (2014). *Silk Road economic Belt: A dynamic new concept for geopolitics in Central Asia.* China Institute of International Studies.
Polo, M. (2003). *The travels of Marco polo [The Venetian].* New York: Liveright.
Prost, M. (2012). *The concept of Unity in public international law.* Oxford: Hart Publishing.
Ren, X. (2016). China as an institution-builder: The case of the AIIB. *The Pacific Review, 29*(3), 435–442.
Rodrik, D. (2011). *The globalization paradox: Democracy and the future of the world economy.* New York: W. W. Norton & Company.
Sautman, B., & Yan, H. (2009). African perspectives on China–Africa links. *The China Quarterly, 199,* 728–759.
Schwartz, B. I. (1985). *The world of thought in ancient China.* Cambridge, MA: Belknap Press.
Slingerland, E. (2003). *Effortless action: Wu-wei as conceptual metaphor and spiritual ideal in early China.* New York: Oxford University Press.
Spahn, P. B. (2004). The Marshall Plan: Searching for 'creative peace' then and now. In J. Agnew & J. N. Entrikin (Eds.), *The Marshall Plan today: Model and metaphor* (pp. 191–213). London: Routledge.
Spence, J. D. (1985). *The memory palace of Matteo Ricci.* London: Penguin.
Valentini, L. (2012). Ideal vs. non-ideal theory: A conceptual map. *Philosophy Compass, 7*(9), 654–664.
Vilaça, G. V. (2014). Badiou's ethics: A return to ideal theory. *Badiou Studies, 3*(1), 271–321.
Vilaça, G. V. (2015). Transnational law, functional differentiation and evolution. *E-Pública, 2*(3), 40–83.
Vilaça, G. V. (2017). China and global governance: 'One Belt One Road,' the New Development Bank and the concept of market state. *Culture-History-Globalization, 22,* 241–258.
Wang, X. (2005). A manifesto for cultural studies. In C. Wang (Ed.), *One China, many paths* (pp. 274–291). London: Verso.
Wang, Y. (2016). Offensive for defensive: The Belt and Road initiative and China's new grand strategy. *The Pacific Review, 29*(3), 455–463.
Ward, E. E. (1951). The Colombo plan. *Australian Outlook, 5*(4), 191–202.
Weigold, A. (2013). Engaging with Asia: The new Colombo plan. *ISAA Review, 12*(2), 13–19.
Xi, J. (2014). *The governance of China.* Beijing: Foreign Languages Press.
Xu, J. (2011). The two poles of confucianism: A comparison of the interstate political philosophies of Mencius and Xunzi. In D. A. Bell & S. Zhe (Eds.), *Ancient Chinese thought, modern Chinese power* (pp. 161–180). Princeton, NJ: Princeton University Press.
Yan, X. (2011). *Ancient Chinese thought, modern Chinese power* (E. Ryden, Trans.). Princeton, NJ: Princeton University Press.
Yu, K. (2004). *From the discourse of 'Sino-West' to 'Globalization': Chinese perspectives on globalization.* Institute on Globalization and the Human Condition 04/1.
Yu, X. (1989). Legal pragmatism in the People's Republic of China. *Journal of Chinese Law, 3*(1), 29–51.
Yuan, Z., Guo, J., & Zhu, H. (2016, November). Confucius institutes and the limitations of China's global cultural network. *China Information, 30*(3), 334–356.
Zhang, M. (2010). The socialist legal system with Chinese characteristics: China's discourse for the rule of law and a bitter experience. *Temple International & Comparative Law Journal, 24*(1), 1–64.
Zhang, Y., & Austin, G. (2013). China and the responsibility of power. In Y. Zhang & G. Austin (Eds.), *Power and responsibility in Chinese foreign policy* (pp. 1–20). Canberra: ANU E Press.

Zhao, J. (2016). The reform of the National Matriculation English Test and its impact on the Future of English in China: Will English lose its predominance in the Chinese foreign language landscape? *English Today, 32*(2), 38–44.

Zhao, T. (2006). Rethinking empire from a Chinese concept 'all-under-heaven' (Tian-xia). *Social Identities, 12*(1), 29–41.

Zhao, T. (2009). A political world philosophy in terms of all-under-heaven (Tian-xia). *Diogenes, 221*, 5–18.

Zheng, B. (2005). *China's peaceful rise: Speeches of Zheng Bijian 1997–2005*. Washington, DC: Brookings Institution Press.

Developing a Sustainable Legal System for the Belt and Road Initiative

Nicholas Morris

1 Introduction

The United Nations Conference on Trade and Development Report (UNCTAD 2009) which followed the first Silk Road Investment Forum, noted that "One of the key problems in much of the Silk Road is the implementation and enforcement of laws" (UNCTAD 2009, p. 26). The Chinese National Development and Reform Commission (NDRC) has also emphasized the need for mutual respect and trust between the countries involved in the 'One Belt One Road' (OBOR) initiative (NDRC 2015, Part VIII). This chapter responds to those challenges by examining how legal and regulatory systems can contribute to developing and supporting sustainable trade and investment. It explores how, in the context of BR, legal and regulatory systems can be developed to encourage and enhance trustworthy behavior.

The countries involved in BR are very varied in their legal and regulatory approaches, ranging from those which rely heavily on religious teachings to those with common law or civil law traditions. Each type of law takes a different approach to matters which are relevant to trustworthiness. Understanding these differences is important in the development of a harmonized legal and regulatory system to underpin the BRI.

Co-editor and author of *Capital Failure: Rebuilding Trust in Financial Services*, published in 2014 by Oxford University Press, and a contributor to *China In The International Economic Order: New Directions and Changing Paradigms*, published by Cambridge University Press in 2015.

N. Morris (✉)
Faculty of Law, University of New South Wales, Sydney, NSW, Australia

The Martin School, University of Oxford, Oxford, UK

China Executive Leadership Academy, Pudong, China
e-mail: c.n.morris@unsw.edu.au

W. Shan et al. (eds.), *Normative Readings of the Belt and Road Initiative*,
https://doi.org/10.1007/978-3-319-78018-4_3

1.1 The Challenge

The UNCTAD Report also observed that "The judicial systems in the region are not all independent from the executive branch, are often inconsistent in their application and interpretation of laws, and some do not operate in a transparent manner", and that "The Central Asian countries have made progress with numerous legal reforms .... such as new commercial legislation .... but the implementation and enforcement of the legal and regulatory frameworks and the governing institutions upholding them have not always kept pace" (UNCTAD 2009, p. 14).

NDRC, in its paper on BRI, spells out the challenge for those who are negotiating the new trading and political relationships:

> The Belt and Road cooperation features mutual respect and trust, mutual benefit and win-win cooperation, and mutual learning between civilizations. As long as all countries along the Belt and Road make concerted efforts to pursue our common goal, there will be bright prospects for the Silk Road Economic Belt and the 21st-Century Maritime Silk Road. (NDRC 2015, Part VIII)

Achieving a sustainable legal and regulatory framework for the 'One Belt, One Road' initiative requires, as a matter of urgency, that attention is given to these matters. In its widest definition, the initiative involves more than 60 countries, around one-third of the world's total economy, more than half the global population and investment of hundreds of billions of dollars. China has allocated $40 bn to a Silk Road Infrastructure Fund, and the new Asian Infrastructure Investment Bank (AIIB), founded in 2014, is also contributing more than $10 bn. Major investments are being made by the Chinese banks China Development Bank (CDB), People's Bank of China (PBOC), Export-Import Bank of China (EXIM) and Industrial and Commercial Bank of China (ICBC). Chinese investment in Belt and Road countries during next few years is expected to exceed $160 billion.[1]

BRI follows a long tradition whereby the Silk Road facilitated interchange between the great civilisations of China, Mesopotamia, Persia, India and Rome, and later Europe. Achieving the objectives of BRI will require that trust between nations is established, not only at the highest levels of government, but also between individuals, companies and communities. The legal and regulatory system is a major tool to encourage, incentivize, implement and police the emergence of trustworthy behaviour. In what follows, we draw on international experience with the development of markets, law and regulation to seek guidance for how sustainable systems may be developed to enable the effective and sustainable development of BR trading relationships.

---

[1]Beijing Review (2015).

2 Why Trustworthiness Matters for BR

Both trade and investment require trustworthy relationships, leading to a degree of trust and shared objectives between participants, without which it is difficult to agree trading terms and finance necessary investments (Arrow 1972; Fukayama 1995; Nelson 2005). Lack of trustworthy behaviour can adversely affect relations between governments (for example, between Greece and Europe), between companies (leading to numerous defaults and corporate failures, including those which accompanied the Global Financial Crisis (GFC)), and between individuals. Various commentators have attributed the Greek crisis to a breakdown in relations between Greece and its European partners and in particular to the erosion of a "credible commitment to future EMU participation under an implicit EMU/German guarantee of Greek fiscal liabilities" (Arghyrou and Tsoukalas 2010). The Greek Debt crisis adversely affected relations between Greece and various EU countries,[2] and has also created serious distrust of the Greek government and its institutions,[3] and of European institutions,[4] among the Greek people.

Even prior to the GFC, the ineffectiveness of relying on competition and market forces to control unethical behaviour was clearly apparent, and ethical misconduct led to corporate scandals of various kinds. Examples include such companies as Arthur Andersen (Smith and Quirk 2004), Enron (Rosen 2003; Healey and Palepu 2003), Health South (Barry 2009), Merrill Lynch (Jickling and Janov 2003), Sears Roebuck (O'Rourke 2009), Tyco (Hamilton and Micklethwait 2006), and WorldCom (Moberg and Romar 2009). Similar problems have affected other capitalist countries, notably Japan, where large-scale accounting scandals emerged at Olympus in 2011 (Aronson 2012) and recently at Toshiba.[5] As the GFC and subsequent events (such as the manipulation of LIBOR and other markets, and continuing problems at institutions such as Societe Generale and J. P. Morgan) have demonstrated, market outcomes that are not based on trustworthy relationships do not create a sustainable economic system.

Shared values (or at least a set of shared beliefs) are also necessary to determine what goals are to be achieved and which means should be used to attain social goals (Dolan and White 2006), both within nations and in groupings of nation states. In

[2]For a description of the various behaviours that culminated in the Greek debt crisis, see http://www.independent.co.uk/news/world/europe/greece-debt-crisis-explainer-a-history-of-how-the-country-landed-itself-in-such-a-mess-10365798.html.

[3]A recent 'Eurobarometer' (November 2015) showed that, at that time, 8 out of 10 Greeks distrusted their Parliament, Government and political parties. See http://greece.greekreporter.com/2016/02/23/eurobarometer-8-out-of-10-greeks-distrust-parliament-government-parties/.

[4]The same survey showed that the percentage of the Greek people who distrusted the European Union was 81%, the European Parliament 71%, the European Commission 75% and the European Central Bank was 78%.

[5]Japanese Finance Minister, commenting on the Toshiba scandal, observed "If [Japan] fails to implement appropriate corporate governance, it could lose market trust... It's very regrettable." (Byford 2015).

practice, ensuring that the behaviour of those in authority is trustworthy varies from country to country, from sector to sector, and under different legal traditions. In some cases, relying on the market and competition between participants can indeed lead to acceptable trustworthy outcomes, especially if market participants care sufficiently about their reputations. However, in other cases, existing laws and regulations have been demonstrated in recent years, notably during the Global Financial Crisis, to permit various types of untrustworthy behaviour. Evidence of the disastrous consequences which resulted from the erosion of appropriate social and legal protection can easily be found in the economic realities of recent years. The steep rise in remuneration which followed 'Big Bang', deregulation, leverage, securitisation, and rapid growth attracted managers to the financial sector who had a very different ethical outlook from their predecessors (Morris and Vines 2014). The result is a trading and financial system that has had a detrimental effect on developing economies in Asia, and most recently on weaker economies such as Greece, Italy and Portugal. Today the environment for investment and trade is, arguably, more challenging than it was in previous epochs, partly because relationships which were previously based on trust and mutual respect have broken down.

Development of trustworthy arrangements for trade and investment in and between the countries involved in the BR is particularly important in order to make the initiative sustainable in the medium- to long-term. There is unfortunately still a legacy of mistrust in some countries. For example, Kazakhstan uses two languages—Kazak and Russian—and academic studies are based on Russian. There is little knowledge of China, a lack of trust in government, and lack of clarity about what is means to be Kazak. There is a fear that "massive imports of Chinese products will significantly limit the development of national production. Chinese traders are thus often victims of cumbersome controls, in particular at the border" (Raballand and Andrésy 2007; Green 2001). The trust which exists between different countries, different parts of society and between the people and their governments all have implications for the effectiveness of business transactions.

In other countries there is evidence of growing nationalism and hostility to the involvement of external countries—such as China—in key economic and social developments. Hellström and Korkmaz (2011) have observed, for example,—about the relationship between India and China—that "there is a general lack of Chinese support for institutionalised efforts to dispel the mutual mistrust and resolve disputes". It is crucial that trusting relationships between BR countries be developed at all levels: governmental, institutional, commercial and individual (Kenny 2015). The legal system has a strong role to play in this objective.

The evolution of legal and regulatory systems in Western nations during the past 40 years has unfortunately had insufficient focus on enhancing trustworthiness. In recent years, pervasive asymmetric information has meant that contracts are nearly always incomplete (Williamson 1985; Epstein 2014), and imperfectly defined or conflicting laws and regulations mean that they are hard to enforce (Winston 2006), especially when the relevant activities transcend jurisdictional boundaries. The introduction of limited liability, securitisation, extensive leverage, 'light handed' regulation and technological complexity, which lacked the fundamental trust that based on shared core values, have all contributed to an inherently unfair and unstable system (Morris and Vines 2014). These problems have emerged in many jurisdictions in the West, under both Common Law and Civil Law systems. Without trustworthy relationships, the confidence to invest gets eroded, gains from trade become more difficult to achieve, and in due course the economic system becomes unsustainable.

3 Encouraging Trustworthy Behaviour Across BR

The so-called 'efficient markets hypothesis' on which global economic policy has been based during the last four decades was believed to be supported by Adam Smith's 'Invisible Hand' (Smith 1776). However, this is now generally accepted to be a misreading of Smith's writings (Smith 1998). In fact, Adam Smith believed strongly in the importance of 'other regarding behaviour', in particular the trustworthy relationships which underpin most economic transactions (Smith 1759). His book, *The Theory of Moral Sentiments*, begins as follows:

> How selfish soever man may be supposed, there are evidently some principles in his nature, which interest him in the fortune of others, and render their happiness necessary to him, though he derives nothing from it except the pleasure of seeing it.

'Other-regarding' motivations include desire for esteem, for the approbation of others, and for the genuine well-being of others (Offer 2014). Such motivations lead to trade and commerce that is mutually beneficial. However, most philosophers agree that trustworthy behaviour must not spring from wholly self-regarding motivations. Gold (2014) distinguishes weak trustworthiness, as studied in neoclassical economics, from strong trustworthiness, which must include a non-self-regarding motivation. Strong trust is ubiquitous, efficient, and often a precondition for effective and sustainable commercial arrangements. Strong trust is particularly important in trade and development because external partners do not usually have a full understanding of the needs of local communities. Mitigating cultural misunderstandings can improve trustworthiness, ensuring that trading partners see strong trustworthiness as expected and appropriate (Morris and Vines 2014).

Different societies have different methods of encouraging trustworthy behaviour. In Britain, prior to deregulation, good behaviour was rewarded through, for example, the honours system and bad behaviour was penalised through exclusion from public activities. Education instilled a sense of public duty and moral values. These mechanisms have become weakened in the past 40 years. Religious practices can also play an important role, as in the teachings of Christianity and in the prohibitions of Islam. Islamic Finance, for example, in its stricter forms seeks to prevent the excesses of usury. In China, *Guanxi* provides a support system for those who adhere to behavioural norms established over thousands of years. The strengths of this system are well described in Fei Xiaotong's *Xiangtu Zhongguo*[6] (Fei et al. 1992), which emphasises how the unique features of Chinese society are reflected in the moral and ethical principles of the population. 'Faithless Guanxi' is penalised by exclusion from public and commercial opportunities. Social relationships have been shown to provide an effective institutional foundation for economic transactions, which has been argued to "enhance economic rationality" (Chung and Hamilton 2001).

4 The Role of the Legal System

The legal system, both at a national and at a global level, has a crucial role to play both in defining what behaviour is acceptable and in holding individuals, firms and countries to account to account for their actions and for the adverse externalities they create (Armour 2008). Properly utilised, it can help to guide the economic and financial system towards a trustworthy equilibrium. Without legal or regulatory constraints, it is easy for those with superior information, or with monopoly access to markets, resources or suppliers, or with superior political power, to take unfair advantage of those who are less privileged. It is the role of the Law, including in bilateral and multilateral trading arrangements, to ensure that relationships between market players and stakeholders are as fair and transparent as possible.

Capital Failure (Morris and Vines 2014) sets out a framework for developing trustworthy structures and behaviours as follows

- the appropriate definition of obligations;
- the identification of corresponding responsibilities;
- the creation of mechanisms by which these responsibilities can be carried out; and
- the holding to account of those involved, in an appropriate manner.

In principle, law can affect behavioural outcomes in many ways, including[7]:

1. Providing guidance on what is regarded as acceptable behaviour.
2. Establishing duties, through, for example, rules imposed on agents, fiduciaries and trustees.
3. Prohibiting certain actions, e.g. murder, theft, insider trading, usury.
4. Regulating specific aspects of commercial operations, e.g. price, return, customs duties, licence fees, charges for public services, disclosure, compliance etc.
5. Incentivising people and companies to act in a trustworthy manner, including through deterrence.
6. Imposing penalties, typically fines or imprisonment, on those who break the law.

[6] Often translated as "From the Soil".

[7] There have been many attempts to define the role of an effective legal system. One of the more authoritative is that of Lord Thomas Bingham (2007), who sets out eight requirements which may be summarized as accessibility, effectiveness, equal access, protection of human rights, resolution of civil disputes, probity of those in authority, fairness and compliance with international law.

The Four Step Strategy

Obligations	Responsibilities	Mechanisms	Holding to Account

→

Contribution of the Law to encouraging Trustworthiness

1. **Providing Guidance** (through legal text, judgements, comments, legislation)	2. **Establishing Duties**, including for fiduciaries, directors, trustees	3. **Prohibition** of certain actions, eg theft, insider trading, usury	4. **Regulation** of price, return, risk, disclosure, compliance etc.	5. Setting and enabling **incentives**	6. **Imposing penalties**, including fines and imprisonment

Fig. 1 Contribution of the law to encouraging trustworthiness

In terms of the four-part framework for improving trustworthiness, (1) and (2) help with the definition of obligations and responsibilities, (2), (3), (4) and (5) set out mechanisms whereby these can be encouraged and enforced, while (6) is an important part of holding to account. The relationship between the four step strategy and these six attributes is illustrated in Fig. 1.

Regulators in many countries are expected to ensure that those they regulate comply with the Law, and often provide detailed guidance on how this may be achieved in complex situations. The courts are expected to resolve disputes and provide suitable arbitration, including across national boundaries, and to hold those who transgress to account.

The different types of legal system also vary in the mechanisms they contain to influence norms, and in their ability to hold those who behave in untrustworthy ways to account. All also specify duties, which they impose in different ways. We discuss how this affects their ability to ensure trustworthy outcomes in the sections below. Working out which type of law is likely to engender the most trustworthy behaviour depends on how well key items above—such as duties, prohibition, regulation and penalties—can be implemented in the relevant legal framework. This will vary from country to country, and also from sector to sector.

China has been seeking to develop inter-governmental arrangements which clarify the legal and regulatory system. This began in 2001 with the Shanghai Co-operation Organisation (SCO), a regional inter-governmental organisation (IGO) under the United Nations (UN) Charter including ('5+1') the Central Asian republics and China, and which was expanded in 2016 to include India and Pakistan. A second initiative is the '16+1' agreement with Central and Eastern European Countries (CEE), for which a third meeting was held in Belgrade in 2014. There have been many other Free Trade Agreements (FTAs), Bilateral Investment Treaties (BITs), agreements and Memoranda of Understanding (MoUs), including the

November 2015 Memorandum of Understanding with Five Central European Countries (Poland, Serbia, Czech, Bulgaria and Slovakia). China has also signed a memorandum of understanding on the EU-China Connectivity Platform with the European Commission.

Some progress already been made in the harmonisation of investment frameworks for BR countries. 100% foreign ownership is now allowed in China, Kazakhstan, Kyrgystan, Tajikistan and Uzbekistan, subject to minima in China and Uzbekistan, and some tax holidays have been agreed (UNCTAD 2009, Table 12). However, foreign ownership of land is not allowed except in Kazakhstan. Some progress has been made with simplifying customs clearance systems and quarantine processes (European Parliament 2016).

Some Chinese authors have called the route of the Maritime Silk Road "the crucial strategic direction of China's rise" (Clemens 2015, p. 7), as it gives China access to three major economic zones (Southeast Asia, South Asia and the Middle East) and is the route for many of China's strategic materials, including oil, iron ore, and copper. In negotiations, China has been particularly concerned to ensure the security of the sea lanes, and the People's Liberation Army (PLA) Navy has been involved in several anti-piracy operations, including the rescue of Chinese nationals.

5 Advantages and Disadvantages of Different Legal Traditions

In what follows, we consider some aspects of how the various legal traditions have emerged, and what their main characteristics are. This is necessary in order to start the process of working out what matters as more harmonious trade relationships are developed between countries with very different legal backgrounds. The discussion is necessarily high-level and only covers these important matters in limited detail.

The different legal traditions—Common Law (United Kingdom (UK), United States (US) and Australia), Civil Law (Europe), Religious Law (Islamic, Hindu, Talmudic) and Technocratic/Administrative Law (China—Taoist and Confucian)—are based on different philosophical frameworks (Glenn 2010) and rely on the different ways that law can intervene to a different extent. All legal traditions have at their heart principles, guidance and prohibitions which are intended to guide the society they serve to a fair, sustainable and trustworthy outcome. In some cases, these emerged from oral traditions, in others from constitutions developed by leaders at a particularly formative time, and in others from revelations from the deity, interpreted by prophets. However, the subsequent evolution of legal traditions, in response to the need to serve much larger populations and deal with more complex situations, has changed and diluted initial clarity. The interaction of different legal systems with each other has also had a large impact, for example between Islam and Christendom,[8] and between China and Europe.

In Common Law jurisdictions the primary duties towards others are contractual or tortious, and in some cases they are fiduciary, a responsibility often arising from the Law of Trusts. Common Law is quite flexible, relying on precedent and the latest set of judges to adapt to new situations (Turcotte 2005). In some areas, judges cite 'public policy' as a reason for changing their interpretation of the law, although there is some resistance to the judiciary usurping the role of legislators in this way (Gleeson 2008). Common law imposes fiduciary duties of loyalty, but this is sometimes set aside where apparently well-informed consent is given, and the courts in many Western courts have recently regarded contracts as taking precedence over common law fiduciary duties. Apparent fiduciary duties have also been eroded by the increasing ability of agents to 'contract around' such duties, as well as the development of Corporate Law to include, for example, the business judgement rule (Arsht 1979).[9] As a result the ability of common law systems to define and uphold obligations and responsibilities, and hence encourage and enforce trustworthy behavior, is somewhat limited. There is now a need to clarify the nature of duties and remedies, and to re-establish the primacy of fiduciary requirements (Getzler 2014), a matter which has received attention since the Global Financial Crisis. This is important in BR trading relationships, especially where one of the countries has less developed legal and regulatory systems, to prevent exploitation by those with greater access to information, to expertise or to relevant knowledge.

Common Law jurisdictions also often resist direct prohibition, regarding this as infringing personal liberty and inhibiting free markets. Regulation in such systems can be ineffective if it is limited to compliance and ensuring disclosure. Incentives for trustworthy behaviour are constrained by the high costs of bringing legal actions. Finally, penalties imposed on multinational corporations tend to be insufficient to deter untrustworthy behaviour. Unless these deficiencies can be overcome, the Common Law system will continue to be ineffective in encouraging and enforcing trustworthy behaviour. Class Actions are seen by some as a solution to this problem.

Civil Law, with origins in Roman Law, relies on a comprehensive system of rules, usually codified. In Civil Law jurisdictions responsibility to others arises as a duty of loyalty to the obligations of, for example, a mandate contract (Frankel 1993). Civil Law jurisdictions usually require evidence of damage or undue profits before condemning a conflicted action (Bahar and Thévenoz 2007). This means that the ability of Civil Law to hold those who behave in untrustworthy ways to account is

[8]For example, the ability of the European renaissance to benefit from the wisdom of Greek and Roman societies was facilitated by the preservation and development of documents and artifacts in Baghdad and other Islamic cities during the Islamic 'Golden Age'.

[9]The business judgment rule, which has been part of the Common Law for two centuries, recognises, at its simplest, that Directors should not be held liable for honest mistakes or unpopular business decisions.

more limited. Civil Law also struggles to impose sufficient penalty and class actions, for example, are harder to bring in such jurisdictions.

Western legal tradition, both in common law and civil law jurisdictions, has sought to place boundaries between politics, morality and the Law, in order to protect individuals from abuse of power by the government (Glendon et al. 2008). The separation of powers between the judiciary, the executive and the legislature is an important part of many legal systems, for example that of Australia (Hunter-Schultz 2005). Unfortunately, this has to some extent eroded the effectiveness of the Law in encouraging trustworthy behaviour, as the lack of a moral basis for legal enforcement reduces its ethical force.

In contrast, Islamic (Shari'a) Law, Hindu Law and Talmudic Law all emphasise the inter-relation between commercial activities and personal morality (Schwartz 2009; Desai and Mulla 2007; Glenn 2010). This makes religious law potentially more useful in defining and encouraging trustworthy behaviour. Religious Law has at its core some immutable beliefs, provided by the deity and interpreted by prophets and religious leaders. Setting norms is thus an important part of the role of Law. Although this primary guidance has been adapted and sometimes superceded by subsequent amendments, for example the Hadiths of Islamic Law, the existence of an underlying moral code does provide some protection from subsequent amendment. Constitutional law, in those countries that have formal constitutions, plays something of the same role in some Common Law and Civil Law jurisdictions (Goldsworthy 1997).[10]

6 Chinese Law and Practice

It has been argued elsewhere that China's superior performance in recent years reflects major differences in approach from most other countries, and derives from fundamental philosophical attitudes developed during the long history of China (Bai and Morris 2014a). The concept of moral values being needed to sustain social stability and prosperity can be traced back to Laotzu and Confucius in 500 BC (Wong et al. 2013), and the concepts derived from both Taoism and Confucianism have provided guidance on how to ensure the trustworthiness of institutions, organisations and individuals (Bai and Morris 2014b). In the Taoist model, which was accepted by Confucianism in later years, Yin and Yang forces create five major subordinate forces (benevolence (*Ren*), propriety (*Li*), faithfulness (*Xin*), justice (*Yi*), and wisdom (*Zhi*). Where legal and regulatory systems are weak or underdeveloped, the basis of

[10]There is considerable debate concerning 'originalism' in constitutional law, with many emphasizing the constitution as protection against subsequent weakening or adjustment of the Law. Goldsworthy cites Gibbs J.: "Our duty is to declare the [Australian] law as enacted in the Constitution and not to add to its provisions new doctrines which may happen to conform to our own prepossessions (AG(Cth); ex rel McKinlay v Commonwealth (1975) 135 CLR 1 at 44 per Gibbs J.).

trust embedded in the values of society can still be used to ensure a fair and efficient outcome. Today, it is argued that value-based principles derived from the ethical framework of Taoism and Confucianism are generally accepted as underpinning the network of interpersonal relationship among leaders and followers in China that cooperate and support one another (Lovett et al. 1999).

Ancient Chinese legal traditions are still dominant in the Chinese system, and norms of behaviour are well understood in Chinese society, as evidenced in Fei Xiatong's writings, discussed above (Fei et al. 1992). Chinese social norms are grounded in ethical principles so it is potentially capable of specifying duties. The planning, governmental control systems, and even informal arrangements that have been effective in China's development over the past four decades are, we believe, a direct result of these Taoist and Confucian philosophical underpinnings, which lead to a beneficial style of economic mechanism which has been called 'Economic Taoism' (Bai and Morris 2015). Formal Chinese law is focused on supporting administrative systems, and often relies on persuasion and relationship-based penalties rather than extensive codification or legal intervention (Glenn 2010). Chinese legal practice also makes extensive use of arbitration, especially in labour disputes, and has a strong impact on social practice and cultural understandings of rights (Diamant et al. 2005).

Confucian legal practice emerged from systems that had persisted for thousands of years. Confucius was the architect of the *li*, which believes that large populations can only be held together by informal and long-term agreement, and which denies the lasting and effective normativity of formal law and formal sanctions (Glenn 2010, p. 321). In developing this, he was reflecting the belief most recently expressed by NDRC, that mutual trust and respect are crucial in the development of sustainable commercial relationships. In modern terms (Gold 2014), Confucius believed trustworthy actions could only emerge from strong trust, that is trust which genuinely emerges from concern for the welfare of others.

Nevertheless, there is a long tradition of formal law and formal sanctions, or *fa*, in Chinese law, dating back to the legalists of at least the eighth century BC (five hundred years before Confucius), and books of punishment existed for at least three centuries before Confucianism became the official doctrine in China, around the late third century BC. *Fa* means imposed standards, which are needed to deal with those who engage in criminal conduct or conduct which does not match the established order. The development of criminal/administrative codes continued through to the last of the dynasties, the Ch'ing, which terminated in 1911, and became greatly admired in Europe, where the final versions were translated into French, Russian and English (Glenn 2010, p. 323).

The way in which these Confucian values of *li* and *fa* affect organizational and management practices has been widely discussed in the management and human resource literature (Wang et al. 2005). Four major impacts of Confucian-based culture that are often identified are hierarchy and harmony; group orientation; relationships; and *mianzi* (face). The contrast between li and fa is often represented as ruling by man (*ren zhi*) versus ruling by law (*fa zhi*). Ruling by man is reflected in

Chinese decision-making processes, where the decisions of top leaders are not challengeable.

China's use of value-based leadership and its associated trustworthy relationship *Guanxi*, underpinned by Taoist and Confucian ethical values, have served it well for thousands of years (Song et al. 2009). Chinese politics and society today are still largely driven by focus on trustworthy relationships (Lovett et al. 1999). With the core values grounded in legislative mandates, national mission, vision statements of leaders, and in political and public will, the ethical framework of Taoism and Confucianism is playing an increasing role in harmonizing Chinese society and keeping it sustainable (Liu et al. 2011; Luo et al. 2012; Shi and Cui 2004). Chinese traditions and system of relationships can serve to enhance trust, which facilitates the social activities which are in due course regulated by law. In addition, the ability of the Chinese system to hold untrustworthy individuals and firms to account can, in certain cases, be greater than the more flexible Common Law system of the US and UK.

As a result, many of the problems with which Western capitalist systems are now struggling do not arise to the same extent in the Chinese system (Kuran 2011; Whalley et al. 2009). This is partly because Chinese society places a greater value on trustworthiness, and does not have the same simple belief that markets in themselves can be left to enforce ethical outcomes. Confucianism gives considerable attention to "virtue, benevolence, social rightness and morality – with harmony as a central goal" (Picker 2011). It is also because the trustworthy relationship *Guanxi* system, reinforced by the apparatus of state control, including specification of 'honours and disgraces' for leaders (Hu 2006; Yang 2010), contains systems for holding 'faithless' individuals and companies to account that the incentives for trustworthy behaviour are stronger (Fu 2013).

7 Potential for Improving Trustworthiness

The legal systems of the various trading partners in BR have an important role to play in setting out acceptable standards of behaviour, defining responsibilities and obligations, and holding countries and multi-national firms to account for their trustworthy adherence to international norms. Consistency between legal systems, in a world in which many economic activities cross national boundaries, is crucial to the development of BR. Effective co-ordination across the BR countries is needed to ensure that unsatisfactory behaviour does not migrate from one country system to another (as, for example, in the misguided use of 'light-handed' regulation that migrated from the UK to other countries prior to the GFC), and that multi-national companies do not engage in 'jurisdiction shopping' to evade their obligations. Piecemeal changes to legal and regulatory systems on a national basis will merely lead to 'forum shopping' and arbitrage between systems (Whytock 2011).

International Law has made some progress in seeking to clarify what constitutes acceptable, trustworthy, behaviour across national boundaries. In the area of contracts, for example, achievements during the past century include the Uniform Laws on the International Sale of Goods, the International Institute for the Unification of Private Law (UNIDROIT) Principles of International Commercial Contracts, the Principles of European Contract Law, and the Vienna Convention for the International Sales of Goods (CISG). However, the drafting of these international texts has been complex because of the need to embrace both Civil Law and Common Law systems. Their development to embrace both the religious-based legal systems of some BR countries, and Chinese legal and regulatory practice will be equally challenging.

There has been some discussion in the literature about which legal tradition provides the best basis for trading arrangements. Barnes (2005), for example, suggests that the Civil Law may provide a more "pragmatic and politically expedient solution" to the development of international trading arrangements. Picker (2008) suggests that International Law works best in countries—such as Scotland, Louisiana, Quebec, South Africa and Israel—which already have legal systems which embrace both Civil Law and Common Law elements. China has been argued to have a major role to play as the international system develops (Allen et al. 2010), a role which its centrality to BR makes even more important.

However, getting consensus as to legal and regulatory standards across the more than 60 countries of BR will be difficult. Vines (2015) has argued that that international cooperation is most effective when there is a global regime in which 'concerted unilateralism' leads to a good outcome. This is because any reforms to economic policymaking are driven by domestic political agendas. That means that national policymakers will not adopt legal and regulatory policies which are in the global interest unless they are also in the national interest. In technical terms we cannot seek a cooperative equilibrium for the whole of the BR which is not also a Nash equilibrium.[11] National policymakers will tend to free ride on such an equilibrium, leading to breakdown. Legal and regulatory cooperation needs to make it possible for there to be different forms of regulation in different countries of a kind which reflects the different industrial, and cultural, forms which exist in different places.

The importance of continued convergence between legal systems is essential to the expansion of BR activities. Sustainability of the BR legal system will, I believe, require that determining what can be achieved through consensus and long-term sustainable relationships, in the manner of Confucian *li*, is given precedence, and that resort to formal penalties and prohibitions, in the manner of Confucian *fa*, is limited to those cases where *li* is genuinely impossible or ineffective. Understanding and taking into account differences both of legal and regulatory systems, and of local culture, is important in the development of a harmonized legal and regulatory system to underpin the Silk Road Initiative.

[11]In Game Theory, a *Nash Equilibrium* is one in which no player has an incentive to change his strategy.

Acknowledgements I would like to thank Deborah Healey, Jeanne Huang, Yongqiang Li, Colin Picker and Rob Nicholls for helpful guidance and comments on previous versions of this chapter. Any errors or misunderstandings are entirely my own.

References

Allen, F., Chakrabarti, R., De, S., Qian, J., & Qian, M. (2010). Law, institutions and finance in China and India. In B. Eichengreen, P. Gupta, & R. Kumar (Eds.), *Emerging giants: China and India in the world economy* (Chapter 5). Oxford: Oxford University Press.

Arghyrou, M. G., & Tsoukalas, J. D. (2010). *The Greek Debt crisis: Likely causes, mechanics and outcomes* (Cardiff Economics Working Papers, E2010/3).

Armour, J. (2008). *Enforcement strategies in UK corporate governance: A roadmap and empirical assessment* (ECGI Working Paper No. 106/2008).

Aronson, B. E. (2012). The Olympus scandal and corporate governance reform: Can Japan find a middle ground between the board monitoring model and management model? *UCLA Pacific Basin Law Journal, 30*(1), 93–148.

Arrow, K. (1972). Gifts and exchanges. *Philosophy and Public Affairs, 1*, 343–362.

Arsht, S. S. (1979). The business judgment rule revisited. *Hofstra Law Review, 8*(1), 93–134.

Bahar, R., & Thévenoz, L. (2007). Conflicts of interest: Disclosure, incentives, and the market. In L. Thévenoz & R. Bahar (Eds.), *Conflicts of interest: Corporate governance and financial markets*. Alphen aan den Rijn: Kluwer Law International.

Bai, X. Z., & Morris, N. (2014a). Leadership and virtue ethics: A Daoist approach. *Public Integrity, 16*(2), 173–186.

Bai, X. Z., & Morris, N. (2014b). *The significance of the ethical framework of Taoism and Confucianism in the Chinese politics and society*. Paper presented at the Asia-Pacific Humanities and Social Sciences Conference (APHSS 2014), Shanghai, November 2014.

Bai, X. Z., & Morris, N. (2015). China, economic Taoism and development: Different paradigms, different outcomes? In C. Picker, L. Toohey, & J. Greenacre (Eds.), *China in the new international economic order: New directions and changing paradigms* (Chapter 13). Cambridge: Cambridge University Press.

Barnes, W. R. (2005). Contemplating a civil law paradigm for a future international commercial code. *Louisiana Law Review, 65*, 677.

Barry, K. (2009). *Healthsouth's corporate accounting scandal: A case study in fraudulent financial reporting*. Management 226: Special Topics in Advanced Accounting. UCLA Anderson School of Management.

Beijing Review. (2015, May 15). Beijing Review, 15. Beijing Review com.cn.

Bingham, T. (2007). The rule of law. *Cambridge Law Journal, 66*(1), 67–85.

Byford, S. (2015, July 21). The Verge. www.theverge.com.

Chung, W. K., & Hamilton, G. (2001). Social logic as business logic: Guanxi, trustworthiness and the embeddedness of Chinese business practices. In R. P. Appelbaum, W. L. F. Felstiner, & V. Gessner (Eds.), *Rules and networks: The legal culture of global business transactions* (pp. 302–349). Oxford: Hart.

Clemens, M. (2015). The Maritime Silk Road and the PLA: Part One. *ChinaBrief, XV*(6).

Desai, S. A., & Mulla, D. F. (2007). *Principles of Hindu law*. New Delhi: Butterworths.

Diamant, N. J., Lubman, S. B., & O'Brien, K. J. (2005). *Engaging the law in China: State, society, and possibilities for justice*. California: Stanford University Press.

Dolan, P., & White, M. (2006). Dynamic well-being: Connecting indicators of what people anticipate with indicators of what they experience. *Social Indicators Research, 75*.

Epstein, W. N. (2014). Facilitating incomplete contracts. *Case Western Reserve Law Review, 65*(2), 297–340.

European Parliament. (2016, July). *One Belt, One Road (OBOR): China's regional integration initiative. Briefing.*

Fei, X., Hamilton, G. G., & Wang, Z. (1992). *From the soil, the foundations of Chinese society: A translation of Fei Xiaotong's Xiangtu Zhongguo, with an introduction and epilogue*. Berkeley, CA: University of California Press.

Frankel, T. (1993). *Fiduciary law: The judicial process and the duty of care*. Paper presented at the 1993 Isaac Pitblado Lectures, University of Manitoba Law School.

Fu, S. Z. (2013). On the application of virtues, competence, hardwork, achievement and cleanness in the performance evaluation of government and party officials. *Journal of Hunan Communication Science and Technology, 39*(1), 98–101.

Fukayama, F. (1995). *Trust: The social virtues and the creation of prosperity*. New York: Free Press.

Getzler, J. (2014). Financial crisis and the decline of fiduciary law. In N. Morris & D. Vines (Eds.), *Capital failure: Rebuilding trust in financial services* (Chapter 9, pp. 193–208). Oxford: Oxford University Press.

Gleeson, M. (2008, January 4). *The role of a judge in a representative democracy*. Speech to the Judiciary of the Commonwealth of the Bahamas.

Glendon, M. A., Carozza, P., & Picker, C. (2008). *Comparative legal traditions in a nutshell*. St Paul, MN: West Academic Publishing.

Glenn, P. (2010). *Legal traditions of the world*. Oxford: Oxford University Press.

Gold, N. (2014). Trustworthiness and motivations. In N. Morris & D. Vines (Eds.), *Capital failure: Rebuilding trust in financial services* (Chapter 6, pp. 129–153). Oxford: Oxford University Press.

Goldsworthy, J. (1997). Originalism in constitutional interpretation. *Federal Law Review, 25*(1).

Green, D. (2001). Regional co-operation policies in Central Asia. *Journal of International Development, 13*, 1151–1164.

Hamilton, S., & Micklethwait, A. (2006). *Greed and corporate failure: The lessons from recent disasters*. New York: Palgrave Macmillan.

Healey, P. M., & Palepu, K. G. (2003). The fall of Enron. *Journal of Economic Perspectives, 17*(2), 3–26.

Hellström, J., & Korkmaz, K. (2011). *Managing mutual mistrust: Understanding Chinese perspectives on Sino-Indian relations*. Stockholm: Swedish Defence Research Agency.

Hu, J. T. (2006). *To set up construct socialist concepts on honors and disgraces* (in Chinese). Beijing: The Peoples Press. Available at: http://politics.people.com.cn/GB/1024/4336318.html.

Hunter-Schultz, T. (2005). Rule of law, separation of powers and judicial decision making in Australia. *The National Legal Eagle, 11*(1), Article 5.

Jickling, M., & Janov, P. H. (2003). *Criminal charges in corporate scandals*. Washington, DC: Congressional Research Service, The Library of Congress.

Kenny, S. (2015). *China and India: A New Great Game founded on historic mistrust and current competition*. Canberra: Centre for Defence and Strategic Studies, Australian Defence College.

Kuran, T. (2011). West is best? Why civilizations rise and fall. *Foreign Affairs, 90*(1), 159.

Liu, J., Wang, Y., & Wu, L. (2011). The effect of Guanxi on audit quality in China. *Journal of Business Ethics, 103*, 621–638.

Lovett, S., Simmons, L. C., & Kali, R. (1999). Guanxi versus the market: Ethics and efficiency. *Journal of International Business Studies, 30*(2), 231–247.

Luo, Y., Huang, Y., & Wang, S. (2012). Guanxi and organizational performance: A meta-analysis. *Management and Organization Review, 8*(1), 139–172.

Moberg, D., & Romar, E. (2009). *WorldCom case study*. Santa Clara, CA: Santa Clara University.

Morris, N., & Vines, D. (2014). *Capital failure: Rebuilding trust in financial services*. Oxford: Oxford University Press.

NDRC. (2015). *Vision and Actions on Jointly Building Silk Road Economic Belt and 21st-Century Maritime Silk Road*. Issued by the National Development and Reform Commission, Ministry of

Foreign Affairs, and Ministry of Commerce of the Peoples Republic of China, with State Council authorization.
Nelson, R. R. (2005). *The limits of market organisation*. New York: Russell Sage Foundation.
O'Rourke, J. A. (2009). *Collection scandal at Sears Roebuck & Company*. Eugene D. Fanning Center For Business Communication 00-05, Mendoza College of Business, University of Notre Dame.
Offer, A. (2014). Regard for others. In N. Morris & D. Vines (Eds.), *Capital failure: Rebuilding trust in financial services* (Chapter 7, pp. 154–171). Oxford: Oxford University Press.
Picker, C. B. (2008). International laws mixed heritage: A common/civil law jurisdiction. *Vanderbilt Journal of Transnational Law, 41*, 1083.
Picker, C. B. (2011). China, global governance and legal culture. In J. Nakagaw (Ed.), *China and global economic governance: Ideas and concepts* (p. 77). ISS Research Series No. 45. Tokyo: Institute of Social Science, University of Tokyo.
Raballand, G., & Andrésy, A. (2007). Why should trade between Central Asia and China continue to expand? *Asian Europe Journal, 5*(2), 235–252.
Rosen, R. (2003). Risk management and corporate governance: The case of Enron. *Connecticut Law Review, 35*, 1157–1184.
Schwartz, S. (2009). *Islam and Communism*. Washington, DC: Centre for Islamic Pluralism.
Shi, W., & Cui, X. L. (2004). *On evaluation of civil servants and the criteria of morality, competence, hardworking, and performance* (in Chinese).
Smith, A. (1759). *The theory of moral sentiments* (Ed. D. D. Raphael, A. L. Macfie). Vol. I of the Glasgow edition of the works and correspondence of Adam Smith. Originally published 1759. Oxford: Oxford University Press.
Smith, A. (1776). *The wealth of nations*. First published 1776. Prometheus Books.
Smith, N. C., & Quirk, M. (2004). From grace to disgrace: The rise & fall of Arthur Anderson. *Journal of Business Ethics Education*, 91–130.
Smith, V. L. (1998, July). The two faces of Adam Smith. *Southern Economic Journal, 65*(1), 2–19.
Song, L. P., Ling, W. Q., & Fang, L. L. (2009). On the cultural roots of moral leadership in China (in Chinese). *Theoretical Field, 5*, 166–169.
Turcotte, K. (2005). Why legal flexibility is not a threat to either the common law system of England and Australia or the civil law system of France in the twenty-first century. *Hanse Law Review, 1*(2), 190–197.
United Nations Conference on Trade and Development. (2009). *Investment guide to the Silk Road*.
Vines, D. (2015). On concerted unilateralism: Raising the global growth rate through macroeconomic policy coordination. In T. Bayoumi, S. Pickford, & P. Subacchi (Eds.), *Managing complexity: Economic policy cooperation after the crisis*. Washington, DC: Brookings Press.
Wang, J., Wang, G. G., Ruona, W. E. A., & Rojewski, J. W. (2005). Confucian values and the implications for international HRD. *Human Resource Development International, 8*(3), 311–326.
Whalley, J., Agarwal, M., Cai, Y., Dong, Y., Tian, H., & Wang, L. (2009). *China and the financial crisis*. Waterloo: CIGI/Chinese Academy of Social Sciences Task Force.
Whytock, C. A. (2011). The evolving forum shopping system. *Cornell Law Review, 96*, 481–534.
Williamson, O. (1985). *The economic institutions of capitalism*. New York: Free Press.
Winston, C. (2006). *Government failure versus market failure*. Washington, DC: AEI-Brookings Joint Center for Regulatory Studies.
Wong, P. S. S., Neck, P. A., & McKenna, B. (2013). *Spiritual wisdom of Taoism in business: Toward a general theory of action*. Cambridge, MA: Harvard University Press.
Yang, D. C. (2010). The present state of evaluation of civil servants and the policy recommendation (in Chinese). *Journal of Chongqing University (Social Science Edition), 6*, 68–73.

The Normative Foundations of the Belt and Road Initiative

Anastas Vangeli

1 Introduction: BRI as a Normative Concept

During the 19th National Party Congress (NPC) held in October 2017, the Belt and Road Initiative (BRI) was enshrined in the Constitution of the Communist Party of China (CPC).[1] With this, the Party effectively put to rest any doubts about the importance of the Initiative. Four years after its official announcement, the BRI today carries unprecedented weight in terms of its relevance to the governance of China and China's relationship with the rest of the world, which in turn makes it a concept relevant for the trajectory of the global political economy as a whole. Moreover, now we have additional information about both the direction and the nature of the BRI. Namely, at the 19th NPC, ideology had the center stage. One of the main outcomes of the Congress was the codification of Xi Jinping Thought on the New Era of Socialism with Chinese Characteristics (hereinafter XJP Thought), a political theory derived from the governance practices under the leadership of Xi Jinping as one of the normative pillars of the CPC.[2] The BRI, as a pet-project of Xi Jinping[3] is inalienable from the development of XJP Thought, thereby having an important normative, if not ideological relevance for global China, even if much of

[1]See Xinhua News (2017).

[2]See Li (2017b). XJP Thought follows Marxism-Leninism, Mao Zedong Thought, Deng Xiaoping Theory, The Important Thought of the Three Represents, and the Scientific Outlook on Development as the foundational ideological inputs of the CPC. The fact that Xi's contribution was codified during, and not after his tenure, that his input carries his name and is categorized as "Thought" (*sixiang*) rather than as a "Theory" (*lilun*), suggests a significant turn to ideology of the Party, after a prolonged period of experimentation and pragmatism.

[3]For example, see Johnson (2016).

A. Vangeli (✉)
Polish Academy of Sciences, Warsaw, Poland

W. Shan et al. (eds.), *Normative Readings of the Belt and Road Initiative*,
https://doi.org/10.1007/978-3-319-78018-4_4

its intended outcomes are believed to be tangible in nature (i.e. increased trade, building of concrete infrastructure projects and so on).

The purpose of the BRI is therefore not only to impact the global political economy but also to change the way others relate to and think about the global political economy and their role in it—in dialogue with China's proposal. As a result, the BRI is not only concept that raises the question of the quantitative changes in the global political economy—it equally concerns the question of qualitative changes, or rather the questions *how* and against *what backdrop* will the China-led interactions along the Belt&Road area develop, and what are their normative implications—both in the terms of reference of Chinese policymakers, and in terms of scholarly inquiry as well. The normative component is in fact visible in the very documents that have outlined the Silk Road vision of China's government.[4] The focus on policy coordination, the promotion of the set of values known as the *Silk Road Spirit*, the critical references to ongoing global developments (all of which will be examined at length below), are all postulates of an emerging paradigm incepted and disseminated by China. In fact, China has itself increasingly pointed to the potential lessons of its own development and its wisdom as a source for voluntary (bot not imposed or coerced) learning by others.

However, in global debates, normative analyses on the BRI are largely overshadowed by more "pragmatic" policy-oriented literature.[5] The BRI is considered a geopolitical maneuver that will "expand China's shadow over regions of the world where hitherto its presence has been relatively modest,"[6] a geo-economic strategy to ensure economic hegemony, and an exercise in soft power or rather "a political marketing concept for world dominance."[7] It is also often cited as one of the sources of China's so called "sharp" power, a contemporary incarnation of the China threat theory that assumes China wants to subvert Western societies, and the hegemony of the United States. Another mainstream approach sees it as an "unclear in design"[8]—perhaps owing to the very nature of the development of the Initiative—the BRI is developed inductively, it is informed by the various practices on the ground, while remaining flexible to the changing circumstances and is open for the comments and proposals from a multitude of actors, including scholars and think tanks. To some outsiders, however, this makes BRI a rather fuzzy, vaguely defined and unspecific concept, often seeming to be a contradiction in terms.

This chapter aims to challenge such assumptions, and provide more nuanced normative reading of the BRI. As a concept, it is rooted in the thinking and practice

---

[4]An important resource where a number of documents and speeches on the BRI can be found is www.yidaiyilu.gov.cn.

[5]A particularly interesting question is what has been the popularity of the BRI. According to one editor of a prestigious Chinese journal, by 2017 there are more than seven million papers written on the BRI, arguably the majority in China itself. One possible future research project would be to systematically assess how well known is the BRI outside China.

[6]Ferdinand (2016).

[7]Fasslabend (2015).

[8]Hall (2017).

of CPC and at the same time a product of a changing Chinese, but also changing global context. The normative side of the BRI can be therefore only grasped if scholars critically analyze China's official discourse and the practice of the BRI in light of broader policy and theoretical debates on China, but also on the trajectories of the global political economic order. A closer look into the discourse and practice of the BRI reveals a multi-faceted concept that creates dialectical relationship between politics and economics, the national and the international, and between the old, reform-era China and the new, ambitious China of the Xi Jinping era that does not shy away from publicly declaring its Communist ideology. That is why it is colloquially called an invitation for a new form of globalization, or at least as a new paradigm of cooperation in the regions it covers (which is predominantly the global South). This chapter, while refraining from any augmentative statements, undoubtedly, belongs to the group of works that are willing to give the BRI in all its ambition—but also its limits—the chance for a fair and critical scholarly assessment.

The BRI, as an object of such critical inquiry, poses a number of challenges. Due to its particularity, it slips away from a lot of the existing theoretical frameworks in the study of global political economy. The BRI—intended to be a global common—is after all explicitly Chinese in nature. In many ways, it is a medium through which the operating logic of the Chinese national policy-making gets diffused throughout the vast number of regions and countries the BRI involves.[9] Yet, while providing a unique challenge, the plasticity of the BRI also offers an opportunity for authors to think outside the box and craft innovative analytical approaches. This chapter, therefore, zooms out and looks towards the BRI from a deconstructionist standpoint in the tradition of the studies of the third dimension of China's power, or rather the power to shape the preferences and behavior of others, or the ability to "win the hearts and minds of others."[10] This chapter in principle follows discussions on the existing literature on the third dimension of China's power,[11] yet at the same it traces the path to a novel approach towards the topic taking in account the new data points from the BRI era. In the times of Xi Jinping, and in particular in the aftermath of the 19 NPC, the established notions on China's potential to influence others deserve re-appraisal and re-contextualization in order to explain the current realities. In the concluding section, the chapter turns to the future scholarship agenda: how to study the social interaction towards which they will (or will not) be internalized by others.

[9]See more in Vangeli (in press-a).

[10]The term has been originally developed by Lukes (2004, 2007).

[11]Some of the important concepts have been as well as the Beijing Consensus (Ramo 2007; Li et al. 2010) and the China Model—and their limits (Zhao 2010; Breslin 2011), their diffusion or lack thereof (Ambrosio 2012) and their exportability under the BRI (Fukuyama 2016), the alternative path to Chinese modernity (Jacques 2012); normative power China (Womack 2008; Kavalski 2013), China's soft power (Barr 2011); Chinese *tianxia*-nism (Godehardt 2016), and China's influence in global governance (Beeson and Li 2016).

2 Normative Sources of the BRI: Global China

2.1 China's Own Development Path

To grasp the essence of China's own development path, which shapes its worldview, the chapter builds upon authors who embrace the dialectics, non-simultaneity as well as the mutually non-exclusive nature of China's seemingly contradictory policy practices. In particular, I emphasize the work of Alvin Y. So and Yin-wah Chu who in order to capture the apparent contradictions between the various practices that constitute China's developmental model coined the term "state neoliberalism."[12] This purposefully self-contradicting concept approximates—even though in a critical way—the Sinified Marxist dialectics whereby divergent and often opposing thoughts and actions do not necessarily cancel or exclude each other, but work in synthesis and are thus complementary with each other, the outcome being a new condition that can be two seemingly mutually exclusive, but practically co-existing things.[13] "State neoliberalism"—a critical take on "socialism with Chinese characteristics"—serves the purpose of operationalizing the contradiction and dialectics that define the Chinese development path.

In terms of the normative grounding of China's development path and its global influence through endeavors such as the BRI, the term "state neoliberalism" captures the dialectics between the state and the market, and the task of the state to ensure the creation of optimal conditions for, and later on to facilitate the unleashing of productive forces—in a manner that even though retains sovereignty and does not allow complete take over from foreign capital, it is still formulating a rather interdependent relationship between the country in question and global capitalism. In practice, this refers to a dynamic process of policy fluctuations between the market-oriented and state-oriented practices, implemented by a strong-armed, sovereign state, which enjoys political stability, has the autonomy to pursue a long-term vision, and is able to steer the process through which it becomes embedded within transnational supply chains and commercial networks.

State neoliberalism hereto differs from terms such as "state capitalism"[14] as it not only refers to a particular mode of production, but also to the neoliberal political technology or governmentality that is knitted into the fabric of the state and society[15]; at the same time, it differs from "developmental state"[16] as the state does not only guide or regulate the market, but plays an active multi-directional role in it; it is not pretending or aiming to enjoy "embedded autonomy" but rather has a pronounced political approach in governing the economy. One way to think of

[12]See Chu and So (2010) and So and Chu (2012, 2015).

[13]For a Marxist analysis see Boer (2017).

[14]On state capitalism, see Bremmer (2008).

[15]On neoliberalism as political technology, see Ong (2012).

[16]On developmental state, see Wade (2004).

state neoliberalism is as a different development on the different levels of policymaking—at some point the national government may pursue a statist (even socialist) direction, while the local government at the same time are pursuing market-oriented approach; or it can have state-owned enterprises that in terms of their operation will follow a neoliberal model. At the same time, "state neoliberalism" differs from Western-style neoliberalism as market fundamentalism in the sense that it serves to strengthen the ruling political class and their project and to introduce controlled flow of investment—while preventing a total take-over by foreign capital; it is also different from post-socialist transitional neoliberalism as it does not serve to privatize state and public assets and move the profits to more affluent parts of the global economy, but to merely create an economic interdependence that would serve as political deterrence and sense of more powerful actors having stakes in the stability and prosperity of the host country among external actors (i.e. due to economic stakes, for a long period of time, the US has had an interest for China to remain stable).

This logic, which underpins China's own development path, also informs the BRI, which is a vision that relies on government-to-government cooperation, with politics moving capital across borders, with the end goal being, paradoxically, to advance globalization.

2.2 *China's New Foreign Policy*

The rootedness of the BRI into China's thinking and practice implies that the BRI adheres to the ongoing trends in China's foreign and domestic policies. In practice, the BRI in many ways is a new umbrella term for a number of existing ideas and policies.[17] In fact, one can often observe that a number of already existing projects or even platforms for cooperation are added the BRI label retroactively, such as infrastructure projects negotiated, or platforms for cooperation (such as the one between China and the sixteen countries of Central, East and Southeast Europe) that had been launched before the official announcement of the BRI—but became part of it afterwards. This implies that the BRI has the purpose of synthetizing and streamlining a number of efforts and endeavors into one comprehensive and more or less coherent global vision. As such, it is the most elaborate concept under the innovative diplomacy developed in the era of Xi Jinping.[18]

The fact that the BRI is constituted by a number of pre-existing elements points to a number of sources that provide insights into how the BRI may develop in the future. The evolution of China's "going global" strategy, China's pro-active and

[17]See the analysis by Pantucci (2016).

[18]For a comprehensive overview on China's new diplomacy under Xi Jinping see the work by Yang (2015), a leading scholar and Yang (2017), China's State Councilor and former Minister of Foreign Affairs.

innovative multilateral regional diplomacy platforms developed in various parts of the world—Africa, Latin America, Central, East and Southeast Europe, China-led international organizations such as the Shanghai Cooperation Organization, groupings such as BRICS and financial institutions such as the AIIB, the "soft power" drive, the efforts to build a new type of major country diplomacy and other tendencies observed in the last several years, are all relevant experiences that have provided lessons in the process of theoretical and practical development of the BRI. In other words, all of the various foreign policy endeavors by China have served as laboratories where Chinese policymakers translated the set of normative beliefs underpinning China's foreign policy intro practice, in their appropriate contexts.

Of particular importance is the tendency present in China's foreign policy under Xi Jinping to create new, China-centered institutions and international organizations. The goal of this undertaking is to give China an ample voice in international affairs, provide it with mobilizing power, fill in the void in global governance and international where it exists, but also help promote its own values while circumventing existing international institutions. The outcome of this has been the creation of a parallel, or "shadow" institutions, that may challenge, but also supplement or even supplant the existing international order.[19] Notably, aside from typical international institutions, China has also created a number of loose institutional mechanisms, which the BRI is a part of, characterized by annual summits and a number of channels for interaction, but so far with no centralized "headquarters" and strong organizational bureaucracy. Nevertheless, this does not prevent the BRI from massively growing as time passes by.

This, however, does not mean that everything China has done at the world stage has had the sole purpose to provide testing ground for the BRI, or that the BRI will serve to replace all existing mechanisms. For one, the BRI is not an eclectic assemblage of various elements from China's foreign policy, but rather than it is an idiosyncratic vision underpinned both by a learning process from other experiences, as well as innovation based on changing circumstances. It is best understood through the concept of multi-channel diplomacy. In this sense, the BRI is one particular channel through which China now communicates with a number of countries in the world; while at the same time other channels remain in place. These other channels include, for instance, regional and policy-specific platforms, and the bilateral relations. The relationship between the channels is as follows: the BRI provides the overarching vision, guidance and generates and disseminates the shared norms; in accord with those norms, the projects are implemented on the bilateral, government-to-government basis; while other diplomatic platforms (such as the 16+1 platform for cooperation between China and the countries of Central, East and Southeast Europe where all members have signed Memorandums to be part of the BRI) serve as to provide the link between the general ideas, and the particular regional context, as well as to streamline the discourse between China and the different countries in question.

[19]On this, see the works by Heilmann et al. (2014) and Qiu (2015a).

While there is certainly some redundancy in the communication, the novel elements of the BRI-level of communication is particularly adding the global layer of interaction between China and the participant countries where they did not exist before. To illustrate with an example, let's take the case of Serbia: the primary level of communication is the China-Serbia bilateral relations; the secondary is the interaction within the China-led 16+1 regional platform, where China already assigns a regional logic based primarily on the mental maps and thinking of Chinese policymakers; whereby the BRI provides additional, macro-regional, global logic and guiding norms to the relationship, by putting Serbia as a country and the 16+1 as a whole into a broader context. In the case of Egypt, it would be: China-Egypt at the bilateral level, FOCAC at the regional/continental level, and BRI at the global level; in the case of Finland, it would be: China-Finland at the bilateral level, Arctic/Nordic formats at the (sub)regional level, BRI at the global level, and so on.

3 Normative Anchoring: Betting on Shared Destiny

As a rising China now has put ahead the objective of the so called *Two Centennial Goals*—to become a *xiaokang* (moderately prosperous) society by 2021, and to "build a modern socialist country that is prosperous, strong, democratic, culturally advanced and harmonious" by 2049,[20] it has also found itself in a position to look beyond its own borders and be a pro-active actor on the international stage. A previously inward-looking China that has kept a low profile in global affairs, and has pursued short-term lucrative interest, now China is in a position to "strive for achievement" and aim for more substantial long-term goals. This has also required for a new framing of China's contribution to the well-being of others, with China assuming a much more responsible posture.[21] While before, China has claimed its own domestic successes in the fight against poverty as its main contribution to the benefit of the whole planet (through colloquial sayings such as "China feeds one fifth of the human population"), a confident China now adopts a much different rhetoric of welcoming others on the "express train of development" and embracing a much more generous approach.[22]

Enter the BRI—a call for collective (rather than unilateral) action issued by China that ultimately aims to contribute to the prosperity not only of China and its people, but rather a number of countries that the initiative involves. While not a poverty-reduction and development aid program,[23] the BRI is based on the idea to tackle macro-level

[20]On the Two Centennial Goals, see the Q&A by Xinhua News (huaxia 2017).

[21]On the changes in China's global posture, see the seminal work by Yan (2014).

[22]See Yang (2015).

[23]Importantly, as China is rising, and aside from the BRI, it is also increasing its commitments in terms of development aid. Arguably, China's development aid has had positive impact on the beneficiaries (Dreher et al. 2017).

economic disparities—within and beyond China.[24] The BRI is to a certain extent framed as an attempt to address the consequences of the global economic crisis, as well as to the unjust form of corporate-led globalization—not with the explicit goal to overthrow the prevailing order, but rather to mitigate the adverse effects such as "the weak recovery of the global economy, and complex international and regional situations" by promoting the so called *Silk Road Spirit*—"peace and cooperation, openness and inclusiveness, mutual learning and mutual benefit."[25]

The BRI in essence brings together the less developed part of China, with the less developed parts of the world economy in general. For China, even though a global vision, the BRI starts at home. The BRI is rooted in China's Great Western Development Program, which aims to bring the Reform and Opening Up to China's inland and remote western areas, and strengthen their links with economic partners from the rest of the world by promoting new transportation routes and economic corridors. This of course, does not mean shifting China's economic core from the East and South coasts to the West hinterland, but rather empowering the Western areas so they can catch up with the more affluent East. Thus, the emphasis is put on places such as Xi'an, Chongqing, Chengdu and the Xinjiang Autonomous Region, which is also facilitated by the narrative of the ancient Silk Road which is associated with these areas. Local governments in these areas, as well as other actors (such as SOEs) have been at the forefront of promoting the BRI.

From a global perspective, the majority of countries and regions that are part of the BRI, and in particular the Silk Road Economic Belt, are post-socialist economies in transition, developing economies, resource-rich countries, and only a small minority are developed economies as defined by the UN—and even fewer members of the OECD—and some of them hardly hit by the 2008 crisis, such as Greece. Another group of countries (and the most numerous one within the BRI countries) are post-socialist economies such as the ones of Eastern Europe that have had limited gains from the post-1990 transition; as well as conflict societies including some of the most severely war torn countries such as Syria and Afghanistan where political instability and war have stunted development. When it comes to the Maritime Silk Road, aside from Southeast Asia, the Initiative includes a number of former colonies whose trajectory in the past has been determined by the legacy of exploitation (such as Africa or Latin America, the newest addition to the BRI). The focus on the less developed parts of the global economy has led some authors to frame the BRI as a modern-day incarnation of the Mao-era Third Worldism.[26]

As an Initiative that bridges China's less developed parts with the less burgeoning countries of the global economy, the BRI perpetuates the ideological drive of "South-South" model of development cooperation, meaning that developing countries with which China cooperates on the basis of a shared sentiment about the global economic order are of primary interest, whereas countries of the global North come as secondary. However, whereas in the past there has been a sharp distinction

[24]Some authors refer to this as a call of an inclusive globalization (Liu and Dunford 2016).

[25]See the official document by China's National Development and Reform Commission (2015).

[26]For instance, Chen (2017).

between the South and the North in China's foreign policy, the BRI tries to synthetize them. Terms like "South-South cooperation with North-South characteristics" and "South-South-North" are ever more present in the Chinese discourse on the BRI. In practice, getting developed countries on board is envisioned as a way to further advance "production capacity cooperation"—which is in effect a strategy of pooling of resources by different parties in order to maximize the outcomes—which can potentially create a path to a "triple win" (one win for each party involved—China, the developing countries, and the developed countries).[27]

Through the BRI, China believes it presents the partner countries with a new opportunity to (further) advance their agency as international actors, and in particular, to find a way to advance their economies, while seeking both short and long term benefits also for China itself. On the short term, the BRI immediately benefits Chinese state-owned enterprises (SOEs) who are contracted for construction projects, Chinese SOEs in sectors with overcapacity (e.g. steel producers), and Chinese financial institutions who are creditors to such projects. On the long run, China's intended "win-win" outcome of the BRI cooperation foresees the creation of a momentum for developing an economically integrated and burgeoning intercontinental market for its exports and sources for its much needed exports (such as food) of unprecedented size (counting India, the Belt&Road would comprise two thirds of the human race). While the implication of the short-term claim (benefits for Chinese SOEs and banks) is self-explanatory, the long-term aspects are underpinned by the idea of mutual interdependence. As China has historically risen into the global system, its economic trajectory of a trading state has become interlinked with the rest of the world (the notion of "common destiny").[28] More specifically, China as the world's largest trader needs an ever-expanding foreign market, where actors thanks to their development will develop a stronger demand, but also an ability to purchase advanced Chinese goods (such as high-speed trains, nuclear power technology, smart technology, etc.).

Hence, as China upgrades its production up the value-chain and gets richer, it needs to world to follow suite—its success depends on the success of others. However, China sees itself as an instigator, animator and contributor—but not the *developer* of other nations. The BRI is therefore sticking to the terminology of "initiative" (*changyi*), or a proposal, and not a strategy or policy.[29] The realization, therefore, requires the participant countries to also commit and invest their resources (according to the deal made with China), meaning that any success depends on the ability of China to ensure that there is a shared sense of ownership of the BRI. Such bold anchoring of the BRI in the idea of shared destiny, and the delegation of so much responsibility about its own future in the hands of others, is in many ways a counter-intuitive development. In the post-Mao era, China has been generally thought of as a

[27]For production capacity cooperation, see Qiu (2015b).

[28]The concept of the community of common destiny is explained in the paper of Zhang (2015).

[29]For the terminology debate, see the contribution by Xie (2015).

risk-averse, reluctant global actor.[30] With the advancement of the BRI, China suddenly engages in an unexpected new form of international cooperation, which many consider economically adventurous, and arguably, not sufficiently rooted in conventional rational choice thinking. Authors in China and outside have even argued that the BRI leads to the "overstretching" of China's capacity.[31]

Yet, with the investment of a significant amount of resources, enshrining the BRI in the CPC Constitution, and linking it with XJP Thought, the BRI—regardless of the risks it carries—is now simply too big to fail—for China and the CPC, and by extension, for the global economy. In that sense, the BRI itself becomes one manifestation of the idea of the "community of shared destiny" in action, but with a particular twist that makes it look more of a wager—China now does not depend only on itself, but also on its joint projects with partner countries, which are of an unprecedented number and scope. With the BRI the nature of the bonds within the (imagined, or rather desired) Sino-centric global community is now ascribed a particular character: the destiny of the BRI is one of China-guided development, which may or may not make sense in the eyes of others. The vision of shared destiny for instance includes a particular stance on trade. For China, rules matter insofar respecting them helps, or at least it does not compromise its interests or harm the potential to achieve strategic goals. The end goal being allowing everyone to achieve economic development, China in principle argues that countries need to pursue openness and trade with each other, on the terms they agree upon. With the rise of protectionism and economic nationalism in the West, and in particular the United States, China has repeatedly made a strong case for maintaining open trade relations, as one of the pillars of global economic prosperity. While not necessarily sharing an identical understanding of free trade as the West, for the time being, China has recently acted as a supporter of the global trade regime with the World Trade Organization (WTO) as its central regulatory body, not the least because it has greatly benefited after joining the WTO, but it has also learned how to rely on the WTO in handling various trade disputes.[32]

Finally, this normative anchoring faces in shared destiny two important challenges rooted in China's practice itself. One is the challenge of distribution of the benefits of whatever will be achieved through the BRI. The BRI addresses primarily the constellations of economic power between countries and regions—and not within countries, except in the case of China (where it empowers the Western inland areas). That means that the BRI, while promoting a rather strong commitment to more equitable developments on the global level, it does not (yet) provide a direct normative nor practical solution on how the new forms of cooperation will benefit the common people on the ground. Nevertheless, some indirect implications are present—for instance, the BRI to a great extent is focused on creating new commons and public goods, such as transportation infrastructure, or energy infrastructure. Yet, the social component of these developments depends on national governments and

[30]For the historic evolution of China as a global actor see Wang (2008).

[31]See Blumenthal (2017).

[32]For illustration, see the speech by Xi Jinping at the World Economic Forum in Davos 2017 (Xi 2017).

their socio-economic policies, which is perhaps a further source of risk for the ideals that underpin the Initiative. The second challenge comes in the form of the question, on perpetuating asymmetries and perpetuating the peripheralization of many of the countries involved in the BRI. One concrete example of this is the "debt trap" of the tied financing infrastructure development model (Chinese banks financing a deal that should include a Chinese state-owned enterprise in the implementation of the project). Recent example of this is the Hambantota Port in Sri Lanka—developed with expensive Chinese loan that Sri Lanka could not afford to repay—instead, in order to alleviate the debt, it leased the port to China, a move that regardless of its economic justification, triggered public outrage.[33]

4 Respecting the Red Lines: Sovereignty-First

The BRI is a state-centric platform. The central role in the development of the BRI is played by China's government, and subsequently, national governments of other participating countries. As a form of inter-governmental cooperation, however, it falls outside the common taxonomy of international institutions and organizations, as it is presented as an open and inclusive, non-coercive form of cooperation, which does not infringe upon the sovereignty of any participating country. The BRI is to be jointly built; even though China at its disposal various forms of lobbying and persuasion if necessary in order to make countries join the Initiative, so far it has coerced anyone into signing up for the BRI. In the official documents, the core normative pillar of the BRI is that it rests on the "Five Principles of Peaceful Coexistence" which have formed the normative basis of China's foreign policy for decades. This reflects continuity rather than a change in China's foreign policy, which has upheld the sovereignty-first, non-intervention and non-interference principles throughout the decades and different eras.[34]

Therefore, while participant countries are expected to play an active role in the construction of the Belt&Road, at the end of the day the BRI is a voluntary mode of participation, whereby the scope of commitment is not a subject to any conditions, and is negotiated on a case-by-case basis. As a result, while some countries have relatively quickly embraced the BRI and started discussing a number of projects (like Pakistan or Belarus), others are still at the level of only formally supporting the BRI without more substantial commitments. In rational-choice terms, this adds on the risk of the BRI for China—its realization depends on the sovereign choices of a number of nations—on whether to join the Initiative, to what extent to commit themselves, and theoretically, when to exit.

In practice, the cooperation under the BRI depends on the level of formalization of both the relationship between participating countries and China, and the formalization of their participation into the BRI via Memorandums of Understanding and other documents. This formalization occurs at the highest political level, and is a

[33]See Reuters (2017).

[34]See Wang (2008).

precondition for the BRI cooperation to commence. After the cooperation is established, however, the Chinese side has a strong preference for communicating via official, state-framed channels. The prioritization of official channels extends to all political and economic aspects of cooperation, but also to the realm of culture and "people to people exchange," which are considered important pillars of the BRI. In the process, in accord with the Five Principles, China does not challenge the domestic circumstances of the participant countries, but adjusts to them—by jointly communicating with the national governments (i.e. be it legal framework for investment, political actors, etc.). Similar adaptation of the participant countries, towards the Chinese framework and practice, is also expected in return. This plays a particular role in developing relations with countries that have different political systems and sets of political beliefs—the partnership requires non-interference in each other's' internal affairs, non-interventionism and avoiding actions that can challenge each other's legitimacy.

This brings us to an important normative principle central to the BRI—the recognition of the sovereign rights of nations to freely choose and pursue their own "path of national development" and exercise their national "policy rights,"[35] and the ideal of a global order that allows for different countries to legitimately pursue diverging and disparate outlooks as well as political and development models.[36] The vision of world as comprised by nation-states that all develop in different, idiosyncratic way, is where China and the BRI diverge, if not contradict the idea of liberal democracy and its universal value and applicability. The political philosophy of the BRI, a consequence of China's exceptionalism is rooted in the objection of the assumed universal values, standards and blueprint rooted in liberal democracy promoted by the Western powers and international organizations.[37] Chinese scholars often observe a global process of a number of countries that in a similar way reject the notion of universality of the Western norms and values, that they call "diversification" of political and economic systems.[38] As of lately, this principle is discussed also as plausible for the growing number of actors—who sometimes even come to power—that stand up for nationalist, nativist, and anti-colonial ideas.[39] In this process, the self-ascribed duty of China is not to provide a particular alternative, but with its own example, to merely show that alternatives can exist successfully.

This, however, is also one point where a particular normative principle that underpins the BRI also poses a potential risk. Namely, what happens when a particular government starts exhibiting transgressions of power? Domestically, China has developed a resilient authoritarian system also in part due to the consistent and thorough anti-corruption efforts. However, by proposing the sovereignty-first

[35]See Li et al. (2010).

[36]See Nathan (2015).

[37]For an overview of China's exceptionalism, but also how it compares to the American and European exceptionalisms, see the work by Bradford and Posner (2011).

[38]Personal interview.

[39]See for example, this controversial piece by Li (2017).

approach, it has accepted the possibility of working with corrupt or simply inept counter-parts. And while not promoting any external reformist or conditional approach, Chinese policymakers and experts have in different occasions expressed their opinions and suggested that a certain course of action should be taken by host governments—but this is far from using it as a basis for systematic analysis. By extension, this leads to the questions of security risks as well as the responsibility for protecting the workers and the projects along the Belt&Road that are built outside China. It poses the puzzle, to what extent can China both maintain the adherence to the Five Principles and help ensure the security along the Belt&Road at the same time, and how it will go about it?

5 Unlocking Potentials: State-Led Growth and Cooperation

The BRI provides new international venue where the national governments have the right of agreeing particular terms and details of cooperation with China, and potentially between each other, on individual and case-by-case basis. This is different compared to the various international organizations, in particular the ones that uphold the market neoliberal Washington consensus, that serve to implement and streamline a set of norms and regulations that delimit the role of the state in the economy, impose certain policies onto participating countries and micromanage their implementation. In the context of the BRI, it is assumed that national interests come first, and that the cooperation is based on the principle of sovereignty-first and non-interference in internal affairs, and fine-tuned according to the national interests of particular governments and their idiosyncratic cultural characteristics.

In China, the CPC and the state have created and guided the market, and determined extent and nature in which China has been involved in global capitalism. The Chinese state has therefore been the major force behind attracting foreign direct investment, creating the regulatory framework to facilitate trade, and fine-tuning the role of market forces and finance in China's economy; it has been also an engineer and driver of China's "going global" policy of making strategic outward investments.[40] This particular developmental path has greatly benefited China, and over time it has been praised both outside of China,[41] and in the country, becoming an important reference for the debates on China's soft power. In particular, it was Westerners who coined terms such as Beijing Consensus or the China Model, but China embraced them as they were signifiers of certain achievement that can be capitalized on.[42] As China's growth and resilience have provided a particular form of prestige, or symbolic capital for the Chinese leadership in international relations, in the era of Xi Jinping China has become ever more confident and boastful about the achievements of the state-led developmental model. On line with the

[40]For the "going global" strategy see Bernasconi-Osterwalder et al. (2013).

[41]See Kirby (2011).

[42]See the work by Zhao (2008).

non-interventionism, China still refrains from exporting its model onto others; however, a novel element is that China now openly suggests that socialism with Chinese characteristics and the Chinese developmental experience can offer lessons, wisdom and solutions for others.[43] China's new foreign policy ventures, and in particular the BRI, will greatly facilitate the spreading of such Chinese solutions happen.

Here, it is important to note that for China (and those who praise it) the role of the state as a driver of economic cooperation is not a goal in itself, but rather seen as an optimal practice to ensure the unlocking of economic potentials and boosting of cooperation and overall economic growth, especially at times of stagnation and sluggish recovery from the global financial crisis largely brought about by austerity practices. The BRI is framed as a response to the global financial crisis, which itself was brought about by market failure and governments getting involved only in the process of sanation rather than prevention; China has notably managed to avoid the detrimental effects of the crisis by relying to a resolute state action in the form of heavy stimulus package as a pre-emptive measure. Nevertheless, China as a "survivor" from the crisis had to face a world in which the majority of its economic partners, especially the advanced Western economies, faced grim economic prospects, which given the level of interdependence at some point would also affect the prospects of the Chinese economy.[44] Chinese policymakers had in this sense utilized the momentum China enjoyed at the international level and managed to champion a global vision in which Beijing would create new environment for cooperation in a way that would help China to unleash its own capacities and make a case for unleashing the capacities of others, contribute to the restoration of economic growth and therefore also reap more lucrative benefits of economic cooperation for itself (as well as others, therefore "win-win").

Thus, one can interpret the BRI as an endeavor that brings (back) the idea of the state as a main driver of economic cooperation on a global level, and as an attempt to harness the power of national governments in participating countries in order to "hack" economic cooperation and the generation of growth the way China knows best: by giving the driver's seat to the ruling institutions (which then is used to boost infrastructure construction through state investment, development of strategically important industries, attraction of foreign investment, (de)regulation the economy in a particular way, etc.). The state can then engage, justify or provide cover for economic policies that are perhaps unjustifiable in a Western liberal context and adhering to the Washington Consensus. For instance, the BRI stands for the principle that if a government presupposes that it needs to build the roads or railways first, by all means it should have the possibility to do so. A railway can be justified as having an added non-monetary value, as it contributes to flow of people, ideas and can therefore inspire new entrepreneurial activity in previously unconnected areas. The promise the new railway holds is something that is worth getting into debt for—China is there to provide a loan, which will be repaid once the railway is built and contributes to the growth of the host country. However, in the Western thinking, if one cannot prove how and when every cent invested in the railway will be paid

[43] See Gitter (2017).

[44] See Overholt (2010).

back, or if the government that wants to build the railway cannot afford the project itself, the project may be deemed unfeasible.[45] And while this can be framed as another form of a "debt trap," often Chinese voices justify it as "borrowing from the future," and Chinese institutions often end up financing projects that had been previously avoided by Western institutions.[46]

In addition to the ability to push for various economic policies, the upholding of the primacy of the state-led economic model also presupposes mainstreaming of different set of political values. In the Chinese case, a strong-armed state with ample maneuvering space in terms of policy-making is the prerequisite of growth—for instance, only a sovereign, strong state can push for resolute moves such as the construction of kilometers long high speed railway. Such strong-armed state requires "stable political environment"[47] and needs to avoid "excessive political competition"[48] in order to be able to steer the economy in one or the other direction, and sometimes to undertake contradicting policies, as well as to reverse previous ones. They way to ensure this is that the state needs to be run by a political elite or party which has a dominant, and in many ways uncontested and uncontestable position in society. In other words, while not definitely incompatible with a liberal democracy, the state neoliberal project often inclines towards authoritarianism, or some form of a "democracy with adjectives," such as managed or sovereign democracy, or illiberal democracy, or some form of hybrid regime. However, this terminology, while in the Western scholarship used in a somewhat derogatory way, among those who adhere to non-Western ideologies are considered to be affirmative (i.e. the Hungarian Prime Minister Viktor Orbán is proudly using the word "illiberal").[49]

In the literature, there have been numerous attempts to discuss the BRI as a medium of authoritarian diffusion,[50] and this is getting new impetus with the debates on China's malicious influence abroad that dominated the news cycles in 2017/2018. However, nuances are important here. The BRI certainly does not explicitly promote authoritarianism, but is even more alien from the promotion of liberal democratic values, always giving priority to political stability and the aptitude of the state. Importantly, however, China's developmental path differs from Western illiberal manifestations that are often accompanied by economic nationalism and anti-globalism, as to a great extent counter-intuitively, for China upholding a central role of the state is important to protect globalization and oppose protectionist tendencies—which was argued in the sections above.

[45]A particular conflict of Chinese vs Western thinking of this sort happens in the region of the Western Balkans, which is the European Union (EU) enlargement area, and therefore closely supervised the by the EU.

[46]Personal interview.

[47]See Li et al. (2010). Interestingly, the criticism of the concept of stability promotion has been growingly present in European Studies, in particular in the debates on European enlargement (Balkans In Europe Policy Advisory Group 2017).

[48]See Sheng and Geng (2017).

[49]See the speech by Viktor Orban (Hungarian Government 2014).

[50]For an exploratory text, see Bryant and Chou (2016).

The principle of state-led growth and cooperation also presupposes certain challenges for the BRI. One of the major ones is rooted in the fact that many of the countries along the BRI area have been considered human laboratories of the neoliberal transition in the 1990s; the consensus on economic development has been the more market, and the less state there is in the economy, the better. This is not only an ideological issue, but also a structural and regulatory one. The latter is of particular importance: for instance, in the BRI countries that are members of the European Union, China has met a number of institutional hurdles to advance the cooperation in infrastructural projects. One of the landmark projects, the Budapest-Belgrade high-speed rail had notable delays, because of incompatibility between the government-led project with European regulations on transparency and competition.[51] At the end, China had to change its approach and adopt the European framework—at least for the Hungarian section of the railway (that is part of the EU)—and agree on opening a public tender in accord with European procurement standards.[52] However, while certainly a limit on the advancement of the principle of state-led economic cooperation, this case also demonstrated the flexibility and the capacity to learn of the Chinese institutions, which will be elaborated in more detail below.

6 Seeking Synergies: Connectivity and New Regionalism

One of the core features of the BRI is that it promotes regional connectivity and cooperation between the various nation-states involved.[53] Connectivity here is a multi-faceted concept: it is a connectivity of physical infrastructure facilities into a trans-continental intermodal transporation network, connectivity of production capacities into supply chains, connectivity of producers and consumers across borders and cultures, connectivity of markets, connectivity of peoples and cultures into networks of interaction and cultural exchange, connectivity between various ideas, and connectivity of the ideas with the means to realize them. Thus, while the main participating units in the BRI are nation-states and the operative framework is based on state-centered and sovereignty-first principles, the main output of the interaction is regional connectivity-based synergy and integration.

In terms of the political economic thinking of the BRI, the notion of regionalism matters as it help in transcending the limits of the economy of nation-states via connecting a number of states together.[54] While this may sound self-evident, again this has a particular underpinning. In the Chinese view, the size of economies and populations are preconditions needed to unleash economic potentials. An ample size of the population however is a privilege only few polities in the world have (most notably, China itself), and therefore the big number of relatively smaller countries

---

[51] See the report by Financial Times (Beesley et al. 2017).

[52] See Peto (2017).

[53] Andornino (2017) calls the BRI a project through which China excercises "connective leadership".

[54] Personal interview.

along the Belt&Road can best prosper if they "pool" together their resources. In this sense, regionalism and connectivity are essential, *sine qua non* of economic prosperity, because of the question of scale.

Moreover, the BRI provides a particular view on the particular regions to be created. Regions in general are socially constructed phenomena; they are certain narrations that assign meanings to a certain geographical space, mediated via asymmetrical power constellations: the resourceful actors are the ones who create narratives of regions. Therefore, the question when it comes to region and "regional thinking" is not what a region is, but who and how establishes the region. In particular, through the BRI, China as a resourceful actor envisions the development of six macro-regional economic corridors (New Eurasian Landbridge, China-Mongolia-Russia Corridor, China-Central Asia-West Asia Corridor, China-Indochina Peninsula Corridor, China-Pakistan Economic Corridor, and Bangladesh-China-India-Myanmar Corridor). These are loosely defined geographical spaces, defined along a functional understanding as much as they are developed based on geographical, spatially determined way.[55] The names, roster of countries involved, and outlined projects are subject to change. In this sense, the BRI envisions a dynamic, ever-evolving regional outlook. Hence, there is no single, definite geographical map of the Belt&Road areas, as the mapping is left to individual actors from China and elsewhere. In the context of China's foreign policy the BRI builds upon a number of previous undertakings in terms of development of regional and global cooperation that China has established or helped establish.

From the perspective of invoking certain narrations of the various areas and regions involved in the BRI, it is important to mention that in the process of developing the platforms for regional cooperation, as well as in the experimentation and development of the BRI itself, China has engaged in various types of practices. In some cases it has engaged with previously defined regions and pre-existing regional platforms, such as China-CELAC, or the Dialogue between China and the Forum of the Pacific Islands. In some cases, it has engaged on macro-level with a comprehensive, "continental" approach such as FOCAC in Africa which includes all countries with which China has established bilateral relations. Finally, China has also designed regional platforms based on its own understanding and mental mapping, the paradigmatic case being the 16+1 platform for cooperation with the countries of Central, East and Southeast Europe.[56]

The latter practice of assembling countries together based on the logic of the Chinese policymakers rather than on pre-existing formats for cooperation is best reflected in the BRI. After all, the BRI promotes a macro-regional vision loosely based on a particular understanding of the global economy today, in combination with a particular interpretation of the ancient Silk Road. As such, the Belt&Road area is a creation of China; it is however, a rather ambiguous one—there is no definite list of countries, no definite map, and an ever evolving outlook (starting from Eurasia and Africa, to Latin America, to the Arctic, now the BRI is a truly global project). However, it is important to note that

[55]For a comparative analysis on China's regionalism as visible in the BRI, see Kaczmarski (2017).

[56]For a comparative study on China's platforms for multilateral cooperation, see Jakobowski (in press).

through its macro-regional approach, the BRI does not aim to create new and exclusive "Silk Road" identity of the countries involved, but rather to create and additional layer to their identification as actors in international affairs, and to strengthen the multi-channel diplomacy, of which BRI is only one level—along with the bilateral relations and regional platforms discussed above.

7 Philosophy of Practice: Flexibility, Experimentation and Exception

The BRI, as argued above, involves a number of countries, clustered in different groups. While many of them have some similarities, overall they have tangible differences related to size and geography, level of economic development, overall political climate, institutional settings, needs and priorities, and resources to cooperate with China. At the same time, China also has different visions, experiences and expectations for each of them. This leads to a rather divergent development of the vision for the BRI across different (sub) regions and countries along the Belt&Road.

Therefore, comprising a great area and a variety of participating countries with various levels of development and political contexts, the BRI in reality will inevitably diversify into projects that correspond to the different local circumstances. There will be no single and most suitable example of the BRI in action, but there will be many different ones, and many of the practices will likely seem disparate, and in some ways even contradictory to one another. This is consistent with the principle of Chinese governance by experimentation, improvisation and pragmatic solution-seeking based on the empirical reality, not blindly following ideology and teleology ("seek truth from facts"). This is in many ways the point where the BRI departs from the Western deductive thinking, which seeks universality, conformity, and consistency, and which expects that global undertakings such as the BRI will remake the world according to the Chinese expectations. In reality, the BRI will change the world very much in interaction within the possibilities of the local circumstances, with the thinking and practice brought by China being in dialogue with both the domestic thinking and practice and the conditions on the ground.

The principle of flexibility defines many of the practices of the cooperation under the BRI. Here we have to go back to the idea of state neoliberalism, which rests on the working of a "particular political technology that actively seeks to create optimal conditions for entrepreneurial activities"[57] by individuals as well as the state. A crucial notion here is one of the exception—the deregulation of particular sectors in an overall highly regulated economy, the creation of special economic zones (SEZs) as physical spaces of exception, the abrupt revision of policies, as well as the disruption of policy sequences. Physical and regulatory spaces of exception, such as SEZs are a common practice of China's domestic development, and a practice that will be exported via the BRI. Jointly constructed SEZs will have a special

[57] Ong (2012).

jurisdiction, allowing for "resolving and overcoming differences" that may arise from the disparities and contradictions between different national legal frameworks and cultures of China and participating countries in the BRI.[58]

A similar form of flexibility exception is the creation of special legal instruments (*lex specialis*) to promote joint BRI projects in host countries. This would have a particular application in existing legal frameworks that closely follow the norms of the Washington consensus in terms of market-orientation, and strong rules on tendering, public procurements and accountability (meaning that their legal framework in general is not friendly towards state-led economic cooperation). Special legal instruments can override general laws when enacting measures on economic or other type of cooperation via the legislative or executive branch of government, using special clauses on the justification or special priority of BRI projects.

Flexibility is thus a key feature of reconciling diverging national development models, as opposed to the Western worldview, according to which there is no particular need or space for significant flexibility or creation of exceptions, as the systems of different countries should rather converge based on the same rules, norms and ideals. The Chinese approach stems from the idea that states based on political will arrange projects, and then they find ways to implement them. If necessary, they can bend the rules or, as argued here, create exceptions. This touches upon the idea of "rule by law" (as opposed to "rule of law")—whereby legal institutions are to serve a particular authority or idea, and are not a goal in itself, but rather the moral expression of power.[59]

In the context of the BRI, this means a flexible legal approach that will develop on case-by-case basis; China will uphold this principle by establishing specialized BRI courts and dispute settlement mechanisms with the primary goal of removing the disputes from the jurisdiction of other international courts. Once the BRI projects fall under the jurisdiction of the Chinese courts, there will be no barriers for application of the "rule by law" logic—political will, and the good political climate in the relations between China and the partner countries will significantly impact the outcome of legal disputes, especially in the context of large scale projects in the BRI framework. In this sense, the BRI will continue to be driven by economics, politics and even political culture, much more than it is driven by an overarching coherent legal or other type of rule-based framework, despite the creation of specialized legal institutions to oversee it.

8 Concluding Remarks and Further Research

In the era of reform and opening up China refashioned itself as a global economic actor, as opposed to the ideological and sectarian, insular foreign policy of the Cultural Revolution. The synthesis of politics and economy in its foreign policy

---

[58]See Vasiliev and Shmigelskaia (2016).

[59]See Castellucci (2007).

after 1978 has allowed it to develop constructive relations in all parts of the world, even with countries that lie on the opposite end of the ideological spectrum (i.e. the United States). With the BRI, China now adds a normative layer to the existing relationships with its partners from different parts of the globe, while also multiplying its capacity to conduct economic diplomacy. This is, without doubt, a significant upgrade of China's foreign policy in the era of Xi Jinping.

Through the BRI and associated mechanisms of multilateral and multi-channel regional diplomacy, and while upholding the sovereignty-first principle, China at the same time exposes a number of countries to economic cooperation as envisioned by the CPC, that determine the ideational development of the BRI. Ultimately, this is a cooperation aimed at achieving common prosperity, in which the notions of interdependence and shared destiny leave China no choice but to put a wager on the ability of others to realize and embrace the potentials of its offer, and to later redistribute the results to their populations. The implementation is to be carried out by states that will not interfere in each other's affairs and will cooperate in a flexible way—given that political will by all sides will persist.

Having laid out the normative foundations of the BRI that essentially constitute the "Chinese wisdom" CPC now offers to the world, the next question for researchers is to trace an approach that would help in uncovering whether, how, and to what extent does the BRI affect the thinking and behavior of external actors directly involved in it, with regards to the way they relate to China, and the way they think on global and domestic and global governance. While China certainly provides a normative concept in the BRI, it is still not clear cut to what extent these norms will be recognized, legitimized and embraced by others.

This offers plenty of space for researchers to follow up. In my own work beyond this chapter, I argue that in order to answer these questions, the interaction within the BRI and its associated China-centric platforms, and their effects are best captured by an innovative analytical approach that combines symbolic domination and principle-diffusion via bounded rationality. This is primarily because within the BRI, given its particular normative framework, but also the impression that within the BRI interactions and power relations operate in concealed manner, the dispositions and adaptation of the actors is as important as is the input from China. In other words, the process would not resemble an open and outspoken type of one-directional "promotion" of norms and values, but rather a long term, gradual and somewhat "subterranean" internalization through dialogue.

Bourdieu(s)ian concepts on power relations and their symbolic mediation emphasizes the centrality of practices, not only of discourse and representations; and the link between symbolic power and the material world.[60] The concept of symbolic domination therefore can help grasping a particular form of influence that is not fully transparent, and therefore belonging in the realm of not so apparent processes. Bourdieu's concepts of symbolic power and symbolic domination have been particularly relevant for the historical study of imperial China's dominance in the East Asian regional order,[61] and can by extension be useful for analyzing contemporary developments.

---

[60]See Leander (2008).

[61]See Lee (2016).

The asymmetrical relationships that comprise the BRI create similar—but not identical—conditions for symbolic domination compared to the East Asian legacy of the dynastic era. While in the past the source of symbolic power of China has been its preponderance and cultural capital thereby referring to practices in a number of areas of governance and life, today, the source of China's symbolic power is rooted in the narrative of its economic success, thereby relating primarily to economic governance (although as argued in this chapter, this has implications in a number of policy areas). In practice, China's call for collective action issued in the form of the BRI is already a first step towards transformation of the thinking and behavior among the participants in the Initiative. The visible and especially the invisible elements of the BRI as a Sino-centric convention of governments are mediated through language and various the social practices that constitute the structured, if not (quasi)institutionalized relationship under the BRI framework. The continuous repetition and the eventual naturalization of these elements in the thinking and behavior of these practices among the participants ultimately constitute the process of symbolic domination.[62]

Through the routinization of the symbolic practices the BRI can facilitate the internalization of new concepts and ideas even if they initially seem puzzling to the recipients. What can originally be ascribed as a somewhat subconscious process, with the time being can also assume a form of a fully deliberate one, which can then lead to a conscious movement of particular norms, ideas and practices into specific forms of governance, policymaking and legislation.[63] The logic of this process can be normative, meaning that actors will start adopting the ideas and practices promoted by China through the BRI based on their acquired belief in their legitimacy; this logic can also be utilitarian—meaning that actors will accept these ideas and practices based on the belief that they work in their economic or political interest. However, in line with the Bourdieu(s)ian approach above, another very likely possibility is that bounded rationality of decision-makers who operate in imperfect conditions, limited knowledge and understanding of the subject and therefore often make biased decisions under the influence of the dominant narrative, can lead to a particular form of diffusion whereby actors will embrace the normative blueprint of the BRI primarily as a result of the continuous engagement with China and simply their fascination with the ongoing "Chinese miracle."

What will be then, the effect of the BRI on the world? A successful diffusion of the normative principles discussed in this chapter would further facilitate the process of diversification of political and economic thinking and practice of international political economy. In this sense, the chapter agrees with the hypothesis of Francis Fukuyama who argues that a successful BRI would mean that a number of countries in the world would start growingly look like China.[64] However, I add a nuance here: while in some policy areas governments will be indeed influenced by China, and perhaps look increasingly like China, this will be far from a consistent, uniform tendency. Countries

[62]For Global China and symbolic power, see Vangeli (in press-b).

[63]This is known as diffusion (Simmons et al. 2008; Gilardi 2013), "transfer" (Stone 2001), "transplantation" (Peerenboom 2013), "translation" (Clarke et al. 2015) and "dissemination."

[64]See Fukuyama (2016).

will indeed, if not because, then greatly encouraged by China, engage in pursuit of national development paths, moving further away from the Universalist assumption of Western liberal democracy. Whether this will be a good or a bad thing, then, it depends on the actual material outcomes, and the convictions and interpretations of the beholders. For China, this will certainly be a welcomed change.

Acknowledgement The author would like to thank the ZEIT-Stiftung Ebelin und Gerd Bucerius for the generous support of their work in the period 2015–2018.

References

Ambrosio, T. (2012). The rise of the 'China Model' and 'Beijing Consensus': Evidence of authoritarian diffusion? *Contemporary Politics, 18*(4), 381–399. https://doi.org/10.1080/13569775.2012.728029.

Andornino, G. B. (2017). The Belt and Road Initiative in China's emerging grand strategy of connective leadership. *China & World Economy, 25*, 4–22. https://doi.org/10.1111/cwe.12211.

Balkans In Europe Policy Advisory Group. (2017). *The crisis of democracy in the Western Balkans. Authoritarianism and EU stabilitocracy*. Balkans In Europe Policy Advisory Group.

Barr, M. (2011). *Who's afraid of China? The challenge of Chinese soft power*. London: Zed Books.

Beesley, A., Byrne, A., & Kynge, J. (2017). EU sets collision course with China over 'Silk Road' rail project. *Financial Times.*

Beeson, M., & Li, F. (2016). China's place in regional and global governance: A new world comes into view. *Global Policy, 7*(4), 491–499. https://doi.org/10.1111/1758-5899.12348.

Bernasconi-Osterwalder, N., Johnson, L., & Zhang, J. (Eds.). (2013). *Chinese outward investment: An emerging policy framework. A compilation of primary sources*. Winnipeg, Manitoba, Canada: International Institute for Sustainable Development and Institute for International Economic Research.

Blumenthal, D. (2017). A strategy for China's imperial overstretch. *American Interest.* Retrieved January 24, 2018, from https://www.the-american-interest.com/2017/03/01/a-strategy-for-chinas-imperial-overstretch/

Boer, R. (2017). Interpreting Marx's capital in China. *Continental Thought and Theory, 1*(4), 177–206.

Bradford, A., & Posner, E. A. (2011). Universal exceptionalism in international law. *Harvard International Law Journal, 52*, 1–40.

Bremmer, I. (2008). The return of state capitalism. *Survival, 50*, 55–64. https://doi.org/10.1080/00396330802173198.

Breslin, S. (2011). The 'China Model' and the global crisis: From Friedrich list to a Chinese mode of governance? *International Affairs, 87*(6), 1323–1343. https://doi.org/10.1111/j.1468-2346.2011.01039.x.

Bryant, O., & Chou, M. (2016). China's New Silk Road: Autocracy promotion in the new Asian order? *Democratic Theory, 3*(2), 114–124. https://doi.org/10.3167/dt.2016.030207.

Castellucci, I. (2007). Rule of law with Chinese characteristics. *Annual Survey of International & Comparative Law, 13*(1), 35.

Chen, G. (陈刚) (2017). *中国"一带一路"战略的外交思想根源– zhongguo yidayilu zhanlue de waijio sixiang genyuan – The Origins of China's Belt and Road Strategy.* 联合早报 Lianhe Zaobao.

Chu, Y., & So, A. Y. (2010). State neoliberalism: The Chinese road to capitalism. In Y. Chu (Ed.), *Chinese capitalisms* (pp. 46–72). International Political Economy Series. Palgrave Macmillan UK. https://doi.org/10.1007/978-0-230-25135-9_3.

Clarke, J., Bainton, D., Lendvai, N., & Stubbs, P. (Eds.). (2015). *Making policy move: Towards a politics of translation and assemblage*. Bristol, England: Policy Press.

Dreher, A., Fuchs, A., Parks, B., Strange, A., & Tierney, M. (2017). *Aid, China, and growth: Evidence from a new global development finance dataset*. Rochester, NY: Social Science Research Network.

Fasslabend, W. (2015). The Silk Road: A political marketing concept for world dominance. *European View, 14*, 293–302. https://doi.org/10.1007/s12290-015-0381-3.

Ferdinand, P. (2016). Westward ho-the China dream and 'One Belt, One Road': Chinese foreign policy under Xi Jinping. *International Affairs, 92*, 941–957. https://doi.org/10.1111/1468-2346.12660.

Fukuyama, F. (2016, January 12). Exporting the Chinese model. *Project Syndicate*. https://www.project-syndicate.org/commentary/china-one-belt-one-road-strategy-by-francis-fukuyama-2016-01

Gilardi, F. (2013). Transnational diffusion: Norms, ideas, and policies. In W. Carlsnaes, T. Risse, & B. A. Simmons (Eds.), *Handbook of international relations* (Chapter 18). London: SAGE Publications Ltd. http://knowledge.sagepub.com/view/hdbk_interntlrelations/SAGE.xml

Gitter, D. (2017, October 28). China sells socialism to the developing world. *The Diplomat*. https://thediplomat.com/2017/10/china-sells-socialism-to-the-developing-world/

Godehardt, N. (2016). *No end of history. A Chinese alternative concept of international order?* (SWP Research Paper). German Institute for International and Security Affairs, Berlin. https://www.swp-berlin.org/en/publication/no-end-of-history/

Hall, I. (2017). Belt and Road: The case for 'wait and see.' *The Interpreter*. Retrieved January 24, 2018, from https://www.lowyinstitute.org/the-interpreter/belt-and-road-case-wait-and-see

Heilmann, S., Moritz, M., Houtari, M., & Buckow, J. (2014). *China's shadow foreign policy: Parallel structures challenge the established international order* (China Monitor no. 28). Mercator Institute for China Studies, Berlin. http://www.merics.org/fileadmin/user_upload/downloads/China-Monitor/China_Monitor_No_18_en.pdf

Huaxia. (2017). CPC Q&A: What are China's two centennial goals and why do they matter? *Xinhua News*.

Hungarian Government. (2014). Prime Minister Viktor Orbán's Speech at the 25th Bálványos Summer Free University and Student Camp. *Government*. Retrieved October 19, 2014, from http://www.kormany.hu/en/the-prime-minister/the-prime-minister-s-speeches/prime-minister-viktor-orban-s-speech-at-the-25th-balvanyos-summer-free-university-and-student-camp

Jacques, M. (2012). *When China rules the world: The end of the western world and the birth of a new global order* (2nd ed.) (Greatly expanded and fully updated). New York: Penguin Books.

Jakobowski, J. (in press). Examining Chinese-led regional multilateralism: the "16+1" platform in the context of China-Africa and China-Latin America relations. *Journal of Contemporary China*.

Johnson, C. K. (2016). *President Xi Jinping's 'Belt and Road' Initiative*. Center for Strategic and International Studies. http://csis.org/publication/president-xi-jinpings-belt-and-road-initiative

Kaczmarski, M. (2017). Non-western visions of regionalism: China's New Silk Road and Russia's Eurasian Economic Union. *International Affairs, 93*(6), 1357–1376. https://doi.org/10.1093/ia/iix182.

Kavalski, E. (2013). The struggle for recognition of normative powers: Normative power Europe and normative power China in context. *Cooperation and Conflict, 48*(2), 247–267. https://doi.org/10.1177/0010836713485386.

Kirby, W. (2011). China's prosperous age: A century in the making. *China Heritage Quarterly* (26). http://www.chinaheritagequarterly.org/features.php?searchterm=026_kirby.inc&issue=026

Leander, A. (2008). Thinking tools: Analyzing symbolic power and violence. In A. Klotz & D. Prakash (Eds.), *Qualitative methods in international relations: A pluralist guide* (pp. 11–28). Palgrave MacMillan.

Lee, J.-Y. (2016). Hegemonic authority and domestic legitimation: Japan and Korea under Chinese hegemonic order in early modern East Asia. *Security Studies, 25*(2), 320–352. https://doi.org/10.1080/09636412.2016.1171970.

Li, E. X. (2017). China, America, and "Nationalism". *American Affairs Journal*. https://americanaffairsjournal.org/2017/10/china-americanationalism
Li, X., Brødsgaard, K. E., & Jacobsen, M. (2010). Redefining Beijing consensus: Ten economic principles. *China Economic Journal, 2*(3), 297–311. https://doi.org/10.1080/17538960903529535.
Li, Y. (2017b, October 25). Xi Jinping thought has global influence. *Belt and Road Portal*. https://eng.yidaiyilu.gov.cn/qwyw/rdxw/31488.htm
Liu, W., & Dunford, M. (2016). Inclusive globalization: Unpacking China's Belt and Road Initiative. *Area Development and Policy, 1*(3), 323–340. https://doi.org/10.1080/23792949.2016.1232598.
Lukes, S. (2004). *Power: A radical view* (2nd ed.). Hampshire, England/New York: Palgrave Macmillan.
Lukes, S. (2007). Power and the battle for hearts and minds: On the bluntness of soft power. In F. Berenskoetter & M. J. Williams (Eds.), *Power in world politics* (pp. 83–97). London/New York: Routledge.
Nathan, A. J. (2015). China's challenge. *Journal of Democracy, 26*(1), 156–170. https://doi.org/10.1353/jod.2015.0012.
National Development and Research Commission. (2015). *Vision and actions on jointly building Silk Road Economic Belt and 21st-century Maritime Silk Road*. National Development and Research Commission of the People's Republic of China. http://en.ndrc.gov.cn/newsrelease/201503/t20150330_669367.html
Ong, A. (2012). Neoliberal as political technology. In *The Wiley-Blackwell Encyclopedia of Globalization*. Wiley. http://onlinelibrary.wiley.com/doi/10.1002/9780470670590.wbeog421/abstract
Overholt, W. H. (2010). China in the global financial crisis: Rising influence, rising challenges. *The Washington Quarterly, 33*, 21–34. https://doi.org/10.1080/01636600903418652.
Pantucci, R. (2016, October 7). How new is the 'Belt and Road'? *China Policy Institute: Analysis (blog)*. https://cpianalysis.org/2016/10/07/how-new-is-the-belt-and-road/
Peerenboom, R. (2013). Toward a methodology for successful legal transplants. *The Chinese Journal of Comparative Law, 1*(1), 4–20. https://doi.org/10.1093/cjcl/cxs002.
Peto, S. (2017). Hungary launches rail link tender as CEE-China summit starts. *Reuters*.
Qiu, Z. (2015a). From 'Game Player' to 'Game Maker': News features of China's Foreign Policy. *China Brief, 15*(14). http://www.jamestown.org/programs/chinabrief/single/?tx_ttnews%5Btt_news%5D=44174&cHash=5953f99bd5b663abf2bf57f8e823b7e3
Qiu, Z. (2015b). The 'Triple Win': Beijing's Blueprint for International Industrial Capacity Cooperation. *China Brief, 15*(18). https://jamestown.org/program/the-triple-win-beijings-blueprint-for-international-industrial-capacity-cooperation/
Ramo, J. C. (2007). *Brand China*. London: Foreign Policy Centre.
Reuters. (2017). Sri Lanka hands over running of Hambantota port to Chinese company. *South China Morning Post*.
Sheng, A., & Geng, X. (2017, October 25). Modernity with Chinese characteristics. *Project Syndicate*. https://www.project-syndicate.org/commentary/19th-congress-xi-jinping-development-plan-by-andrew-sheng-and-xiao-geng-2017-10
Simmons, B. A., Dobbin, F., & Garrett, G. (2008). *The global diffusion of markets and democracy*. Cambridge University Press.
So, A. Y., & Chu, Y. (2012). The transition from neoliberalism to state neoliberalism in China at the turn of the twenty-first century. In C. Kyung-Sup, B. Fine, & L. Weiss (Eds.), *Developmental politics in transition* (pp. 166–187). International Political Economy Series. Palgrave Macmillan UK. https://doi.org/10.1057/9781137028303_9.
So, A. Y., & Chu, Y. (2015). *The global rise of China*. Cambridge, England/Malden, MA: Polity Press.
Stone, D. (2001). *Learning lessons, policy transfer and the international diffusion of policy ideas* (CSGR Working Paper 69/01). Centre for the Study of Globalisation and Regionalisation,

The University of Warwick, Warwick. http://wrap.warwick.ac.uk/2056/1/WRAP_Stone_wp6901.pdf

Vangeli, A. (in press-a). A framework for the study of the One Belt, One Road Initiative as a medium of principle-diffusion. In X. Li (Ed.), *Mapping China's "One Belt One Road" Initiative.* Palgrave.

Vangeli, A. (in press-b). Global China and symbolic power: The case of 16+1 cooperation. *Journal of Contemporary China.*

Vasiliev, I. A., & Shmigelskaia, N. A. (2016). The revival of the Silk Road: Brief review of the 4th China-Eurasia Legal Forum. *Vestnik of Saint Petersburg University. Law*, (2), 94–101. https://doi.org/10.21638/11701/spbu14.2016.209.

Wade, R. (2004). *Governing the market: Economic theory and the role of government in East Asian industrialization, with a new introduction by the author.* Princeton, NJ: Princeton University Press. 2. pbk. edn.

Wang, G. (2008). China and the international order: Some historical perspectives. In G. Wang & Y. Zheng (Eds.), *China and the new international order* (pp. 21–31). Routledge.

Womack, B. (2008). *China as a normative foreign policy actor* (CEPS Working Documents). Centre for European Policy Studies, Brussels. http://aei.pitt.edu/11662/1/1607.pdf

Xi, J. (2017). Jointly shoulder responsibility of our times, promote global growth. Keynote Speech at the Opening Session of the World Economic Forum Annual Meeting 2017. *CGTN Am.* Retrieved January 24, 2018, from https://america.cgtn.com/2017/01/17/full-text-of-xi-jinping-keynote-at-the-world-economic-forum

Xie, T. (2015). Is China's "Belt and Road" a strategy? *The Diplomat.*

Xinhua News. (2017). "Belt and Road" incorporated into CPC Constitution. *Xinhua News.*

Yan, X. (2014). From keeping a low profile to striving for achievement. *The Chinese Journal of International Politics, 7*, 153–184. https://doi.org/10.1093/cjip/pou027.

Yang, J. (2015). China's 'New Diplomacy' under the Xi Jinping administration. *China Quarterly of International Strategic Studies, 01*(01), 1–17. https://doi.org/10.1142/S2377740015500013.

Yang, J. (2017). *Study and implement General Secretary Xi Jinping's thought on diplomacy in a deep-going way and keep writing new chapters of major-country diplomacy with distinctive Chinese features.*

Zhang, J. (2015). China's new foreign policy under Xi Jinping: Towards 'Peaceful Rise 2.0'? *Global Change, Peace & Security, 27*, 5–19. https://doi.org/10.1080/14781158.2015.993958.

Zhao, S. (2010). The China Model: Can it replace the western model of modernization? *Journal of Contemporary China, 19*(65), 419–436. https://doi.org/10.1080/10670561003666061.

Zhao, Y. (2008). Neoliberal strategies, socialist legacies: Communication and state transformation in China. In P. Chakravartty & Y. Zhao (Eds.), *Global communications: Toward a transcultural political economy* (pp. 23–50). Rowman & Littlefield.

The Belt and Road Initiative as Global Public Good: Implications for International Law

Chi He

1 Introduction

In 2013, Chinese president Xi Jingping in different occasions proposed two initiatives aiming to better integrate the Eurasia countries by dense infrastructure construction and close economic cooperation.[1] After a period of careful elaboration and adjustment, the two initiatives merged into what we now call the "Belt and Road Initiative" (BRI).[2] Although the exact scope and depth of the BRI are yet to be defined, its appeal as a grand design is increasingly remarkable. Various literatures in the fields of international relations, finance as well as law are devoted to exploring the boundaries, possibilities, and challenges ahead.

As a relatively recent theory in the international development literature, the concept of global public good(GPG) is heeded by Chinese policy makers as well as scholars to make sense the BRI by denoting its main aims as to provide infrastructure construction, economic integration, financial cooperation, environmental protection that satisfy the non-rival and non-exclusive characteristics which a GPG

The chapter benefited greatly from three referees' detailed comments and feedback. The views expressed herein are personal and do not necessarily reflect those of the organizations with which the author is or was affiliated. All errors remain the author's.

[1]The two initiatives are called the Silk Road Economic Belt and the twenty-first-Century Maritime Silk Road and were respectively proposed in September and October 2013 when President Xi was visiting Central Asia and Southeast Asia.

[2]Previously it was called the One Belt and One Road Initiative ("OBOR") but later the word "one" was deleted for the semantic confusion it may cause. Another major change is in the official usage, the Belt and Road should be called an "initiative" rather than "strategy". The reason is that the word "strategy" is too aggressive and did not match the ethos of the BRI as a friendly and mutual benefit project.

C. He (✉)
Peking University Law School , Beijing, China
e-mail: hechi@pku.edu.cn

W. Shan et al. (eds.), *Normative Readings of the Belt and Road Initiative*,
https://doi.org/10.1007/978-3-319-78018-4_5

entails. According to the spokesperson of the Ministry of Foreign Affairs, Hua Chunying, the BRI as a platform for international cooperation can itself be treated as an important global public good.[3]

The GPG narrative is profound for it hits the very core of the BRI: coordinating collective actions to solve common problems. However, successful collective actions in international stage can never be easily attained. States rely on international law to facilitate cooperation with each other. But the "weak law" identification renders international law unable to satisfactorily ensure the provision of GPG needed to solve these common problems. As an initiative which involves expansive geographical area, the BRI faces the same challenge on effectively resolving the dilemma of collective actions and therefore, the role of international law in this process should be seriously scrutinized. International law is never a set of static rules but a fluid discourse that can be shaped by various actors and that gives chances for China, the initiator and major supporter of the BRI, to navigate in the current international legal system and make its own voices to materialize its GPG agendas along the Belt and Road. In this sense, the BRI provides a vivid case to reflect and imagine the theoretical underpinning as well as normative structure of international law from a Chinese standpoint.

This chapter argues that by viewing the BRI through the lens of global public good, it provides a useful perspective to critically examine the role of international law in the course of international cooperation and meanwhile, opens a space of imagination to envisage a Chinese perspective of international law based on the Chinese conception of world order to better address the GPG needs of the Belt and Road area as well as the world. The Chinese conception of world order is deeply embedded in the old Chinese philosophical concept "Tian-xia" (All- under-Heaven) which prioritizes the oneness of the world. The "Tian-xia" philosophy shaped the world view of Chinese people and attached an idealistic ethos of the Belt and Road Initiative and more importantly, it is echoing the GPG narrative. However, a Chinese perspective of international law also faces challenges since the nation-state based international order prevails in contemporary international politics as well as the relatively limited practices of the BRI so far.

It is necessary to bear in mind that the research about the BRI, GPG and international law is largely an explorative one and the research result is tentative rather than exhaustive given the complexity, dynamics, and enormity of the BRI. This paper tries to shed some light on how to view the BRI and its potential influences on the international legal order.

[3]Foreign Ministry Spokesperson Hua Chunying's Regular Press Conference on August 16, 2017. http://www.fmprc.gov.cn/mfa_eng/xwfw_665399/s2510_665401/2511_665403/t1485231.shtml. Accessed on 18 October 2017.

2 Global Public Good: Concept, Law and the BRI

2.1 *Global Public Good: What's in a Concept?*

Public goods, in economic sense, refer to the goods that are characterized as non-rival and non-exclusive.[4] The phenomenon of free-riding can be traced to the works of Adam Smith and David Hume and it was Paul Samuelson who systematically brought up the concept "public goods" to explain the dilemmas concerning the management of the commons.[5] Since it is non-rival, the consumption of a public good would not diminish its use to others and the non-exclusive character implies that everyone can freely enjoy the benefits of the goods without exclusion, even those who did not pay for it. Due to the above two characteristics and with the presumption of *homo economics*, it lacks incentives to supply public goods for people tend to free ride others' efforts. Market failure serves as a case in point when it comes to public goods in economic analysis.

As a neo-classical economics concept, public good can be perceived as externalities in extreme cases and works in relatively limited economic conditions.[6] However, the concept exerted a spillover effect and amassed attentions from scholars in other fields, especially those in political science. In *The Logic of Collective Actions*, Olson pioneered the idea of public goods in his analysis of the failure of collective actions in various levels of groups and applied it in explaining the state's responsibility to provide national defense, legal order, public healthcare, education and etc.[7] These above, as Olson defined, are all public goods that only can be provided by a central authority with the monopoly of taxation and legal enforcement. Otherwise, the market would fail if it was bestowed to provide such public goods for it cannot overcome the free-riding impulses of individuals.

Afterwards, the concept of public goods was used to address the incentives of international cooperation and GPGs began to emerge in international arena.[8] Sponsored by the United Nations Development Programme (UNDP), three seminal volumes concerning global public goods were published and the International Task Force on Global Public Goods which led by some leading experts on international development, produced an extensive study on its theoretical underpinnings and practical relevance.[9] By their definition, "Global public goods are goods with

---

[4]This definition has been widely accepted among mainstream microeconomics economic textbooks. See Gravelle and Rees (1992) and Varian (1978).

[5]See Samuelson (1954), pp. 387–389.

[6]See Coussy (2005), pp. 177–178.

[7]See Oslon (1965), pp. 9–10.

[8]See Olson (1971) and Kindleberger (1986).

[9]The three volumes are: Kaul et al. (1999, 2003) and Kaul and Conceição (2006). See also International Task Force on Global Public Goods (2006) Meeting Global Challenges: International Corporation in the National Interest. Some governments and international organizations also initiated studies on GPGs. See Kaul (2013). See also, Gavas (2013).

benefits and/or costs that potentially extend to all countries, people, and generations."[10] The concept unifies a diverse collection of topics, suggesting a common collective action problem and large potential benefits to international cooperation.[11] In this sense, the BRI as a project to foster international cooperation and tackle common problems facing the region and the world, can be viewed as initiative to facilitate the provision of various GPGs. Above all, one prominent feature of GPG is that it hinges on international rules to ensure the proper international cooperation needed in its provision process and that requires us to first consider the theoretical connections between GPG and international law.

2.2 *Global Public Good and International Law*

In domestic setting, there exists a government to wield the necessary power to collect taxes and enforce legal rules to provide public goods. But transferring to international domain, it is not difficult to find that such an organ as world government doesn't exist. States enjoy the supreme sovereignty in international society and there is no higher authority above them. When it comes to the provision of global public goods, it mainly depends on the cooperation between states involving decentralized forms of implementation and enforcement to advance collective goals. Nordhaus, a prestigious economist, drew a worrisome picture by stating that:

> One of our major challenges is to devise mechanism that overcome the bias toward the status quo and the voluntary nature of current international law in life-threating issues. To someone who is an outsider to international law, the Westphalian system of states seems an increasingly dangerous vestige of a different world.[12]

To some scholars, International law and Global public goods inherited the same symptoms of the Westphalia system.[13] Based on the consensual structure and scarce effective enforcement measures, international law is relatively a weak law which relies on the voluntary compliance of individual states. In certain areas, state consent is beginning to recede given the peculiarities of the problem addressed, in general, the consensual structure of the international remains resilient.[14] However, not all international lawyers are that pessimistic about the role of international law concerning global public goods. As Daniel Bodansky notes, since it (GPG) cannot

---

[10]See Kaul (2011), p. 37.

[11]See Petersmann (2012), p. 710.

[12]See Nordhaus (2005), p. 8.

[13]See Kaul (2012).

[14]See Krisch (2014), pp. 39–40.

be provided by markets, we need international law and institutions to provide.[15] Despite the Westphalian dilemma, growing literatures now focus on the role of international law in facilitating the cooperation of states and international institutions to provide GPGs.

To better cope with the provision problem, international law scholarship has adopted the typology that was initiated by Scott Barrett in his influential book *Why Cooperate? The Incentives to Supply Global Public Goods*.[16] Based on the cooperation models of states, three categories of public goods are set up: single best effort goods, weakest link goods, and aggregate efforts goods.[17] Each type of public good askes for different legal frameworks for the distinct production technologies required.[18] By differentiating different production technologies, international law finds its role to play in the GPGs discourse.[19] It provides a goods lens to analyze the BRI and different legal frameworks concerning the provision of relevant GPGs along the Belt and Road. However, prior to that, the thing needs to be addressed first is to identify the exact GPG characters the BRI entails.

2.3 *The BRI and Global Public Good*

Some scholars are critical of the concept "GPG". For them, it has departed from its economic origin and risks being used as formalistic cover to gain certain degree of scientific justification. Further, they contended, the concept is not without confusions and obscureness when applied in concrete circumstances and the prevalence of this hollow concept lies on its rhetorical power that maybe exploited by politicians.[20] Beyond the criticisms, the appeal of the concept lies in that it arouses people's imagination and expectation to boost cooperation in solving the common problems ahead the humankind and by doing so, it gains moral attractiveness as well as explanative power towards the turbulent world in which the under-provision of

---

[15]See Bodansky (2012), p. 657.

[16]See Barrett (2007).

[17]This typology has been widely accepted by scholars and policy makers alike. See, Too Global to Fail: The World Bank at the Intersection of National and Global Public Policy in 2025, pp. 13–51. https://elibrary.worldbank.org/doi/10.1596/978-1-4648-0307-9_ch2. Accessed 19 October 2017.

[18]For the single best effort good, it relies on the one single state which has the resources or ability to provide. For example, in the case of the deflection of an asteroid which was about to hit the earth, only limited states have the technology to accomplish that goal. For weakest link goods, such as eradication of communicable diseases, nuclear non-proliferation or anti-terrorism, the success relies on the weakest link countries to provide the above GPGs. If the weakest link failed to provide, the whole success would be in peril. In the case of aggregate efforts goods, their provisions rely on aggregate efforts of all the parties concerned. An obvious example is the common effort to tackle climate change.

[19]See Shaffer (2012).

[20]See Long and Woolley (2009).

GPGs is a salient phenomenon. Viewing the BRI against the political and economic background of contemporary world, the BRI can be conceived as an important initiative to provide necessary GPGs to the Belt and Road region as well as the world.

The Belt and Road region has long been neglected by the dominant West and is in shortage of various GPGs. Thus, most countries along the BRI are haunted by poverty, social turbulences, and lagging infrastructure. According to the Action Plan on the Belt and Road Initiative, the BRI inherited the Silk Road spirit which highlights peace and cooperation, openness and inclusiveness, mutual learning and mutual benefit, and its objective is to cope with the gloom world economy that has not fully recovered since the 2008 international financial crisis.[21] The BRI comprises five pillars of according policies aiming to strengthen interconnectedness and economic integration: policy coordination, facilities connectivity, unimpeded trade, financial integration, people-to-people bond.[22] Although more detailed cooperation plans are needed to give the BRI blood and flesh, from the existing framework it is not difficult to discern the GPGs orientation of the BRI. Each of the five pillars is connected to the necessary GPGs that are desperately needed in the Belt and Road region to boost economy growth and facilitate trade circulation.

Currently, China has cooperated with many countries on infrastructure construction projects such as renovating roads, opening up new ports, building new railways and setting up power plants which would lay the foundations of local economic development and close economic integration along the Belt and Road. Infrastructure construction is a typical public good and in the BRI setting, can be viewed as a GPG. Meanwhile, China has initiated the Asia Infrastructure Bank (AIIB) in order to finance the relevant development projects.[23] International financial institutions such as AIIB and Silk Road Fund are also typical GPGs. What's more, the BRI highlights free trade and advocates for a more equitable international economic and trade system and that, can also be considered as an important GPG.[24] In areas such as environmental protection, China has issued Belt and Road Ecological and Environmental Cooperation Plan to better incorporate environmental protection into the BRI

[21] Action Plan on the Belt and Road Initiative, issued by the National Development and Reform Commission, Ministry of Foreign Affairs, and Ministry of Commerce of the People's Republic of China, with State Council authorization, on March 28, 2015.

[22] Ibid.

[23] See Article 1of The Articles of Agreement of the Asian Infrastructure Investment Bank: The purpose of the Bank shall be to: (1) foster sustainable economic development, create wealth and improve infrastructure connectivity in Asia by investing in infrastructure and other productive sectors; and (2) promote regional cooperation and partnership in addressing development challenges by working in close collaboration with other multilateral and bilateral development institutions.

[24] See Mendoza (2003).

projects in order to build a green Silk Road.[25] What's worth mentioning is that the BRI stresses cultural exchange and the cohesion of different civilizations and aims to foster the Community of Common Destiny for all Mankind. It is a reflection of providing intangible and paramount GPG that is much needed in the BRI region which is deeply entangled with terrorism and extremism forces.

The above examples attest to the GPG face of the BRI. Since the provision of GPGs hinges on international law, the success of the BRI should work hand in hand with a set of international rules to make sure the realization of the above-mentioned GPGs. The following part will first critically examines the role of international law in the course of international cooperation by digging into its past and present and then tries to rediscover and revitalize its value as an important intermediary to facilitate the provision of GPG against the background of the BRI.

3 Juxtaposing International Law with the BRI: A Critical Study

3.1 International Law: Some Reflections

Before analyzing the BRI and the relevant international rules which could be utilized to promote the supply of GPGs, it is necessary to bear in mind international law is never only a set of objective rules. Originated from Europe and spread out to the entire world in the process of colonialization, international law was largely shaped by the preferences of the dominating powers, mainly the western countries. Martti Koskenniemi contends that international law is essentially Eurocentric and that continues to today.[26] It is not hard to discern that although some GPGs are universally recognized, relying on international law alone still cannot ensure a proper solution to their provisions. If one GPG is not incompatible with or has no direct or urgent linkage to the interests of the powerful states, it would be neglected or compromised. One salient example is the recent withdrawal of the Paris Accord by the Trump administration.[27]

If there was no surprise that international law is a weak law and could not resist the influences of power politics and ideological differences, what makes things worse is that international law may work as accomplice in the process of covering some private interests as GPGs. That means some *prima facie* GPGs, in reality, work

---

[25]The Belt and Road Ecological and Environmental Cooperation Plan, issued by the Ministry of Environment Protection, on May 14, 2017. https://eng.yidaiyilu.gov.cn/zchj/qwfb/13392.htm. Accessed 19 October 2017.

[26]See Koskenniemi (2011), p. 158.

[27]Statement by President Trump on the Paris Climate Accord. https://www.whitehouse.gov/the-press-office/2017/06/01/statement-president-trump-paris-climate-accord. Accessed 18 October 2017.

to promote the interest of the powerful and international law exists only to stamp this process. Take US dollar as an example, after the collapse of the Bretton Woods system, dollar becomes the *de facto* global currency and constitutes as a GPG for it provides the reliability and conveniences for international trade and financial settlement.[28] However, as a GPG provided by the single best effort of one country, the US has taken advantage of dollar against the interests of the rest of the world. After the sub-prime debt crisis, the US initiated quantitative easing which caused a global flood of liquidity and led to European debt crisis as well as mined the bomb for global financial instability that continues to affect the world today.[29] It is just one example that the powerful states could disguise their private interests through GPGs. Although some international theorists proposed the hegemonic stability theory and deemed the privatization of some GPGs as the price paid to a stable world order.[30] Let alone the plausibility of this theory, it does not mean that it is not necessary to reflect upon the role of international law in such a process. On the contrary, the complicity committed by international law should be thoroughly exposed in order to substantially reform the unequal international order and ensure the genuine global public goods are always timely provided.

Throughout history, international law has played a suspicious role in the expansion of colonialism and maintained the western-dominated world order. The Westphalia system unveiled a world view constituted by nation states and initiated the international law to regulate the relations among them. At the very beginning, international law is premised on fragmented individual entities rather than viewing the world as a whole. With the set of boundaries among nation states comes with endless struggles and conflicts and partial interests always triumph the common interests.[31] That is exactly what Carl Schmitt judged the core of the politics as the distinction of friend-enemy.[32] Influenced by the monotheistic Christian religious tradition, international law was stigmatized by the partial western conception of world order and was made universal with the western conquest of the globe. By defining the "self" and "other" and portraying self as the center and other as the periphery, this binary has become an everlasting theme in every encounter between West and the rest of the world, geographically, emotionally as well as politically.[33] International law has become a tool for the West to justify its superiority in the process of colonization as well as its contemporary dominance. In Said's detailed study of orientalism, one can get to know the logic of how the so called academic

[28]See Tavlas (1997).

[29]See Neely (2015).

[30]See Eichengreen (1989).

[31]See Kennedy (2016).

[32]See Schmitt (1996). To be specific, the distinction (friend-enemy) is Schmitt's overarching understanding of the political realm: it is precisely the distinction "to which political actions and motives can be reduced".

[33]See Greene (1990) and Kennedy (2016), pp. 199–217.

subject "orientalism" was used to justify self's conquest over others.[34] International law played a similar role by adapting its key concepts such as "sovereignty", "civilization" to the needs of imperialism and that continues by adopting the concept of "development", "progress", "human rights" to discipline the less developed and developing countries in the post-colonial age.[35] The civilizing mission based on self and other is deeply embedded in the international institutions such as UN, World Bank as well as IMF.[36] Thus, international law cannot be viewed as a set of neutral rules but a ruling technique of the western powers. Bearing the above analysis in mind, the undersupply of GPGs in contemporary world is not difficult to understand.

3.2 *Assessing the BRI Within Contemporary International Legal Order*

China has long been an "other" in international society and played a limited if not marginal role in the formation and development of international law. Firstly, China's initial encounter with the "civilized" world was not voluntary. As an ancient civilization maintained its own self-sufficient world view, China had a dynamic system to conduct relations with its neighbors and aliens which is not necessarily rule-based but more resembles a process of moralization and persuasion. It is an important feature in Chinese philosophy to distinguish Shu (rules or norms) and Dao (moral principles) and the latter is accredited with higher status. When China was dragged into the then world order, it had gone through a though process of resistance, adaptation, and re-interpretation of the international legal system which was largely alien to it. This process even continues to today.[37] Secondly, after gaining independence from a semi-colonial and semi-feudal society by winning the hard fought Sino-Japanese War and National Emancipation War, China adopted a totally different ideology compared to the West and thus was largely excluded from interacting with and contributing to the international legal system at that time. It was at this background, the Five Principles of Coexistence was brought up together with the mind-liked third world countries to conduct friendly relations with each other. Thirdly, after the Reform and Opening up, although China started to engage

[34]See Said (1978).

[35]See Anghie (2007). Anghie made detailed study on the continuing influence of imperialism from the nineteenth century to contemporary war on terror and expressed his suspicion on the role of international law in different stages of history in maintaining the rule of different imperialistic powers.

[36]See Orford (2003). Take humanitarian intervention as example, Orford provided insightful ideas on the role of international institutions, especially the financial institutions, in instigating the local conflicts and the failure of their responses to provide necessary help to the local people after the crisis. The reason, is due to the civilizing mission attached to these institutions at the beginning of their establishments by the dominating powers.

[37]See Yi (2016), p. 180.

with the outside world, as a developing country with the main focus on economic development under the huge pressure to feed its enormous population, China considered the international law as western dominated discourse and chose to passively get involved in it. This period was characterized as "Hide one's capacities and blind one's time" in Chinese policy narrative.[38] Since there is room for China to rely or "free-ride" on the international norms to boost its economy, there is no need to challenge it. That mentality can be inferred from China's voting behavior in the UNSC since it resumed its lawful seat in 1972.[39] As international law is always intermingled with certain power structures, for quite a long time, China has neither the willingness nor the ability to shape international legal order.

The BRI can be perceived as a bold departure from China's previous gentle stances and according to the observations of some western theorists, it is the Chinese version of "Marshal Plan" and is an intentional statecraft based on the geo-political calculations.[40] Since an important feature of the western understanding of world order is premised on the belief that international society resembles the "Hobbesian Jungle" and international politics is a zero-sum game, it is no wonder that they would stick to such an observation. This observation partly reflects the complicated feelings the western countries have on the BRI as the former colonizers. In fact, the area covered by the BRI mostly was inflicted by the traumas of colonization and is still kept underprivileged because of the unequal world political and economic order.

The BRI, although initiated by China, can be more understood as an experiment to fill the gap in the supply of GPGs. In two aspects the BRI is different from the Marshal Plan. Firstly, China does not match the US as the sole big power after the World War Two. Although China has ranked as the second largest world economy, its overall influence is relatively limited compared to the US and the EU on international stage. Concerning the contents of the BRI, from the beginning China sent a very clear signal that the spirit of cooperation and inclusiveness is the guiding principle and those who are interested, including the western countries, are welcomed to work together. Take the AIIB as an example, its member states are now over 80 and geographically well represented.[41] Since the BRI is an open project, it is not likely China could dominate it. Secondly, in initiating the BRI, partial economic gains or the expansion of sphere of influence is not China's prime consideration. That is quite different from the Marshal Plan for China has long established and

---

[38]"Hide one's capacities and blind one's time" was first proposed by Den Xiaoping and has been China's basic foreign policy maxim since the Reform and Opening up. The succeeding leadership did not deviate from this principle for almost 30 years and entering into the reign of President Xi, it begins to experience some changes.

[39]See Shichor (2006), pp. 4–6.

[40]See Joseph Nay: Xi Jinping's Marco Polo Strategy, in Project Syndicate, June 12, 2017. https://www.project-syndicate.org/commentary/china-belt-and-road-grand-strategy-by-joseph-s--nye-2017-06?barrier=accessreg. Accessed 19 October 2017.

[41]As of October 13, total approved membership of AIIB is 80. Members and Prospective Members of the Bank. https://www.aiib.org/en/about-aiib/governance/members-of-bank/index.html. Accessed19 October 2017.

adhered to the Five Principles of Co-existence as the cornerstone of its foreign policy and in conducting the BRI projects, mutual benefits rather than partial gains of one side are prioritized. Meanwhile, the BRI has also put a lot of business unrelated measures, such as environmental protection, cultural exchange, and civilizational cohesion as its important agendas.

Based on above analysis, it is not difficult to discern the irreconcilable discrepancy when assessing the BRI within contemporary international legal order. What China aspires through the BRI is not acquiring a dominant position but promoting the common good. However, according to the basic logic of western conception of international law, it is inconceivable and the BRI as a holistic strategy must come with China's political ambitions and a shift of world order. How could one country reconcile its own interests in one hand and the common interests in another hand? Sometimes, a question unanswerable is just because people asked the wrong question. Examining this question against the Chinese conception of world order originated in the very beginning of the civilization, one may expect a comprehensible answer.

4 The BRI as Global Public Good and the "Tian-xia" (All-Under Heaven): A New Paradigm to International Law?

4.1 The "Tian-xia" as the Bedrock of Chinese Conception of World Order

Before being integrated into the western dominated world order, China has sustained its own way of life orderly and peacefully. Among the various characteristics that can be attached to the Chinese conception of world order, one prominent feature is its unique way to apprehend the relationships between family, state and the world which constitute the main content of Tian-xia (All-under-Heaven). To be simple, the main argument of Tian-xia is that the world is unified as a whole. It presupposes the oneness of the world and nothing is considered as being "foreign" or "pagan".[42] For a state to live peacefully, it needs to consider the interest of the world first.

The Tian-xia is the center and starting point in Chinese political concepts and defines the world as a rethinking unit of viewing and interpreting political life, constitution, and institution.[43] That is different from the western conception of

[42]See Zhao (2009). Prof. Zhao Tingyang is a leading philosopher in China and he authored several books on applying the Chinese philosophy to interpret and reconstruct the world order. His main argument is the Tian-xia (All-under-heaven) may provide another world order that worth envisioning given the contemporary failure of the world based on western thoughts. See Zhao (2016).

[43]Ibid. Zhao (2016), p. 11.

world order which put the nation state as its central concept. From this perspective, the western imagination of the world is nothing higher and greater than international allies or unions of nation states.[44] In western perception of world politics, national interest occupies the paramount position and works as the baseline to evaluate other interests when conflicts arise.[45] When universal interest contradicts with national interest, the latter prevails. On contrary, in Tian-xia, the world is always the priority and the realization of any individual interest hinges on the realization of the universal interest. The ethics of Tian-Xia follows the Chinese family-ship ethics which comes from the "very essence of humanity".[46] When conflicts arise within one family, each family member's interest is deferential to the interest of whole family. There is an ethnical transposition in the level of family, state, and the world.[47] That's to say, the moral codes applied in the family level should be transferred to the state and world level.[48] That does not exist in the West given the Machiavellian perception of politics dominates.

According to the study of some historians, Tian-xia as an ideal political order was practiced in the ZHOU dynasty in a limited geographical area 3000 years ago. That time was deemed as the most peaceful and harmonious governance ever existed in Chinese history. However, due to moral decay and corruption, Tian-xia collapsed and the world spilt into separate states ruled by feudal lords. One major theme and aspiration of Confucius is to restore the Tian-xia and after years of persuasion and teaching around various states, he failed.[49] Although no records left how the world was exactly organized based on Tian-xia, the concept has been a core political principle that was carved into the very foundation of Chinese conception of world order. It is no wonder with Tian-xia as its basic world-view, China had never developed a sophisticated international law system as Europe for states are not the central element in the whole arrangement of politics, what matters is the world as a

[44]It is no wonder the "Westphalia system" is always considered as the starting point of the western conception of world order. And this phenomenon was called the "Westphalian myth".

[45]See Giddens (1985).

[46]See Zhao (2006).

[47]See *supra* note 42, Zhao (2016), p. 12.

[48]One can take a glimpse of the essence of Chinese philosophy on binding the ethics of family and the ruling of the world together in the opening clause of *Daxue*(大学), an essential reading for every Chinese elite: "From ancient times, those who want to promote great virtue to the world, first need to govern their states; in order to govern their states, they need to first manage their family; in order to manage their family, they need to first improve themselves; in order to improve oneself, they need to regulate their mind; in order to regulate their mind, one needs to maintain sincere intention; in order to maintain sincere intention, one needs to exhaust one's knowledge; in order to exhaust one's knowledge, one needs to study the essence of the physical world. Study the physical world, learn everything you can learn, be sincere with your intentions and regulate your mind; with your mind at the right place, you'll be able to improve yourself. After you improve yourself, you can manage your family, after your family is managed, you can govern your states and bring justice and virtue to the World."

[49]The time after the Zhou was decried by Confucius as "rites collapsed and music disappeared". The rites and music are all essential ingredients for a harmonious society based on Tian-xia.

whole under Tian-xia (or All-under-heaven). And if conflicts arose, there were a set of moral rules and mechanisms such as the tributary system based on Tian-xia to deal with the conflicts and reach a plausible solution. Throughout history, China has sustained peaceful relations with neighboring countries by practicing the ideals of Tian-xia. When its door was cracked open by the British colonizer, China's instinct reaction was to conduct relations with the aliens based on its own conception of the world order but not to apply international law. Even when later China started to learn the international law in order to better engage with the colonizers, it never took it as something to be honored.[50] What matters is the world view that inherited from Tian-xia.

4.2 BRI and Global Public Good: An Interpretation from the "Tian-xia"

The idea of Global Public Good can be seen as perfect illustration of Tian-xia. Put GPG in the context of the Westphalia system, as analyzed before, the so called global public is a dubious existence. Some theorists questioned the very idea of "public" and differentiated between public as "a category of analysis" and "a category of practice". As a category of analysis, public denotes a particular configuration of accountability and capacity, which can, in principle, be found at the global level. As a category of practice, public is a claim to universality and responsibility that different types of actors use to legitimize what they do.[51] Therefore, if we base our analysis of GPG on a world order that constituted by states as the primary actor, there would be no global public for states would be only responsible for its particular territorially defined constituency and the claim to global public only works as a shield to whitewash its private considerations. However, in Tian-xia, the idea of GPG takes hold for it echoes the common interests that always come as priori. The two prominent features denote the Tian-xia are its universalness and the publicness and the concept of GPG entails both characteristics. The main problem Tian-xia aspires to address, to be phrased in modern language, is to provide GPGs. Put the BRI under this circumstances, a clear picture begins to emerge. As an initiative that was proposed according to the Chinese conception of world order, it can be interpreted as a GPG and more importantly it is aimed to provide various other GPGs.

Although GPG is a relatively recent theoretical construct, similar expressions existed in Chinese traditional culture and were practiced by the political elites in dealing with external relations under Tian-xia. The opening clause of Shang Shu,

---

[50]See Sato (2014). The book surveyed the Chinese intellectuals' struggles when encountering the western civilization and their works to modify their world-views to counteract the shocks. International law was one of the important themes at that time.

[51]See Eriksen and Sending (2013), p. 177.

one of the most influential political writings in China, is "Tian Xia Wei Gong", which dictates the main purpose of the Tian-xia is for the public rather than private interests.[52] When dealing with the conflicts between public interest and private interest, public interest comes first and the public is not confined to the national sphere but refer to the world level for all the political thoughts in Chinese philosophy are concerned with the ultimate good of the world. So it is not difficult to understand that as an old civilization which was the leading power for very long time, China had never embarked on the path of expansionism. At the great voyages led by Zheng He in the Ming dynasty, China outreached to as far as East Africa along the Pacific and Indian oceans, however, the purpose for the voyages was not for conquest but for delivering the good intentions by sending gifts and conducting preferential trade. From a western perspective, it didn't make sense. But from Chinese perspective, we can get a plausible explanation for territorial expansion is never a priority in Tian-xia, what matters is the overall improvement. Another example is China's foreign aids to Africa which was initiated from the very beginning of the establishment of the PRC. China poured enormous aids to help Africa on infrastructure construction, provision of medical facilities and services, disaster relief as well as education development.[53] Given China was also a relatively poor country when it decided to send aids to Africa, it formed a stark contrast against the period of colonization by the West. To conclude, there exists a continuum of China's adherence to the Tian-xia which displayed different modalities in different time and the BRI can be comprehended as the newest phase of that belief. The provision of GPGs echoes that phase.

4.3 Evaluating the Impact of the BRI on International Law

Since the BRI is built upon a different philosophy, without doubt, it would cast pressure on contemporary international legal order. To evaluate the impact of the BRI on international law, one needs to abandon the idea of viewing international law as a set of tactic rules but a fluid discourse.[54] International law as the language adopted by states to conduct relations with each other, the BRI would add some new elements to this language. A question needs to be asked is to what extent the BRI would exert its influences. Is China seeking to revive the world order based on Tian-xia and hoping to set up a new international legal discourse through the BRI? Or would China adhere to the existent system and incrementally push the changes in the hope for building a more equal international legal order? If we closely examine the

[52]*Shang Shu* (《尚书》) is one of the oldest Chinese books, dating from approximately 3000 years ago, recording the words and anecdotes of the greatest kings of yesteryear. Quoted from Zhao (2009).

[53]See Zhang (2017).

[54]See Kennedy (1987) and Koskenniemi (2005).

discourse and practices of the Chinese government, it is not difficult to find that it is adopting a pragmatic approach to international law. On one hand, treating the BRI as an initiative to provide GPGs, it is trying to formulate an idealistic tone that shows its dissatisfaction with existing international legal system and exhibits its ambition to correct the moral deficit of that system. However, the BRI is also deeply embedded in the current nation-state system and to better cater to the interests of various partners, there should be sophisticated rules to coordinate and conciliate heterogeneous interests and the existing international legal system must be utilized to realize that aim. In this sense, the BRI has its realistic face that deeply integrated into the contemporary world order. Bearing the idealistic and realistic sides in mind, it is worth envisaging an emerging Chinese perspective of international law under the BRI.

5 An Emerging Chinese Perspective of International Law Under the BRI: Opportunities and Challenges

5.1 Five Principles of Peaceful Coexistence, the BRI and Global Public Good

The five principles of peaceful coexistence have long been regarded as the cornerstone in China's engagement with other countries.[55] First brought up jointly with India to solve their territorial disputes, it was reaffirmed in the Bandung Conference and gained widespread support among the third world countries.[56] The main content of the five principles are mutual respect of territorial sovereignty and integrity, mutual non-aggression, mutual non-interference, equality and cooperation for mutual benefit, peaceful coexistence. Though the international situation and China itself has gone through tremendous changes, the five principles are consistently followed and reiterated in different circumstances. In the Action Plan for the BRI, the five principles are also prioritized as the guiding principles to conduct peaceful and cooperative relations with the Belt and Road related countries.[57]

The five principles can be considered as the first expression of Chinese conception of international law and formed the basic structure of the Chinese perspective of international law by the means of succession and continuum.[58] Paying close attention to the content of the five principle, it is not difficult to find they are mainly concerned with territorial integrity and peaceful coexistence. It is understandable

[55]See Liu (2014).

[56]The Five principles of co-existence was incorporated in the preamble of the agreement of Trade and Intercourse between India and the Tibet region of China. It was the first time that the Five Principles appeared in a document of international relations on April 29, 1954.

[57]See the Action Plan for the Belt and Road Initiative.

[58]See Chen (1984) and Wang (1990).

given the anti-colonialism waves and ideological confrontations when it was brought up. However, in the context of the BRI, the five principles are lack of concrete contents to deal with the complicated economic activities as well as an unstable world order that is shaped by growing agendas and intermingled interests. So a Chinese perspective of international law should move beyond the five principles and cater to the real needs of the BRI.

Since the BRI may facilitate the provision of GPGs, there is room for international law to maneuver and that gives China opportunities to shape some international rules that may not be sufficient to or even obstruct the provision of GPGs. The BRI covers all the three types of GPGs. For single best effort goods which may rely on the effort of China alone, China would need to correct the prior practices of other hegemonic or dominated countries on misusing its power. For example, in the process of the internationalization of RMB along the BRI, China may carefully design its currency policy to provide a stable and reliable tool for international transactions and investments to promote mutual benefits. In this sense, China can contribute to a more equal international financial governance and express its voices to the existing rules that can easily fall into abuses. At the same time, there are some goods which cannot be provided by China alone but need to incorporate the efforts of all the countries concerned. In the environmental protection along the BRI, it is possible to develop new rules for international cooperation on environmental impact assessment, cross-country environmental inspection as well as coherent trans-boundary damage compensation. Another case to the point is the establishment of the AIIB. As a supplement to the existing international financial system, AIIB differs with other major contemporary financial institutions on the conditionality clauses, project assessment standards as well as the loan criteria. In the future, as the founding member of the AIIB, China may use it as a platform to voice its opinion on existing unequal financial system along with other developing countries. At the same time, the success of the BRI also hinges on the provision of GPGs which can be classified into the weakest link type. Most of the heavily involved countries are developing countries and what make things worse is some of them are facing unstable security situations due to the activities of terrorist groups and ethnic extremists. To ensure a secure environment, China may cooperate with these countries on fighting terrorism and eliminating extremism in different platforms such as the Shanghai Cooperation Organization. As a traditional civilization comprised by heterogeneous ethnic groups, China may share its experience in promoting ethnic harmony and contribute to the current practices on fighting against terrorism which was heavily criticized and proved useless or even futile. The BRI is a comprehensive project and each field of it provides opportunities for china to shape international law and develop a systematic Chinese perspective of international law.

5.2 *Fostering the Chinese Perspective of International Law: Ambiguities and Challenges*

In various occasions, President Xi jingping has proposed the idea of building a Community of Common Destiny for All Mankind (hereinafter "the common destiny discourse") and the BRI is considered as a bold move to put it into practice.[59] The common destiny discourse is not only a rhetoric but also a long believed ideal that originated from the Tian-xia conception. To foster a Chinese perspective of international law, normative changes do not suffice. There should be fundamental changes towards the basic principles organizing the international legal order and the common destiny discourse can be perceived as a good inroad for it aims to uplift the moral ground of contemporary world order. However, there are no details on what constitute the common destiny and in what aspects this common destiny would fundamentally differ with the current international order. Without further clarifications and bearing with ambiguities, the common destiny discourse is hardly compelling. The practices of the BRI would provide concrete cases to illustrate how to build a common destiny through the provision of GPGs, but at the moment these practices are limited and fragmented and cannot provide sufficient clues. If a Chinese perspective of international law is to develop into a complete and independent system, more practices are needed as solid evidences. That depends on the further development of the BRI, the scope and depth it brings to the world order.

Another challenge for a Chinese perspective for international law is rooted in a more fundamental cause: the different world views that divide the East and West. The Chinese world view tends to put the world as the starting point as its way of thinking. Both the Tian-xia conception and the common destiny discourse are examples for that. A Chinese perspective of international law is not only comprised of rules but also a set of moral maxims that would set a high moral standard for the rules. However, the basic logic beneath contemporary legal order is the competition of individual interests and the international rules are utilized to reconcile the various interests. The moral element of the rules is largely omitted given its unfeasibility in a complicated world as international law turned from natural law to positivism in the late nineteenth century. Since state interests always come as the priority, there is always a moral deficit when it comes to the common interests. In this sense, the common destiny discourse, by nature, is in conflict with existing international legal system. For the BRI, despite its global public goods orientation, there are inevitably competing national interests and how to harmonize these interests and integrate these individual interests within the common interests, is a paradox awaits to be solved and that constitutes an acute theoretical as well as practical challenge to a Chinese perspective of international law.

[59]See Xi Jingping (2017).

6 Conclusion

For a chapter about the BRI, at this point, any "conclusion" would be inappropriate. The BRI is an ongoing process and entails a broad space for imagination. For Chinese government, through the BRI, it is projecting its power to so many unknown places and fields that previous experience provides little reference. China has exhibited its good intentions in the BRI, but living in a world of struggle, the effective communication of the good intentions would be a major challenge. Resorting to history, as an old civilization that lasted for thousands of years, China would not lack intellectual resources to support and justify a bigger role it can play in the international stage. Unearthing the concept of Tian-xia (All-under-Heaven) provides a connecting point with the global public goods narrative that is comprehensible to the world today and also necessitates a new approach to international law which has long ruled out other possibilities. The BRI provides a vivid case for envisioning a Chinese perspective of international law which would contributes to a genuine Community of Common Destiny for All Mankind. And at the same time, the continuing advancement of the BRI hinges on an emerging Chinese perspective of international law to better communicate with the outside world. With challenges ahead, the future of a new world order is to be expected.

References

Anghie, A. (2007). *Imperialism, sovereignty and the making of international law*. Cambridge: Cambridge University Press.

Barrett, S. (2007). *Why cooperate?: The incentive to supply global public goods*. New York: Oxford University Press.

Bodansky, D. (2012). What's in a concept? Global public goods, international law, and legitimacy. *European Journal of International Law, 23*, 651–668.

Chen, T. (1984). The People's Republic of China and public international law. *Dalhousie Law Journal, 8*, 3.

Coussy, J. (2005). The adventures of a concept: Is neo-classical theory suitable for defining global public goods? *Review of International Political Economy, 12*, 177–194.

Eichengreen, B. (1989). Hegemonic stability theories of the international monetary system (NBER Working Paper No. 2193). In R. Bryant (Ed.), *Can nations agree? Essays on international economic cooperation*. Washington, DC: The Brookings Institution.

Eriksen, S. S., & Sending, O. J. (2013). There is no global public: The idea of the public and the legitimation of governance. *International Theory, 5*, 213–237.

Gavas, M. (2013). *The EU and global public goods, challenges and opportunities* (DIIS Report 5). Danish Institute for International Studies (DIIS).

Giddens, A. (1985). *The nation-state and violence*. Cambridge: Polity Press.

Gravelle, H., & Rees, R. (1992). *Microeconomics*. Harlow: Longman Group UK Ltd.

Greene, J. P. (1990). *Peripheries and center: Constitutional development in the extended polities of the British Empire and the United States 1607–1788*. New York: W.W. Norton & Company.

Kaul, I. (2011). Rethinking public goods and global public goods. In B. Siebenhüne, E. Brousseau, & T. Dedeurwaerdere (Eds.), *Reflexive governance for global public goods*. Cambridge: The MIT Press.

Kaul, I. (2012). Global public goods: Explaining their under provision. *Journal of International Economic Law, 15*, 729–750.

Kaul, I. (2013). *Global public goods, A concept for framing the post-2015 Agenda*. Discussion Paper for German Development Institute (D.I.E) 2.

Kaul, I., & Conceição, P. (Eds.). (2006). *The new public finance: Responding to global challenges*. Oxford, England: Oxford University Press.

Kaul, I., Conceição, P., Le Goulven, K., & Mendoza, R. U. (Eds.). (2003). *Providing global public goods: Managing globalization*. Oxford, England: Oxford University Press.

Kaul, I., Grunberg, I., & Stern, M. (Eds.). (1999). *Global public goods: International cooperation in the 21st century*. Oxford, England: Oxford University Press.

Kennedy, D. (1987). *International legal structures*. Baden-Baden: Nomos Verlagsgesellschaft.

Kennedy, D. (2016). *A world of struggle: How power, law, and expertise shape global political economy*. Oxford: Princeton University Press.

Kindleberger, C. P. (1986). International public goods without international government. *The American Economic Review, 76*, 1–13.

Koskenniemi, M. (2005). *From apology to Utopia: The structure of international legal argument*. Reissue with a new epilogue. Cambridge: Cambridge University Press.

Koskenniemi, M. (2011). Histories of international law: Dealing with Eurocentrism. *Rechtsgeschichte, 19*, 152–176.

Krisch, N. (2014). The decay of consent: International law in an age of global public goods. *American Journal of International Law, 108*, 1–40.

Liu, Z. (2014). Following the five principles of peaceful coexistence and jointly building a community of common destiney. Speech made at the international colloquium commemorating the 60th anniversary of the five principles of peaceful coexistence in Beijing on 27 May 2014. *Chinese Journal of International Law, 13*, 477–480.

Long, D., & Woolley, F. (2009). Global public goods: Critique of a UN discourse, global governance. *A Review of Multilateralism and International Organizations, 15*, 107–122.

Mendoza, R. U. (2003). The multilateral trade regime: A global public good for all? In P. Conceição, I. Kaul, K. Le Goulven, & R. U. Mendoza (Eds.), *Providing global public goods: Managing globalization*. New York: Oxford University Press.

Neely, C. J. (2015). Unconventional monetary policy had large international effects. *Journal of Banking & Finance, 52*, 101–111.

Nordhaus, W. N. (2005). *Paul Samuelson and global public goods: A commemorative essay for Paul Samuelson* (p. 8). Retrieved October 18, 2017, from www.econ.yale.edu/~nordhaus/homepage/PASandGPG.pdf

Olson, M. (1971). Increasing the incentives for international cooperation. *International Organization, 25*, 866–874.

Orford, A. (2003). *Reading humanitarian intervention: Human rights and the use of force in international law*. Cambridge: Cambridge University Press.

Oslon, M. (1965). *The logic of collective action: Public goods and the theory of groups*. Cambridge, MA: Harvard University Press.

Petersmann, E. (2012). Introduction and overview: A research Agenda for making "global public goods theory more policy relevant" in "mini-symposium on multilevel governance of interdependent public goods". *Journal of International Economic Law, 15*, 710.

Said, E. (1978). *Orientalism*. New York: Vintage Books.

Samuelson, P. A. (1954). The pure theory of public expenditure. *The Review of Economics and Statistics, 36*, 387–389.

Sato, S. (2014). *The intellectuals and civilization in modern Chinese history (in Chinese)*. Nanjing: Jiangsu People's Press.

Schmitt, C. (1996). *The concept of the political* (G. Schwab, Trans.). Chicago: University of Chicago Press.

Shaffer, G. (2012). International law and global public goods in a legal pluralist world. *European Journal of International Law, 23*, 669–693.

Shichor, Y. (2006). China's voting behavior in the UN security council. *China Brief, 6*, 4–6.

Tavlas, G. S. (1997). The international use of the US dollar: An optimum currency area perspective. *The World Economy, 20*, 709–747.

Varian, H. R. (1978). *Microeconomic analysis.* New York: W.W. Norton & Company.

Wang, T. (1990). International law in China: Historical and contemporary perspectives. In *Recueil Des Cours.* Netherlands: Hague Academy of International Law.

Xi Jingping. (2017). *Building a community of common destiny for all Mankind.* Speech delivered in the UN Headquarters Geneva.

Yi, P. (2016). Swan song, or a phoenix rising. *Journal of the History of International Law, 18*, 147–180.

Zhang, J. (2017). China's aid to Africa. In H. Zhou & H. Xiong (Eds.), *China's foreign aid: 60 year in retrospect.* Singapore: Springer.

Zhao, T. (2006). Rethinking empire from a Chinese concept 'all-under-heaven' (Tian-xia). *Social Identities, 12*, 29–41.

Zhao, T. (2009). A political world philosophy in terms of all-under-heaven (Tian-xia). *Diogenes, 56*, 5–18.

Zhao, T. (2016). *A possible world of all-under-heaven system: The world in the past and for the future.* (In Chinese). Beijing: Citics Publishing House.

A Tale of Ending Poverty: The New Financial Institutions and China's Global Strategy

Kangle Zhang

1 Introduction

On 12 October 2017, I attended a panel titled "The Belt & Road Initiative: Building Bonds Across Asia, Europe and Beyond", at the Annual Meetings of the Boards of Governors of the World Bank Group (WBG) and the International Monetary Fund (IMF). Guest speakers at the panel include President of World Bank (WB), Jim Yong Kim, President of Asia Infrastructure Investment Bank (AIIB), Jin Liqun, and (vice-)ministers of finance of China, Kazakhstan and Indonesia. Entering the Preston Auditorium where the panel was hosted, the background picture with title of the panel strikes me. The picture, presenting four faces, tells the economic suffering of individuals. At the lower part of the background picture, marked two hashtags: #endpoverty #BeltAndRoad.

At the panel, "end poverty" seems to be the consensus of the speakers on the mission of the BRI. The WB is positively open to collaborate with the AIIB to fill in the gap in infrastructure investment,[1] and the (vice-) ministers of finance of the three attending countries are taking the BRI as an opportunity for local development. The adoption of such a term at the panel intrigues my interest in the following question: Is "end poverty" the middle-ground between China and other actors involved in the BRI, in the grand project of Chinese global strategy?

[1]Kynge (2017), "Asia must invest $26 tn in infrastructure by 2030"; Asia's infrastructure gap, estimated by the Asian Development Bank, requires $26 trillion of investment from 2016 to 2030, see: Asian Development Bank (2017).

K. Zhang (✉)
The Erik Castrén Institute of International Law and Human Rights, University of Helsinki, Helsinki, Finland
e-mail: kangle.zhang@helsinki.fi

W. Shan et al. (eds.), *Normative Readings of the Belt and Road Initiative*,
https://doi.org/10.1007/978-3-319-78018-4_6

"End poverty" was deployed by WB in Jim Yong Kim's statement published by *China Daily* in 2015.[2] As a major multilateral development bank (MDB) established in the aftermath of the 1944 United Nations Monetary and Financial Conference (the Bretton Woods conference),[3] its policy toward the AIIB largely represents the policies of the traditional and established international institutions, in particular the MDBs,[4] concerning the new financial institutions. The geo-political factors among, and economic interests of, major state actors as members of the traditional and new institutions respectively, certainly lead to frictions among the countries and institutions. This chapter considers the term "end poverty" serving as the mediator by offering the space for action amid competitive struggles. Confirmative toward the connection between the agenda of the multilateral development banks (MDB), as "to provide financial support to investments in human and physical capital that promote development,"[5] the term "end poverty" enables traditional international institutions to further their respective interests by engaging with the BRI.

David Kennedy states, "the result of continuous struggle is an eerie stability it is hard to imagine challenging or changing."[6] By struggle, Kennedy refers to the process of strategic actions taken to further the interests of relevant actors based on their own field of expertise. In the BRI context, "end poverty" offers the space of manoeuvre to the actors, to continuously further their respective interest.

Kennedy contends, on expertise, that "the usefulness of its indeterminacy [is] more appreciated than its analytic rigor."[7] In the context of the BRI, the term "end poverty", a term developed and deployed by the expertise of WB, is useful because of the term's indeterminacy. "End poverty" enables the new international institutional actors involved in, as well as China, the initiator of, the BRI to be "unhitched from the promise of decisive clarity,"[8] to engage with the BRI and further their respective interests without needing to question the agenda of others, without tackling the concrete meaning and effectiveness of the term. We are left with a term of moral high-ground, and that only. "End poverty" is not much about poverty, and

---

[2]Kim (2015).

[3]The Bretton Woods conference established the International Bank for Reconstruction and Development, which has evolved into five institutions, making up the World Bank Group and the International Monetary Fund.

[4]The multilateral development finance evolved dramatically in the past decades, with a multitude of development banks and funds established: The African Development Bank, Asian Development Bank, European Bank for Reconstruction and Development, European Investment Bank, and Inter-American Development Bank. See, Wihtol (2014).

[5]Arezki et al. (2016). For further elaboration on the initial mandates of MDBs, see Yeyati et al. (2004).

[6]Kennedy (2016), p. 5.

[7]David Kennedy explores the struggles at the level of the works of the experts and their perception of order in a governed system, to "explore the role of expertise and professional practice in the routine conflicts through which global political and economic life takes shape." See Kennedy (2016), p. 2. Such a tackling-angle enriches the understanding of the global political economy and the shape of it by various actors with their own particular interests, and the perception of expertise by revealing the indeterminacy therein.

[8]Kennedy (2016), p. 2.

the risks resulted by the struggles are borne, essentially, by the peripheries that are largely neglected.

This chapter focuses on the financing mechanism of the BRI, which involves financing from the newly-established and traditional international/regional institutions, and financing from Chinese banks, including commercial banks, policy banks, and other financial institutions in China.

Section 2 of the chapter focuses on the new institutions established with a link to the BRI. The new institutions engage with the BRI projects out of the member countries conviction in furthering their respective interest. The new institutions are established to challenge the world order of development financing, and the structural of governance within the traditional MDBs established by the Bretton Woods Conference. It's a picture of struggle, instead of one in which the new institutions are jointly built to fill in the gap of infrastructure investment in certain regions. Section 2 continues to point out the downsides of the struggles. First, despite the governing structure of the new institutions, the political objectives and impacts of particular countries are inevitably present in the functioning of the institutions and the financing of the projects. Second, while the term "end poverty" enables the struggles, the concrete meaning of the term is neglected. Without analytical engagement with the term, the BRI risks further strengthening the elites and their power in the recipient countries over their populations.

Section 3 presents the BRI as one aspect of China's global strategy, as a project designed to further the interest of China in a world of struggle. The financing mechanism of the BRI reveals that the majority of the financing is from domestic banks in China, that the BRI projects are financed through contract-based infrastructure financing, together with political objectives-defined development financing.

2 The New Institutions' Story of Ending Poverty

The financing mechanism of the BRI presents the role of the new institutions in BRI. While the mainstream tells a narrative of ending poverty, that the new institutions fill in the gap of infrastructure investment in certain regions, this part contradicts with the narrative by telling a story of new institutions built out of challenging the governing structure of the traditional MDBs. Despite the term "end poverty" deployed, each actor is endeavouring to further its respective interest in a world of struggle.

2.1 Financing of the BRI and the New Institutions

In May 2017, Financial Times (FT), with its sources from company statements and Oxford Economics, estimates that the overall $292bn of funding for the BRI, of outstanding loans or equity investment at the end of the year 2016, is composed of the following: $150bn from the big four state-owned commercial banks, $110bn from China Development Bank (CDB), $24bn from Export-Import Bank of China

(Eximbank of China), $4bn from the Silk Road Fund (SRF), $2bn from AIIB, and $2bn from New Development Bank (NDB).[9]

According to FT's estimation, the new financial institutions involved in the financing mechanism of the BRI, the AIIB, NDB, and SRF, contribute 0.6%, 0.6%, 1.3% to the overall financing of the BRI respectively. Among the three, the SRF[10] is designed to operate "as a private equity venture, but with a smaller group of investors committed for longer terms", so as to "help avoid riskier politically-driven deals that are not always in the best economic interests."[11] Admittedly, the political impacts of contributing members within the SRF play a role in its strategic actions taken to further its interests and the interests of the members. Yet the private entity nature of it leaves it outside the scope of this paper's inquiry: It is not a development bank. Then, with the AIIB and NDB left, the two take 1.2% of the overall financing of the BRI according to the FT report in May 2017. Despite the relatively small share of the two institutions in the overall financing of the BRI, the institutions engage with the BRI out of the member countries' interest, politically, economically, and more, in the BRI projects.

The AIIB is a multilateral financial institution with 56 member countries as of June 2017, with 37 regional members and 19 non-regional members covering Europe, Oceania, Africa and south America, focusing on supporting infrastructure construction. According to Jin Liqun, the AIIB "plans to increase operation gradually, investing $1.5bn-$2bn in infrastructure this year", and investing "$3bn-$5bn next year and around $10bn in 2018".[12]

The NDB is a multilateral development bank operated by the BRICS states (Brazil, Russia, India, China and South Africa), with a primary focus on lending to infrastructure projects.[13] It was established in 2014, "with an initial subscribed capital base of $50 billion, with each of the five countries contributing $10 billion and receiving equal voting rights".[14] The bank "has a brief to provide no-strings loans to Emerging Market and Developing Countries (EMDCs), principally for major infrastructure and sustainable development projects."[15] The NDB is "accompanied by a Contingent Reserve Arrangement (CRA) comprising a pool of $100

[9]Wildau and Ma (2017).

[10]The Silk Road Fund is an investment fund established in 2014. The fund's initial $10bn is from the State Administration of Foreign Exchange, China Investment Corporation, China Development Bank and Export-Import Bank of China. Out of the four entities contributing the initial $10bn, China Investment Corporation is the Chinese sovereign wealth fund, established in 2007 as a state-owned company, with registered capital of $200bn, responsible for managing part of the country's foreign exchange reserves.

[11]Chhibber (2015), p. 2.

[12]Kynge (2016).

[13]"The bank's primary focus of lending will be infrastructure projects with authorized lending of up to $34 billion annually." See Chhibber (2015), p. 2.

[14]Wihtol (2014).

[15]Dixon (2015), p. 1.

billions of currency swaps".[16] The CRA is established to provide protection against global liquidity pressures,[17] that when the members' national currencies are being adversely affected by global financial instability, the CRA will provide financial support in case of short-term balance of payments pressures and other cases of liquidity pressures.[18]

The $100bn AIIB offers financial support to the BRI together with the $50 billion NDB and the $100 billion Contingent Reserve Arrangement (CRA).[19] The new international financial institutions finance the BRI through offering credit and loan, bonds, equity investment, insurance, and other financing instruments.

2.2 *Ending Poverty or Strategic Struggle?*

The establishment of the AIIB was linked with "ending poverty" through the narrative of satisfying the need of the investment gap in infrastructure in Asia.[20] With the shortage of basic facilities, various Asian countries desire infrastructure investment. The existing development banks, namely the Asian Development Bank (ADB) and the WB, have a capital base of about $160bn and $220bn respectively, yet the capital are largely deployed "in existing projects and their mandates are much broader than infrastructure".[21] While the need for improvement in physical infrastructure, in particular as the consequence of neglect after the collapse of the Soviet Union in Central Asia, provides the incentive for governments in the region to provide political stability and a positive investment climate,[22] there exists an investment gap. The establishment of AIIB has been praised for its potential in achieving the goal of gaping the needs for infrastructure-financing in Asia.[23] With its infrastructure focus, the AIIB projects would benefit the social and economic development of the regions and countries along the BRI. Supporting such a view, it's argued that the model for attracting "the flow of long-term savings towards long-term

[16]Wihtol (2014). The $100bn of currency swaps is consisted of the PRC contributing $41 billion; Brazil, the Russian Federation, and India $18 billion each; and South Africa $5 billion.

[17]"The CRA is a framework for the provision of support through liquidity and precautionary instruments in response to actual or potential short-term balance of payments pressures. It will provide financing similar to the IMF but not under an IMF agreement." See Chhibber (2015), p. 2.

[18]The CRA is designed as "an external account support facility to help developing countries manage balance of payments crises", see Biswas (2015), p. 3.

[19]Chhibber (2015), p. 2.

[20]Kynge (2017), "Asia must invest $26tn in infrastructure by 2030"; Asia's infrastructure gap, estimated by the Asian Development Bank, requires $8 trillion through 2020, see World Economic Forum (2014).

[21]Arezki et al. (2016), p. 36.

[22]Fallon (2015).

[23]For a detailed narrative on the infrastructure investment needs in Asia, see Inderst (2016).

infrastructure assets" facilitates AIIB's efforts in promoting infrastructure investment.[24] It is as well noticed that since its establishment, it has been successfully co-operating with the traditional multilateral development banks (MDBs),[25] thus would join the efforts to promote development and end poverty.

The NDB, with a primary focus on infrastructure projects, is as well considered to be able to promote development. While the narrative centering "end poverty" in the establishment and functioning of the AIIB and NDB presents the new institutions as filling in the gaps in existing international and regional efforts in promoting development, this section contradicts with such a narrative, and contends that establishment of the AIIB and NDB challenges the traditional system of development financing, that the founding members of the new institutions were dissatisfied with the governing structures within the traditional MDBs.[26]

The traditional system of development financing, and the structure of governance within multilateral lenders, refer to the international institutions and their internal governing system, established following the Bretton Woods Conference in 1944. With a total of 44 founding members establishing the IMF and the IBRD, the voting powers were largely resided with the US and some European countries. Through the years, while the number of member countries of the IMF and the World Bank rose to 188, and the percentage of developing countries in the share of world GDC increased tremendously, the governance structure of the IMF and World Bank hardly evolved.[27] At the same time, in the World Bank and the IMF, "the number of votes assigned to member countries is determined by a combination of their contributed capital and the size and stability of their economies."[28] The result of such a power structure being, for instance, China's vote-share lower than that of the United Kingdom, despite its larger economy.[29] The bias of the current system, "as a

[24]Arezki et al. (2016), p. 36. As the article argues: "with a higher projected leverage it is likely that the AIIB will not just be issuing AAA rated bonds to long-term investors, but also lower rated bonds with a higher yield, which should make these particularly attractive to long-term investors in the current global low yield environment."

[25]The co-financing of projects in Asia by World Bank and the China-led Asian Infrastructure Investment Bank is an example of such cooperation. "Since the AIIB began business at the start of 2016, it has co-financed five projects with the World Bank". See Kynge (2017).

[26]"To the extent that the AIIB succeeds, it will secure the buy-in of its clients and member states, and the new bank may even exert pressure on the established multilateral lenders to change." See Chin (2016).

[27]For a detailed narrative of the share of GDP and of voting rights in IMF, and the discontent of BRICS with the Bretton Woods structure of governance, see Biswas (2015).

[28]Lioa (2015).

[29]The latest argument is made by Jiajun Xu by tracing the play out of power transition in the World Bank over the last five decades, which shows the US's hegemonic role in the World Bank that drives the rising China to "initiative the AIIB and NDB, putting competitive pressures on the US-centred multilateral institutions to adapt." See Xu (2017). Jiajun Xu focuses on the role of the emerging financial institutions challenging the traditional financial institutions due to the power play, including voting rights and internal structure, within the financial institutions.

continuation of the politics of war and economic struggle",[30] naturally incentivizes the actors in a disadvantaged position to challenge the system.[31]

The internal governance structures of the new institutions reflect the endeavours of the emerging market and development countries in challenging the governing structure of the traditional institutions. AIIB has developed the governance structure that "the voting shares are based on the size of each member country's economy (GDP PPP) (and whether they're an Asian or Non-Asian Member) and not contribution to the Bank's authorized capital."[32] Following such an approach, countries with larger economies would take a higher voting share, which promotes the interests of the larger economies. The establishment of the new institutions also poses a challenge to the traditional global development financing.[33] Despite the limited capability of the individual BRICS country and other development countries in providing development finance,[34] "the NDB, AIIB and Silk Road Fund combined ... will give developing countries a greater voice in governing global development finance in the next decade and beyond."[35]

This narrative tells that the new institutions involved in financing the BRI are built out of dissatisfaction with the structure of governance within the traditional MDBs, and the structure of traditional global development financing. It's not about, at least not just about, filling in the infrastructure investment gaps in certain regions. Undeniably, however, the term "end poverty" enables both the traditional and new institutions to be involved in the BRI projects.

2.3 *Strategic Struggles and the Downside*

"End poverty" is deployed by WB in promoting its collaboration with the AIIB. The moral high-ground of the term "end poverty" makes it highly marketable. The term serves as a middle ground for involved actors to make strategic moves, to further their respective interests. As in the case of the AIIB and NDB, being involved in the BRI under the tag "end poverty", the member countries are challenging the governing structure within the traditional MDBs, and expanding opportunities for themselves in development financing. The structure of internal governance of the

[30]Kennedy (2013), p. 37.

[31]In practice, when the 2007–2008 global financial crisis hit the world, certain countries resort to financial agencies other than assistance from IMF. Indonesia, for instance, obtained "the necessary funds through currency swaps with the Bank of China and the Bank of Japan". See Dixon (2015), p. 4.

[32]Chhibber (2015), p. 2.

[33]"The founding of these new agencies must be seen as an implicit challenge to the established international financial system" See Dixon (2015), p. 2.

[34]This is largely due to the constraints on the foreign exchange reserves of most of the large developing countries.

[35]Biswas (2015), p. 11.

new institutions reflects the member countries' discomfort in the over-powerful influence of certain countries in the traditional institutions. For instance, the governance structural within the AIIB presents an institutional guarantee that "China's influence will be checked... by the equal percentage of voting rights given to founding members."[36] It's an effort to avoid any country furthering its interest without the institutional check of other (founding) members of the institutions. Despite the institutional design as such, the new institutions cannot escape from political objectives and impacts of particular countries in their projects of development financing. The first downside of the struggle for interests is the inevitable political impacts in the new institutions despite the institutions built out of dissatisfaction of political impacts within the traditional institutions. This section draws on the abolition of conditionality clauses in the new institutions, and argues that despite the abolition of conditionality clauses in the new institutions, political objectives and impacts of particular countries are inevitably present in (the projects of) the institutions. In other words, despite the institutional design to avoid any country having a larger say in the new institutions so as to further the interests of each member country equally, certain countries would inevitably have a larger impact. In fact, conditionality clauses are utterly excluded in all the financing mechanisms for the BRI. Yet, the extent to which the institutional setting of abolishing conditionality clauses would alleviate the political impact is rather questionable.

The financing for the BRI projects do not have conditionality clauses at all. The loans from the state-owned commercial banks to Chinese companies investing in infrastructure projects along the BRI, as private flow of investment that are commercial-interest driven, do not contain conditionality clauses in the investment. The Chinese policy banks' financial support to the BRI projects, as well, do not contain conditionality clauses. The White Paper on Foreign Aid published in April 2011 and July 2014 respectively, containing the concessional loan issued by the Eximbank of China as a financial source of foreign aid, explicitly lists the five aspects of China's principles on foreign aid,[37] which largely follow China's Five Principles of Peaceful Coexistence, claiming no attachment of political conditions. That's to say, the concessional loan issued by the Eximbank of China as a means of BRI financing mechanism does not contain any conditionality clause.

The financing for BRI projects through the emerging financial institutions, namely the AIIB and NDB, do not contain conditionality clauses as well. The

[36]Lioa (2015). As Lioa introduces, "Other sources of voting shares include the amount of paid-in capital. If China pays in 30 percent of the bank's capital, as it is slated to, it will still only receive 26 percent of the organization's voting shares."

[37]The five principles are: 1. Help recipient countries build their self-development; 2. Impose no political conditions; 3. Adhere to principles of equality, mutual benefit and common development; 4. Strive for the best whilst remaining realistic; 5. Keep pace with the times, pay attention to reform and innovation.

AIIB's *Articles of Agreement* explicitly "bar members from influencing political affairs."[38] The NDB was as well established by the EMDCs expressing their reluctance to the conditionality of both World Bank and IMF.

In the traditional MDBs, conditionality is closely attached. With IMF, for instance, loans were given "only to those who promised to slash national budgets to avoid running deficits (with welfare programs usually the first to go), lower tariffs, and increase the openness of financial markets."[39] The Millennium Development Goals, a set of information criteria within the World Bank, evaluate how well a country has put its funds to use. These criteria include infant morality, the prevalence of epidemics, democratic practices, government transparency, and so on.[40] The loan conditionality attached by the World Bank and the IMF focus, in general, on liberalization—of trade, investment, finance—, deregulation and privatization of the economic sectors of the countries requesting the loans.[41]

The new institutions' detachment of conditionality clauses has invited several narratives. To overly simplify the narratives, they can be categorized into the following. The first narrative links it with China's Five Principles of Peaceful Coexistence, claiming that an emphasis to economic development and integrity of the sovereign has long been the practice of Chinese diplomacy. Admittedly, the BRI is the first published master plan of the People's Republic on external affairs, thus it is reasonable to see the financing mechanisms not setting any formal political or economic conditionality, following the diplomatic practices. The narrative claims that "the 'one belt one road' vision reflects Chinese leaders' vision for 'peaceful co-existence with difference' and commitments for providing global public goods, peace and security, and sustainability". The second narrative seeks inspiration from traditional Chinese philosophy. The narrative contends that such an approach to infrastructure finance represents the long-existing mentality of development in China: mutual beneficial, sustainable development,[42] and peaceful rise. These mentality of development, it is argued, is based in the Chinese culture and philosophy. The third set of narrative is more critical toward the detachment of conditionality, that in effect, not only those investments will not get any return for the investors, but also not changing the local social standards.

---

[38]Lioa (2015).

[39]Lioa (2015).

[40]Lioa (2015).

[41]The conditionality clauses have been under criticism. Those criteria of conditionality have lead to unwanted consequences. For instance, during the Asian financial crisis of 1997, "as a condition of IMF bailout, Indonesia and Thailand both had to slash their fiscal budgets, doing away with critical social services in the process, so that the interest on the loans could be repaid," leading to the criticism over IMF for "forcing the country to open up its financial markets before there was a proper regulatory infrastructure in place." See Lioa (2015), Gold (1979), Dell (1981), Nowzad (1981), Spraos (1986) and Best (2012).

[42]Sustainability is listed as one of the goals of finance for development is incorporated into the AIIB: to be "leaner, cleaner, greener".

The three narratives capture, to an extent, an aspect of the detachment of conditionality clauses in projects under the umbrella of BRI. However, the political objectives and political effects of the projects are overlooked. Detachment of the wording conditionality does not free the projects from the political objects and effects at all. The first two narratives' reading of the detachment of the conditionality clauses, linking the detachment with either Chinese foreign policy or Chinese philosophy, by default, recognizes the political impact of China over the BRI projects. While countries and institutions involved in the BRI struggle for their own interests, leading the AIIB and NDB to come up with the detachment of the conditionality clauses, the infrastructure-focus of the two institutions are structurally linked with China and China's vision of development. Indeed, the selection of the projects, in particular due to the connection between the AIIB and the BRI, has been noticed as promoting China's influence across the world, facilitating the BRI in achieving "China's politico-strategic and soft power influence through strengthening of regional and global integration."[43] China's economy position and political influence will, inevitably, have an impact on the new institutions—all the international/regional banks and financial institutions seek to "promote the national interests and political worldviews of their most powerful members."[44] There is nothing surprising or hypocritical that the establishment of the AIIB furthers the political objective of China. With the establishment of the AIIB, China has been deemed, by some, as "a potential vanguard for an alternative economic world order".[45]

Another downside of the countries and institutions deploying the term "end poverty" to enable their own struggle for interests, along with the inevitable political objectives and effects within the BRI and the new institutions, is the lack of focus on poverty itself. While the indeterminacy of the term enables the involved actors to stand at a morally high ground, what the term really entails seems not to be the concern of the actors involved. The *Articles of Agreement* of the AIIB,[46] for instance, does not contain the term—not that mentioning the term would provide the actual procedural guarantee to work toward ending poverty though. While it is taken for granted, as a hypothesis, that promoting development and reducing poverty could be a possible impact of the AIIB and NDB in satisfying the need of the investment gap in infrastructure building, such a hypothesis takes the populations within countries and regions as a whole, without differing the elite and privileged with the rest of the population. Without a particular analytical rigor on the term "end poverty," the BRI projects risks sacrificing the interests of the disadvantaged in the recipient countries of the BRI projects.

[43]Mishra (2016), p. 169.

[44]Lioa (2015).

[45]Lioa (2015). Similar to this line of argument, it is argued that the AIIB "will not be a true multilateral institution committed to common objectives", but rather "a vehicle for China to advance its own unilateral strategic objectives in Asia". See Callaghan and Hubbard (2016), p. 116.

[46]Articles of Agreement (2015).

3 Exploring China's Global Strategy: Through the Financing Mechanism of the BRI

While Sect. 2 of the chapter draws special attention on the financial institutions involved in the financing mechanisms of the BRI, the institutions contributed only a small percentage in the overall BRI financing till 2017. The largest percentage of contributions are from the state-owned commercial banks and the policy banks in China.[47] The small percentage of the institutions' financial contribution to the overall financing of the BRI presents them more as China the rising power exploring its potential in innovative ways of international institutional governance and project-financing. The main vehicles of BRI, a governmental initiative, a master plan on foreign affairs, are financing through domestic Chinese banks.

The chapter contextualizes the BRI in China's global strategy. China's global strategy is characterized, with relevance to the BRI, as the project of "national rejuvenation" and "major-country diplomacy".[48] The BRI projects, launched at the times of excess capacity in China,[49] offer opportunities of further development and growth for Chinese companies and in large, the macro-economy of China.[50] The BRI's potential in promoting trade and in facilitating infrastructure investment, in connecting people and regions along the BRI, in promoting an image of China as an alternative to development and governance,[51] in increasing its soft and hard competitiveness, makes it an essential aspect of the country's global strategy.

This section shows that the BRI promotes China's global strategy through a combination of infrastructure financing and development financing. The infrastructure financing is supported by domestic banks offering loans to companies conducting infrastructure projects along the Belt and Road (BR). Essentially, it is contract-based, economic-driven, and revenue-oriented. The infrastructure financing mechanisms expands the market of investment for Chinese companies and industries. Meanwhile, development financing, including financing through policy banks of China and the new institutions, is closely tied with the political objectives of China.

---

[47]Wildau and Ma (2017). For other summaries of the financing mechanism of the BRI, see Weinland (2017) and Wells and Weinland (2017). It is estimated that the BR infrastructure projects took place with the amount of $900bn, planned or underway, of investment on ports, roads, rail lines popping up across Asia.

[48]"National rejuvenation" 民族复兴 (Min Zu Fu Xing), and "major-country diplomacy" 大国外交 (Da Guo Wai Jiao), are included in Chinese President Xi's report to the 19th National Congress of the Communist Party of China. For an analysis of national rejuvenation and major-country diplomacy, see, for instance Baijie (2017) and Yi (2017a).

[49]Dollar (2015).

[50]Liu and Dunford (2016). Such a view, though, is not undisputable. As Dollar writes, "the contributions that these initiatives together make to China's demand are likely to be too small to be macroeconomically meaningful." See Dollar (2015).

[51]Similar narratives include, for instance, "a community of shared future for mankind," and promoting "benefit-sharing world through partnerships worldwide." See Xinhuanet (2017).

3.1 *Financing Mechanism of BRI: Domestic Banking*

3.1.1 State-Owned Commercial Banks

The domestic commercial banks, in particular the big four state-owned commercial banks, with their branches along the BR, offer multiple ways of financing. $150bn out of the overall $292bn of outstanding loans or equity investment for BRI at end of 2016 is from the big four state-owned commercial banks.[52] In the state-owned Chinese commercial banks, the state has the majority holding. The four state-owned commercial banks are: The Bank of China (BoC), the China Construction Bank (CCB), the Agricultural Bank of China (ABC), and the Industrial and Commercial Bank of China (ICBC). The Law of the People's Republic of China on Commercial Banks was adopted in 1995 to commercialize the operation of the four state-owned banks, and amended in 2003.[53]

The China Banking Regulatory Commission (CBRC) released the Guidance to the Banking Sector on Supporting Major Projects (CBRC no.43, 2015) in August 2015,[54] enlisted the BRI as one of the important projects that the banking sector shall provide support to. President of BoC announced that in the year 2016, BoC had released the loan of $60bn to BRI projects.[55] In the year 2017, president of the ICBC announced that ICBC had contributed to the infrastructure projects in foreign countries with the amount exceeding $80bn[56]; ICBC had release loan of $23.5bn for projects along the BRI, CCB with the loan of $6bn for 46 projects in 14 countries along the BRI in recent years.[57] Reports from the Phoenix Financial Daily Report summarizes that by 2017, BoC is involved in about 460 projects along the BR region

[52] Wildau and Ma (2017).

[53] According to the Law of the People's Republic of China on Commercial Banks, the state-owned commercial banks may have the following business (Art.3 of the Law of the People's Republic of China on Commercial Banks): Absorb public deposits; issue short-term, medium-term and long-term loans; arrange settlement of both domestic and overseas accounts; handle the discount of negotiable instruments; issue financial bonds; issue cash and sell government bonds as agents; buy and sell government bonds; do inter-bank lending and borrowing; buy and sell per se or as agents foreign exchanges; provide credit card service and guarantee; handle receipts and payments and insurance businesses as agents; provide safe boxes; undertake other businesses approved by the People's Bank of China.

[54] Non-official translation. 关于银行业支持重点领域重大工程建设的指导意见 [Guanyu Yinhangye Zhichi Zhongdian Lingyu Zhongda Gongcheng Jianshe de Zhidao Yijian], 银监发[2015]43号, 中国银监会国家发展和改革委员会发布, 2015年8月21日 (CBRC no.43, 2015, released by the National Development and Reform Commission of the CBRC). The CRBC is China's banking regulator.

[55] 杨中华: 境外贷款增速加快, 国有大行布局"一带一路"区域, [Yang Zhonghua, Jingwai Daikuan Zengshu Jiakuai, Guoyou Dahang Buju Yidaiyilu Quyu] 界面新闻, 2017年4月10日 Yang (2017b).

[56] 易会满: 商业银行要做"一带一路"金融服务生力军, [Yi Huiman, Shangye Yinhang Yaozuo Yidaiyilu Jinrong Fuwu Shenglijun] 2017年5月19日, 财新网 Yi (2017b).

[57] Yang (2017b).

or countries, with investment in projects exceeding $437.2bn, ICBC offered the amount of loan of $67.4bn, and ABC is engaging with foreign business with the amount of $92.5bn.[58] The amount of investment by BoC has been confirmed by the news released by BoC, that by 2016 an amount of $60bn of loans is provided to projects along the BR, leveraging investment exceeding $400bn; BoC has as well issued BRI bonds totaling $7bn outside of China, attracting international investors.[59]

3.1.2 Policy Banks

The domestic policy banks, namely the China Development Bank (CDB) and Eximbank of China, offer long-term loans with low interest rate and conduct equity investment in China-foreign cooperative investment funds. By 2017, the Chinese policy banks contributed $134bn to the overall $292bn, with $110bn from CDB and $24bn from Eximbank of China.[60] CBD has provided loans to more than 1200 projects along the BR, in more than 50 countries, while the Eximbank of China financing more than 1000 projects in 49 countries involved in the BRI and established foreign investment special loans for the BRI.[61] Indeed, the financing mother lode for BRI "will continue to come from bilateral lending by the Chinese policy banks".[62]

Funded mostly by state revenue and expenditure, the policy banks are not interest-oriented. They focus on the common good and social benefit.[63] Aside from the state revenue, the CDB issues mid-to-long term bonds to finance the investment. Both the CDB and Eximbank of China belong directly to the State Council of China.

3.1.3 Others

Other financial supports to BRI include funding through the new financial institutions as elaborated in Sect. 2, and support from joint-equity banks and mid-size

[58]金融事业部出品，金融机构参与"一带一路"高峰论坛舆情研究报告，[Jinrong Jigou Canyu Yidaiyilu Gaofeng Luntan Yuqing Yanjiu Baogao]凤凰财经，2017年5月25日 Phenix Financial News (2017).

[59]田国立：构建金融大动脉，助力"一带一路"建设再上新台阶，[Tian Guoli, Goujian Jirong Dadongmai, Zhuli Yidaiyilu Jianshe Zaishang Xin Taijie] 2017年6月14日，中国银行网站 Guoli (2017).

[60]Wildau and Ma (2017).

[61]Kynge (2016).

[62]Kynge (2016).

[63]Another policy bank in China, the Agriculture Development Bank of China, focuses on agriculture development in China, and is not much involved in the BRI.

commercial banks in China,[64] the China Export and Credit Insurance Corporation,[65] and traditional international financial institutions.[66] Credit insurance mechanism, mostly through the China Export Credit Insurance corporation, provides credit insurance services to help export enterprises to identify and control risks.

3.2 BRI: Projects of Infrastructure Financing

The BRI projects and their financing mechanisms have constantly been linked with development financing. Development financing, as defined by OECD,[67] highlights the "promotion of the economic development and welfare of developing countries as its main objective".[68] OECD statistics define official development finance as a combination of official development assistance (ODA),[69] "grants and concessional

[64]For instance, China CITIC Bank, the seventh largest lender in terms of total assets in China, is actively involved in the BRI, providing loans to projects along the belt and road. Reportedly, President TIAN Liguo of BOC said that, there are nine Chinese commercial banks setting up 62 branches at provincial level, providing loans exceeding $1000bn. See, 林琦, 中行将尝试通过并购扩大一带一路沿线的网络布局--董事长 [Qi Lin, Zhonghang jiang Changshi Tongguo Binggou Kuoda Yidaiyilu Yanxian de Wangluo Buju] Qi (2017).

[65]The China Export and Credit Insurance Corporation is the only state-owned policy insurance corporation dealing with export and credit insurance, providing insurance service, including short-term export credit insurance, mid-term export credit insurance, and overseas investment insurance. The China Export and Credit Insurance Corporation also offers consultation to Chinese companies investing outside of China. Reportedly, by June 2017, China Export and Credit Insurance Corporation has supported 1097 export and investment projects along the Belt and Road, exceeding the amount of $320bn, covering fields including transportation, oil equipment, electrical engineering, and so on. It has the paid the amount of $1.67bn as indemnity to companies and banks along the Belt and Road, covering projects in 60 countries along the Belt and Road. See, XIAO Yang, 政策性信用保险为"一带一路"建设增添新动能 [Zhengcexing Xinyong Baoxian wei "Yidai Yilu" Jianshe Zengtian Xingongneng] Policy Credit Insurance Adds New Engine to the Construction of the Belt and Road (2017a).

[66]Jim Yong Kim, the World Bank Group President, announced at the opening plenary session of the Belt and Road Forum for International Cooperation, that "in partnership with China, other countries, and multilateral development banks, we've initiated the Global Infrastructure Facility and the Global Connectivity Alliance to provide project preparation funds, and transaction structure advice to help accelerate project readiness." See: World Bank (2017).

[67]OECD's definition of development financing does not lack criticism against such definition, and proposals to broaden the definition have been put forward. See, for instance, "the OECD-DAC definitions of ODA and OOFs are a good starting point, but they need to be reformed to clarify and to take into account all forms of finances aimed to support development". This part, however, does not aim to categorize the various channels of funding in the financing mechanism of BRI into the terms OECD statistics provide; nor does this article wish to explore the evolvement of such definition of the OECD through the practices of the financing mechanism of BRI.

[68]See ii. (a) of the definition of the official development assistance by OECD.

[69]The official development assistance (ODA) is defined as those flows to countries and territories on the DAC List of ODA Recipients and to multilateral institutions which are i. provided by official agencies, including state and local governments, or by their executive agencies; ii. Each transaction

and non-concessional development lending by multilateral financial institutions", and other official flows (OOF).[70,71]

Admittedly, to an extent the financing mechanisms of BRI and development financing overlap. The policy banks provide financial support to companies and projects involved in the BRI through providing commercial loans and preferential credit, foreign aid loans,[72] setting up investment funds for specific countries or industries, conduct equity investment,[73] and so on. The China Eximbank and its financing mechanism, the "two preferential facilities" (the government concessional loan and preferential export buyers' credit) are examples of development financing. The two preferential facilities are designed to facilitate development, and the China Eximbank provides financial support to the BRI largely through such mechanism,[74] together with debt financing and setting up investment funds for particular countries or projects. The AIIB and NDB as multilateral financial institutions also provide development financing.

That said, there is a section of the financing mechanism of the BRI that falls under the category of neither ODA nor OOF: the financing through state-owned commercial banks. State-owned commercial banks take the largest sharing in financing the BRI projects till 2017. The main financial mechanisms through which the state-owned commercial banks finance the BRI include bank credit, syndicated loans, bond financing both domestically and in foreign countries, and other financial services. Bank credit is mostly provided by the commercial banks to foreign companies and industries in purchasing electromechanical products. The state-owned commercial banks initiated syndicated loans to join international pension funds, insurance companies, sovereign wealth funds, private equity funds and others

---

of which (a) is administered with the promotion of the economic development and welfare of developing countries as its main objective; and (b) is concessional in character and conveys a grant element of at least 25% (calculated at a rate of discount of 10%).

[70]The other financial flows (OOF) are defined as official sector transactions that do not meet official development assistance criteria.

[71]OECD (2017).

[72]The Chinese government's definition of foreign aid enlists financing mechanisms that overlap with the financing mechanism of the BRI. According to the State Council White Paper on China's Foreign Aid, China provides grants, interest-free loans, and concessional loans, with 8 forms of foreign aid: complete (turn-key) projects, goods and materials, technical cooperation, human resource development cooperation, medical teams sent abroad, emergency humanitarian aid, volunteer programs in foreign countries and debt relief'. State Council (2011) White Paper on China's Foreign Aid. pp.8. Financial resources for Chinese foreign aid, as written in the white papers, are, (a) grant, (b) interest-free loan from the government budget, and (c) concessional loans issued by the Exim Bank of China. The BRI projects, with concessional loans issued by the Eximbank of China, have an element of foreign aid.

[73]An example of such funds set up the CDB, though not for the BRI, is the China-Africa Development Fund set up by CDB, conducting equity investment in Chinese companies and projects investing and trading in Africa, to provide financial support to the companies and projects.

[74]The two preferential facilities provide loans with low interest rate (2–3%), and long period (15–20 years, with the option of only paying back the interest for a period, and paying back certain amounts every half a year). Such financial mechanism is, thus, preferred by developing countries.

in issuing loans, so as to reduce the risk in investment. An example being CCB partnering with IE Singapore, a state-owned trade development board, to finance BR projects. The state-owned commercial banks issued bonds to finance the BRI projects as well. The ABC issued RMB bond in mid-East in 2014; the CCB issued Maritime Silk Road Bond of RMB1bn in 2015 to finance the BRI, which was rated as A2 by the rating agency Moody's; the BoC issued bonds of $4bn to finance the BRI.[75] Other financial services provide by these commercial banks include insurance, equity investment, external guarantees, fund and financial leasing, and so on.[76]

The vehicles through which the state-owned commercial banks finance the BRI projects reveal the nature of the projects, that they are conducted by private entities seeking to increase their revenues through joining the BRI projects. The projects are revenue-oriented, and based on contracts between various entities both in the implementation and financing of the projects. The percentage of financing from these state-owned commercial banks exceeds the percentage of it through development financing. Thus, the largest portion of the BRI projects are revenue-oriented infrastructure businesses. Infrastructure financing fundamentally focuses on building infrastructures and financing mechanisms supporting such building activities,[77] and seeks mutual—not necessary equal—benefits.[78]

Such an exploration of the financing mechanism of the BRI reveals the financing of BRI projects consisted of development financing and infrastructure financing. Development financing reflects the political objectives of China: the financing through policy banks are policy-oriented, and the political objectives and impact of China are inevitably present in the new institutions, as argued in Sect. 2 of the chapter. Infrastructure financing takes the largest share in the financing mechanism. It's a contract-based, revenue-oriented mechanism of financing.

3.3 China's Global Strategy Through Infrastructure Financing and Development Financing

Infrastructure financing, together with development financing, for the BRI projects emerged when the traditional "western" banks and financial institutions are constrained to provide much financing for infrastructure projects. Since the 2007–2008 global financial crisis (GFC), the banking regulations of major "western"

[75]朱振鑫, "一带一路"融资机制全梳理, 民生证券研究院, [Zhu Zhenxin, Yidaiyilu Rongzi Jizhi Quan Shuli] 2017年3月22日 Zhu (2017).

[76]For a detailed narrative on the financing mechanism and the current situation of the financing of the BRI, see Zhu (2017).

[77]There are clear indications of commercial and diplomatic interests attached to the project: it is the Ministry of Foreign Affairs rather than the Ministry of Commerce that deals with strategic plan in finance for development. For a detailed narrative on the institutional arrangement within China on development cooperation, see Gu (2015), pp. 2–3.

[78]Gu (2015).

countries had the effect of reducing the amount of syndicated bank loans, which was the traditional source of finance for infrastructure investment. The GFC has as well left surge in domestic liquidity in various "western" countries, especially in the following years of the GFC, leaving the institutional investors cautious with risks. In terms of the loan maturity, "nowadays, banks tend to limit loan maturity to five or eight years, while infrastructure projects typically require amortization of debt over 15 to 20 years".[79] "Western" banks are disappearing from the market of the Asian infrastructure activities. "By the end of 2016, just one western bank was in the league tables for the top 20 bank financiers for infrastructure in Asia, data from Dealogic shows".[80]

While the banks are playing a lesser role in long-term investment, it paves the way for a greater role of long term investors.[81] Against the drop of capital market-based finance, especially of it in Asia, China is stepping in and playing a huge role. Among the top 10 bank financiers for infrastructure in Asia, Dealogic shows that "Chinese banks took seven places, up from one the year before."[82] Banks from China, mostly state-owned commercial banks and policy banks, are taking, by estimation, 60% of the market of infrastructure finance in Asia in the year 2016.[83] For China, with the largest domestic development banks among emerging markets—a joint capital base of over $100bn, worth nearly 70% of the total capital base of the domestic development banks in BRICS—the country is well equipped with the financial power.[84] In this era of political uncertainty and increasing protectionism, the benefiter of globalization, in this case, China, created by globalization, will be in defence of it.[85]

The space for China to step in meets China's global strategy, one that highlights national rejuvenation and major-country diplomacy. Through the infrastructure financing and development financing involved in the BRI, China's strategy could be largely put in practice.

Such an expansion of infrastructure financing through Chinese capital raises questions toward the risk of debt to international financial stability. The "world is

---

[79] Arezki et al. (2016), pp. 7–8.

[80] "Crédit Agricole retained the number 18 spot on the list, with $854m." See Weinland (2017).

[81] Such investors include, sovereign wealth funds, pension funds, and insurance companies. See Arezki et al. (2016).

[82] Weinland (2017).

[83] "In 2012, banks from China that made it into the top 20 did $4.47bn in infrastructure finance in Asia, holding 11.2 per cent of the total market. Four years later, Chinese banks did $38.4bn, more than 60 per cent of the market." See Weinland (2017).

[84] EPSC (2015).

[85] Globalization has led to optimistic results. As Martin Sandbu writes, in the quarter-century from 1990, "the absolute number of people living in 'extreme poverty' has fallen from 2bn to less than half that"; "rich countries made up 80 percent of nominal global economic output in 1990", and now "that number is barely 60 per cent." Through this process, "globalisation has created its own defenders. Thanks to economic integration, (much of) the developing world has become richer — which constitutes both a benefit and a source of power to shape world affairs." See Sandbu (2017).

today more awash in debt than ever".[86] Since the financial crisis, the world is left with an enormous accumulation of debt. Figures from Dealogic shows that the debt issuance by supranational organizations has doubled in the last decade.[87] At the times of 2007–2008, facing the financial crisis, the Chinese government started "an enormous wave of easy loans channeled through the state-owned banking system", leading to it today that "in absolute terms, China's total debt has ballooned from about $6tn at the time of the financial crisis to nearly $28tn by the end of last year," and "as a percentage of GDP, total debt has risen from 140 per cent to almost 260 per cent over the same period."[88] With the big economies, including USA and China, largely on debt, the impact of debt to financial stability, with the BRI projects adding up on the debt, remains to be seen.

4 Conclusion: BRI in a World of Struggle

The BRI has encountered obstacles since the launch of it. Financial Times investigated three projects of the BRI in Laos, Indonesia, and between Serbia and Hungary respectively, finding obstacles facing each project. The affordability of the project in Laos was doubted, given Lao's "capacity to take on and absorb debt"; the one in Indonesia is facing obstacle with the political systems of Indonesia, in particular its "vibrant democracy with strong land tenure laws"; the Chinese high-speed rail project in Europe faces official suspicion with an investigation on-going, checking the viability of the funding as well as "whether it has violated EU laws stipulating that public tenders must be offered for large transport projects."[89] The nuclear export projects are, as well, facing challenges.[90] The underlying premise of infrastructure financing, that it will work because it worked in China, might be challenged for the differences between countries and regions along the BRI and China: The huge population, collective political system, and ample debt capacity of China make it a rather special case. Besides, there are unpredictable factors along the BRI that are risking the projects.[91] In the year 2017, the Chinese investment in the initiative slowed: "Outbound foreign direct investment to BRI countries fell 2 per cent in 2016", "outstanding loans from CDB fell by $1bn in 2016 to $110bn" by the end of

[86]Sandbu (2017).

[87]Allen (2017).

[88]Anderlini (2017).

[89]For detailed analysis, see Kynge et al. (2017).

[90]Cottee (2017). The major obstacles for nuclear projects include environmental consciousness and the dwindling market competition in nuclear energy providing industry.

[91]"In Libya, for instance, the outbreak of civil war in 2011 put paid to a $2.6bn project to build a line from Tripoli to Sirte, hometown of the late dictator Muammer Gaddafi." See: Kynge et al. (2017).

2016,[92] and "the role of the Asia Infrastructure Investment Bank... is comparatively tiny".[93]

China, the rising power, holding the second largest GDP and with experience of investment activities in Africa and Latin America, is eye-catching with whatever it does. Its economic and political influences challenge the dominant economic powers and put a threat to the established structural biases in the system of international economic order. Meanwhile, while the governing party of China takes pride in economic achievement, such development has encountered challenges domestically with the increasing income-gap, industrial surplus and challenges from the side of environment and other social standards.

The BRI project, a governmental initiative, is part of China's global strategy. In a world of struggle, each and every actor is taking actions, making strategic moves, to further its interests. It's a constant competition for power and interest. Taking the decision on the balance of representation in the board of AIIB as an example. Reportedly, Beijing "offered to forgo the veto power and reduce its voting rights to less than one-quarter if Japan or the United States had been willing to join the new bank as founding members."[94] While March 31, 2015 was set as the deadline for founding membership of AIIB, in that month, a three-way foreign minister's meeting was held in Seoul for China, Japan and the Republic of Korea to exchange views on AIIB-related issues. "Out of complex considerations, Japan and the USA decided not to join, at least for the moment."[95] Apparently, both Japan and the USA's decisions are based on interest-consideration. Another example being the process of AIIB membership application within the European context. United Kingdom applied for membership shortly after informing GC members of its decision,[96] while France, Germany and Italy coordinated their own applications a few days after United Kingdom's application. Various other European nations applied before the applications closed on 31 March 2014 to become founding members.[97] As the European Political Strategy Centre, the European Commission's in-house think tank states, "14 EU Member States have signed up for the AIIB but not in a coordinated manner and without ensuring representation for European institutions such as the European Investment Bank or the European Commission".[98] It's a world of struggle, in which each actor makes decisions based on its expertise for the purpose of furthering its interests. The BRI is, essentially, the strategic move of China.

---

[92]China Development Bank is the largest of China's three state-owned non-commercial "policy banks".

[93]Wildau and Ma (2017).

[94]Chin (2016).

[95]Xiao (2016), p. 437.

[96]Reportedly, The United Kingdom was interested in attracting Chinese finance to London rather than Frankfurt. See: Anderlini (2015, 17 March).

[97]For details of the response of major European countries, US, Japan, Australia, South Korea, see: Callaghan and Hubbard (2016).

[98]EPSC (2015).

In a world of struggle, the term "end poverty" is deployed by the expertise of WB for engaging in the BRI projects, to work with other actors, and for each actor involved in BRI to further its respective interests. Section 2 of the chapter shows the struggle at the level of international financial institutions: the establishment of the new institutions challenges the traditional MDBs in development financing; the new institutions are inevitably influenced by the political objectives and impacts of particular countries in its projects as well. China, namely, plays a major role in the design of the BRI projects. Section 3 introduces the BRI in the context of China's global strategy, and contends that the financing mechanism of the BRI shows that it is a combination of infrastructure financing, which is contract-based and economic interest driven, and development financing, which is inevitably connected with the political objectives of China.

It is not a tale of ending poverty. "End poverty" is deployed by actors in the BRI projects, for their interests in a world of struggle.

Indeed, the tale of ending poverty is, a tale. The question that came to me after attending the panel is answered: "End poverty" is the middle-ground between various actors, including the sovereign nations, new and established financial institutions involved in the BRI. The moral endowment and indeterminacy of the term enables WB and other international institutions to engage with the BRI for the purpose of its own agendas. The term offers a narrative of the establishment of the AIIB and NDB, that they filled in the gap in financing for infrastructure building along the BRI, disguises the story of the struggle of the member countries of the new institutions for strategic advantages in multilateral lending, and conceals the political objectives and effects of particular countries within the new institutions. The term, as well, facilitates China to deploy its global strategy in the political economy of the contemporary world. It is claimed as a win-win, as various policy analysis emphasizes,[99] but the essential meaning of ending poverty is not of concern. Who cares when the elites' power over their populations are strengthened through the BRI projects, that the living standards, the social well-being of those suffering from the consequences of economic globalization, deteriorate further?

Doubts over the impact on the disadvantaged in the recipient countries of the BRI projects is not unfounded. In the context of China's development cooperation with the South, it is argued that "Chinese aid projects seem to have generated few local employment opportunities".[100] If not carefully, analytically planned, the BRI projects could deepen the disadvantage of the neglected population in the receiving countries, risk the economic sustainability of the project itself, and add pressure on the global financial stability.

Finally, it is necessary to notice here, that with the BRI, a project in its development, the readings into the BRI offered in this chapter are cautionary in nature. Empirical issues include, for instance, how to safe-guard the interests of the

[99] See, for instance Xinhua News (2017).

[100] "Many African officials are concerned that Chinese workers are displacing local workers". See Monga and Lin (2015), p. 807.

disadvantaged in the peripheries of the project, how to build regulatory regimes to avoid corruption in the receiving countries, are not touched on here. With the vast majority of research works on the BRI, both in the field of political science and law, focusing on the legal infrastructure, the geopolitics and interest defined by power, or praising the project by digging into Chinese traditional philosophy,[101] this paper is an endeavour to add a critical voice into the bigger picture, to focus on the involved actors' pursuit of interests and the struggle among the actors, to caution the social impacts of the project, with the hope of contributing to this project.

References

Allen, K. (2017, August 9). Supranational debt issuance more than doubles in a decade. *Financial Times.*

Anderlini, J (2015, March 17). China will not thank perfidious Albion for joining its New Bank. *Financial Times.*

Anderlini, J. (2017, August 15). China's economy is addicted to debt. *Financial Times.*

Arezki, R., Bolton, P., Peters, S., Samama, F., & Stiglitz, J. (2016). *From global savings glut to financing infrastructure: The advent of investment platforms, economy policy*. 63rd Panel. Meeting hosted by the De Nederlandsche Bank, Amsterdam, 22–23 April 2016.

Articles of Agreement. (2015). *Asian Infrastructure Investment Bank.* Retrieved September 18, 2017, from https://www.aiib.org/en/aboutaiib/basic-documents/_download/articles-of-agreement/basic_document_english-bank_articles_of_agreement.pdf

Asian Development Bank. (2017). *Meeting Asia's infrastructure needs.* Mandaluyong City, Philippines: Asian Development Bank.

Baijie, A. (2017, October 26). March to rejuvenation. *China Daily.* Retrieved October 26, 2017, from http://www.chinadaily.com.cn/china/2017-10/26/content_33715396.htm

Best, J. (2012). Ambiguity and uncertainty in international organizations: A history of debating IMF conditionality. *International Studies Quarterly, 56*(4), 674–688.

Biswas, R. (2015). *Reshaping the financial architecture for development finance: The new development banks* (Working Paper No. 2/2015). LSE Global South Unit.

Callaghan, M., & Hubbard, P. (2016). The Asian Infrastructure Investment Bank: Multilateralism on the Silk Road. *China Economic Journal, 9*(2), 116–139.

Chhibber, A. (2015). *China's One Belt One Road strategy: The new financial institutions and India's options* (Working Paper No. 2015-155). National Institute of Public Finance and Policy.

Chin, G. T. (2016). Asian Infrastructure Investment Bank: Governance innovation and prospects. *Global Governance, 22*, 11–26.

Cottee, M. (2017, August 3). China's nuclear export ambition run into friction. *Financial Times.*

Dell, S. (1981). *On being grandmotherly: The evolution of IMF conditionality. Essays in international finance*. Princeton, NJ: Princeton University Press.

Dixon, C. (2015). *The new BRICS Bank: Challenging the International financial order?* (Policy Paper No. 28). Global Policy Institute.

[101]See, for instance, Nicholas Morris, Developing A Sustainable Legal System for the Belt and Road Initiative; Guilherme Vilaça, Strenghtening the Cultural and Normative Foundations of the Belt and Road Initiative: The Colombo Plan, Yan Xuetong and Chinese Ancient Thought, both included in this volume. By no means this chapter considers such readings into BRI by referring to the Chinese philosophies unjustified; quite a contrary, those readings offer an alternative approach to reading into Chinese activities on the global arena, and to global governance in general.

Dollar, D. (2015). *The AIIB and the 'One Belt, One Road'*. Brookings. Retrieved October 26, 2017, from https://www.brookings.edu/opinions/the-aiib-and-the-one-belt-one-road/

European Political Strategy Centre (EPSC). (2015, April 24). *The Asian Infrastructure Investment Bank: A new multilateral financial institution or a vehicle for China's geostrategic goals.* EPSC Strategic Notes, 1.

Fallon, T. (2015). The New Silk Road: Xi Jinping's grand strategy for Eurasia. *American Foreign Policy Interests, 37*(3), 140–147.

Gold, J. (1979). *Conditionality*. Washington, DC: International Monetary Fund.

Gu, J. (2015). In R. Chandran, & H. Cooper (Eds.), *China's New Silk Road to development cooperation: Opportunities and challenges*. United Nations University Centre for Policy Research.

Guoli, T. (2017, June 14). *Construct financial lifeline, facilitating the BRI to a new stage.* Bank of China.

Inderst, G. (2016). *Infrastructure investment, private finance, and institutional investors: Asia from a global perspective* (ADBI Working Paper Series, No. 555). Asian Development Bank Institute.

Kennedy, D. (2013). Law and the political economy of the world. *Leiden Journal of International Law, 26*, 7–48.

Kennedy, D. (2016). *A world of struggles: How power, law and expertise shape global political economy*. Princeton, NJ: Princeton University Press.

Kim, J. Y. (2015). *Welcoming AIIB to fight poverty*. The World Bank. Retrieved September 18, 2017, from http://www.worldbank.org/en/news/opinion/2015/06/08/welcoming-aiibto-fight-poverty

Kim, J. Y. (2017). *Remarks of World Bank Group President Jim Yong Kim at the Belt and Road Forum for International Cooperation – Opening Plenary Session*. World Bank. Retrieved October 31, 2017, from http://www.worldbank.org/en/news/speech/2017/05/14/remarks-of-world-bank-group-president-jim-yong-kim

Kynge, J. (2016, May 10). How the Silk Road plans will be financed. *Financial Times.*

Kynge, J. (2017, June 16). Finance will create new alliances across Asia. *Financial Times.*

Kynge, J., Peel, M., & Bland, B. (2017, July 17). China's railway diplomacy hits the buffers. *Financial Times.*

Lioa, R. (2015, 27 July). Out of Bretton Woods: How the AIIB is different. *Foreign Affairs.*

Liu, W., & Dunford, M. (2016). Inclusive globalization: Unpacking China's Belt and Road initiative. *Area Development and Policy, 1*(3), 323–340.

Mishra, R. (2016). Asian Infrastructure Investment Bank: An assessment. *India Quarterly, 72*(2), 163–176.

Monga, C., & Lin, J. Y. (2015). *The Oxford handbook of Africa and economics: Policies and practices.* New York: Oxford University Press.

National Development and Reform Commission of the CBRC. (2015). CBRC no. 43.

Nowzad, B. (1981). *The IMF and its critics* (Essays in International Finance No. 146). Princeton, NJ: Princeton University Press.

OECD. (2017). *Glossary of key terms and concepts*. Retrieved September 26, 2017, from http://www.oecd.org/dac/dac-glossary.htm#ODA

Phenix Financial News. (2017, May 25). *Research report on the financial institutions' participation in the BRI forum*. Retrieved September 18, 2017 from http://finance.ifeng.com/a/20170526/15412635_0.shtml

Qi, L. (2017, May 18). *Bank of China will try to expand the network along the Belt and Road through Merger*. Reuters. Retrieved September 26, 2017, from http://cn.reuters.com/article/boc-b-r-plan-0518-thursday-idCNKCS18E053

Sandbu, M. (2017, March 27). Globalisation and its defences. *Financial Times.*

Spraos, J. (1986). *IMF conditionality: Ineffectual, inefficient, mistargeted* (Essays in International Finance No. 166). Princeton, NJ: Princeton University Press.

Weinland, D. (2017, May 4). Asia's regional banks lend where their western rivals dare not. *Financial Times.*

Wells, P., & Weinland, D. (2017, January 26). Fitch warns on expected returns from One Belt, One Road. *Financial Times.*

Wihtol, R. (2014). *Whither multilateral development finance?* (Working Paper Series No. 491). Tokyo: Asian Development Bank Institute.

Wildau, G., & Ma, N. (2017, May 11). Charts: China's Belt and Road initiative. *Financial Times*.

Xiao, R. (2016). China as an institution-builder: the case of the AIIB. *The Pacific Review, 29*(3), 435–442.

Xinhua News. (2017, May 16). Spotlight: Belt and Road initiative brings win-win results. *Xinhua News*. Retrieved September 26, 2017, from http://news.xinhuanet.com/english/2017-05/16/c_136288592.htm

Xinhuanet. (2017). *19th CPC National Congress*. Retrieved October 31, 2017, from http://www.xinhuanet.com/english/special/19cpcnc/index.htm

Xu, J. (2017). *Beyond US Hegemony in international developments: The contest for influence at the World Bank*. Cambridge: Cambridge University Press.

Yang, X. (2017a, June 14). Policy credit insurance adds new engine to the construction of the Belt and Road. *Financial News*. Retrieved September 26, 2017, from http://www.financialnews.com.cn/bx/jg/201706/t20170614_119131.html

Yang, Z. (2017b, April 10). Loans to foreign territorial projects increase, big commercial banks set banking framework along BRI. *Jiemian News*.

Yeyati, L., Alejandro, E., Panizza, M., & Panizza, U. (2004). *Should the Government Be in the Banking Business? The Role of State-Owned and Development Banks* (Research Department Publications 4379). Inter-American Development Bank, Research Department.

Yi, H. (2017a, May 19). Commercial banks will be pillaring the financial service of the BRI. *Financial News*.

Yi, W. (2017b, October 19). *Talks about general goal of major country diplomacy with Chinese characteristics in new era: To promote the building of a community with shared future for mankind*. Retrieved October 26, 2017, http://www.china-un.org/eng/zgyw/t1503758.html

Zhu, Z. (2017, March 22). *A scrutinization of the financing mechanism of the BRI*. Minsheng Securities Research Center.

Planning for a Sustainable Belt and Road Initiative (BRI): An Appraisal of the Asian Infrastructure Investment Bank (AIIB) Environmental and Social Safeguards

Daniele Brombal

1 Introduction

The Belt and Road Initiative (BRI) aims at enhancing connectivity between the Asia-Pacific region, Central Asia, and Europe. It will therefore largely revolve around infrastructural projects, bringing massive investments throughout the Eurasian region in the fields of transport, logistics, and energy. The initiative has been hailed by many as a game changer in the field of economy. Other observers however are concerned about its environmental and social costs (Liu 2016; Ma 2014). BRI routes[1] will touch areas that are both environmentally fragile and socially vulnerable. The transnational nature of the initiative adds to its complexity, since many projects will require integrated transnational planning. Another cause for concern lies in that many BRI projects will be implemented in countries where public participation and environmental rights remain curtailed. Finally, environmental activists have warned against poor environmental records of Chinese companies operating abroad, and the risk that China may use the initiative to delocalize polluting industries (Simonov 2016a, b). Affected communities and the civil society have begun advocating for a careful consideration of the initiative's environmental and social impacts. In 2016, the Egiin Gol hydropower project in Mongolia was halted due to the opposition by local communities, the civil society, and the Russian government, concerned about the environmental impacts of the project on the Selenge river and the Baikal lake (RwB 2016a, b).[2] How the BRI will cope with these challenges will depend upon the

[1] At present, there is no 'standard' BRI chart. One of the most informative and complete was prepared by the Mercator Institute and is available online here: https://www.merics.org/en/merics-analysis/infographicchina-mapping/china-mapping/.

[2] The project is being funded by EXIM Bank of China.

D. Brombal (✉)
Department of Asian and North African Studies, University Ca' Foscari Venice, Venice, Italy
e-mail: daniele.brombal@unive.it

W. Shan et al. (eds.), *Normative Readings of the Belt and Road Initiative*,
https://doi.org/10.1007/978-3-319-78018-4_7

capacity of concerned actors (governments, financial organizations, companies and State enterprises, civil society, and the public) to carry out integrated and inclusive planning.[3] A major role will be played by organizations funding the initiative. They may have substantial leverage on government actors and companies, by setting socio-environmental conditions for project approval and loan disbursement. Moreover, international financial organizations have historically played a crucial role in establishing environmental and social assessment standards in recipient countries, through capacity building and transfer of knowledge (Kennedy 1999; Estevens et al. 2016).

2 Aims and Methods

The aim of this chapter is to appraise the rationale, scope, legitimacy, and decision-making structure of environmental and social policies applicable to BRI. To pursue this aim, the Asian Infrastructure Investment Bank (AIIB) is taken as a case representative of progress made and challenges ahead. The AIIB is a multilateral financial organization founded in 2015 under the auspices of the Chinese government. Currently it comprises of 57 member countries, with a total capital of 90 billion US dollars (AIIB online a, b). China is the major shareholder, with 32.4% of total subscriptions and 27.8% of the voting shares (AIIB online b). AIIB is going to play a major role in funding BRI. Xi Jinping first laid out the Bank's role in the initiative during the eighth meeting of the Leading Group for Financial and Economic Affairs of CPC's Central Committee, held on November 4, 2014. Here Mr. Xi stressed the importance of the AIIB in providing financial support to the initiative, promoting economic cooperation throughout the region (People's Daily 2016). In fact, a considerable part of AIIB's initial capital has been earmarked to fund BRI projects (Soong 2016). In February 2016, the Bank approved its "Environmental and Social Framework" (henceforth ESF), to streamline environmental and social requirements applicable to its projects (AIIB 2016). The framework has been described as having the potential to set, rather than follow, international standards (Kim 2016). While this claim might be optimistic, it is entirely possible that the ESF will indeed set a standard among organizations funding the BRI. Moreover, the very nature of AIIB as a multi-lateral development bank (MDB) makes it an ideal platform to enhance and harmonize socio-environmental planning in recipient countries, similarly to the role played by the World Bank (WB) and the Asian Development Bank (ADB) since the 1990s (Kennedy 1999; Estevens et al. 2016. On the topic, see also Wang 2016). The chapter is subdivided into four sections. The first provides an overview of AIIB's goals and projects. The second section characterizes the ESF against four attributes, i.e., rationale, scope, legitimacy, and decisional process (see Table 1).

[3]On the importance of the role played by partner countries in shaping the BRI, see Brown (2017).

Table 1 Attributes used to characterize the AIIB "Environmental and Social Framework"[a]

Attribute	Explanatory notes
Rationale	The rationale is categorized into three typologies: (a) instrumental, whereby the ESF is intended as a tool to ensure smooth project implementation, minimize conflict, and safeguard the Bank from risks; (b) substantial, whereby the assessment of environmental and social aspects is carried out to ameliorate projects, avoiding and/or mitigating negative impacts on the environment and society; and (c) empowering, based on principles of institutional transformation and ownership within/by recipient countries[b]
Scope	The scope of the ESF is mainly appraised based on the sustainability criteria used to assess and manage environmental and social impacts of projects, and on the spatial scale to which the ESF are applicable
Legitimacy	This attribute refers to the source(s) of formal legitimation of the ESF. A key aspect in this respect is the function attributed in the process of project assessment to country regulatory systems for environmental and social planning
Decisional process	This attribute refers to the procedural characteristics of project assessment and management. Key characteristics include the timing, actors, and responsibilities laid out in the ESF vis-à-vis the different stages of the decision-making processes in project approval and implementation

[a]Attributes' definitions have been normalized based on literature concerning environmental and social assessments in international projects. See in particular Estevens et al. (2016), Kim (2016), IAIA (2015a), and Kennedy (1999)
[b]Categorization is drawn from literature on decision making processes in environmental planning. The distinction between an instrumental, substantial, and normative (i.e., empowering) rationale is made by Glucker et al. (2013) with reference to public participation in Environmental Impact Assessments (EIAs). Conceptually, the characterization is suitable to characterize the role of environmental and social assessment in project planning and approval (see also Arnstein 1969; Brombal et al. 2017)

The third section discusses findings against the background of recent development of MDBs social and environmental policies. The discussion refers primarily to the WB, which in 2016 introduced new environmental and social safeguards (IAIA 2015a; WB 2016a, b. See also NDB 2016). The conclusive section outlines the potentials and pitfalls of the AIIB's environmental and social policies, and delineates possible directions for future research.

3 AIIB's Goals and Areas of Intervention

The declared aim of the AIIB is to "promote interconnectivity and economic development in the region through the development of infrastructure and other productive sectors" (AIIB online c. See also AIIB 2016, p. 1). The Bank has individuated six thematic areas for intervention, including transportation and telecommunications, energy and power, rural infrastructure and development, water supply and sanitation, urban development and logistics, and environmental protection (AIIB online d; Weiss 2017). Figure 1 provides a breakdown of AIIB's current portfolio, including both submitted and approved projects. The lion's share is

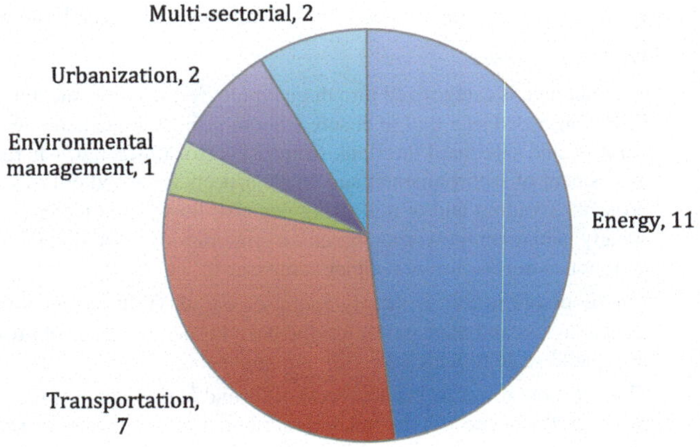

Fig. 1 AIIB's project portfolio by sector as for May, 2017 (n.) (Author's figure, based on AIIB online e, f)

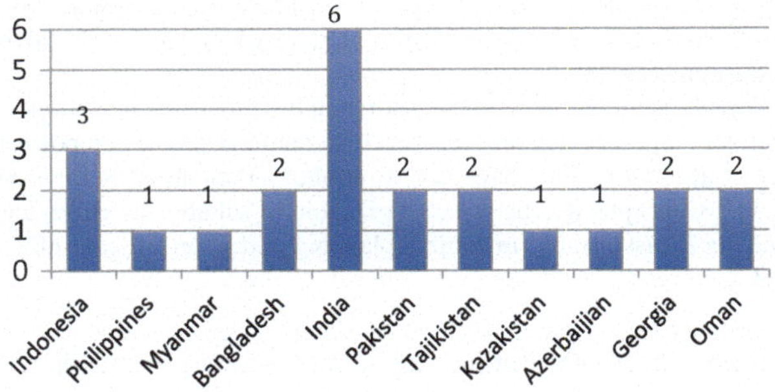

Fig. 2 AIIB's project portfolio by country as for May, 2017 (n.) (Author's figure, based on AIIB online e, f)

composed by the energy and transportation sectors, that makes for over three-fourths of the total. Projects included in AIIB's pipeline are distributed across a wide area, from Indonesia to Georgia (Fig. 2).

Among AIIB's projects, several are deemed as likely to have significant adverse impact on the environment and society. They include the Trans Ananotolian Natural Gas Pipeline Project (Azerbaijan); the Myngyan Power Plant Project (Myanmar); the National Motorway M-4 Project (Pakistan); and the Tarbela 5 Hydropower Extension Project (AIIB online e). The latter, co-financed by the WB, has already been the source of social tensions and opposition by local communities, due to expected impacts on local communities and their access to traditional livelihoods (EJAtlas 2017).

4 Case Study: Appraising the AIIB Environmental and Social Framework (ESF)

4.1 Rationale

By rationale we hereby intend the objectives pursued by the AIIB through the establishment of its environmental and social framework (AIIB 2016).[4] The three rationales (instrumental, substantial, and empowering) should not be understood as mutually exclusive. Rather on the contrary, they are positioned along a continuum, ranging from basic organizational objectives of AIIB and project proponents—ensuring smooth project implementation and avoiding conflicts, to a normative conceptualization of sustainable development, in tune with nature and human communities (see Glucker et al. 2013). The ESF comprises both instrumental and substantial objectives, as well as—though to a lesser extent—goals consistent with an empowering rationale. One of the key objectives of the ESF is to provide "a robust structure for managing operational and reputational risks of the Bank and its shareholders in relation to projects' environmental and social risks and impacts" (AIIB 2016, p. 2). This provision is clearly inspired by an instrumental rationale. To take into consideration environmental and social issues throughout the project cycle is indeed vital to ensure smooth implementation. This is particularly true for large infrastructures, where the emergence of social and environmental concerns is often cause of disruption of project activities. This instrumental approach is accompanied by a substantial role attributed to sustainability considerations in informing decision making. In fact, the ESF endorses the logic of integrated planning, intended as a set of processes and procedures aimed at fostering comprehensive development, inclusive of different dimensions of sustainability (see in particular AIIB 2016, pp. 2, 3, 7, 13). The pursue of holistic objectives of development is framed in the ESF both in terms of local impacts, and with reference to global challenges, especially climate change (AIIB 2016, pp. 2, 3). The substantial role attributed to sustainability considerations is reflected in provisions relevant to public participation and stakeholders' engagement.[5] The ESF recommends the establishment of "meaningful" forms of consultation, which should be "inclusive, accessible, timely [...] open," and conveying "adequate information" (AIIB 2016, pp. 4, 30). Besides directly affected individuals and communities, the ESF recommends consultations with actors of the civil society (AIIB 2016, p. 39). It is not clear to what extent these principles may relate to normative ideas of empowerment, enabling people and communities to influence decisions affecting their lives. In fact, on this point the ESF is rather ambivalent. On the one hand, ample reference is made to social inclusion,

[4]The rationale defined in the ESF may differ from the actual objectives pursued by AIIB and its clients during project implementation. On the gap between principles and practice in environmental planning, see Brombal et al. (2017).

[5]For the purpose of this study, the term 'public' should be understood as inclusive of all kinds of stakeholders, i.e., those having an interest or stake in an issue, including individuals, interest groups, communities (Brombal et al. 2017).

which the Bank defines as "*empowering* people to participate in, and benefit from, the development process" (AIIB 2016, p. 3). On the other, no explicit reference is made to the role of AIIB in enabling affected communities to play a role in decision making. The document appears therefore skewed towards the socio-economic dimension of empowerment, avoiding commitment towards the provision of institutional conditions enabling participation into decisional processes. This may relate to the Bank's willingness of keeping clear of issues related to power and politics in recipient countries. Objectives of empowerment may easily assume connotations of political conditionality, which so far AIIB has carefully tried to avoid (Qing 2015).

4.2 Scope

The scope of the ESF can be appraised based on three criteria: (a) spatial coverage; (b) applicability to different phases of the project cycle; and (c) integration of criteria of environmental and social sustainability. Spatially, the ESF extends its scope to cover the entire area of influence of projects, or the area "likely to be affected by the Project, including all its ancillary aspects [. . .] as well as unplanned developments induced by the Project"(AIIB 2016, pp. 9, 27, 53). As for different project phases, the ESF applies to both project preparation, implementation, and management. Clients[6] are required to assess expected environmental and social impacts, and to develop relevant mitigation and management measures (AIIB 2016, p. 14). Such measures should be provided for in an Environmental and Social Management Plan (ESMP) or in a Environmental and Social Management Planning Framework (ESMPF),[7] to be submitted during project application. The compliance with the ESMP (or ESMPF) would be thereafter monitored periodically by the AIIB (AIIB 2016, pp. 14, 21). With reference to sustainability criteria the ESF requires that clients carry out assessment and mitigation of impacts on the following aspects: environmental quality of air and water, environmental health, quality and quantity of land and water resources, ecosystems and habitats integrity, biodiversity, and ecological functions, greenhouse gases emissions (AIIB 2016, pp. 5, 27, 30–33). The social component focuses on socioeconomic conditions of local communities, social vulnerability, gender, access to natural resources and traditional livelihoods, cultural resources, workers' and community health and safety (AIIB 2016, pp. 28, 33–35). No specific metrics or indicators are provided for in the ESF. However, the document recommends to employ a cumulative impact assessment approach, within and across the environmental and social dimension (AIIB 2016, p. 12). Detailed

[6]The definition of 'client' applies to both recipients of AIIB funding, and any other entity responsible for project implementation. Clients may be either public or private entities (AIIB 2016, p. 8).

[7]An ESMPF is required when projects consist of a number/series of activities whose details are "not yet identified at the time the Project is approved by the Bank" (AIIB 2016, p. 17).

provisions are made however for involuntary resettlement, and for impacts on indigenous peoples. The section on involuntary resettlement covers both physical and economic displacement. Clients are required to assess and mitigate to the maximum possible extent[8] the negative impacts of projects on losses of residential land and dwellings resulting from relocation, as well as to avoid restrictions to the access to sources of income and natural resources (AIIB 2016, pp. 38–41). Consistently with this approach, the ESF requires clients to "improve, or at least restore" the livelihoods of those displaced by the project, to build skills facilitating employment, and to protect cultural institutions (AIIB 2016, pp. 38, 40). Targeted consultations—involving both local communities and the civil society—are recommended (AIIB 2016, p. 39). The standard on indigenous people applies to "distinct indigenous cultural group," possessing peculiar "customary cultural, economic, social or political institutions" and a distinct language (AIIB 2016, p. 42). Requirements focus on the assessment and mitigation of cultural impacts, to avoid jeopardizing the culture-economy nexus embedded in traditional societies (AIIB 2016, pp. 42–43). As in the case of resettlement, additional requirements for public consultations are put forward. In particular, the ESF requires the integration in project planning and execution of customary decision making structures in place among indigenous communities (AIIB 2016, p. 44).

4.3 Legitimacy

The ESF applies to all projects submitted for funding to the AIIB. Its requirements therefore constitute an integral part of project review (AIIB 2016, p. 8). As shown in Sect. 4.2, the ESF do not consist of specific, compulsory procedures for assessment and management of impacts. It rather includes general requirements, principles and objectives, which clients should abide to during project preparation and implementation (AIIB 2016, pp. 3–4). Against this background, the ESF attaches importance to country regulatory systems as sources of legally binding procedures and standards (AIIB 2016, p. 4). The Bank "may selectively provide the Client the option of using all or part of such systems [. . .] in place of all or part of this [ESF]" (AIIB 2016, p. 4). The choice of whether or not to make use of local systems is made by the Bank based on their capacity to meet requirements set forth by the ESF. Additional country requirements should be applied, if they are found to be more stringent than those provided for in the ESF (AIIB 2016, p. 9). In case co-financed projects, the Bank may also determine to use procedures adopted by the other organization(s) involved (AIIB 2016, p. 9). Apart from encouraging the adoption of country systems, the ESF commits the Bank to support the strengthening of relevant regulatory frameworks in recipient countries (AIIB 2016, pp. 4, 11). The concrete application of these

[8]In the introductory paragraph to the involuntary resettlement section, the ESF explicitly makes reference to the "avoidance" of resettlement as the optimal solution to be pursued (AIIB 2016, p. 38).

principles will largely depend upon the legal and institutional context in which projects will be implemented. All countries eligible for AIIB funding have in place Environmental Impact Assessment (EIA) regulations. First introduced in Western countries in the 1970s,[9] EIA procedures gained ground in the Greater Asia-Pacific region and in Central Asia during the 1990s and early 2000s (ELaw online; MER online; WB 2002; Li 2008; Dorjsuren 2010; Karimi 2015).[10,11] Although EIA provisions may vary to a considerable degree, they share the same rationale: (a) EIA is the main tool to assess harms which private and public projects may cause to the environment, and (b) development consent is granted to project proponents based on the appraisal of EIA by a competent authority. Moreover, all legislations foresee public participation in the EIA process, albeit its key features (timing, scope, inclusiveness) may vary from one country to the other (ELaw online; MER online; WB 2002; Li 2008; Dorjsuren 2010; Karimi 2015). Public participation is pursued also in authoritarian or semi-authoritarian countries: in China, EIA public participation is one of the most important institutionalized form of participation in public decision-making processes, albeit its influence remains limited (Brombal et al. 2017). Similarly, Vietnam's legal requirements are stringent when it comes to consulting the public during EIAs (Li 2008). The adoption of Social Impact Assessment (SIA) in the region is weaker if compared with EIA. In some countries, the assessment of social impacts[12] is carried out routinely as part of the EIA process (Li 2008; ELaw online). Others have set up ad-hoc procedures targeting specific sectors, such as in India's mining sector (Shaikh 2014). A number of pilot SIAs have been conducted across the region in the framework of projects funded by MDBs, in particular WB and ADB (see e.g. the case of Bangladesh, in Momtaz 2003. See also Zaman n.d.). Standards set by donor agencies have been often used as a benchmark to improve SIA practices (see e.g. the case of Pakistan, in FATA 2012). A SIA has been reportedly carried out for the China-Pakistan Economic Corridor, included in the BRI initiative (Zhang and Shi 2016). The scope of SIAs varies: while there tends to be a general agreement in carrying out SIAs for involuntary resettlement and loss of livelihoods, different practices remain with respect to political inclusiveness, personal rights, and the development of aspirations of communities (Momtaz 2003; Li 2008; IAIA 2015b). The development of Strategic Environmental

[9]EIA was first introduced in the USA in 1970. In Europe, Community-level EIA legal provisions were enacted in 1985 (Moorman and Zhang 2007; EC 1985).

[10]The first countries to introduce formal EIA requirements in the region were Pakistan (1983), India (1986), and Indonesia (1986) (MER online; Nadeem and Fischer 2011).

[11]The Netherlands Commission for Environmental Assessment has recently developed a tool to map relevant policies. Information are (partially) available online at: http://www.eia.nl/en/our-work/eia-mapping-tool. With reference to transboundary issues, cfr. http://www.unece.org:8080/fileadmin/DAM/env/eia/ratification/convmap.htm.

[12]The International Association of Impact Assessment (IAIA) devised in 2015 a definition of social impact as "everything that affect people", including the following: people's way of life, culture, community, political systems, the environment, health and wellbeing, personal and property rights, fears and aspirations (IAIA 2015b, p. 2).

Assessment (SEA) is yet another element which will impact on AIIB's activities. SEA differs from EIA and SIA in that it aims at individuating the environmental and social consequences of policies, plans, and programs, rather than projects. It has therefore a wider scope and it takes place upstream in the decision making process (WB 2002, 2009, p. 1). As in the case of SIA, also SEA's adoption in the region is uneven and heterogeneous, with a substantial role played by MDBs in establishing SEA practices (WB 2009). This does not mean that substantial national experiences are absent: SEA systems in China, Vietnam, and Indonesia are fairly developed. Malaysia, Thailand, Philippines, Laos, and Cambodia have widely experimented with strategic assessment as well. SEAs are being piloted also in Central Asian countries, with the support of international organizations (WB 2009; OECD 2016). Finally, with reference to transboundary impacts, there is a substantial lack of common regulatory in the region. Among countries targeted by the AIIB, the UNECE Espoo convention on transboundary environmental impacts has been ratified only by Kazakhstan, Kirghizistan, Azerbaijan, and Armenia (UNECE: online). Overall, AIIB will therefore operate in a context characterized by: (a) extensive presence of regulatory frameworks for the assessment of environmental impacts; (b) increasingly large adoption of frameworks for the strategic assessment of policies and plans; (c) relatively weak adoption of SIA; (d) weak adoption of frameworks for the assessment and management of transboundary impacts. The last two points will clearly constitute a major criticality in the implementation of AIIB activities. In particular, the ESF will constitute the major source of binding requirements for the assessment of social impacts. The establishment of social impact assessment procedures may therefore constitute a key aspect of AIIB's commitment to strengthen country systems.

4.4 Decision Making Process

After project submission, the AIIB categorizes projects into three categories, based on their expected impacts on the environment and on social conditions (AIIB 2016, pp. 9–10):

- Category A. Projects in this category are estimated to have "significant adverse [...] impacts that are irreversible, cumulative, diverse or unprecedented" which "may affect an area larger than the sites or facilities subject to physical works."
- Category B. Projects with a "limited number of potentially adverse [...] impacts" which are "not unprecedented; few if any of them are irreversible or cumulative; they are limited to the Project area."
- Category C. Projects with minimal or absent adverse impacts.

Categorization is the key phase in defining subsequent steps in the decision making process. Projects falling under category A are required to undergo a full Environmental and Social Impact Assessment (ESIA) and to prepare an Environmental and Social Management Plan (ESMP) or an Environmental and Social

Management Planning Framework (ESMPF)[13] (AIIB 2016, p. 10). On the other hand, for projects falling under category C clients may proceed directly to negotiation, provided that project documents do introduce projects' environmental and social implications (AIIB 2016, p. 10). As for projects under category B, there remains significant uncertainty. The definition of the appropriate procedure to assess impacts and their mitigation, is left to consultations between the Bank and the client (AIIB 2016, p. 10). Once these consultations are held, the "Bank may determine that an environmental and social assessment or another similar instrument is appropriate [...] The scope of the assessment may vary from Project to Project" (AIIB 2016, p. 10). For projects implying involuntary resettlement and those having adverse impacts on indigenous peoples, clients are required as well to prepare relevant assessment and management plans, to be included in documents submitted for AIIB review (AIIB 2016, pp. 14–15). The ESF mandates that the public is engaged by the client in consultations, both during the process of assessment, and in the definition of mitigation and management measures (AIIB 2016, p. 21). At this respect, the client is requested to provide affected communities with information over project impacts and project alternatives. Although this is not specifically provided for in the ESF, it appears that for projects under category A, the scope of consultations should also cover the "zero option" (i.e., no project implementation), since clients are required to include such an option among alternatives considered in the ESIA (AIIB 2016, p. 10). Consultation should be particularly extensive in the case of impacts on indigenous people, showing "evidence of broad community support [...] on the outcome of the negotiations" (AIIB 2016, p. 22).[14] Once completed, the ESIA (or another similar instrument for category B projects), complete with ESMP (or ESMPF) and records of consultations are all submitted to the Bank for review (AIIB 2016, p. 11). The review appraises projects based on (a) the degree into which all potential impacts are reflected and assessed in the documents submitted by the client; (b) appropriate and feasible measures for their avoidance and/or mitigation are foreseen; and (c) appropriate consultations have been held, and their results incorporated in documentation (AIIB 2016, pp. 11, 21–22). In this stage, the Bank may also appraise the extent into which the client has committed to and made preparations for strengthening its technical and institutional capacities (AIIB 2016, p. 11). If the ESIA is deemed by the Bank as appropriately addressing above mentioned aspects, the Bank and the client may proceed to negotiation and contracting. Otherwise, the Bank may require additional information to be incorporated in the ESIA, or further assessment and planning work to be conducted. This may also result in the preparation of a revised ESIA, complete with supplemental assessment or studies, to be resubmitted to the Bank. The Bank may also require to held additional consultations (AIIB 2016, p. 12). After the signature of the contract and the inception of project activities, it is the client's responsibility to provide periodical

[13]On the difference between ESMP and ESMPF, see note 9.

[14]Although consultations fall under the clients' responsibility, the Bank may take part in consultations (AIIB 2016, p. 22).

reports to the Bank, pursuant to the mitigation and management of adverse environmental and social impacts (AIIB 2016, p. 22). The Bank reviews periodical reports, appraising their consistency with measures defined in the ESMP (or ESMPF). If clients fail to comply with it, the Bank may require corrective measures, or resort to the use of legal instruments provided for in the contract binding the two parties (AIIB 2016, pp. 22, 24). In parallel with the monitoring process by the Bank, the client is required to establish grievance mechanisms to facilitate the resolution of conflicts which may arise during project implementation (AIIB 2016, p. 23) (Fig. 3).

5 Discussion

The potential of the AIIB in fostering sustainable development has been subject to differing judgments. Sceptics argue that it would replicate flaws of the development model of its main shareholder—China, whose growth has been achieved at tremendous environmental and social costs (see e.g. Ma 2014; Simonov 2016a, b). On the other hand, optimists welcome AIIB as a badly needed contribution to socio-economic development of Eurasia (UN 2015). Such widely differing positions are not surprising. Even though some critiques might be inspired by politicized concerns over China's growing geopolitical influence, it is nonetheless clear how the very nature of projects in the AIIB's portfolio may be controversial. Large-scale infrastructural projects do have a positive potential in bringing about economic benefits. However, they are intrinsically contentious in terms of environmental and social impacts. The discussion on the capacity of AIIB to contribute to sustainable development can be best understood if contextualized within the wider debate on the role of international organizations in fostering sustainable development. Activities of MDBs have been historically characterized by a pro-development bias, which has often resulted in serious environmental damage (Rich 1985. On the potential of MDBs to promote development, see also Perry 2009). MDBs however should not be used as the scapegoat for everything that goes wrong: projects funded by MDBs are proposed by borrowing countries, which play a key role both in project planning, implementation, and management. The murder in 2016 of Honduran environmental activist Berta Cáceres due to her strenuous opposition to a hydropower project backed by the WB, is a dramatic epitome of the complex interactions unfolding between MDBs, governments, companies, and communities.[15] In recent years, the debate on how to ensure that MDBs pursue development objectives consistent with the environment and societal needs has intensified. The debate has translated in the revision of environmental and social safeguards adopted by many large MDBs. In 2009, the ADB enacted its new "Safeguard Policy Statement" (ADB 2009). In 2012, the World Bank launched a review process of its policies. The process involved an

[15]The Environmental Justice Atlas (EJAtlas), accessible online at https://ejatlas.org, is a good resource to know more about environmental and social conflicts triggered by infrastructural projects. The online tool allows to refine search by projects' funding institutions.

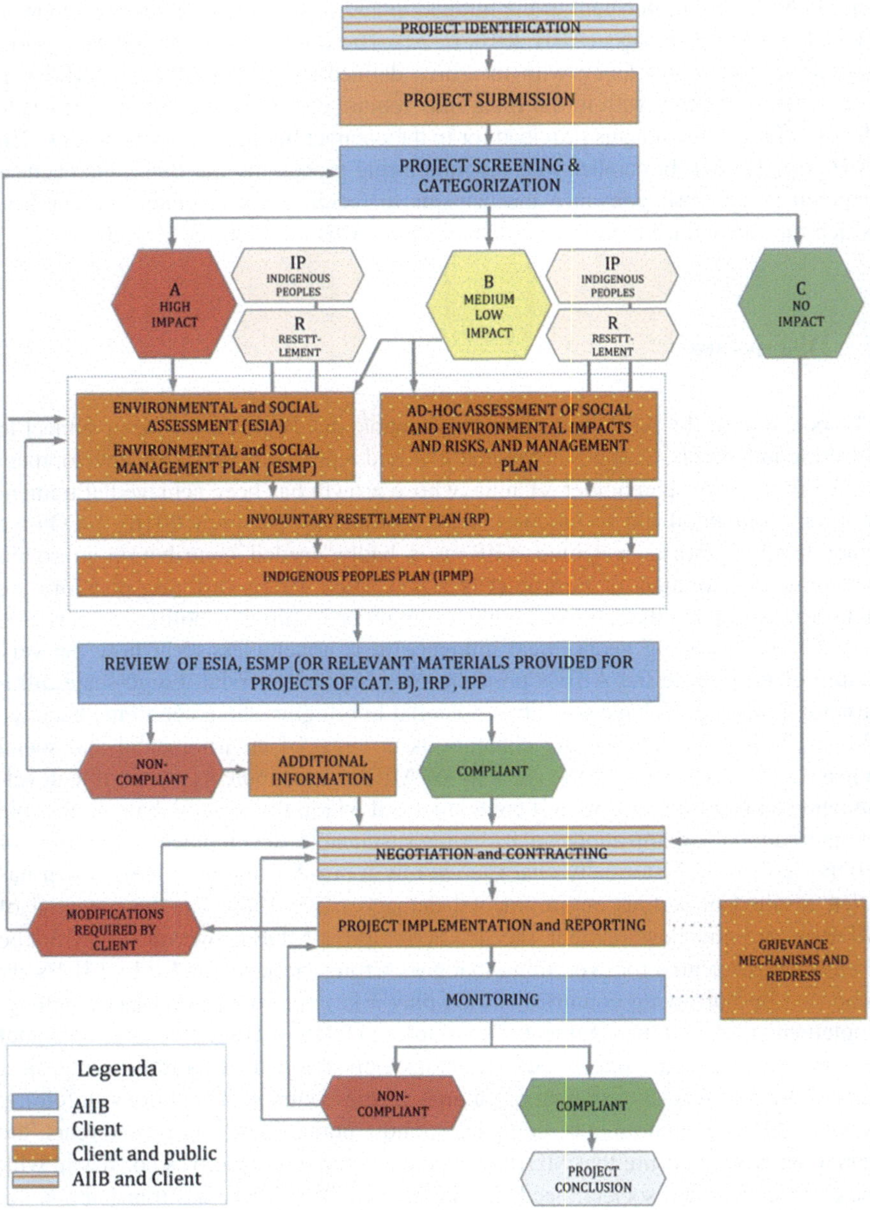

Fig. 3 Main steps in decision making process for AIIB projects (Author's figure, based on AIIB 2016, pp. 9–23)

approximate 8000 stakeholders and eventually produced a new environmental and social framework, adopted in August 2016 (WB 2012, 2016a, b). AIIB's ESF were born in this context. It should not be overlooked that AIIB's activities will be often carried out in coordination with other international organizations: out of nine projects approved by early 2017, six are to be co-funded by either the WB (four projects), ADB (two projects), and the European Bank for Reconstruction and Development (one project).[16] The need to provide for common rules of the game—or at least shared principles—has been recognized by AIIB and China. The Bank's ESF are consistent with international practice with respect to rationale, scope, sources of legitimacy—including the interaction with country systems, and decision-making processes. The framework also endorses core principles of integrated territorial planning that has been widely applied in international practice, often as a result of interventions made by MDBs. The logic of integrated planning, encompassing different dimensions of sustainability, is reflected by the wide scope of the ESF, both in spatial terms, and with reference to different kinds of impacts taken into consideration. Moreover, the attention put in establishing safeguards for vulnerable groups—relocated communities, indigenous peoples—is consistent with wider developments observed in the field. In recent years, awareness has grown among practitioners and the general public over the need to ensure inclusiveness of development projects, both in socio-economic and political terms. The ESF does not represent an exception in this regard, nor it does the ambivalence on political issues noted in Sect. 4.1. The possibility to use country systems to complement AIIB's ESF is both a recognition of the current state of development of environmental and social planning in the region, and an endorsement of the principle of ownership. The concept is well established in mainstream discourses and practice of development cooperation, based on the assumed positive nexus between greater ownership, strengthening of country institutions, and durable development outputs. This approach is endorsed also by other major MDBs (Estevens et al. 2016). As a matter of fact, implications of ownership for decision making has been subject to heated debate. The attribution to clients of an increasingly large role in ensuring project's environmental and social sustainability is seen by many observers as a Trojan Horse, which may introduce laxer social and environmental requirements for projects' approval. Critiques to the revised WB ESF focus on the fact that the Bank replaces "its own mandatory safeguards and accountability mechanisms with vaguely worded aspirational standards and an over-reliance on borrowers' national systems" (Oxfam 2015). Uncertainty and vagueness, both in terms of responsibilities and applicable standards, can in fact be found also in AIIB's ESF, as shown in Sect. 4.4 with reference to projects categorization.

6 Conclusion

Main features of AIIB's environmental and social safeguards are aligned with international practice. To produce outcomes consistent with a sustainable approach to development, the Bank therefore shares challenges similar to those faced by other MDBs. These difficulties are inherent to the logic of compromise which inform large

[16] In the case of Myanmar's Myngyan power plant, both WB and ADB are co-funding the project.

scale infrastructural projects: between different interests, value systems, perceptions of what may deemed desirable in terms of development, and understandings of sustainability. The decisional process outlined in the ESF provides the Bank with leverage on its clients. The framework could skew the balance towards considerations of social inclusion and environmental protection. Its effectiveness in promoting sustainability will depend from the Bank's political commitment towards institutional change, and its interaction with institutions in client's countries. The case study introduced in this chapter does not claim to be representative of the overall approach which BRI's key player—China—will take on sustainability issues. However, it does contain some indications worth considering in future research. BRI's socio-environmental implications should not be merely seen as a reflection of limits in China's development. Rather on the contrary, their appraisal should be grounded on the analysis of institutional contexts in which BRI's projects will be implemented. The debate on BRI has so far been characterized by a substantial Sino-centrism. This is understandable, since the initiative was rolled out by China's leaders. However, with reference to its environmental and social consequences, efforts should be made to focus more specifically on the interactions between funding institutions, clients, and local communities: this is the locus where BRI's capacity to produce a development tuned with sustainability will come to a test.

References

Arnstein, S. (1969). A ladder of citizen participation. *Journal of the American Planning Association, 35*(4), 216–224.

Asian Development Bank (ADB). (2009). *Safeguard policy statement.* Retrieved March 14, 2017, from https://www.adb.org/sites/default/files/institutional-document/32056/safeguard-policy-statement-june2009.pdf

Asian Infrastructure Investment Bank (AIIB). (2016). *Environmental and social framework.* Retrieved January 31, 2017, from https://www.aiib.org/en/policies-strategies/_download/environment-framework/20160226043633542.pdf

Asian Infrastructure Investment Bank (AIIB). Membership status (online a). Retrieved February 14, 2017, from https://www.aiib.org/en/about-aiib/who-we-are/membership-status/index.html

Asian Infrastructure Investment Bank (AIIB). Members of the bank (online b). Retrieved February 14, 2017, from https://www.aiib.org/en/about-aiib/who-we-are/members-of-bank/index.html

Asian Infrastructure Investment Bank (AIIB). Who we are (online c). Retrieved February 14, 2017, from https://www.aiib.org/en/about-aiib/index.html

Asian Infrastructure Investment Bank (AIIB). Our work (online d). Retrieved February 14, 2017, from https://www.aiib.org/en/about-aiib/who-we-are/our-work/index.html

Asian Infrastructure Investment Bank (AIIB). Approved projects (online e). Retrieved February 14, 2017, from https://www.aiib.org/en/projects/approved/index.html

Asian Infrastructure Investment Bank (AIIB). Proposed projects (online f). Retrieved February 14, 2017, from https://www.aiib.org/en/projects/proposed/index.html

Brombal, D., Moriggi, A., & Marcomini, A. (2017). Evaluating public participation in Chinese EIA. An integrated public participation index and its application to the case of the New Beijing Airport. *Environmental Impact Assessment, 62*, 49–60. https://doi.org/10.1016/j.eiar.2016.07.00.

Brown, K. (2017, April 16). Belt and road initiative invites interpretation. *China Daily*. Retrieved August 03, 2017, from http://www.chinadaily.com.cn/newsrepublic/2017-04/16/content_28950405.htm

Dorjsuren, D. (2010). *Environmental impact assessment system and transboundary context of Mongolia*. Paper presented at the 13th session of the UNECE Working Group on Environmental Impact Assessment, Geneva, 17–19 May 2010. Retrieved February 16, 2017, from http://www.unece.org/fileadmin/DAM/env/eia/documents/WG13_may2010/Mongolia_EIA_system_and_Transboundary_May2010.pdf

EIA legal framework. ELaw (online). Retrieved February 16, 2017, from https://eialaws.elaw.org

Environmental Justice Atlas (EJAtlas). (2017). *Tarbela dam, Pakistan*. Retrieved January 31, 2017, from https://ejatlas.org/conflict/tarbela-dam-pakistan

Estevens, P., Zoccal Gomes, G., & Torres, G. (2016). *The new multilateral development banks and the socio-environmental safeguards*. BRICS Policy Center, Plataforma SocioAmbiental, Rio De Janeiro. Retrieved January 31, 2017, from http://bricspolicycenter.org/homolog/uploads/trabalhos/7197/doc/1912915104.pdf

European Communities (EC). (1985). Council Directive of 27 June 1985 on the assessment of the effects of certain public and private projects on the environment (85/337/EEC).

Glucker, A. N., Driessen, P. P. J., Kolhoff, A., & Runhaar, H. A. C. (2013). Public participation in environmental impact assessment: Why, who and how? *Environmental Impact Assessment, 43*, 104–111.

Government of Pakistan Works & Service Department Peshawar (FATA). (2012). *Environment and social impact assessment of Federally Administered Tribal Areas Emergency Rural Roads Project (FATA ERRP)*. Retrieved January 31, 2017, from http://documents.worldbank.org/curated/en/966101468288636421/Pakistan-Multi-Donor-Trust-Fund-Federally-Administered-Tribal-Areas-Emergency-Rural-Roads-Project-environmental-and-social-impact-assessment

International Association for Impact Assessment (IAIA). (2015a). *Review of the World Bank 2014 environmental and social framework*. London Expert Roundtable. Summary Report. Retrieved January 31, 2017, from http://www.iaia.org/pdf/WB%202014%20ESF%20Review.pdf

International Association for Impact Assessment (IAIA). (2015b). *Social impact assessment: Guidance for assessing and monitoring the social impacts of projects*. Retrieved January 31, 2017, from https://www.iaia.org/uploads/pdf/SIA_Guidance_Document_IAIA.pdf

Karimi, E. P. (2015). *Environmental rules and policies in Iran*. Retrieved January 31, 2017, from http://www.unep.org/delc/Portals/119/documents/Iran-presentation.pdf

Kennedy, W. V. (1999). EIA and multi-lateral financial institutions. In J. Petts (Ed.), *Handbook of environmental assessment* (pp. 98–120). Oxford: Blackwell Science.

Kim, J. (2016). Regulating economic development: Environmental and social standards of the AIIB and IFC. *Harvard International Law Journal*, 21. Retrieved January 31, 2017, from http://www.harvardilj.org/2016/04/regulating-economic-development-environmental-and-social-standards-of-the-aiib-and-the-ifc/

Li, C. (2008). *Environmental impact assessment in developing countries: An opportunity for greater environmental security?* USAID and FEES Working Paper, 4. USAID, FESS, Washington, DC and Falls Church. Retrieved February 15, 2017, from http://www.fess-global.org/workingpapers/eia.pdf

Liu, Q. (2016, January 6). China needs to pave 'One Belt One Road' with green finance, say experts. *China Dialogue*. Retrieved January 31, 2017, from https://www.chinadialogue.net/article/show/single/en/8532-China-needs-to-pave-One-Belt-One-Road-with-green-finance-say-experts-

Ma, Y. (2014, December 5). The environmental implications of China's new bank. *The Diplomat*. Retrieved February 15, 2017, from http://thediplomat.com/2014/12/the-environmental-implications-of-chinas-new-bank/

Momtaz, S. (2003). The practice of social impact assessment in a developing country: The case of environmental and social impact assessment of Khulna-Jessore drainage rehabilitation project in

Bangladesh. *Impact Assessment and Project Appraisal, 21*(2), 125–132. https://doi.org/10.3152/147154603781766347.
Moorman, J. L., & Zhang, G. (2007). Promoting and strengthening public participation in China's environmental impact assessment process: Comparing China's EIA law and U.S. NEPA. *Vermont Journal of Environmental Law, 8*, 282–335.
Nadeem, O., & Fischer, T. B. (2011). An evaluation framework for effective public participation in EIA in Pakistan. *Environmental Impact Assessment, 31*, 36–47.
Netherlands Commission for Environmental Assessment (MER). *Countries and profiles*. Retrieved January 31, 2017, from http://www.eia.nl/en/countries
New Development Bank (NDB). (2016). *Environment and social framework*. Retrieved January 31, 2017, from http://www.ndb.int/wp-content/themes/ndb/pdf/ndb-environment-social-framework-20160330.pdf
Organization for Economic Co-operation and Development (OECD). (2016). *Applying strategic environmental assessment. Good practice guidance for development co-operation*. Retrieved February 17, 2017, from http://www.oecd.org/environment/environment-development/37353858.pdf
Oxfam. (2015, August 5). *Dangerous rollback by World Bank in environmental and social protections*. Oxfam International. Retrieved March 17, 2017, from https://www.oxfam.org/en/pressroom/pressreleases/2015-08-05/dangerous-rollback-world-bank-environmental-and-social
People's Daily. (2016, November 7). *Jian yi dai yi lv dai yanxianguo qincheng hui rong* 建一带一路待沿线国亲诚惠容 The construction of the One-Belt-One-Road awaits for mutual benefit and inclusiveness of countries along the route. *People's Daily*, 07 Nov 2014. Retrieved February 14, 2017, from http://paper.people.com.cn/rmrbhwb/page/2014-11/07/01/rmrbhwb2014110701.pdf
Perry, G. (2009). *Beyond lending: How multilateral banks can help developing countries manage volatility*. Washington: Center for Global Development. Retrieved February 14, 2017, from https://www.cgdev.org/sites/default/files/9781933286327-Perry-Beyond-Lending.pdf
Qing, K. G. (2015, September 1). Exclusive: China's AIIB to offer loans with fewer strings attached – Sources. *Reuters*. Retrieved March 21, 2017, from http://www.reuters.com/article/us-aiib-china-loans-idUSKCN0R14UB20150901
Rich, B. (1985). The multilateral development banks, environmental policy, and the United States. *Ecology Law Quarterly, 12*(4), 681–745. Retrieved January 31, 2017, from http://scholarship.law.berkeley.edu/cgi/viewcontent.cgi?article=1261&context=elq
Rivers without Boundaries RwB. (2016a). *Hope for Selenge and Baikal: Dam construction stopped, consultations planned*. Retrieved January 31, 2017, from http://www.transrivers.org/2016/1750/
Rivers without Boundaries RwB. (2016b). *Lake Baikal locals appealed to China's agencies*. Retrieved January 31, 2017, from http://www.transrivers.org/2016/1634/
Shaikh, A. (2014). *Social impact assessment*. Retrieved February 17, 2017, from https://www.slideshare.net/ArifShaikh11/social-impact-assessment-35420285
Simonov, E. (2016a). *Silk road strategy and public participation in development process*. Paper presented at the 20th Meeting of the Working Group of the Parties of the Aarhus Convention, Geneva, 15–17 June 2016. Retrieved January 31, 2017, from http://www.unece.org/fileadmin/DAM/env/pp/wgp/WGP-20/Statements_and_Presentations/Silk_Road_Strategy_and_Public_Participation_in_Development_Process.pdf
Simonov, E. (2016b). *Would ecological civilization take the silk road?* Rivers without Boundaries, 27 March 2016. Retrieved January 31, 2017, from http://www.transrivers.org/2016/1650/
Soong, J. J. (2016). The political economy of development between China and the ASEAN states: Opportunity and challenge. *The Chinese Economy, 6*, 395–399. Retrieved January 31, 2017, from http://www.tandfonline.com/doi/full/10.1080/10971475.2016.1207972
United Nations. (2015). *World economic situation and prospects 2015*. Chapter III. Retrieved January 31, 2017, from http://www.un.org/en/development/desa/policy/wesp/wesp_archive/2015wesp-ch3-en.pdf

United Nations Economic Commission of Europe (UNECE). *Espoo convention ratification status as a map*. Retrieved January 31, 2017, from https://www.unece.org/env/eia/ratification/convmap.html

Wang, H. (2016). Development banks. Opportunities and challenges for global governance. In M. Kahler, C. R. Henning, C. P. Bown, H. Wang, E. Voeten, & P. D. Williams (Eds.), *Global order and the new regionalism, discussion paper series on global and regional governance* (pp. 41–54). New York: Council on Foreign Relations. Retrieved January 31, 2017, from http://i.cfr.org/content/publications/attachments/Discussion_Paper_Series_Kahler_et%20al_Global_Regional_Governance_OR.pdf

Weiss, M. (2017). Asian Infrastructure Investment Bank (AIIB). Congressional Research Service, 7-5700, R44754. Retrieved August 04, 2017, from https://fas.org/sgp/crs/row/R44754.pdf

World Bank (WB). (2002). *Environmental impact assessment systems in Europe and central Asian countries*. Retrieved January 31, 2017, from http://documents.worldbank.org/curated/en/771381468749086135/pdf/300670PAPER0English0EIA0in0ECA.pdf

World Bank (WB). (2009). *Strategic environmental assessment in east and southeast Asia. A progress review and comparison of country systems and cases*. Retrieved January 31, 2017, from http://documents.worldbank.org/curated/en/385961468247268166/Strategic-environmental-assessment-in-East-and-Southeast-Asia-a-progress-review-and-comparison-of-country-systems-and-cases

World Bank (WB). (2012). *The World Bank's safeguard policies. Proposed review and update*. Retrieved January 31, 2017, from https://consultations.worldbank.org/Data/hub/files/consultation-template/review-and-update-world-bank-safeguard-policies/en/materials/safeguardsreviewapproachpaper.pdf

World Bank (WB). (2016a). *Environmental and social framework*. Retrieved January 31, 2017, from http://www.bankinformationcenter.org/wp-content/uploads/2016/07/third_draft_esf_for_disclosure_july_20_2016.pdf

World Bank (WB). (2016b). *Review and update of the World Bank safeguard policies*. Retrieved January 31, 2017, from https://consultations.worldbank.org/consultation/review-and-update-world-bank-safeguard-policies

Zaman, M. (n.d.). *Social impact assessment practices: Case studies of four mega-projects and lessons learned*. Retrieved February 17, 2017, from https://www.global-assembly.org/wp-content/uploads/2015/11/Zaman-Ideas_MZ-BKK.pdf

Zhang, R., & Shi, G. (2016). *Social impacts assessment for China-Pakistan economic corridor investment activities*. Retrieved February 17, 2017, from http://conferences.iaia.org/2016/Final-Papers/Zhang,%20Ruilian%20-%20SIA%20for%20China-Pakistan.pdf

Developing China's Investor-State Arbitration Clause

Discussions in the Context of the 'Belt and Road' Initiative

Shu Zhang

1 Introduction

Although many scholars have expressed their doubts as to the nature of investor-state arbitration,[1] it is now a popular option in investment law dispute resolution and has become a common component of BIT and other international investment agreements ('IIAs').[2] China is now the second-largest economy in the world and is an active player in negotiating BITs and IIAs,[3] most of which contain an ISA clause. China's foreign investment and economic cooperation policy has developed and shifted significantly during the last few decades, and recent moves include the

An earlier version of the chapter was published in The Chinese Journal of Comparative Law (2017, Vol. 5, Issue 1) by Oxford University Press.

[1]For example, 11 criticisms are identified in recent European research. See EFILA (2015). Criticisms include that ISA infringes the state's sovereignty and their power to regulate; arbitrators are manipulating the ISA practice and getting benefits by favouring investors; and that ISA is used as a weapon of the investors from Western developed countries against the developing countries who would like to attract FDIs. See for example Bernasconi-Osterwalder (2005), Chung (2007), Odumosu (2007), Eberhardt et al. (2012) and Van Harten (2012). These concerns, however, are to some extent addressed by others. See for example Brower and Blanchard (2014).

[2]See Reed et al. (2010). See also Höffken (2014), which refers to the generally positive understandings on including an ISA clause from both the EU and the US. Doubts in some countries, however, remain in many countries in South America and Pacific; see a summary provided in Trakman (2012).

[3]Salomon and Friedrich (2015).

S. Zhang (✉)
Deakin Law School, Deakin University, Melbourne, VIC, Australia
e-mail: shu.zhang@deakin.edu.au

W. Shan et al. (eds.), *Normative Readings of the Belt and Road Initiative*,
https://doi.org/10.1007/978-3-319-78018-4_8

negotiation of BITs with the European Union and the US,[4] the establishment of the Asian Infrastructure Investment Bank ('AIIB'),[5] and the Silk Road Economic Belt and the twenty-first-Century Maritime Silk Road ('the Belt and Road') Initiatives. The Belt and Road Initiative was first raised by President Xi Jinping when he visited Central Asia and Southeast Asia, and aims to "promote the economic prosperity of the countries along the Belt and Road and regional economic cooperation, strengthen exchanges and mutual learning between different civilizations, and promote world peace and development".[6] Promoting unimpeded trade and investment, as well as establishing mechanisms of cooperation among the members in the 'Belt and Road' region, are the key elements of this initiative,[7] in which the ratification and function of BITs and IIAs may play a significant role. It is particularly notable that risks to investment are significant in many countries in the Belt and Road region, and that ISA is a particularly important tool for investors to protect their interests in these countries.

This paper reviews the ISA clauses in China's investment agreements with the Belt and Road countries and regions, discusses issues arising from these ISA clauses, and evaluates the impacts of the current sets of ISA clauses on China's recent moves in international trade and investment, as well as its development of regional and global economic cooperation relationships. Section II introduces China's BIT and IIA activities, and ISA practices, focusing on the 'Belt and Road' region. Section III reviews China's ISA clauses in accordance with the time when they are signed and their scope. Section IV, V, VI and VII further discuss key features of these ISA clauses: the selection of institutions, rules and applicable law, the pre-conditions of submitting an ISA claim, the enforceability of an ISA award, and the issue of concurrent and transition of IIAs. Section VIII concludes by recognising the high degree of flexibility and divergence illustrated in China's ISA clause drafting and highlights the risks caused by such ambiguities and inconsistencies, suggesting that China should take initiatives in converging its treaty-making. It further suggests on the possible negotiations in which China may propose its new ISA clauses and converge its ISA arrangements with its 'Belt and Road' partners. A more predictable and consistent rule-setting for ISA practice, would contribute to, and be a part of, the development of China's inbound and outbound investment activities under the 'Belt and Road' Initiative.

---

[4]The 9th round of China-EU BIT negotiation took place in Beijing, January 2016c, see http://english.mofcom.gov.cn/article/newsrelease/significantnews/201601/20160101234801.shtml. The 23th round of China-US BIT negotiation took place in Washington, November 2015, http://www.mofcom.gov.cn/article/ae/ai/201511/20151101195891.shtml.

[5]China's role in AIIB, for example, see Wong (2016).

[6]The State Council of the People's Republic of China (2015).

[7]Ibid.

1.1 *International Investment Agreements (IIAs) and Investor-State Arbitration (ISA): China and the 'Belt and Road' Countries*

1.1.1 China's IIA: Developments and Features

Since its first BIT, the China-Sweden BIT (1982),[8] China has been active in reaching BITs and other international investment agreements in recent decades. According to UNCTAD, China now has 145 BITs and currently 111 of them are in effect.[9] In addition, China has recently reached many international trade and investment agreements, 8 of which include a substantive set of rules on investment.[10] China also made arrangements regarding its cross-border investment with Hong Kong, which also included a unique set of dispute settlement provisions.[11] The following chart shows China's BITs and other IIAs signed since 1982 (Fig. 1):[12]

China's activities of concluding BITs and IIAs are roughly divided into different phases by scholars in accordance with different versions of BIT provisions.[13] The first phase started with the China-Sweden BIT (1982) and reached its peak in late 1980s and early 1990s. During this period China reached BITs with most of the Western European countries, such as Germany, France, Italy and then with many other developed and developing countries around Europe, Asia-Pacific and South America.[14] The investment agreements concluded in this phase only covered limited issues and did not touch complicated or sensitive issues such as national treatment;

---

[8]China-Sweden BIT, signed and in force on 29 March 1982, http://investmentpolicyhub.unctad.org/IIA/country/42/treaty/976. Years of IIAs and BITs noted in this paper is the date of conclusion, not ratification, which suits the purpose of this paper of analysing the development of China's approach of drafting and negotiating IIAs (and the ISA clause contained in such IIAs).

[9]See http://investmentpolicyhub.unctad.org/IIA/IiasByCountry#iiaInnerMenu. It shows 145 BITs in total and 110 in force. According to MOFCOM, the China-Congo Democratic Republic BIT (2011) is now in force.

[10]These include the China-Australia Free Trade Agreement ('FTA') (2015), the China-Korea FTA (2015), the China-Costa Rica FTA (2010), the China-Peru FTA (2009), the China-New Zealand FTA (2008), the China-Japan-Korea Trilateral Investment Agreement (2012), the ASEAN-China Investment Agreement (2009) and the China-Pakistan FTA (2006).

[11]China Mainland and Hong Kong Closer Economic Partnership Arrangement (2017). Its Article 19 provides a unique dispute settlement scheme for investment disputes between investor and governments between Mainland China and Hong Kong. However, it does not refer to the investor-state arbitration, but only refer to administrative methods, mediation and judicial procedure, so this Arrangement will not be covered in the statistic studies in relation to the ISA clauses in this chapter.

[12]A list of China's BITs and other investment-related instruments, see http://investmentpolicyhub.unctad.org/IIA/CountryBits/42#iiaInnerMenu.

[13]For example, Dulac (2010) and Berger (2015).

[14]Some scholars further divided the first phase to two: first with developed countries (1982–1990) and then with developing countries (1991–1998). For example, Berger (2015), p. 845.

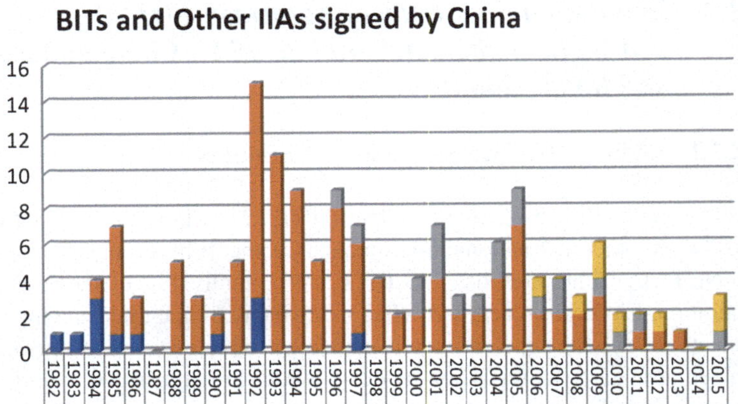

	1982	1983	1984	1985	1986	1987	1988	1989	1990	1991	1992	1993	1994	1995	1996	1997	1998
Other IIAs																	
BIT: Not Ratified	0	0	0	0	0	0	0	0	0	0	0	0	0	0	1	1	0
BIT:In force	0	0	1	6	2	0	5	3	1	5	12	11	9	5	8	5	4
BIT: Terminated	1	1	3	1	1	0	0	0	1	0	3	0	0	0	0	1	0

	1999	2000	2001	2002	2003	2004	2005	2006	2007	2008	2009	2010	2011	2012	2013	2014	2015
Other IIAs								1	0	1	2	1	0	1	0	0	2
BIT: Not Ratified	0	2	3	1	1	2	2	1	2	0	1	1	1	0	0	0	1
BIT:In force	2	2	4	2	2	4	7	2	2	2	3	0	1	1	1	0	0
BIT: Terminated	0	0	0	0	0	0	0	0	0	0	0	0	0	0	0	0	0

Fig. 1 BITs Signed by China (according to the dates on which the BITs were signed)

nor did they provide an expansive or comprehensive Investor-State Arbitration clause.[15] During this period, China also became a member country of the New York Convention and the Washington Convention, showing its friendliness to foreign investors.[16] The second phase started from the China-Barbados BIT (1998) in which an advanced version of investment obligations was adopted. During this phase, China concluded BITs with more countries around the world and updated its BITs with several major developed countries in Europe such as Germany, France, Belgium-Luxemburg, Portugal, Spain, Finland and Switzerland. The most recent phase started from the late 2000s, beginning with the China-New Zealand FTA (2008) and the China-Mexico BIT (2008). Treaties reached in this phase provide comprehensive provisions on investment obligations and dispute resolution, following the NAFTA country's treaty model.[17]

[15]Further discussed in Section III.

[16]The Convention on the Recognition and Enforcement of Foreign Arbitral Awards (New York, 1958); The Convention on the Settlement of Investment Disputes between States and Nationals of Other States (Washington, 1965). China signed the agreement to join in the Washington Convention on 09 Feb 1990 and such commitment entered into force on 06 Feb 1993. China's commitment under the New York Convention is further discussed in Section VI.

[17]Berger (2013).

1.1.2 China's Investment Activities and IIAs with the 'Belt and Road' Countries

As defined by the Chinese government, the 'Belt and Road' Region generally covers Asia, Europe and Africa; although the Chinese government has further clarified that the Initiative is open to all countries to join the regional economic cooperation.[18] This paper limits its discussion to 130 BITs and IIAs between China and its partners from Asian, European and African regions, a significant proportion of China's 153 investment instruments.[19]

China has been one of the largest host countries for FDI in recent years, with FDI of 133.7 billion USD in 2016.[20] China's outbound investment has also increased significantly in the recent decade, and was the second largest capital-export amount in 2016 (183.1 billion USD).[21] According to MOFCOM's report (which limits the Belt and Road region to several developing countries), since the initiation of the 'Belt and Road' strategy, China's investment in the 'Belt and Road' region in 2016 reached 14.53 billion USD.[22] The foreign investment from 'Belt and Road' regions in China also experienced a rapid growth in 2015, with the establishment of 2164 new enterprises (an increase of 18.3%), and investments worth 8.46 billion USD (an increase of 23.8%).[23] Till the end of 2016, the most favoured target of Chinese investors includes several Asian, African and European countries, such as Singapore, Netherlands, UK, Russia, Indonesia, Luxembourg, Germany, South Africa, Laos, Kazakhstan, France, Vietnam and the UAE.[24]

Countries covered by this research include 43 European countries, 36 Asian countries and 34 African countries. Among the 130 investment instruments we examine, 52 were reached with European countries, 42 with Asian countries, and 36 with African countries. A glance at the 130 investment instruments shows that most of them are BITs (121), although a few are FTAs or other investment agreements (9). The predominant role of bilateral agreements is consistent with worldwide practice in investment treaty drafting and negotiation.[25] The only two regional agreements were reached with ASEAN and Japan-Korea accordingly, showing

---

[18]National Development and Reform Commission, Ministry of Foreign Affairs, and Ministry of Commerce of the People's Republic of China (2015).

[19]A list of these instruments, see Annex A. There are some countries in the middle of both Europe and Asia and the categorisation of these countries is also listed in Annex A. IIAs reached between Mainland China and Hong Kong or Mainland China and Macau, as well as IIAs reached by Hong Kong and Macau with other jurisdictions are excluded from this research.

[20]See http://unctad.org/en/Pages/DIAE/World%20Investment%20Report/Annex-Tables.aspx, also UNCTAD (2015).

[21]http://unctad.org/en/Pages/DIAE/World%20Investment%20Report/Annex-Tables.aspx.

[22]MOFCOM, Investment and Cooperation with the 'Belt and Road' Countries in 2016a, http://hzs.mofcom.gov.cn/article/date/201701/20170102504429.shtml.

[23]Ibid.

[24]MOFCOM (2016b).

[25]A summary of the worldwide investment treaty making, see Kinnear (2015), pp. 10–11.

China's eagerness to maintain its peaceful development strategy within the Asia-Pacific region.

There are, however, some concerns. One is an observation that China's IIA drafting lacks a consistent pattern, or strategy.[26] It is also notable that, although there are massive numbers of BITs and IIAs, the effectiveness of China's treaty-making has not actually been tested given the small number of treaty-based disputes that has arisen.[27] Also, despite China's progress in opening the Africa market, 16 of 36 Chinese BITs with African countries have not yet been ratified, illustrating a significant risk for Chinese investors.

1.1.3 ISA Experiences: China and the 'Belt and Road' Countries

The volume of ISA cases is not large but has experienced a significant increase during the last decade. At the end of 2016, ICSID registered 597 cases in total and 48 cases in the full year of 2016.[28] There are many sources of investor-state arbitration: investment contracts; domestic investment law; BITs and IIAs; regional and international agreements, for example, the Energy Charter Treaty; agreements on a case-by-case basis, etc.[29] China's connection to ISA, however, is largely limited to its BITs and IIAs that include an ISA clause.[30]

Compared with the massive number of China's BITs and IIAs, most of which contain an ISA clause, China's experience in ISA practice is not extensive. So far China has been involved in only a handful of ISA cases: ICSID reports 5 cases brought by Chinese parties, 3 of which were BIT-based,[31] and 3 cases in which

[26]Berger (2013), p. 850.

[27]Chi and Wang 2015, pp. 869–898, 871–73, 898.

[28]See ICSID, The ICSID Caseload Statistics, Issue 2017-1, available at: https://icsid.worldbank.org/en/Documents/resources/ICSID%20Web%20Stats%202017-1%20(English)%20Final.pdf. The number includes the cases registered under the ICSID Convention and Additional Facility Rules, and excludes the non-ICSID cases administrated by ICSID.

[29]See ICISD's website, https://icsid.worldbank.org/en/Pages/cases/searchcases.aspx.

[30]China is an observer but not yet a member of the International Energy Charter (2015). There are however, some investment agreements made between Chinese investors and foreign states/stated owned companies. See for example, the two claims brought by Hong Kong investors towards Tanzania: ICSID Case No. ARB/10/20 and ICSID Case No. ARB/15/41.

[31]Tza Yap Shum v the Republic of Peru, ICSID Case No. ARB/07/6 (relying on China-Peru BIT); Ping An Life Insurance Company of China Ltd. and Ping An Insurance (Group) Company of China Ltd. v Kingdom of Belgium, ICSID Case No. ARB/12/29 (relying on China-Belgium and Luxembourg BIT); Beijing Construction Group Co Ltd. v Republic of Yemen, ICSID Case No ARB/14/30 (relying on the China-Yemen BIT). The other two claims brought by Hong Kong investors relying on investment contracts are not discussed here.

Table 1 ISA claims

Country/ Region	As claimant	As respondent	Claims from Africa	Claims from Asia	Claims from Europe
China	5	3	0	2	1
Africa	43	140	40	14	91
Asia	79	101	2	49	61
Europe	452	280	0	12	191

China is the respondent subject to its BITs.[32] In addition, there are two ad hoc arbitration cases brought on the basis of China's BITs (Table 1).[33]

Among the Belt and Road countries and regions, there is no doubt that the European countries are the most active users of ISA clauses. European investors have brought 452 claims in total.[34] Specifically, major Western European countries have played a significant role in bringing claims: Dutch investors brought the most claims (73) and were followed by investors from the UK (63), Germany (42), Spain (41), France (37) and Italy (35). Other European countries, however, are not so active: 28 countries have brought no more than 5 claims and 6 of them have brought no claims at all. Asian and African investors are generally not experienced users of this mechanism, with significantly less claims than the European countries—overall, 79 claims from Asia and 43 claims from Africa. A significant portion of them are cases in which claimants and respondents are from the same nationality, and these are actually claims brought by local enterprises established by foreign investors against their host country. Except Turkey (which is arguably a member of the European economy), no Asian or African countries have brought more than 10 claims.

Viewing these countries which have been the target of ISA claims, it is surprising that European countries have been the respondents of 280 claims, more than African countries (140) and Asian countries (101). It is particularly notable that claims against European countries have grown significantly in recent years; an example is that Spain has received 31 claims since 2012, all except one of which are still pending. Many Asian, African and European countries have limited exposure to

[32] Ekran Berhad v People's Republic of China, ICSID Case No. ARB/11/15 (relying on China-Malaysia BIT); and Ansung Housing Co Ltd. v People's Republic of China, ICSID Case No. ARB/14/30 (relying on China-Korea BIT); Hela Schwarz GmbH v People's Republic of China, ICSID Case No.ARB/17/19 (relying on China-Germany BIT 2003).

[33] China Heilongjiang International Economic & Technical Cooperative Corp, Beijing Shougang Mining Investment Company Ltd. and Qinhuangdaoshi Qin Long International Industrial Co Ltd. v Mongolia (relying on China-Mongolia BIT), UNCITRAL, PCA, https://pcacases.com/web/view/48, Sanum Investments Ltd. v Lao People's Democratic Republic (relying on China-Laos BIT), UNCITRAL, PCA Case No.2013-13.

[34] The calculation was made on the basis of the statistics on 24 October 2017. The number of cases and claims are collected from the ICSID website. When there are claimants from different jurisdictions, it is recorded for each different jurisdiction. Turkey is regarded as an Asian country in this research, although the uniqueness of its active ISA practices should be noted.

ISA claims, except 7 of them which have faced 10 or more claims: Spain (31), Egypt (30), Ukraine (15), Hungary (14), Romania (13), Kazakhstan (13), Turkey (10); 33 of these countries have never been the respondent of an ISA claim.

It is also notable that intra-regional ISA cases form the majority of all ISA cases. A predominant number of claims against European countries have been made by European countries (191 claims in 280 cases); a similar trend can also be observed in intra-regional claims in Asia (claims in 89 cases). Even African countries, which are traditionally considered as the main target of investors from developed countries, also have 40 out of the 140 claims from African countries. On the other hand, the frequency of inter-regional activities varies: while European claimants are extremely active against Asian and African countries, and brought 61 claims and 91 claims accordingly, Asian and African claims against European countries are rare; there are only 8 claims from Asia and none from Africa. Interactions between Asian and African countries in ISA activities are not significant: despite the considerable investment activities between these two regions, there were only 14 claims from Asian to African countries and 2 from African countries to Asian countries, as reported by ICSID.

Two conclusions are to be drawn from these statistics: first, most Asian, African and European countries have limited involvement in ISA practices. This is partly because of the late inclusion of the investment arbitration schemes, especially an expansive ISA clause, by most of these countries,[35] as well as the cultural reasons underlying the reluctance of Asian countries (including China) in getting involved in a formal dispute resolution scheme like ISA.[36] There is still a generally observed cautiousness in these countries in utilising ISA as their dispute settlement method. Secondly, a higher frequency of ISA claims is observed in intra-regional than inter-regional contexts, showing a closer connection of investment-related activities at regional level rather than inter-regional level.[37] From this point of view, a trend of convergence in ISA practice and ISA clause-drafting would be more likely to be achieved within a region. This could then be expanded to inter-regional contexts in accordance with the promotion of inter-regional trade and investment activities.

2 Three Generations of ISA Clauses: Change of Scope

Alongside the development of China's international investment instruments as discussed in II.A above, ISA clauses in these instruments have also developed, reflecting the change of China's position and policy-making. Roughly three generations of ISA clauses have been adopted, and the core features of these different generations of ISA clause are discussed below.

[35] Salomon and Friedrich (2015), p. 840.

[36] Nottage and Weeramantry (2012), p. 31.

[37] See also Salomon and Friedrich (2015), pp. 835–838.

Most of China's BITs (and their protocols) in the first phase included a simple ISA clause that limited the scope of arbitration as to a "dispute in regard to the amount of compensation caused by expropriation",[38] while others did not include an ISA clause at all.[39] The China-South Africa BIT (1997) signalled China's second phase of BIT-drafting and for the first time included expansive ISA clauses.[40] According to that type of ISA clause, "any dispute" or "any legal dispute" in connection with a covered investment can be submitted to investor-state arbitration. The first third generation ISA clause is to be found in the China-Korea BIT (2007), which for the first time limits the scope of arbitrable disputes to the breaches of BIT provisions. As the foundation of the third-generation Chinese ISA clause, the 2010 New Model BIT of China contains a tailored ISA clause that limits the scope of arbitrable disputes to certain types of breaches of BIT provisions. A more advanced version of this ISA clause can also be found in the ASEAN-China IIA (2009).[41]

China's BITs with Asian, European and African countries also follow this general track. In all BITs that are currently in force, almost all BITs made before 1997 contain a restrictive clause; and BITs made after 1998 and before 2006 contain an expansive clause. Among all 130 IIAs covered in this research, 74 contain a restrictive ISA clause, 65 of which are currently in effect[42]; 41 contain an expansive ISA clause, 28 of which are currently in effect[43]; 6 IIAs contain a tailored ISA clause that limits the arbitrable disputes to certain breaches of the IIA provisions and 5 of them are currently in force.[44] A few IIAs do not contain an ISA Clause or require further consent for submission of an ISA claim.[45] It is notable that there are exceptions of the general timeline: the tailored ISA clause was already adopted in the China-Korea BIT (2007) and the China-ASEAN IIA (2009), and the expansive clause is still used in many other BITs, such as the China-Mali (2009), the China-Malta (2009), the China-Switzerland (2009) and the China-Libya (2010).

For the first generation of China's ISA clause, which only provides for disputes of "amount of compensation for expropriation", there are concerns whether a preliminary issue of the existence of expropriation could be decided by the tribunal. In *European Media Ventures S.A. v Czech Republic*,[46] the tribunal referred to the

[38]For example, the China-France BIT (1984).

[39]For example, the China-Romania BIT (1983) and the China-Thailand BIT (1985).

[40]For example, China-Germany BIT (2003); China-India BIT (2006).

[41]Article 4, 5, 7–10 of the ASEAN-China Investment Agreement, signed at 15 August 2009, in effect at 1 January 2010.

[42]Among the other 9, 8 are terminated and 1 is signed but not in force.

[43]All the other 13 were signed but not enter in force yet.

[44]A detailed list of these IIAs and the types of their ISA clauses, see Annex A. The texts of these IIAs, see www.investmentpolichub.unctad.org and www.lawinfochina.com. There are four BITs with no ISA clauses and 5 IIAs whose texts are not available.

[45]For example, the China-Turkmenistan BIT (1992) and China-Romania BIT (1994) require further consent for ISA.

[46]European Media Ventures SA v Czech Republic, UNCITRAL Award on Jurisdiction, not published.

international law principles of treaty interpretation (such as the Vienna Convention) and interpreted a similar clause reached by Belgium & Luxembourg and Czechoslovakia in the Soviet Era as it was broad enough to allow the tribunal to decide on whether there was expropriation taking place before deciding on the amount of compensation resulted from an alleged expropriation. Such a decision was subsequently upheld by the English High Court.[47] However, international practices on this regard were not consistent; in contrast to the expansive interpretation adopted in the *European Media Case*, a restrictive approach was adopted by the tribunals in *RosInvest Co. UK v. The Russian Federation*[48] and *Berschader v. The Russian Federation*.[49]

Expansive interpretations have been observed in two China-related cases so far. In *Tza Yap Shum v The Republic of Peru*, the tribunal endorsed an expansive interpretation of the wording "involving the amount of compensation for expropriation" in the China-Peru BIT.[50] A similar approach was found in *Sanum Investment Ltd. v Government of the Lao People's Republic* which dealt with an identical ISA clause, which was subsequently upheld by the Court of Appeal of the Singapore High Court.[51] In the Sanum case, however, the High Court of the Singapore Supreme Court (the court of first instance in Singapore Supreme Court) adopted a restrictive approach.[52] In addition to the text-based analysis, Edmund Loew JC added several reasons supporting the restrictive approach: One was the communist nature of Chinese government (as well as the Lao government). His Honour commented that "communist regimes possessed a certain degree of distrust regarding investment of private capital and were concerned about the decisions of international tribunals on matters over which they have no control".[53] Also, the shift from the first-generation BITs to the second-generation BITs in China's treaty drafting might imply that the first-generation BITs intended a restrictive rather than expansive approach. Although Loew JC's opinion was later overturned by the Court of appeal, it should be accepted that his reasoning supporting the restrictive approach would also reflect thoughts and opinions in practice. It is therefore difficult to conclude, from both international practice and China's ISA experiences, that the controversy regarding the restrictive or expansive interpretation of the first-generation Chinese ISA clauses has been totally solved, and such a controversy will continue because of the existence of a significant number of first generation

[47]The English High Court, Czech Republic v European Media Ventures SA [2007] EWHC 2851.

[48]SCC Case No. V070/2005, Award of October 2007.

[49]SCC Case No. V080/2004, Award of 21 April 2006.

[50]ICSID Case No. ARB/07/6, Award of 7 July 2011.

[51]Sanum Investments Ltd. v Government of Lao People's Democratic Republic, UNCITRAL, PCA Case No.2013–13; Sanum Investments Ltd. v Government of Lao People's Democratic Republic [2016] SGCA 157.

[52]Sanum Investments Ltd. v Government of Lao People's Democratic Republic [2015] SGHC 15.

[53][2015] SGHC 15.

BITs between China and countries that are traditionally not active in reaching comprehensive investment agreements that contain an expansive ISA clause.

For the second-generation of China's ISA clause, which covers all disputes that relate to investment, there are language issues. Languages used by different BITs may vary from "any disputes in connection with investment", or "any legal disputes" that reflect the language of the Washington Convention. The generally broad language raises concerns that such a definition is too broad and therefore problematic as it may cause massive arbitration claims against the Chinese government in the future.[54] It is also argued that such an expansive approach is not consistent with China's Art 25(4) Notification under the Washington Convention, which also limits its consent to arbitrate to disputes over compensation for expropriation.[55] It is, however, the general opinion that the restrictive approach in the Notification would not negate the validity of China's liberalised treaty-making after 1998.[56]

The most recent generation of ISA clauses follow the features of the new US Model BIT and limit the scope of claims to the breach of certain treaty obligations. Even within this generation of ISA clauses, the scope of arbitrable disputes can vary. Among the 6 IIAs involved in this research, there are two approaches adopted: in all three documents between China and other East Asian countries (Korea and Japan), the ISA clauses generally refer to breaches of any obligations of states under the IIA, and only the China-Japan-Korea Trilateral Investment Agreement (TIA) (2012) lists two exceptions: matters in relation to establishment and maintenance of a transparent intellectual property regime and matters in relation to prudential measures taken in regulating financial services.[57] On the other hand, the ASEAN-China IIA (2009), the China-Chad BIT (2010) and the China-Uzbekistan BIT (2011) adopt the Model BIT's approach and list the IIA provisions covered by this ISA clauses: the China-Chad and the China-Uzbekistan BITs cover provisions including promotion and protection of investment, fair and equitable treatment, national treatment, most-favourable-nation treatment, expropriation, compensation for losses, transfer, sub-rogation, and any other commitment in writing made with investors in the form of agreement or contract[58]; while China-ASEAN IIA only covers states' obligations under national treatment, most favourable nation treatment, treatment of investment, expropriation, compensation for losses, transfers and repatriation of profits.[59] A more extreme variant of this type of ISA clause is to be found in the

[54]For example, Yanru (2006), p. 109, Chen (2006), p. 899, Wen (2013).

[55]Notification of 7 January 1993.

[56]Gallagher and Shan (2009), p. 331.

[57]See China-Korea BIT (2007), arts 9(1) and 9(5); China-Japan-Korea Trilateral Investment Agreement, arts. 15(1) and 15(2)(b) referring to arts 9(1)(b) and 20; China-Korea FTA (2015), art 12.12.

[58]China-Chad BIT (2010) Art 12.2 and China-Uzbekistan BIT (2011) Art 12.2.

[59]ASEAN-China IA (2009) Art14.1.

China-Australia BIT(2015), which only allows claims against breaches of national treatment to be arbitrated.[60] The tailored ISA clause suits the needs of different counterparties and is consistent with China's shift from a capital importer towards a capital exporter.[61] It is arguable, however, that the shift towards a more balanced investment policy could be achieved in this regard (given the small number of IIAs) with the tailored ISA clauses developed in the recent decade.

3 Selection of Institutions, Rules and Applicable Law

In terms of selection of arbitration institutions, rules and applicable law, the Chinese ISA clauses have also shown significant discrepancies. Both arbitration administrated by famous arbitration institutions, such as the International Centre for Settlement of Investment Disputes (ICSID) and the Arbitration Institute of Stockholm Chambers of Commerce (SCC), and ad hoc tribunals are relied upon. Among all 130 IIAs, 16 nominated ICSID as the only institution of ISA, and 66 only choose an ad hoc tribunal; 38 provide both ICSID and ad hoc tribunals, or transition from ad hoc to ICSID when some or both of parties become members of the Washington Convention.[62] The preferred mechanism also changes along with China's treaty drafting policies and was influenced by China's ratification of the Washington Convention in 1993. Most of the ISA clauses choosing only ad hoc arbitration are made before 2000 (62 out of 66); and ISA clauses choosing ICSID only or providing ICSID as an option only started to be used since 1993. In the recent decade (2006–2016), China included 2 'ICSID only' clauses and no 'ad hoc only' clause, but 13 ISA clauses that provides various options for investors, showing shift towards a higher degree of flexibility in China's clause drafting. In only one BIT (China-Madagascar 2005), a domestic arbitration institution of the host country is provided as an option.

In non-ICSID arbitration, the choices of arbitration rules also diverge. Early Chinese BITs provided that the ad hoc tribunal should form their own rules but could refer to the institutional rules, for example, ICSID rules and sometimes SCC rules; between 1982 and 1989, most of the ISA clauses choose SCC as the appointing authority and ICSID Rules as the reference (in 13 BITs); while after 1989 and before 1993, most ISA clauses preferred the same institution, either SCC (on 6 occasions) or ICSID (on 10 occasions), to be the appointing authority and the provider of procedural rules for reference. After 1993, ICSID played a predominant role in fulfilling these functions, and was chosen in 31 BITs till 2004. UNCITRAL Rules was not a popular choice in BITs made before 2004 and was only chosen

[60]China-Australia FTA, Art 12.2(1) and (2).

[61]See for example, Gallagher (2016), pp. 88, 90–91.

[62]The rest 10 IIAs are not available, not do not include an ISA clause, or do not specify the mechanism of ISA.

16 times in 98 BITs, but it become the default feature in all 21 IIAs that provided an option for ad hoc arbitration.[63]

Chinese BITs with countries within a region and within a certain period of time also show similar features in choosing rules and appointing authorities. For example, China's BITs with many central Asia and East Europe countries reached in early 1990s refer to the SCC rules and to SCC's role in the appointment of arbitrators, while such choice is rare in any other BITs.[64] It is uncertain, however, whether such a limited trend of convergence was initiated by China or influenced by its counterparties based on their similarities.

Applicable law is also a key feature in most of the ISA clauses. Among all IIAs, 87 of them have provided that the tribunal should decide on the substance of the case on the basis of certain international and domestic law rules.[65] Other IIAs do not specify the applicable law.

Regarding the choice of applicable law, options referred to by these IIAs include the provisions of the IIA and sometimes other agreements between the contracting states, the domestic law of the host country (including its conflict of law rules), international law rules and accepted principles of international law. Some restrictive ISA clauses only provide the option of the treaty or the domestic law of the host country,[66] while others provide more than one sources of law for the tribunal. It is particularly notable that different languages are used when referring to the principles of international law: while 28 ISAs refer to "universally accepted" principles,[67] another 38 ISAs emphasise the acceptance of the principles by both contracting parties.[68] This divergence starts from the earliest BITs and extends to the most recent FTAs and may create concerns as to what kind of international law principles are universally accepted, and what are accepted by both parties. In addition, a reference to "applicable principles of international law" was adopted in 13 IIAs between 1999–2005, although the "applicable" principles were not defined and would also add ambiguities in interpretation and application.[69] The recent China-Chad and

[63]This number includes the China-Sweden BIT 1982, the ISA clause of which was inserted by a protocol in 2004.

[64]This include: China-Armenia BIT (1992), China-Kazakhstan BIT (1992), China-Kyrgyzstan BIT (1992), China-Ukraine BIT (1992), China-Uzbekistan BIT (1992), China-Tajikistan BIT (1993). Most of BITs reached in 1992 and 1993 agree that the tribunal should refer to ICSID Rules or UNCITRAL Rules in setting their own rules, and refer to ICSID as an appointing party.

[65]Examples of this type of clause could be found in Gallagher and Shan (2009), 356, fn 223.

[66]For example, China-France BIT (1984).

[67]For example, China-Kazakhstan BIT (1992), China-Iceland BIT (1994) and China-Libya BIT (2010).

[68]For example, China-Italy BIT (1985), China-South Africa BIT (1997) and China-Mali BIT (2009).

[69]China-Bahrain BIT (1999), China-Botswana BIT (2000), China-Congo BIT (2000), China-Cyprus BIT (2001), China-Kenya BIT (2001), China-Mozambique BIT (2001), China-Myanmar BIT (2001), China-Netherlands BIT (2001), China-Sierra Leone BIT (2001), China-Cote d'Ivoire BIT (2002), China-Djibouti BIT (2003), China-Finland BIT (2004), China-Korea DPR BIT (2005).

China-Uzbekistan BITs provide a new version of applicable law clause, which respects the choice of law agreed by the disputed parties, and in absence of such choice, the application of the domestic law of the host country (including its conflict of law rules) and any applicable international law rules (including this IIA). Arguably, this is a more liberal approach than the earlier versions; yet all four types of language are ambiguous and may invite subjective interpretations by the tribunal and therefore create uncertainties for both investors and states.

4 Pre-conditions for Submitting an ISA Claim

Another common feature of the ISA clauses in China's IIAs is the pre-conditions for submitting an ISA claim to the arbitration tribunal. It is usually agreed that the parties should firstly request consultation and negotiation for a certain period of time. A requirement of 6-months consultation before submitting an arbitration claim is a common feature in 96 of the IIAs. The length of time varies in different IIAs, for example, 1 year in 5 BITs,[70] 5 months in the China-Bahrain BIT (1999), 4 months in 3 IIAs in East Asia,[71] and 3 months in the China-Finland BIT (2004). Many of those IIAs also provide that the parties shall exhaust the local administrative review process before submitting an arbitration claim, or provide the contracting states the power to impose such a requirement, with a promise of completion of such administrative review within a certain period of time (usually 3 months).[72] It is not certain whether such requirements should be purely procedural or jurisdictional, but a promise of the completion of such an administrative review would be likely to be an indicator of the relaxation of this requirement.[73]

Almost half of these IIAs also adopt the "fork in the road" clause and requires that a choice between domestic courts and ISA should be final. Two major types of such clauses are used: in early IIAs, it is provided that ISA would not apply if the disputed party has chosen the domestic court first.[74] IIAs since 2000 usually state that a choice between a domestic court and ISA should be final.[75] A shift from the first type to the second type might happen simultaneously with the transition of the first generation to the second generation of ISA clauses in China. There are however, some variations from these two types of clauses. For example, the China-Qatar BIT (1999) provides that a submission to ISA could only be made as long as neither party referred to the domestic courts. Also, 7 IIAs allow the disputed party to submit an

[70]China-France BIT (1984), China-Poland BIT (1988), China-Pakistan BIT (1989), China-Turkey BIT (1990), China-Syria BIT (1996).

[71]China-Korea BIT (2007), Japan-Korea-China TIA (2012) and China-Korea FTA (2015).

[72]China-Netherlands BIT (2001), Protocol Ad Article 10.

[73]Gallagher and Shan (2009), p. 338.

[74]For example, the China-Mongolia BIT (1991), Art 8.3.

[75]For example, the China-Bosnia and Herzegovina BIT (2002), Art 8.2.

ISA claim if they withdraw from a local court before the final decision has been rendered by the court; 6 of them are between China and European countries and one is between China and ASEAN, showing some extent of regional convergence on this respect.[76]

These clauses, however, are still different from the "no U-turn" clause adopted by the NAFTA countries.[77]

Despite the variations provided in China's IIAs in regard of the pre-conditions, it is arguable that these pre-conditions, if considered as a pure procedural matter, it might be easily bypassed by referring to a broadly drafted most-favour-nation clause and those Chinese BITs without such a pre-condition.[78] In order to impose a compulsory "cooling off" period, a stronger clause might be necessary for China's future treaties.

5 Enforceability of the ISA Award

Enforcement of an ISA award is a more problematic issue, although this issue is touched on in China's ISA clause drafting. There are several types of language used in these instruments illustrating that China has recognised the finality of the award and has committed to enforce the award, although no detailed mechanism is provided.

A reference to domestic law in enforcement of arbitral awards is adopted in 65 of the IIAs, becoming the most common feature. Particularly, it was adopted in most of BITs made before 1999 (the first-generation BIT).[79] Such a reference to domestic law has become less frequently used in the recent decade but is still found in the recent China-Korea FTA (2015). It is notable that, however, despite China becoming a member of the Washington Convention it has never promulgated a domestic law in fulfilling its obligations of recognising and enforcing a ISA award.

The enforcement of awards rendered by non-ICSID tribunals seems difficult in China in the absence of a particular domestic law. The New York Convention is referred to in several BITs as a possible solution, although its applicability to the enforcement of an ISA award is doubtful. The China-Czechoslovakia BIT (1991) provides that the arbitral award should be enforced in accordance with the New York Convention and such provision still binds Slovakia. Similarly, the 2004 Protocol between China and Sweden regarding the China-Sweden BIT (1982) states that the

[76]China-Latvia BIT (2001), China-Netherlands BIT (2001), China-Germany BIT (2003), China-Sweden BIT (2004 Protocol), China-Czech BIT (2005), ASEAN-China IA (2009), China-Switzerland BIT (2010).

[77]Such a clause requires a written waiver to be signed by the party before an ISA claim could be made. See Gallagher and Shan (2009), pp. 338–339.

[78]Gallagher and Shan (2009), pp. 334, 367.

[79]Particularly, since the China-Hungary BIT (1991) till 1999, most of the BITs provides that clause.

enforcement of an award by an ad hoc tribunal under UNCITRAL Rules should be enforced in accordance with the New York Convention. It is notable, however, that China has made the commercial reservation under Art I(3) of the New York Convention, and further clarified in the Supreme People's Court's Notice of Implementation of the New York Convention that the disputes of a "commercial nature" should not include the disputes between an investor and its host country.[80] Such commercial reservation was made before China's ratification of the Washington Convention but still stands as a bar of the enforcement of ISA awards in China.

Without the New York Convention or any applicable domestic law, the only rule supporting the recognition and enforcement of a foreign award in China seems to be the principle of reciprocity.[81] However, this provision only refers to an award made by a "foreign arbitration institution" and says nothing about an ad hoc tribunal[82]; it is also not certain that the application of principle of reciprocity in this context requires the recognition and enforcement in the opposite state of a Chinese award in commercial disputes, or of an ISA award.

Enforcement of ICSID awards is less problematic in China compared with ad hoc awards even in the absence of a specific domestic law, because the Washington Convention provides its own enforcement mechanism in its Arts.53–55, and further requires every member party, including China, to take necessary measures to implement the ICSID within its territory accordingly. China's commitment to the Washington Convention, therefore, might provide sufficient basis for the enforcement of an ISA award.

It is also notable that some more recent BITs only simply provide an obligation to "commit with themselves to the enforcement of the award" and no longer refers to a domestic law. Such type of clause became popular after 1998; among all IIAs, 32 adopted this type of clause, and 27 of them were made after 1998. Such a clause may indicate that obligations under these treaties may be considered as could be directly implemented in China without the assistance of any domestic law. However, the applicability of BITs and IIAs on this regard in domestic enforcement proceedings may not cover other IIAs that refer to domestic law.[83]

Another solution might be to adopt an approach that admits the direct applicability of international treaties in the recognition and enforcement of awards, including the Washington Convention and the BITs and IIAs. This solution could be established on the basis of Art 282 of China's Civil Procedure Law, which allows the

[80]The SPC's Notice in Relation to the Implementation of the Convention on the Recognition and Enforcement of Foreign Arbitral Awards, of which China Becomes a Party, Fa Jing [1987] No.5, 10 April 1987.

[81]It is provided by the Art 283 of Chinese Civil Procedure Law.

[82]Although in the practices in relation to international commercial arbitration, China now recognises the enforceability of a foreign award made by an ad hoc tribunal (see for example, the SPC's Notice in Relation to the Enforcement of Hong Kong Arbitration Award in Mainland China, Fa [2009] No.45), it is doubtful whether such practice would extend to the recognition and enforcement of an ISA award.

[83]As discussed around above n 79.

enforcement of foreign awards in accordance with international treaties, though this does not fully solve the enforcement problem. As discussed, IIAs are not like the New York Convention, which provided a comprehensive mechanism in relation to the court proceedings and a standard of judicial review in relation to the enforcement. Even under the Washington Convention, the enforcement towards a particular piece of property still largely relies on the domestic law and the national courts.[84] For both ICSID and ad hoc awards under ISA, it is suggested that the status and applicability of the Washington Convention and the IIAs should be further clarified in China either in legislation or in judicial interpretations, and the detailed judicial review proceedings and standard of judicial review should be provided.[85]

6 Concurrent ISA Clauses and the Transition of ISA Clauses

Generally, all IIAs provide that they apply to investment made before or after the entry into force of that treaty, or have a retrospective effect to investment made before it came into force. However, the parties may exclude certain investments and limit the time effect of the treaty. Forty five out of all IIAs made such exclusions. Such exclusion is meaningful when there are concurrent ISA clauses or transition of ISA clauses between two states, and may influence the investor's choice of ISA clauses when making a claim. Within the scope of this research, 13 states have more than one concurrent IIA with China,[86] and 15 have old IIAs replaced by new ones,[87] which makes the issue of concurrent and transitions of ISA clauses significant.

There are two categories of exclusions. The first provides the period of time when an investment made during the period would be covered. IIAs set an earliest date for a covered investment. These starting dates are usually made for political reasons,[88] and would not likely influence the application of an ISA clause in the situation of concurrent or transited IIAs. The second excludes certain investment disputes that arise, or being in the process of dispute settlement, before the entry into force of the IIAs. Three modes of language are used, as listed in the following Table 2:

[84] See Art 54(3) of the ICSID Convention. See also Baldwin et al. (2006), p. 5.

[85] Xiao (2011), p. 100.

[86] The ten countries of ASEAN, Japan, Korea and Pakistan.

[87] See the terminated BITs listed in the Annex.

[88] For example, the date referred to in China-Korea BIT 1992 for investment in China is the date of foundation of the People's Republic of China.

Table 2 Modes of languages used in excluding certain disputes

Mode 1	BITs shall not apply to any dispute which 'has arisen' before its entry into force
Mode 2	BIT shall not be applicable to claims or disputes arising out of events which occurred prior to its entry into force
Mode 3	BIT shall not apply to any dispute or any claim concerning an investment which was already under judicial or arbitral process before its entry into force.

Among all IIAs covered in this research, 24 adopt Mode 1; 3 adopt Mode 2; and 6 adopt Mode 3.[89] Among 15 states that have replaced old BITs with new ones with China, 4 adopt Mode 1, 2 adopt Mode 2, 6 adopt Mode 3 and 2 have kept silent on this issue.[90] China-ASEAN IA adopts a combination of Mode 2 and 3. It is noteworthy that all 6 clauses under Mode 3 were made between China and Western European countries during 2000s, and were made in dealing with the transition of BITs, showing some degree of convergence; but in general, there is no convergence among all these IIAs on this regard, as the clauses in other IIAs do not follow either time or geographic indicators.

Even though the different language used in these clauses illustrate the treaty drafter's intention in distinguishing time of occurrence of the disputes (Mode 1), occurrence of the events that cause disputes (Mode 2) and the time when the dispute is subject to judicial or arbitral process (Mode 3), such an intention may not be appreciated by the tribunals in applying these ISA clauses. For example, a clause which follows Mode 3 in the China-Belgium &Luxembourg BIT (2005) can be explained by the tribunals as to exclude its application to the disputes that have arisen and are brought to their attention by sending a dispute notice but not yet subject to an arbitration proceeding when the new BIT comes into force as illustrated by *Ping An v Belgium.*[91]

In this case, the dispute arose in 2007–2008, which was before the new China-Belgium & Luxemburg BIT came into effect in 1 December 2009 replacing the old BIT reached in 1984. Ping An only brought its claims before ICSID in 2012 and

[89]Mode 1: China-Sweden BIT (1982), China-Mongolia BIT (1991), China-Romania BIT (1994), China-Serbia BIT (1995), China-Lebanon BIT (1996), China-South Africa BIT (1997), China-Jordan BIT (2001), China-Myanmar BIT (2001), China-Bosnia and Herzegovina BIT (2002), China-Latvia BIT (2004), China-Tunisia BIT (2004), China-Uganda BIT (2004), China-Equatorial Guinea BIT (2005), China-Madagascar BIT (2005), China-Namibia BIT (2005), China-Portugal BIT (2005), China-Russia BIT (2006), China-Korea BIT (2007), China-Seychelles BIT (2007), China-Mali BIT (2009), China-Malta BIT (2009), China-Chad BIT (2010), China-Libya BIT (2010), China-Uzbekistan BIT (2011).

Mode 2: China-Ethiopia BIT (1998), China-Czech BIT (2005), China-Japan-Korea TIA (2012).

Mode 3: China-Netherlands BIT (2001), China-Germany BIT (2003), China-Finland (2004), China-Belgium and Luxembourg BIT (2005), China-Spain BIT (2005), China-France BIT (2007).

[90]Mode 1: Korea BIT (2007), Portugal (2005), Russia (2006), Uzbekistan (2011). Mode 2: Czech Republic (2005). Mode 3: See above n 89.

[91]Ping An Life Insurance Company of China Ltd. and Ping An Insurance (Group) Company of China Ltd. v Kingdom of Belgium, ICSID Case No. ARB/12/29.

based its claims on the ISA clause in the new BIT. The ICSID tribunal decided that the dispute was not covered by the new BIT based on the fact that Ping An had sent complaint letters to Belgium government firstly based on the old BIT (on 14 Oct 2009), and that both parties agreed that the dispute arose before the new BIT came into effect. It concluded that the wording of the new BIT did not provide that the broad ISA clause under the new BIT should apply to this dispute. Rather than relying on the specific agreement following Mode 3, the tribunal emphasised in Art 8.1 of the new BIT,[92] focusing on the point that the new BIT did not intend to include any dispute arise prior to its commencement date. This interpretation has been heavily criticised as it is a departure from the literal meaning of the Mode 3 type of transition clause, and the intention of the treaty maker illustrated by the differentiated languages adopted in China's three modes.[93]

Ping An v Belgium may remind the investors the risks in dealing with concurrent or transited IIAs even if there is a transition clause provided. It also reminds the ISA tribunals that, the interpretation of such kind of clauses in an IIA should be made with great caution and the true intention of the treaty makers should be understood from a context of the comprehensive treaty-drafting practice of the involved states. For treaty-drafters, it is also be a lesson that, while adopting various modes of clauses in different treaties would suit needs of different business partners, a detailed and precise language used in treaties and a consistent approach of using one particular mode of clause would be a strong indicator of its true intention.

7 Summarising and Commenting on China's Current ISA Clause and Its Network

A review of the previous major aspects of the ISA clauses of the 130 IIAs between China and the 'Belt and Road' countries suggests a high degree of divergence and flexibility in China's approach in drafting the ISA clauses. Despite of some significant shifts from old generation to new generation ISA clauses (for example, the scope of arbitrable dispute), a generally consistent approach that covers all or substantive aspects of China's ISA clause drafting is not observed. In many aspects, such as the preferred institutions and arbitration rules, the pre-conditions of submitting a claim, the enforcement schemes and the transition clauses, differences are significant in different generations of IIAs, and are also found among IIAs within the same generation. Also, there is much ambiguous language used in China's ISA clauses which allows subjective interpretation of arbitration tribunals, and unresolved issues such as the enforcement of arbitral awards. Even the most recent

[92]Art 8.1 of the China-Belgium-Luxembourg BIT (2005): "When a legal dispute arises between an investor of one Contracting Party and the other Contracting Party, either party to the dispute shall notify the other party to the dispute in writing."

[93]Ren (2016).

version of China's ISA clauses lacks some popular or leading features in worldwide ISA practice, such as the transparency of arbitration proceedings, joinders, the acceptance of submissions from interested parties, etc.[94]

Reasons for the diverged network of China's ISA clauses are multiple. The complicated history, the mixed use of different generations of ISA clauses, the rapid development of China's economy and inbound and outbound investment, as well as the lack of comprehensive domestic law governing China's foreign investment law and enforcement of the ISA schemes, have all contributed to China's complex nexus of ISA clauses. The complexity will consequently influence China-related ISA practice and create uncertainties and risks for the protection of both the Chinese investors' interests and China's power of regulating foreign investments, as well as China's reputation as a host country and its ability to attract FDIs in the future.[95]

This high degree of divergence and flexibility in China's treaty-making might suit the needs of different contracting partners, but at the same time leave massive unsolved problems for possible ISA practice in the future. Limited trends of convergence within a certain period or within a region on some aspects of ISA clauses are observed, but it is hard to tell if China, in the treaty-negotiations during the last few decades, have actively taken initiatives to converge its IIAs, or have been merely influenced by its counterparties.[96]

Another significant issue arising from the divergent network of China's ISA clauses is that, despite that China has adopted a few advanced features in its most recent ISA clauses, they might still need to face potentially massive claims arising from the out-of-fashion ISA clauses that exist in such a network. It would take significant time and costs for China to update its ISA clauses with each of its BIT partners, and before that, the risk of old version ISA clauses remains. Such risk includes the arguable expansive approach in understanding the scope of the first-generation ISA clauses that limit arbitration to amount of compensation for expropriation (as illustrated by the Sanum case), as well as the problem of the ambiguous language used in transition clauses (as illustrated by the Ping An case). Due to the ad hoc nature of ISA arbitration in general, each tribunal will have their own opportunity to review the particular language of the ISA clauses involved in a dispute, and inconsistent or even surprising outcomes would arise. Thus, the uncertainty in China's ISA cases cannot be easily eliminated under China's current nexus of ISA clauses.

---

[94]For example, the transparency of investor-state arbitration proceedings, see the UNCITRAL Rules on Transparency in Treaty-based Investor-State Arbitration, effective on 1 April 2014; United Nations Convention on Transparency in Treaty-based Investor-State Arbitration (New York, 2014) (the "Mauritius Convention").

[95]As provided by an empirical study, emergence of actual ISA cases will negatively influence the country's ability and reputation to attract further FDIs. Aisbett et al. (2016).

[96]For example, the influence of NAFTA countries such as Canada and Mexico might be the cause of China's most recent version of IIA. See Berger (2013).

These conclusions are particularly crucial in the context of the 'Belt and Road' initiative. For China and its partners in this region, their long-term economic cooperation would rely on a stable, friendly and advanced investment environment that strengthens their geographic advantages and enhances their joint economic competitiveness. Divergence of China's current ISA clauses may bring uncertainties and risks to investment practice. Lack of a comprehensive and consistent ISA clause network may be one significant restraint to the development of China's investment agreement and China's inbound and outbound investment.

8 Development of a Converged ISA Clause Network in the Context of the 'Belt and Road' Perspective: Possible Platforms, Approaches and Features

The urge for an increasingly convergent investment instrument is illustrated by the adoption of some new and advanced features in some recent Chinese IIAs. For example, similarities have been observed between the China-Chad BIT (2010) and the China-Uzbekistan BIT (2011), and the identical clauses adopted in the China-Korea BIT (2007), the Japan-Korea-China TIA (2012) and the China-Korea BIT (2015). Even the China-Australia FTA (2015), which is considered as containing an extremely narrow ISA clause,[97] followed the same model ISA clause and has some extent of similarities with the previous treaties. This might be a signal that China would take initiative to converge its complicated nexus of ISA clauses, particularly in China's trade and investment relationships with its Asian, East-European and African partners within the context of the 'Belt and Road' Initiative.

It is notable that, the convergent ISA clauses established in the most recent Chinese BITs and FTAs provide a more carefully drafted set of rules, and demonstrate a more balanced inbound and outbound investment policy. Including a carefully tailored scope of arbitrable matters, and the introduction of the transition clauses, etc. This is consistent with the significant shift of China's role from a capital-importer in 1990s to both a capital-importer and capital-exporter recently, especially in the context of China's trade and investment relationship with the 'Belt and Road' countries. It might be expected that the development of a more converged ISA clause within the 'Belt and Road' regime would suggest a shift of China's investment policy from openness and flexibility to a more balanced approach between liberalisation and regulation, which might serve the more comprehensive needs of the Chinese government in making its new investment policy.

There are now more than 30 agreements between China and the 'Belt and Road' Countries regarding their cooperation, declaring the positions of the governments,

[97]See Art 9.12 of the China-Australia Free Trade Agreement.

expressing the mutual understandings of a long-term collaborative relationship and identifying the areas of cooperation in the future.[98] None of these agreements contain a comprehensive scheme regulating rights and obligations in international trade and agreements.[99] Furthermore, China has not yet released any plan for drafting and negotiating investment or trade agreement with legal effects for the particular purpose of the Belt and Road Initiative. Thus, the convergence of China's international investment instrument and its ISA clauses would rely on its existing BITs, IIAs and its recent negotiations with other countries. Chinese government is always active in bilateral negotiations, but within the context of the Belt and Road region, it would take decades of time in bilateral negotiations in reaching new international investment instrument and in updating the existing BITs and IIAs with each of its treaty partners.

Therefore, it would be more convenient for China to utilise the current trend of regional developments of trade and investment instruments when promoting its consistent ISA clause drafting in the future. Negotiations of trade and investment agreements, including the ISA clauses they contain, witnessed the convergence within regions as illustrated by the success of NAFTA, ASEAN, and possibly the Lisbon Treaty for the EU, and the development of intraregional investment framework is considered as consistent with "flourishing intraregional trade and investment" in the last two decades[100] The focus is now moving towards interactions between regions: the proposed TPPA from between NAFTA countries and the broad Asia-Pacific,[101] CETA and proposed TTIP between the two sides of the Atlantic,[102] and emerging investment cooperation around ASEAN represented by RECP.[103] It is notable, however, that China, as well as many countries in the 'Belt and Road' region, is not a leading player of most regional level IIA negotiations and the practice of investment arbitration. The establishment of the 'Belt and Road' initiative might provide both China and the developing countries in this region to form their own

[98]The Xinhua News Agency (2016).

[99]For example, the Joint Declaration of the Government of the People's Republic of China and the Government of Republic of Uzbekistan (2016), the Joint Declaration of the Government of the People's Republic of China and the Government of the Republic of Belarus regarding the Establishment of a Comprehensive Strategic Partnership with the Understanding of Mutual Trust and Win-win Cooperation (2016).

[100]Salomon and Friedrich (2015). An analysis of the role of Lisbon Treaty, see Shan and Zhang (2010), p. 1049.

[101]Trans-Pacific Partnership and the US's initiative in leading the treaty-making in Asia-Pacific, see: https://ustr.gov/tpp/overview-of-the-TPP, Executive Office of the President (2017).

[102]The EU-Canada Comprehensive Economic and Trade Agreement, http://ec.europa.eu/trade/policy/in-focus/ceta/, The Transatlantic Trade and Investment Partnership, http://ec.europa.eu/trade/policy/in-focus/ttip/, European Commission (2017a, b).

[103]ASEAN's framework of and progresses in cooperation under the Region Comprehensive Economic Partnership, http://asean.org/?static_post=asean-framework-for-regional-comprehensive-economic-partnership and http://asean.org/storage/2016/09/56-RCEP_Joint-Leaders-Statement_8-September-2016.pdf, which affirms the possibility of a potential regional agreement on this regard Association of South East Asian Nations (2012, 2016).

platforms of investment rule-making and to shape the ISA scheme that suits their own needs.

It is uncertain, however, as to what regional or international investment treaty-negotiation platform would China choose, and to what extent it would affect China's future model investment treaty drafting. Possible options for China are many. According to Berger, China's current Model BIT is similar to the NAFTA countries' investment treaties in many aspects[104]; it is also argued that the next generation Model BIT might be significantly influenced by the TPP and the ongoing negotiation of China-US BIT, which would also be similar to the NAFTA countries' Model BITs. After the US's withdrawal from the TPP framework, many think that China might join it and even take a leading role, and may utilise this platform in promoting its regional investment policies.[105] However, it is notable that current version of China's Model BIT, including its ISA, is significantly different from the standard practice provided by the investment chapter of TPP in many aspects, including the definition of the scope of arbitrable issues, the transparency of arbitration and the acceptance of amicus curiae submissions, the application of the Minimum Standard of Treatment, the use of interim measures and injunctions, etc.[106] It would be a tremendously difficult task for China to either fit itself in this high-level ISA framework, or to persuade the other lingering parties of TPP to modify this ISA framework in order to protect China's own interests and represent China's investment policy in the new era.[107]

One additional multinational platforms for China is Energy Charter Treaty (ECT), which also contains a comprehensive ISA clause that covers all member countries. China is currently an observer to the Energy Charter Conference and recently signed the International Energy Charter (2015), illustrating its intention to deepen its collaboration with the ECT. One major reason for China's hesitation in joining the ECT, however, is the potential risks of being sued under ECT's ISA clauses, particularly after the famous cases filed by the Yukos shareholders against Russia.[108] Some Chinese scholars argue that ECT over-protects the investors and would create enormous risks for Chinese government.[109] It is argued that China's current ISA clause network based on BITs has covered most of the ECT members,

---

[104]Berger (2013).

[105]Kelly (2017).

[106]Chapter 9, Section B of the Trans-Pacific Partnership Agreement (TPP).

[107]The concerns regarding the high level ISA practice in the TPP drafts and its impacts to China, see for example, Gong (2013).

[108]Yukos Universal Limited (Isle of Man) v The Russian Federation, PCA Case No.AA 227. The award made on 28 July 2014 awarded the major shareholders over $50 billion damages, but such an award was quashed by the District Court of the Hague on the ground of lack of jurisdiction.

[109]Bai (2012).

and ECT's ISA scheme established 20 years ago does not exceed the comprehensive ISA scheme in China's current Model BIT, joining ECT would not significantly increase the risk of being sued under the ECT's ISA clause. Thus, it might be a convenient platform for China to converge its ISA clauses with the ECT members, and that would fit China's 'Belt and Road' map in particular as most ECT members are within the 'Belt and Road' region.[110] It is notable, however, that ECT only covers the energy-related investment, which takes a relatively small portion of China's current international investment but may increase in the future.[111] Also, China did not participate in the negotiation and drafting process of the current ISA scheme under ECT; in order to promote China's investment policy and its own priorities in ISA, China would need to be more actively involved in the negotiation and drafting of the next generation of ECT. Thus, regarding the convergence and advancement of China's ISA network, the contribution of becoming a member of ECT is limited in short term, but significant in the long run.

In the meanwhile, other regional negotiations and organisations are suggested as a possible platform for China's attempt to converge its current investment treaties and to facilitate the 'Belt and Road' Initiative. China is actively seeking leadership or a significant bargaining power in a few negotiations and organisations in different regions, including Africa—the China-Africa Economic and Trade Cooperation activities,[112] Asia Pacific—the APEC Meetings and the RCEP negotiation, and the East Europe and Central Asia—the Shanghai Cooperation Organisation (SCO).[113] As Africa, Asian-Pacific and Central Asia are all covered by China's 'Belt and Road' Initiative, and many of the countries in these regions do not have a significant leading bargaining power in trade negotiations, it would be convenient if China could utilise these regional opportunities to promote its own investment policies. The limited degree of convergence of China's BITs and IIAs within these regions, for example, in Central Asia and in Africa respectively, could possibly be a start of establishing a regional investment and ISA framework. Evidently, a general attitude of supporting and facilitating trade and investment cooperation within the framework of the 'Belt and Road' Initiative has already been observed in these negotiations, for example, in the Joint Declaration of 14th Meeting of the Government

[110]Shan et al. (2016), pp. 43–45.

[111]Ibid.

[112]It is generally considered that China-backed RCEP is competing with the US-promoted TPP in controlling the trade rules in the Asia-Pacific Region. See for example, Gantz (2016), p. 57. Also, achievements made by the China Africa Economic and Trade Cooperation, see Information Office of the State Council (2013).

[113]The Shanghai Cooperation Organisation (SCO) (2017). It is recognised that the creation of new models of economic cooperation among members in the context of the 'Belt and Road' Initiative should be one of the focuses of the member countries. See the Joint Declaration of the Councils of State Government Officials of SCO (2016).

Official (Prime Minister) Council of the SCO.[114] Although these platforms may not originally established for the primary purpose of promoting trade and investment partnership, communications at this level may result in some collaborative moves for the purpose of establishment of trade and investment treaties in the future.

Among them, many thinks that RCEP would be the framework comparable to the TPP framework and may result in a comprehensive regional model legal instrument of free trade and investment.[115] In that context, China's opportunity in the ongoing RCEP negotiations to shape the investment rules and influence the new ISA regime in the Asia-Pacific would be precious. China may take into account its recent FTAs with Australia, as well as the China-Korea BIT and FTA, as well as China-Japan-Korea Investment Agreement, all of which contains the most advanced version of Chinese ISA clauses. A more balanced approach in shaping the investment policy and the ISA scheme within this region and taking into consideration of the 'Belt and Road' collaboration, therefore, might be a good start. To what extent the outcome of RCEP would impact the worldwide international investment policy-making, and to what extent China's investment policy and the 'Belt and Road' collaboration would be considered, however, still depend on the mutual understandings among the RCEP countries, which are not easy to reach.[116]

A more flexible approach in converging and advancing ISA schemes, as suggested by Professor Gabrielle Kaufmann-Kohler, is the Mauritius Convention approach, which provides a multilateral treaty for parties to 'Opt-in' features of the ISA practice.[117] It is argued that this approach would be helpful for the acceptance of one or several advanced features of ISA, such as the rules in relation to transparency (as illustrated by the Mauritius Convention), or as suggested, regarding the establishment of a permanent tribunal or an appellant system. The flexibility provided by this approach is consistent with China's treaty-negotiation practice. It is doubtful, however, to what extent China would utilise the Mauritius Convention approach to converge its ISA clauses with its hundreds of partners. For one thing, the Mauritius Convention is promoted by UNCITRAL, which is a more neutral and multilateral platform than that led by a particular nation or several nations. Even if so, the Mauritius Convention is hardly a success as it is only signed by 22 countries and ratified by 3.[118] The other important thing is that advancement of the ISA scheme is

---

[114]Xinhua News Agency (2015).

[115]For example, Kelly (2017).

[116]For example, the countries might have different opinion regarding China's 'Belt and Road' collaboration; while New Zealand becomes the first Western country to reach the agreement with China regarding the 'Belt and Road' collaboration, Australia rejected China's proposal on 'Belt and Road'. See Morning Report (2017) and Smyth (2017).

[117]Kaufmann-Kohler and Potesta (2016).

[118]United Nations Commission on International Trade Law (2014), its status, see: http://www.uncitral.org/uncitral/en/uncitral_texts/arbitration/2014Transparency_Convention_status.html, retrieved on 10 November 2017.

still quite controversial; it is not sure whether China would prefer these advanced features in its current ISA practice at all. Insofar China has not yet actively moved towards the adoption of the Mauritius Convention,[119] and only mentioned the possibility of establishing an appellant system in one IIA, the China-Australia FTA.[120]

In addition, China's exploration for alternatives and different features in investor-state dispute settlement might also be considered as part of China's comprehensive and flexible approach in reaching ISA clauses in the future. For example, regarding the selection of arbitration administrators, or institutions, the Chinese arbitration institutions provide a new option by providing their own rules facilitating the possible disputes. In September 2017, China International Economic and Trade Arbitration Commission (CIETAC), the prominent international arbitration institution in China, published its Investment Arbitration Rules and standard Arbitration Clause, aiming to promote the development of ISA in China, and facilitate the 'Belt and Road' Initiative. In addition, the specific culture of emphasising the importance of mediation in China and East Asia[121] is also referred to in many occasions. Not only mentioned in the CIETAC Investment Arbitration,[122] but also the China Mainland-Hong Kong Closer Economic Partnership Arrangement,[123] referred to institutional mediation for dispute resolution. The promotion of a combined med-arb or arb-med model might be attractive to Asian countries. These developments provide that the future of China's ISA clause-drafting might be more comprehensive, covering more options, providing additional flexibilities and serving more versatile needs along the increasing and expanding investment activities along the 'Belt and Road' region.

After discussing these negotiation platforms and approaches in relation to the of China's ISA clauses, a few points could be addressed. Following the trend of moving from bilateral to multilateral agreements, opportunities of converging China's ISA clauses are seen in both regional and multinational contexts, in currently existing trade and investment negotiations as well as other organisations or platforms established for other purposes at governmental levels. China's decision of choosing from these platforms and utilising the ongoing negotiations, however, would depend on a few key factors: whether there are existing ISA clauses, and if so, whether and to what extent would China accept these clauses, including the advanced and controversial features; the flexibility provided by the existing framework, including

[119]Ibid.

[120]Art.9.23 of the China-Australia FTA (2015).

[121]Buhring-Uhle et al. (2006), Ali (2011) and Fan (2014), p. 777.

[122]Art 11 of the CIETAC Investment Arbitration Rules (2017).

[123]China Mainland and Hong Kong Closer Economic Partnership Arrangement (2017), Article 19.

the stage of negotiations and the 'opt-in' approach; the coverage of that platform and negotiation power of China within it, the culture differences or similarities with these partners, and the costs of actively promoting China's priorities in that negotiation. Considering all these key factors, a more realistic approach for China is to promote a comprehensive version of ISA clauses with flexible options and moderate features, which would facilitate its own balanced investment policy, and to obtain consents in some regional and industrial-specific negotiations, such as in RCEP and in ECT.

9 Conclusion

After more than 30 years of treaty-negotiation and treaty-related practices, it is a lesson for China that, although flexibility provided in the various IIAs suits the needs of different states and contributes to China's rapid growth of inbound and outbound investment activities, delicateness, preciseness and consistency in ISA clause drafting would be the foundation of a predictable and balanced approach of ISA practice, and fit China's goal of peaceful development in the future. As the second-largest economy in the World, China needs to, and should have the confidence to take initiatives in making its own voice in the treaty drafting in the future and make its unique contributions to the convergence of ISA treaty drafting and ISA practices at the regional and international level. On the basis of the observations and discussions made in this paper, it might be concluded that the 'Belt and Road' Initiative provides China such an opportunity as well as a platform to promote its trade and investment policy and to establish its preferred regulatory framework on ISA, which may have huge impacts on not only the 'Belt and Road' countries but also on the global economy.

In achieving further and deeper economic cooperation in the context of the 'Belt and Road' Initiative, a comprehensive, adaptable, and predictable ISA mechanism should be in place, and the unsolved ambiguities, concerns and risks arising from the diverged 130 IIAs should be eliminated. Taking into considerations of China's existing treaties, ongoing negotiations and its current needs for both promoting and protecting its inbound and outbound investments, it is suggested that China may utilise its current negotiations and cooperation within certain regions to reach some consensus, for example, the RCEP countries, the Central Asian countries, to shape and promote is next generation of ISA clauses with more comprehensive and balanced provisions. In the meanwhile, the next generation of the ISA clauses should also contain certain features and provide sufficient flexibility, so that it can accommodate the needs of both China and its partners in the 'Belt and Road' region. Such practice would not only serve for the promotion of economic cooperation within the 'Belt and Road' Initiative, but also provide the blueprint of the next generation of influential regional or even multilateral investment agreements (Table 3).

Table 3 Annex A: China's investment instruments with Asian, Europe and African countries and regions (Investment Policy Hub, UNCTAD and China Law Info Data 2016)[a]

Country	Region	Instrument	Year signed	ISA clause type
Albania	Europe	BIT	1993	Restrictive
Algeria	Africa	BIT	1996	Restrictive
Armenia	Europe	BIT	1992	Restrictive
ASEAN	Asia	IIA	2009	Tailored
Austria	Europe	BIT	1985	Restrictive
Azerbaijan	Europe	BIT	1994	Restrictive
Bahrain	Asia	BIT	1999	Restrictive
Bangladesh	Asia	BIT	1996	Restrictive
Belarus	Europe	BIT	1993	Restrictive
Benin	Africa	BIT	2004 (not in force)	Expansive
Belgium-Luxembourg	Europe	BIT	1984 (terminated)	Restrictive
Belgium-Luxembourg	Europe	BIT	2005	Expansive
Bosnia and Herzegovina	Europe	BIT	2002	Expansive
Botswana	Africa	BIT	2000 (not in force)	Expansive
Brunei Darussalam	Asia	BIT	2000 (not in force)	Expansive
Bulgaria	Europe	BIT	1989	Restrictive
Cambodia	Asia	BIT	1996	Restrictive
Cameroon	Africa	BIT	1997	Restrictive
Cape Verde	Africa	BIT	1998	Restrictive
Chad	Africa	BIT	2010 (not in force)	Tailored
Congo, Democratic Republic of the	Africa	BIT	1997 (not in force)	Restrictive
Congo, Democratic Republic of the	Africa	BIT	2011 (in force in 2016.6)	Text not available
Congo	Africa	BIT	2000	Expansive
Cote d'Ivoire	Africa	BIT	2002 (not in force)	Expansive
Croatia	Europe	BIT	1993	Restrictive
Cyprus	Europe	BIT	2001	Expansive
Czech Republic	Europe	BIT	1991 (terminated)	Restrictive
Czech Republic	Europe	BIT	2005	Expansive
Denmark	Europe	BIT	1985	Restrictive
Djibouti	Africa	BIT	2003 (not in force)	Expansive
Egypt	Africa	BIT	1994	Restrictive
Equatorial Guinea	Africa	BIT	2005	Expansive
Estonia	Europe	BIT	1993	Restrictive

(continued)

Table 3 (continued)

Country	Region	Instrument	Year signed	ISA clause type
Ethiopia	Africa	BIT	1998	Restrictive
Finland	Europe	BIT	1984 (terminated)	Restrictive
Finland	Europe	BIT	2004	Expansive
France	Europe	BIT	1984 (terminated)	Restrictive
France	Europe	BIT	2007	Expansive
Gabon	Africa	BIT	1997	Restrictive
Georgia	Europe	BIT	1993	Restrictive
Germany	Europe	BIT	1983	Restrictive
Germany	Europe	BIT	2003	Expansive
Ghana	Africa	BIT	1989	Restrictive
Greece	Europe	BIT	1992	Restrictive
Guinea	Africa	BIT	2005 (not in force)	Text not available
Hungary	Europe	BIT	1991	Restrictive
Iceland	Europe	BIT	1994	Restrictive
India	Asia	BIT	2006	Expansive
Indonesia	Asia	BIT	1994 (terminated)	Restrictive
Iran, Islamic Republic of	Asia	BIT	2000	Expansive
Israel	Asia	BIT	1995	Restrictive
Italy	Europe	BIT	1985	Restrictive
Japan	Asia	BIT	1988	Restrictive
Japan-Korea-China	Asia	IIA	2012	Tailored
Jordan	Asia	BIT	2001 (not in force)	Expansive
Kazakhstan	Asia	BIT	1992	Restrictive
Kenya	Africa	BIT	2001 (not in force)	Expansive
Korea, Democratic People's Republic of	Asia	BIT	2005	Expansive
Korea, Republic of	Asia	BIT	1992 (terminated)	Restrictive
Korea, Republic of	Asia	BIT	2007	Tailored
Korea, Republic of	Asia	FTA	2015	Tailored
Kuwait	Asia	BIT	1985	Restrictive
Kyrgyzstan	Asia	BIT	1992	Restrictive
Lao People's Democratic Republic	Asia	BIT	1993	Restrictive
Latvia	Europe	BIT	2004	Expansive
Lebanon	Asia	BIT	1996	Restrictive
Libya	Africa	BIT	2010 (not in force)	Expansive

(continued)

Table 3 (continued)

Country	Region	Instrument	Year signed	ISA clause type
Lithuania	Europe	BIT	1993	Restrictive
Macedonia, the former Yugoslav Republic of	Europe	BIT	1997	Restrictive
Madagascar	Africa	BIT	2005	Expansive
Malaysia	Asia	BIT	1988	Restrictive
Mali	Africa	BIT	2009	Expansive
Malta	Europe	BIT	2009	Expansive
Mauritius	Africa	BIT	1996	Restrictive
Moldova, Republic of	Europe	BIT	1992	Restrictive
Mongolia	Asia	BIT	1991	Restrictive
Morocco	Africa	BIT	1995	Restrictive
Mozambique	Africa	BIT	2001	Expansive
Myanmar	Asia	BIT	2001	Expansive
Namibia	Africa	BIT	2005 (not in force)	Expansive
Netherlands	Europe	BIT	1985 (terminated)	Restrictive
Netherlands	Europe	BIT	2001	Expansive
Nigeria	Africa	BIT	1997 (terminated)	Restrictive
Nigeria	Africa	BIT	2001	Expansive
Norway	Europe	BIT	1984	Restrictive
Oman	Asia	BIT	1995	Restrictive
Pakistan	Asia	BIT	1989	Restrictive
Pakistan	Asia	FTA	2006	Expansive
Philippines	Asia	BIT	1992	Restrictive
Poland	Europe	BIT	1988	Restrictive
Portugal	Europe	BIT	1992 (terminated)	Restrictive
Portugal	Europe	BIT	2005	Expansive
Qatar	Asia	BIT	1999	Expansive
Romania	Europe	BIT	1983 (terminated)	No
Romania	Europe	BIT	1994	Conditional-further consent needed
Russian Federation	Europe	BIT	1990 (terminated)	Text not available
Russian Federation	Europe	BIT	2006	Expansive
Saudi Arabia	Asia	BIT	1996	Restrictive
Serbia (Yugoslav)	Europe	BIT	1995	Restrictive
Seychelles	Africa	BIT	2007 (not in force)	Expansive
Sierra Leone	Africa	BIT	2001 (not in force)	Expansive

(continued)

Table 3 (continued)

Country	Region	Instrument	Year signed	ISA clause type
Singapore	Asia	BIT	1985	Restrictive
Slovakia	Europe	BIT	1991	Restrictive
Slovenia	Europe	BIT	1993	Restrictive
South Africa	Africa	BIT	1997	Expansive
Spain	Europe	BIT	1992 (terminated)	Restrictive
Spain	Europe	BIT	2005	Expansive
Sri Lanka	Asia	BIT	1986	Restrictive
Sudan	Africa	BIT	1997	Restrictive
Sweden	Europe	BIT	1982 (2004 protocol)	Expansive
Switzerland	Europe	BIT	1986 (terminated)	Restrictive
Switzerland	Europe	BIT	2009	Expansive
Syrian Arab Republic	Asia	BIT	1996	Restrictive
Tajikistan	Asia	BIT	1993	Restrictive
Tanzania, United Republic of	Africa	BIT	2013	Text not available
Thailand	Asia	BIT	1985	No
Tunisia	Africa	BIT	2004	Expansive
Turkey	Europe	BIT	1990	Restrictive
Turkey	Europe	BIT	2015 (not in force)	Text not available
Turkmenistan	Asia	BIT	1992	Conditional-further consent required
Uganda	Africa	BIT	2004 (not in force)	Expansive
Ukraine	Europe	BIT	1992	Restrictive
United Arab Emirates	Asia	BIT	1993	Restrictive
United Kingdom	Europe	BIT	1986	Restrictive
Uzbekistan	Asia	BIT	1992 (terminated)	Restrictive
Uzbekistan	Asia	BIT	2011	Tailored
Vietnam	Asia	BIT	1992	Restrictive
Yemen	Asia	BIT	1998	Restrictive
Zambia	Africa	BIT	1996 (not in force)	Restrictive
Zimbabwe	Africa	BIT	1996	Restrictive

[a]Sources of texts of BITs and IIAs: UNCTAD: http://investmentpolicyhub.unctad.org/IIA/CountryBits/42 and China Law Info Data: http://www.chinalawinfo.com/ accessed 10 September 2016. Armenia, Azerbaijan Cyprus, Georgia and Turkey in this research is categorised as European countries due to their close economic relationship with EU

References

Aisbett, E., Busse, M., & Nunnenkamp, P. (2016). *Bilateral investment treaties do work; Until they don't* (Kiel Working Paper No. 2021). Retrieved April 2, 2017, from https://www.ifw-members.ifw-kiel.de/publications/bilateral-investment-treaties-do-work-until-they-don2019t/kwp_2021

Ali, S. (2011). The morality of conciliation: An empirical examination of arbitrator "role moralities" in East Asia and the west. *Harvard Negotiation Law Review, 16*(1).

Association of South East Asian Nations. (2012). *Framework for regional comprehensive economic partnership*. ASEAN. Retrieved April 2, 2017, from http://asean.org/?static_post=asean-framework-for-regional-comprehensive-economic-partnership

Association of South East Asian Nations. (2016). *Joint leaders statement*. ASEAN. Retrieved April 2, 2017, from http://asean.org/storage/2016/09/56-RCEP_Joint-Leaders-Statement_8-September-2016.pdf

Bai, Z. (2012). *Research on the dispute settlement scheme in the energy charter treaty*. Hubei: Wuhan University Press.

Baldwin, E., Kantor, M., & Nolan, M. (2006). Limits to enforcement of ICSID awards. *Journal of International Arbitration, 23*(1), 5.

Berger, A. (2013). Investment rules in Chinese PITAs—Partial "NAFTA-ization". In R. Hofmann, S. Schill, & C. Tams (Eds.), *Preferential trade and investment agreements* (pp. 297–334). Baden-Baden: Nomos Verlagsgesellschaft.

Berger, A. (2015). Hesitant embrace: China's recent approach to international investment rule-making. *Journal of World Investment and Trade, 16*, 843, 845.

Bernasconi-Osterwalder, N. (2005). Who wins and who loses in investment arbitration? Are investors and host states on a level playing field? The Lauder/Czech Republic legacy. *Journal of World Investment and Trade, 6*(1), 69–71.

Brower, C. N., & Blanchard, S. (2014). What's in a Meme? The truth about investor-state arbitration: Why it need not, and must not, be repossessed by states. *Columbia Journal of Transnational Law, 52*, 689–779.

Buhring-Uhle, C., Kirchhoff, L., & Scherer, G. (2006). *Arbitration and mediation in international business* (2nd ed.). New York: Kluwer Law International.

Chen, A. (2006). Should the four great safeguards in Sino-foreign BITs be hastily dismantled? Comments on provisions concerning dispute settlement in model US and Canada BITs. *Journal of World Investment and Trade, 7*, 899.

Chi, M., & Wang, X. (2015). The evolution of ISA clauses in Chinese IIAs and its practical implications. *Journal of World Investment and Trade, 16*, 869–898.

Chung, O. (2007). The lopsided international investment law regime and its effect on the future of investor-state arbitration. *Virginia Journal of International Law, 47*(4), 953–976.

Dulac, E. (2010). The emerging third generation of Chinese investment treaties. *Transnational Dispute Management, 7*(4), 1.

Eberhardt, P., Olivet, C., Amos, T., & Buxton, N. (2012). *Profiting from Injustice: How law firms, arbitrators and financiers are fuelling an investment arbitration boom*. Corporate Europe Observatory (CEO). Retrieved April 2, 2017, from http://corporateeurope.org/sites/default/files/publications/profiting-from-injustice.pdf

European Commission. (2017a). *The EU-Canada Comprehensive Economic and Trade Agreement*. EC. Retrieved April 2, 2017, from http://ec.europa.eu/trade/policy/in-focus/ceta/

European Commission. (2017b). *The transatlantic trade and investment partnership*. EC. Retrieved April 2, 2017, from http://ec.europa.eu/trade/policy/in-focus/ttip/

European Federation for Investment Law and Arbitration. (2015). *A response to the criticism against ISDS*. EFILA. Retrieved April 2, 2017, from http://efila.org/wp-content/uploads/2015/05/EFILA_in_response_to_the-criticism_of_ISDS_final_draft.pdf

Executive Office of the President. (2017). Trans-Pacific Partnership and the US's initiative in leading the treaty-making in Asia-Pacific. Office of the United States Trade Representative. Retrieved April 2, 2017, from https://ustr.gov/tpp/overview-of-the-TPP

Fan, K. (2014). An empirical study of arbitrators acting as mediators in China. *Cardozo Journal of Conflict Resolution*, 15, 777.

Gallagher, N. (2016). Role of China in investment: BITs, SOEs, private enterprises, and evolution of policy. *ICSID Review, 31*(1), 88, 90–91.

Gallagher, N., & Shan, W. (2009). *Chinese investment treaties: Policies and practice* (p. 331). Oxford: The Oxford University Press.

Gantz, D. (2016). The TPP and RCEP: Mega-Trade Agreements for the Pacific Rim. *Arizona Journal of International and Comparative Law, 33*, 57.

Gong, B. (2013). Commentary on the investor-state dispute settlement scheme in the TPP agreement. *World Trade Organization Focus, 1*. (in Chinese).

Harten, G. V. (2012). Arbitrator behaviour in asymmetrical adjudication: An empirical study of investment treaty arbitration. *Osgoode Hall Law Journal, 50*(1), 211–268.

Hela Schwarz GmbH v People's Republic of China, ICSID Case No.ARB/17/19 (relying on China-Germany BIT 2003).

Höffken, J. (2014). Global policy, more than regional investment protection – ISDS in the EU-US trade agreement. *Global Policy Journal*. Retrieved April 2, 2017, from http://www.globalpolicyjournal.com/blog/08/05/2014/more-regionalinvestment-protection-%E2%80%93-isds-eu-us-trade-agreement

Information Office of the State Council, China-Africa Economic and Trade Cooperation. (2013). Retrieved April 2, 2017, from http://news.xinhuanet.com/english/china/2013-08/29/c_132673093.htm

International Energy Charter. (2015). Retrieved April 2, 2017, from http://www.energycharter.org/who-we-are/members-observers/countries/china/

Jing, F. (1987). The SPC's Notice in Relation to the Implementation of the Convention on the Recognition and Enforcement of Foreign Arbitral Awards, of which China Becomes a Party, No. 5.

Kaufmann-Kohler, G., & Potesta, M. (2016). Can the Mauritius Convention serve as a model for the reform of investor-State arbitration in connection with the introduction of a permanent investment tribunal or an appeal mechanism: Analysis and roadmap. *Geneva Center for International Dispute Settlement*. Retrieved April 2, 2017, from http://www.uncitral.org/pdf/english/CIDS_Research_Paper_Mauritius.pdf

Kelly, J. (2017). Malcolm Turnbull opens door to China to join TPP after Donald Trump pulls out. *The Australian*. Retrieved April 2, 2017, from http://www.theaustralian.com.au/national-affairs/malcolm-turnbull-opens-door-to-china-to-join-tpp-after-donald-trump-pulls-out/news-story/3852ae4996049d18a15925c6f19a0882

Kinnear, M. (2015). ICSID and international investment treaty arbitration: Progress and prospects. In W. Shan & J. Su (Eds.), *China and international investment law: Twenty years of ICSID membership* (pp. 9–22). Leiden: Brill Nijhoff.

Ministry of Commerce, People's Republic of China. (2015). *The 23th round of China-US BIT negotiation*. MOFCOM. Retrieved April 2, 2017, from http://www.mofcom.gov.cn/article/ae/ai/201511/20151101195891.shtml

Ministry of Commerce, People's Republic of China. (2016a). *Investment and Cooperation with the 'Belt and Road' Countries in 2016*. MOFCOM. Retrieved April 2, 2017, from http://hzs.mofcom.gov.cn/article/date/201701/20170102504429.shtml

Ministry of Commerce, People's Republic of China. (2016b). *National Bureau of Statistics and State Administration of Foreign Exchange, Report on China's Foreign Direct Investment*. MOFCOM. Retrieved October 24, 2017, from http://fec.mofcom.gov.cn/article/tjsj/tjgb/201709/20170902653690.shtml

Ministry of Commerce, People's Republic of China. (2016c). *The 9th round of China-EU BIT Negotiations*. MOFCOM. Retrieved April 2, 2017, from http://english.mofcom.gov.cn/article/newsrelease/significantnews/201601/20160101234801.shtml

Morning Report. (2017). Belt & Road initiative could be huge opportunity for NZ. *Radio NZ*. Retrieved April 2, 2017, from http://www.radionz.co.nz/national/programmes/morningreport/audio/201838213/belt-and-road-initiative-could-be-huge-opportunity-for-nz

Nottage, L., & Weeramantry, J. (2012). Investment arbitration in Asia: Five perspectives on law and practice. *Arbitration International, 28*(1), 19–62.

Odumosu, I. (2007). The antinomies of the (continued) relevance of ICSID to the third world. *San Diego International Law Journal, 8*(2), 345–386.

Reed, L., Paulsson, J., & Blackaby, N. (2010). *Guide to ICSID arbitration* (pp. 6–7, 57). Austin: Kluwer Law International.

Ren, Q. (2016). Case comment on ping An v Belgium: Temporal jurisdiction of successive BITs. *ICSID Review,* 1.

Salomon, C., & Friedrich, S. (2015). A statistical analysis of bilateral investment treaties, other international investment agreements and investment arbitrations in the region. *Journal of World Investment and Trade, 16*(5–6), 800–842.

Shan, W., Wang, P., & Wang, H. (2016). The cost-benefit analysis of China being a member of the energy charter treaty in the context of the belt and road initiative. *Chinese Review of International Law, 1*, 39, 43–45.

Shan, W., & Zhang, S. (2010). The treaty of Lisbon: Half way toward a common investment policy. *European Journal of International Law, 21*(4), 1049.

Smyth, J. (2017). Australia rejects China push on Silk Road strategy. *Financial Times*. Retrieved April 2, 2017, from https://www.ft.com/content/e30f3122-0eae-11e7-b030-768954394623

The ICSID Caseload Statistics. Issue 2017-1. Retrieved April 2, 2017, from https://icsid.worldbank.org/en/Documents/resources/ICSID%20Web%20Stats%202017-1%20(English)%20Final.pdf

The Shanghai Cooperation Organization. (2017). Retrieved April 2, 2017, from http://www.cfr.org/china/shanghai-cooperation-organization/p10883

The State Council of the People's Republic of China (with the National Development and Reform Commission, Ministry of Foreign Affairs and Ministry of Commerce of the People's Republic of China). (2015). *Action plan on the belt and road initiative*. The State Council of the PRC (with the National Development and Reform Commission, Ministry of Foreign Affairs and Ministry of Commerce of the PRC). Retrieved April 2, 2017, from http://english.gov.cn/archive/publications/2015/03/30/content_281475080249035.htm

Trakman, L. (2012). Choosing domestic courts over investor-state arbitration: Australia's repudiation of the Status Quo. *UNSW Law Journal, 35*(3), 979–1012.

United Nations Commission on International Trade Law. (2014). *Status of the Mauritius Convention*. UNCTAD. Retrieved April 2, 2017, from http://www.uncitral.org/uncitral/en/uncitral_texts/arbitration/2014Transparency_Convention_status.html

United Nations Conference of Trade and Development. (2015). *World Investment Report*. UNCTAD. Retrieved October 24, 2017, from http://unctad.org/en/PublicationsLibrary/wir20156_en.pdf

Wen, X. (2013). Commentary on China's model BIT draft: Part III. *Journal of International Economic Law, 19*(2), (in Chinese).

Wong, S. L. (2016). *China launches new AIIB development bank as power balance shifts*. Reuters. Retrieved April 2, 2017, from http://www.reuters.com/article/us-asia-aiib-investment-idUSKCN0UU03Y

Xiao, F. (2011). Recognition and enforcement of the international investment arbitration award in China. *The Jurist, 6*, 94–107. (in Chinese).

Xinhua News Agency. (2015). Retrieved April 2, 2017, from http://www.gov.cn/xinwen/2015-12/15/content_5024468.htm

Xinhua News Agency. (2016). *China has signed governmental-level cooperation agreements on the 'Belt and Road' initiative with more than 30 countries*. XNA. Retrieved April 2, 2017, from http://news.xinhuanet.com/world/2016-09/26/c_1119627176.htm
Yanru, W. (2006). On the impropriety of China's recent complete acceptance of ICSID jurisdiction. *Chinese Journal of International Economic Law, 13*(1), 109.
Yukos Universal Limited (Isle of Man) v The Russian Federation, PCA Case No. AA 227.

On the Environmental Responsibility of Chinese Enterprises for Their FDIs in Countries Within the Belt and Road Initiative

Desheng Hu, Jun Ou, and Xueyue Hu

1 Introduction

The Belt and Road Initiative (BRI) proposed by Chinese President Xi Jinping in 2013 is not only an 'action plan' or a 'development strategy' for China but also a 'cooperation initiative' for the international community. The key objectives of the BRI include the 'four core concepts' (peace, cooperation, development, and mutual benefit), the 'five cooperative priorities' (policy coordination, facilities connectivity, unimpeded trade, financial integration, and people-to-people bonds), and the 'three communities' (shared interests community, human destiny community, and responsibility community).[1] The 2015 'Vision and Actions on Jointly Building a Silk Road Economic Belt and a 21st Century Maritime Silk Road', which was issued by the Chinese government, clearly indicates that the jointly built new Silk Road is going to be a green one.[2] It also proposes to enhance cooperation in the fields of environmental protection, biodiversity, and climate change while requiring Chinese

---

The chapter was published in The Chinese Journal of Comparative Law (2017, Vol. 5, Issue 1) by Oxford University Press.

[1]See Liu (2014), pp. 538–544.

[2]The Vision and Actions on Jointly Building Road and Belt Initiative was jointly issued on 28 March 2015 by the National Development and Reform Commission (NDRC), the Ministry of Foreign Affairs, and the Ministry of Commerce (MOFCOM) under authorization from the State

D. Hu (✉)
Law School, Silk Road Institute for International and Comparative Law, Xi'an Jiaotong University, Xi'an, China

J. Ou
Law School, Xi'an Jiaotong University, Xi'an, China

X. Hu
Department of Geography and Environment, London School of Economics and Political Science, London, UK

W. Shan et al. (eds.), *Normative Readings of the Belt and Road Initiative*,
https://doi.org/10.1007/978-3-319-78018-4_9

enterprises investing in other Belt and Road (BR) countries (including various regions) to highlight the concept of ecological civilization. This is the key to embedding the concept of green development into China's comprehensive national strength and international competitive advantage.[3]

Environmental protection is to provide public goods, on the one hand. Diversity of participation and collaboration is necessary for achieving this from the perspective of good governance. The issue of environmental responsibility arises from the negative repercussions of industrial production activity. On the other hand, growing concerns about the environment have been changing the perception of the responsibility of multinational companies, particularly for their FDIs.[4] Therefore, examining and dealing with environmental responsibilities arising from Chinese FDIs in other BR countries is vital for making them green. This article discusses environmental responsibility determination and intends to propose potential and practical solutions to this issue. This article intends to innovatively contribute to this field of study by: (1) developing a theoretical dimension by incorporating FDI development transition, green development, and good environmental governance; (2) discussing environmental responsibility determination; and (3) proposing possible solutions that could be useful references for governmental bodies, enterprises, and tribunals.

2 FDI and Environmental Protection Issues

2.1 FDI of Chinese Enterprises in Other BR Countries

The implementation of the reform and opening-up policy since the late 1970s has been making China a vigorous participant in the world economy. China has transformed itself from simply 'bringing in' to 'bringing in' and 'going out' and is now one of the largest FDI recipient countries as well as one of the biggest FDI outflow countries.[5] On the one hand, this accomplishment demonstrates that China has the ability to operate and compete internationally, while, on the other hand, it characterizes the significant change in China's development pattern in both its economy and society. China's overseas investment is positively correlated with its international trade, market size, economic growth, opening-up level, and natural resources.[6] Through outward FDIs, China has significantly increased its position in the global value chain. Major characteristics of China's outward FDIs include a

Council of the PRC. An English version can be found on the NDRC's website http://en.ndrc.gov.cn/newsrelease/201503/t20150330_669367.html accessed 20 October 2016.

[3]See Wang (2016).

[4]See Bazillier et al. (2013), pp. 1–33.

[5]See United Nations Conference on Trade and Development (2015), p. 41.

[6]See Zhang and Daly (2011), pp. 389–398.

relatively later start, rapid growth, a large volume, state-owned enterprise leadership, and intensive focus on industries and regions.

Chinese enterprises have to face complex domestic and international circumstances, which may affect their process of 'going out'. Domestically, China has entered into a stage of 'promoting a new round of high-level opening up'. China's thirteenth Five-Year Plan proposes to improve the strategic layout of its opening up, form a new opening-up system, build the new BR, and actively participate in global economic governance. As globalization advances, trade liberalization, investment facilitation, regional integration, green development (sustainable development), ecological civilization, and good governance will be formed, advanced, and perfected. The BRI embodies the above contexts and realities. Chinese enterprises should understand and comprehend its intention when investing directly in foreign countries.

The features of China's current 'going-out' could be characterized from the following three dimensions: enterprise, industry, and culture.[7] Regarding the theory of comparative advantage, capturing China's comparative advantages in enterprise, industry, and culture at each stage is the key to successfully 'going out'. Outward FDI is a comprehensive competitive process that implements one's comparative advantages, seeks resources to improve one's value chain, or creates strategic linkages for a specific purpose in a different region from one's own. Although China's outward FDI has increased significantly, many issues, such as poor quality, unreasonable structure, low internationalization, unsatisfactory performance index, and inadequate regulation have been increasingly exposed.[8] The inadaptability of China's FDI is becoming more obvious due to a lack of sufficient attention to environmental welfare and environmental risks from Chinese enterprises.

As of December 2015, China's accumulated outward FDI in other BR countries had neared US $185 billion, accounting for almost 20% of China's outward FDI stock.[9] The geographical distribution shows the following pattern: Southeast Asia > West and Central Asia > South Asia > Central and East Europe. Energy, mining, manufacturing, and infrastructure construction exhibit the main fields of industrial concentration.[10] The above distributions show that China's outward FDI is highly environmentally sensitive. Industrial capacity cooperation, energy revolution, and the Asian Infrastructure Investment Bank proposed by the Chinese government will significantly influence outward FDI behaviour patterns in all BR countries. Predictably, environmental issues will still be challenging to Chinese enterprises when they make outward FDIs in the future.

---

[7]See Yang et al. (2012), pp. 75–85.

[8]See Liu and Su (2014a), pp. 37–41.

[9]MOFCOM, National Bureau of Statistics, State Administration of Foreign Exchange (2016) and MOFCOM-PRC (2016).

[10]See Zheng and Liu (2015), pp. 563–570.

2.2 Issues of Environmental Protection

Environmental protection should be an indispensable aspect of jointly building the BRI. First, environmental protection is the basis of, as well as a support to, green development in BR countries. Sustainable development should take into account the carrying capacity of the local environment. Many BR countries face severe environmental problems; therefore, environmental protection should be prioritized in sustainable cooperation and FDI. Second, BR countries have been orienting themselves towards the value of environmental protection. For example, the European Union (EU) is an active promoter and a leader of environmental protection and has formulated[11] stringent environmental standards, laws, and regulations. Due to unsustainable production modes and lifestyle behaviours in the past, the majority of Asian countries are being confronted with severe environmental problems and are seeking change. Third, environmental cooperation (supply of public goods) is a promising aspect of the BRI. As an integrated mechanism, the BRI has attributes of local and/or regional public goods (for example, environmental governance, biodiversity conservation, and green energy cooperation).[12] Last but not least, environmental protection has a synergistic effect that can boost the construction and development of other affairs related to the BRI. Environment-related risks and threats are major challenges to cooperation projects in question; therefore, focusing on environmental protection can fundamentally prevent, or even eliminate, many environment-related problems.

However, although there are significant achievements in Chinese outward FDI, its unsustainable aspects have been recognized. First, the quality of outward FDI is unsatisfactory. China's outward FDI performance index is relatively low (that is, less than one), indicating that its outward FDI is not in parallel with China's economic development level.[13] The behaviour patterns show that seeking resources in high-risk areas is still the dominant approach of China's outward FDI, despite moving towards a value chain extension.[14] Second, the investor structure of outward FDI is very singular. The fact that the state-owned enterprises are the dominant investors reflects the fact that the internationalized level of Chinese private enterprises is limited and that China's outward FDI is mainly due to national planning and motivated by politics. Third, outward FDI lacks attention on the social and environmental responsibilities of enterprises. The traditional paradigm of emphasizing the 'top/official cooperation mechanism' while ignoring the 'grassroots/civil cooperation mechanism' has resulted in heavy losses for Chinese enterprises (such as

[11]The idea and expression about Pollution Haven are inspired from Marconi's paper "Environmental Regulation and Revealed Comparative Advantages in Europe: Is China a Pollution Haven?"

[12]See Huang (2015), pp. 138–155.

[13]See Liu and Su (2014b), pp. 37–41.

[14]See Kolstad and Wiig (2012), pp. 26–34.

shelving events like the Myanmar Myitsone hydropower station and the Letpadaung copper mine).[15]

As an enhanced concept of sustainable development—a well-supported concept worldwide—green development for FDI is the logical means by which Chinese enterprises will move in the direction of environmental protection. The concept of sustainable development reflects an important shift in understanding the relationship between mankind and nature.[16] Green development is a series of value and behaviour modes and requires that the economic, social, and environmental benefits are maximized under a series of constraints.[17] Environmental protection has become a fundamental objective in national and international politics.[18] Green development requires enterprises to balance their pursuit for profit with environmental protection when acting in the market. FDI could be understood as a simple externalization of an economic philosophy, but value creation, development promotion, and development sustainability are its more profound aspects. With advances in globalization, the advocacy of a 'community of human destiny' has been emerging. Self-interested behaviour with a lack of necessary regulation and coordination will easily lead to a 'tragedy of the commons' or a 'zero-sum game'. In regard to the development process and encountered risks of Chinese outward FDIs, the 'zero-sum' mentality has not been discarded. In the context of global integration and governance, green development is the approach that Chinese enterprises should take when investing directly abroad.

3 Determination of Environmental Responsibility

In terms of law, liability refers to the responsibility that someone should suffer from his or her actions, especially for a breach of contract or a violation of law. However, the term 'responsibility' is employed here in a more inclusive and flexible way to substitute for 'liability'. Environmental responsibility includes not only the obligations provided by relevant agreements and/or norms (such as international law, international soft law, international custom, and domestic law and policies) but also other responsibilities based on ethics, justice, and undertaking. The BRI involves multiple jurisdictions and different cultures as well as political and legal systems, in addition to different societies with different developmental levels and situations. Therefore, the determination of environmental responsibility is full of complexity and uncertainty. FDIs by Chinese enterprises in other BR countries face environmental regulations from both home (China) and host (other countries). Clarifying the sources of environmental responsibility is therefore a foundation for determining

[15]See Li (2014), pp. 35–38.

[16]See Hopwood et al. (2005), pp. 38–52.

[17]See Rogers et al. (2012), p. 46.

[18]See Hu (2014), pp. 1–8.

environmental responsibility, while the logic of different environmental dispute settlement mechanisms should also be examined.

3.1 Sources of Environmental Responsibility

According to juridical logic, liability is the precondition of obligation; however, with respect to positive law, legal liability is the precondition for the legal subject to undertake liability. Environmental responsibility sources of Chinese enterprises for their FDIs in other BR countries are diverse, and they can be classified either as formal and informal, domestic and foreign, or static and dynamic.

The Chinese government has set a series of environmental protection responsibility requirements that apply to Chinese enterprises for their FDIs. As mentioned above, Chinese outward FDI in the past has been unsustainable; the social and environmental responsibilities of enterprises was not taken into proper account by most Chinese enterprises; and they led to accusations that were disturbing to the Chinese government such as 'pollution haven', China threat theory, neo-colonialism, and so on.[19]

By progressing towards a transformation in the domestic development mode and participation in international economic governance—although governmental supervision needs to respect enterprises as the dominant market players and promote 'going out'—enforcing environmental regulation on outward FDI is an inevitable trend. In order to encourage enterprises 'going out', the Chinese government has deregulated various regulatory measures on outward FDI. However, there are still stringent requirements on environmental protection in a number of fields, such as finance, insurance, foreign exchange, state guarantees, state-owned asset management, taxation, and project bidding. In addition, the relevant working departments of the State Council have issued some introductory and normative documents. For example, the Ministry of Commerce (MOFCOM) and the Ministry of Environmental Protection (MEP) have jointly issued the Guidelines for Environmental Protection in Foreign Investment and Cooperation in 2013, and MOFCOM, along with nine other ministries, jointly issued the Interim Measures for Bad Credit Records in the Fields of Foreign Investment Cooperation and Foreign Trade in the same year. Table 2 at the end of this article summarizes, by current Chinese laws and policies, what environmental responsibilities concerning outward FDI have been imposed on Chinese enterprises and how the relevant authorities shall perform their duties, where appropriate, to regulate or promote Chinese enterprises complying with these responsibilities.

Some of this legislation, such as the 2008 Notice on Further Regulating the Overseas Investment Cooperation of Chinese Enterprises, touch directly on environmental protection, while most indirectly promote environmental protection

[19]See Marconi (2012), pp. 616–635.

through risk assessment and management. It could be expected that the issue of environmental protection will be an important focus when legislating Chinese outward FDI regulations. Due to environmental sensitivity, requirements on environmental responsibility from the Chinese government on Chinese outward FDI in other BR countries will likely increase and become more stringent.

There are various environmental responsibilities required by the host country and international community. The BRI embraces countries and areas on several continents that have different environmental foundations, environmental protection priorities, and conditions of law and implementation. All of these lead to various requirements on FDI. For example, the EU and its member states have always been leaders in international environmental policy; therefore, their environmental protection responsibility requirements are numerous and stringent in regard to FDI.[20] However, many countries in Eastern Europe and Asia are developing nations that have little or even no requirements on environmental protection responsibility in FDI. Due to continuous regional integration, environmental protection is being emphasized by many regional cooperation mechanisms and institutions. In the 1970s, global environmental governance began to form a system of relatively sufficient institutions and norms.[21] Responsibilities from international environmental protection treaties, regulations, and other documents have greatly influenced FDI.

There are various informal sources of environmental responsibility. Lack of adequate attention to informal sources of environmental responsibility is among the main reasons why Chinese enterprise FDIs have suffered major failures in the past. For example, in June 2014, a Chinese FDI project in South Korean Chejudo Island was suspended, and, in February 2015, the Sino-Cambodian cooperative dam project was suspended by the prime minister of Cambodia. Informal sources of environmental responsibility mainly refer to requirements from local residents, local communities, non-governmental organizations (NGOs), industrial self-governance agencies, and political pressure groups. For instance, the Sino–Burmese railway project has been stranded since July 2014 due to opposition from residents along the railway and NGOs in Burma. In this regard, outward FDI should combine the 'top/official cooperation mechanism' with the 'grassroots/civil cooperation mechanism', obtaining consent from both the government and society. The rise of environmental rights, 'NIMBY' (not in my backyard) movements, and good environmental governance provide the means and legitimacy for cases of grassroots undertakings. Although these responsibilities do not appear as compulsory public powers, they may lead to public power outcomes (for example, the government may be forced to stop a project due to public pressure).

It is worth pointing out that sources of environmental responsibility should be treated from a dynamic and differentiation perspective. Enterprises are key components of the market; their operation decisions have to serve multiple values and objectives, and when considering environmental responsibilities, multiple factors

[20]See Kelemen (2010), pp. 335–349.

[21]See Nanda and Pring (2012), p. 97.

need to be balanced properly. Environmental standards within other BR countries have many differences, which is a challenge, as well as an opportunity, for Chinese enterprises. As long as Chinese enterprises adhere to appropriate developmental concepts and approaches, environmental risks can be overcome.[22] Meanwhile, environmental responsibility is always evolving; therefore, Chinese enterprises should be able to foresee and respond effectively to changes. FDI regulations are being reshaped worldwide. The desire to promote sustainable development and to balance benefits between host countries and investors is shared by the international community. In the new generation of bilateral and multilateral FDI treaties, inclusion of environmental clauses is the 'new normal'.[23] Investment treaties between China and other BR countries in the past has rarely paid close attention to environmental items, but in the process of updating and renegotiating, issues of environmental regulatory rights of the host country, environmental responsibility of investors and home countries, and environmental standards are increasingly mentioned. Items on environmental protection in future FDI rules will undoubtedly increase significantly.[24]

3.2 *Settlement of Environmental Disputes*

Each stakeholder in a (potential) dispute wishes that the dispute will have a successful resolution. However, different settlement mechanisms for an existing dispute, with different operation logic and value orientation, usually lead to different—sometimes significantly different—results of responsibility determination. For dispute settlement in FDI, there are many institutional arrangements at the international level, including relevant procedures in the World Trade Organization, the International Centre for Settlement of Investment Disputes (ICSID), and Energy Charter Treaty (ECT).[25] Generally, dispute settlements between private investors embrace negotiation, mediation, and arbitration, while dispute settlements between investors and host countries seek solutions from judicial systems, diplomacy, and arbitration. With the nature of FDI disputes transiting from 'political' to 'administrative', the arbitration approach is becoming a mainstream approach for settlements.[26] Environmental disputes arising from Chinese enterprise FDIs usually involve multiple stakeholders, leading to diverse settlement measures and/or approaches.

Under the notion of pursuing successful dispute resolutions, including the prevention of disputes, for environmental dispute settlement, the following should be explored by Chinese enterprises. First, the environmental standard should be applied

[22]See Liu (2015), pp. 108–112.

[23]See Han (2013), pp. 103–115.

[24]See Liu (2011), pp. 90–93.

[25]See Brewer (1994), pp. 633–672.

[26]See Xu (2010), pp. 143–153.

as a reference. In the light of the 'invisible hand', investors (particularly in pollution-intensive industries) are rational and are affected by complicated market factors that encourage them to seek 'pollution havens'—namely, the phenomenon of a 'race to the bottom' from the perspective of environmental protection.[27] Environmental standards (formal responsibility sources) directly influence the FDI decision making of an enterprise. Some countries deregulate their environmental regulations and standards in order to attract (more) FDIs. Following an approach of positive law, any action following these should not be prosecuted for negative environmental impacts and damages. However, on the one hand, the challenge in practice is that environmental regulations or standards are sometimes absent, ambiguous, elastic, and so on. For example, the absence of environmental standards could lead to inaccurate or wrong diagnoses by Chinese enterprises. On the other hand, in theory as well as in practice, in the pursuit of justice, the approach of positive law is not always followed since other elements are often taken into consideration.[28] Environmental standards that contain suspicious elements cannot help but reduce risks being faced by Chinese enterprises since they may be held to be responsible by examining the sources of environmental responsibility. Elastic environmental standards leave room for random explanations, causing uncertainty in the determination of responsibility, while low environmental standards may trigger protest and conflicts from local communities and opposition parties. The protest against the Las Bambas copper project in southern Peru is a good example. Environmental standards determine the particular responsibilities as well as the ways in which responsibilities should and shall be taken by Chinese enterprises.

Second, the rationality and legitimacy of environmental regulatory measures is enacted by the host country.[29] The right of a host country to regulate FDIs for environmental protection has been increasingly supported by international law and policy. In practice, whenever the environmental regulatory measures of a host country are in due process, in good faith, consistent with the objectives of environmental protection, scientifically supported, and accompanied by the principles of non-discrimination and proportion, they are usually supported by tribunals in FDI dispute settlement.[30] In terms of procedural justice, governments should not justify themselves in the process of dispute settlements, while the importance of an independent dispute settlement mechanism cannot be over-estimated. Even so, some countries (for example, Argentina) are still considering abolishing international mechanisms in relevant treaties that allow investors to sue host countries in order to avoid outcomes against them. Undoubtedly, this could severely affect

[27]See Dong et al. (2012), pp. 216–237.

[28]Eg, Holmes pointed out that 'the felt necessities of the time, the prevalent moral and political theories, intuitions of public policy, avowed or unconscious, even the prejudices which judges share with their fellow-men, have had a good deal more to do than the syllogism in determining the rules by which men should be governed'. See Holmes (1991), p. 1.

[29]See Hu (2012), pp. 656–660.

[30]See Han (2010), pp. 22–27.

environmental dispute settlements. There is an interactive relationship between FDI and host country regulations; the former may produce negative external results (for example, pollution), while the latter produces internal results. Thus, to judge fairly and justly the validity and rationality of host country environmental regulations, this relationship must be taken into account.

Third, the actual environmental consequences and imputation principles will apply to FDIs. The principle of striving for, and safeguarding, legitimate rights is a key principle that a FDI investor should uphold. With the emergence or intensification of nationalism, populism, protectionism, pan-politicization, geopolitics, and other elements, various illusory environmental disputes relating to FDI have been in the making. For example, based on the grounds of 'need[ing] to see the feasibility study' and 'need[ing] to see the environmental impact assessment and reassess the tax concessions given to it and land ownership issues', the new Cabinet of Sri Lanka in March 2016 decided to temporarily suspend work on the Colombo Port City Project, which had been invested in by China Communications Construction Company.[31] Although the project restarted after renegotiations, the Cabinet spokesperson admitted in August 2016 that the suspension decision had been made under great pressure from India. A similar example is India's speculation on the purpose of China's investment of building the Gwadar Port in Pakistan, suggesting that it had a military, rather than a commercial, purpose.[32]

It is acknowledged that an objective and scientific appraisal of environmental consequences from FDI has been helpful for resolving the problems mentioned above. In the process of dispute settlement, the doctrine of liability fixation is an important concept, as it determines not only the classification of torts but also the components of liability, onus of proof, exemptions from liability, the principles and means of compensation, and reasons for reducing liability.[33] Fault liability, strict liability, and equity liability are among the most common types of liability fixation. Regarding environment-related torts, both the civil law system and the common law system have experienced transition from fault liability to presumed-fault liability, equity liability, strict liability, or mixed liability.[34] These five doctrines are briefly summarized in Table 1. Among them, the doctrines of presumed-fault liability, strict liability, and mixed liability are widely applied doctrines in the field of environment-related tort litigation, while the doctrine of fault liability can also be applied between a host state and a foreign investor or its home state.

Regarding investor–state environment-related disputes, although a host state is under an obligation to comply with the investment treaty or treaties in which it participated—particularly when there is a stabilization clause—it could employ ambitious requirements (for example, good production practices and environmental impact assessment) to develop in detail an investor's responsibilities or liabilities or

[31]See Pothmulla (2016).

[32]See Ghouri (2016), pp. 36–68.

[33]See Wang (2008), pp. 3–15.

[34]See Zeng and Zhao (2011), pp. 135–139.

Table 1 Environmental imputation principles under five major doctrines of liability fixation

			Onus of proof at the first round	
	Loss	Negligence	Existence of negligence	Causal relationship
Fault liability	The claimer	The claimed should be at fault	The claimer	The claimer
Presumed-fault liability	The claimer	The claimed should be at presumed fault	The claimer	The claimer or According to precise legal provision(s)
Equity liability	The claimer	Both the claimer and the claimed are at no fault	Both	The claimer
Strict liability	The claimer	n/a	n/a	According to precise legal provision(s)
Mixed liability	For licensed operation, the doctrine of strict liability is applied. For unlicensed operation, only when the doctrine of presumed fault liability is un-applicable, the principle of fault liability is applied.			

a prerequisite for investments. This is well illustrated by *Pac Rim Cayman LLC v Republic of El Salvador*.[35] In this case, the dispute arose from the environmental permit required by the law of El Salvador, along with which an environmental impact study or environmental diagnostic was required. However, in March 2008, the El Salvador government placed a *de facto* ban on all metallic mining, based mainly on environmental considerations. It is our understanding that the government of El Salvador adopted the doctrine of strict liability in its legislation and set up more stringent burdens on the investor. An ICSID tribunal, in its award issued in October 2016, believed that, according to the doctrine of fault liability, the claimant bore the burden of proof in regard to liability, causation, and injury, and, therefore, it supported El Salvador's standing.

There are some typical domestic environment-related litigations concerning FDI involving the above doctrines of liability fixation. For example, in *Sithole and Others v Thor Chemicals Holdings and Another*, the UK Court of Appeal, Civil Division, believed that there was negligence in the design and transfer of hazardous chemical technology to South Africa as well as in the monitoring and supervision of the health of the South African workers, both by the parent company and by the directors and employees for whose conduct it made the parent company liable for mercury poisoning of South African workers under the doctrine of fault liability.[36] The plaintiffs in *Oguru, Efanga and Milieudefensie v Royal Dutch Shell Plc and Shell Petroleum Development Co Nigeria*, according to the doctrine of strict liability, alleged that the defendants (foreign investors) were liable essentially for their duty of care to the Nigerian farmers (the potential harm was foreseeable) and for their ability to ensure that adequate steps were taken to avoid the harm.[37]

[35]See ICSID (2016).

[36][1999] All ER (D) 102.

[37]ECLI:NL:RBSGR:2009:BK8616.

When evaluating and deciding the environment-related liability of Chinese enterprises for their FDIs in other BR countries, the above logic and paths should be followed. The environmental standard systems in other BR countries are complicated, and environmental regulations are becoming increasingly stringent. Taking into account the environmental sensitivity of Chinese enterprise FDIs, disputes are unavoidable. Therefore, the operational logic of different dispute settlement mechanisms has to be taken into consideration when determining liability.

4 Strategies for Chinese Enterprises in Dealing with Environmental Responsibility

The social and environmental responsibilities of enterprises are related not only to voluntary behaviour, self-discipline, and self-governance of enterprises but also to governmental regulation, international governance, and social norms.[38] The issue of environmental responsibility from Chinese enterprise FDIs in other BR countries has both domestic and international dimensions, for it concerns corporate governance, economic transition, rule of law, sustainable development, environmental protection, and good governance. Strategically, Chinese enterprises should pay attention to the following three aspects when conducting FDI in other BR countries.

4.1 Changing the Notion of Operation: From Domestic to Abroad

Many Chinese enterprises follow unsustainable notions when doing business in China; this notion could be termed as a 'domestic operation notion', which is opposite to an 'abroad operation notion'. These two terms could be understood based on the concept of best practice. The best practice of enterprises refers to the operational practices taken under the highest environmental standards of international law, including customary international law. Most Chinese enterprises do not operate best practices; when specific environmental standards are absent in Chinese law, enterprises simply operate, ignoring the possible negative externalities on the environment. We would like to suggest that when Chinese enterprises invest directly abroad, they should abide by the best practice principle—that is, operate to higher, or the highest, environmental standards internationally—this being the 'abroad notion'. According to the Path Dependency Theory (which refers to a social process grounded in a dynamic of 'increasing returns', or where we go next depends not only on where we are now but also upon where we have been),[39] if a Chinese

[38]See Brammer et al. (2012), pp. 3–28.

[39]See Pierson (2000), pp. 251–267 and Liebowitz and Margolis (2000), p. 981.

enterprise practices unsustainable development patterns abroad, not only will its own development become obstructed, but it will also negatively affect China's efforts to enhance its 'discursive power', establish a responsible image, and improve its position of international leadership. The BRI proposes concepts of 'peace and cooperation', 'openness and inclusiveness', and 'mutual learning and mutual benefit'. Therefore, ignoring environmental protection when pursuing economic interests is not compatible with the concepts proposed above. Chinese enterprises should plan cautiously because their development in other BR countries concerns not only their individual development prospects but also China's national strategy. Although there are various development priorities in other BR countries, enterprises should emphasize environmental responsibility in regard to green development and the supply of public goods.

In order to change a domestic operation notion in direct investment to an abroad notion, Chinese enterprises should undertake the following measures. First, halt risk taking, speculating, and 'free-riding' behaviour. The absence of necessary institutional and comprehensive arrangements for environmental protection can easily lead to a tragedy of the commons.[40] When investing abroad, Chinese enterprises should link their fortunes with the fortunes of the local community and build a community of human destiny. Second, follow the concept of green development. FDI development should balance immediate and long-term interests in regard to objectives of the enterprise itself and the local community. Third, improve comprehensive competitive ability. The common development of the host country and enterprises should be achieved through fair competition and enhanced environmental risk management.

4.2 Performing Due Diligence and Prudence

Due diligence and prudence in performance could help to ensure the success of Chinese enterprises when investing in other BR countries. As discussed earlier, due to the dominant position of state-owned enterprises in China's investment structure, additional censorship and harsh requirements have been put upon Chinese outward FDIs. For example, on 25 February 2015, the Philippines decided to end its cooperation with the National Grid Company due to 'national security concerns'. Therefore, Chinese enterprises need to improve their operation philosophy, management methods, and service objectives. The environment is the common ground between Chinese FDI and the development of other BR countries; it is also the key to avoiding, eliminating, or reducing conflict. Environmental responsibility is not a burden but, rather, a mechanism that motivates self-improvement. Enterprises should perform due diligence and prudence to partially avoid environmental risks

[40]See Hardin (1968), pp. 1243–1248.

and unnecessary environmental liabilities because due diligence and prudence are important aspects of examination by tribunals.

It is essential for Chinese enterprises to perform due diligence and prudence following the four measures listed below. First, perform due diligence and make comprehensive valuation. Adequate investigation of environmental policies, environmental law, and social conditions in the host country should be conducted, and international and regional environmental policy and policy prospects should be fully understood. Second, strictly abide by environmental regulations. It is necessary to carry out environmental impact assessments before launching projects in question, and, where applicable, environmental accidents should be promptly reported and addressed. Third, establish a stringent internal control mechanism. It is useful to include environmental risks in risk management and to examine the environmental impacts of major decisions. Finally, establish an information disclosure mechanism. Many disputes stem from asymmetric information, and, therefore, updating information to local residents, communities, NGOs, and government bodies is helpful in forming good relationships with or between stakeholders and resolving environment-related conflicts (Table 2).

4.3 *Utilizing Multiple Dispute Resolution Mechanisms*

Environmental responsibility—in particular, obligations—usually arises from environmental disputes. On the one hand, as mentioned above, different dispute settlement approaches may lead to different responsibility distributions; therefore, the choice of the dispute settlement approach requires comprehensive balancing of various factors. On the other hand, forum shopping has existed widely since environment-related disputes came into being.[41] Therefore, Chinese enterprises should pursue successful dispute resolutions, which could be categorized essentially as the following: product oriented, politically oriented, interest oriented, responsibility oriented, and relationship oriented. According to Susan Moore, '[s]uccessful resolution generally include[s] more than one category of success, with one category often preceding another'.[42]

However, for any good enterprise, the methodology regarding disputes should be prevention first, and, whenever a dispute arises, it has sufficient justice and legal bases to support its standings through whatever dispute settlement mechanism is selected. That is to say, a preventive- and judicial-oriented methodology should be adopted and should be applied in the field of environmental protection.

To prevent disputes, social licensing mechanisms are very important when trying to decrease risks in both environmental responsibility and issues associated with, or

[41] See Namballa (2014), pp. 181–205 and Nwapi (2014), pp. 24–43. Also see Hu and Xu (2013), pp. 21–26.

[42] See Moore (1996), pp. 151–169.

Table 2 Major provisions in current laws and policies on Chinese enterprises' environmental responsibility concerning outward FDI

Field	Requirement	Title of laws and policies	Issuing authority
Finance	National development and reform commission (NDRC) and the export-import Bank of China (EXIMBANK) shall jointly set up a credit support mechanism for overseas investments (article 1). Strict risk review shall be made when an enterprise applies for the support-related fund(s) (article 3, 4, 6).	Notice on giving credit support to the key overseas investment projects encouraged by the state (entered into force: 27 October 2004)	NDRC, EXIMBANK
	Domestic commercial banks and their overseas branches shall, after making adequate assessment and effective control of risks, provide financing facilities for non-state-owned enterprises to develop international markets (section 3, Para. 3).	Opinions on encouraging, supporting and guiding the overseas investment cooperation of non-state-owned enterprises (entered into force: 10 May 2007)	Ministry of Finance (MOF), PBOC, MOFCOM, all-China Federation of Industry and Commerce
Insurance	1. With respect to a project with significant country-related risks, the domestic investor is required to make full use of the existing overseas investment insurance mechanism to go through relevant procedures for buying the insurance, and actively avoid overseas investment risks (article 4).	Notice on giving credit support to the key overseas investment projects encouraged by the state (entered into force: 27 October 2004)	NDRC, EXIMBANK
	2. NDRC shall promote relevant entities to improve their overseas investment risk guarantee mechanisms so as to further improve overseas investment insurance (article 5).		
	1. NDRC and the China export and credit insurance corporation (SinoSure) shall jointly set up a risk prevention mechanism for key overseas investment projects (article 1).	Notice concerning relevant issues on setting up a risk prevention mechanism for key overseas investment projects (entered into force: 25 January 2005)	NDRC, SinoSure
	2. A Chinese investor may apply for risk prevention services for its overseas investment projects (article 3).		
Foreign exchange	When processing registration and\or approval for its outward FDI and outbound remittance of funds, a Chinese investor shall, in addition to submitting the relevant materials for review as required, explain to the bank the sources of the funds for investment and the purposes (use plan) of such funds, and provide the relevant resolution(s) of the board of directors (or the relevant resolution of the partners), and the relevant	Notice on further promoting the reform of foreign exchange administration and improving authenticity and compliance review (entered into force: 26 January 2017)	State Administration of Foreign Exchange

(continued)

Table 2 (continued)

Field	Requirement	Title of laws and policies	Issuing authority
	contract(s) or other materials for proving the transaction authenticity. Banks shall strengthen authenticity and compliance review in accordance with business principles (article 8).		
State guarantee	EXIMBANK shall, for the projects that have passed the risk review and under intended use of special loans for overseas investments, provide project-related financial services including performance guarantee, prepayment guarantee, quality guarantee, and international settlement, etc., and also provide certain preferences in respect of counter guarantee or guarantee bond in consideration of the situation about the domestic investor and the projects (article 7).	Notice on giving credit support to the key overseas investment projects encouraged by the state (entered into force: 27 October 2004)	NDRC, EXIMBANK
	1. The enterprise shall study and strictly abide by laws, regulations and policies on China's overseas investment cooperation, and delve into and abide by laws and regulations of the host country, especially the provisions on environmental protection, labor and employment, exit-entry administration, production safety, bidding and so on (article 2).	Notice on further regulating the overseas investment cooperation of Chinese enterprises (entered into force: 6 June 2008)	MOFCOM, FMPRC, SASAC
	2. When enterprises violate laws and regulations and causing serious consequences, MOFCOM, the Ministry of Foreign Affairs (FMPRC) and the state-owned assets supervision and administration commission (SASAC) shall handle or punish them according to the relevant provisions. MOFCOM shall handle or punish them by circularizing a notice of criticism, giving a warning, denying an enterprise's pass of annual inspection, and suspending and even cancelling the qualification for business operation according to relevant provisions. FMPRC shall impose restriction on the relevant enterprise's or competent authority's right to approve foreign affairs, right to apply for passport and right to apply for visa on its own or in proxy, according to the relevant provisions. SASAC shall impose corresponding punishments		

	on the enterprises and relevant liable persons causing adverse effects (article 5).		
	MOFCOM shall, in conjunction with relevant departments, promulgate environmental protection guidelines, and urge enterprises to conduct business operations in compliance with laws and regulations overseas (article 27). An Enterprise shall not be eligible for the support of relevant state policies for 3 years if its overseas investment falls under any of the circumstances prescribed by these 'measures' (article 32).	Measures for overseas investment management (entered into force: 6 October 2014)	MOFCOM
State-owned asset administration	1. Reinforce comprehensive regulation on overseas investment activities throughout the investment process (article 3).	Measures for the supervision and Administration of Overseas Investment by central government-owned enterprises (entered into force: 7 January 2017)	SASAC
	2. Strengthen the management and control of overseas risks, formulate a negative list of overseas investment projects by central government-owned enterprises (article 4).		
	3. Central government-owned enterprises shall comply with the laws and regulations, business rules and cultural practices of China and the host countries (regions) of its investment (article 6).		
	4. The SASAC shall establish and perfect the mechanism for joint operations of investment regulation, and display the concerted efforts of relevant regulatory functions such as strategic planning, legal compliance, financial supervision, property rights management, appraisal and distribution, capital operation, cadre management, supervision by dispatched board of supervisors, disciplinary inspection and supervision, audit and tour inspection, etc. (article 10)		
	5. Any central government-owned enterprise shall establish a proper concept of public good and profitability, and actively fulfil its social responsibilities (article 28)		
	Central government-owned enterprises shall further strengthen their awareness of social responsibilities, and play an exemplary role in abiding by law, operating in good faith, conserving resources, and promoting environmental protection (article 4).	Notice on further regulating the overseas investment cooperation of Chinese enterprises (entered into force: 6 June 2008)	MOFCOM, FMPRC, SASAC
	Public institutions shall strictly implement the approval procedures for overseas investment, and strengthen the risk control (section 5, article 15).	Opinions on further regulating and strengthening the Administration	MOF

(continued)

Table 2 (continued)

Field	Requirement	Title of laws and policies	Issuing authority
		of State-owned Assets of administrative institutions (entered into force: 23 December 2015)	
Taxation	Taxation plays an important role in promoting regulation on overseas investments of Chinese enterprises (section 1, Para. 1). Local tax authorities shall, in accordance with the provisions, strictly implement the policies for calculating overseas incomes, making up the losses, calculating taxable incomes, deducting overseas taxes as well as reducing and exempting overseas taxes, etc. (section 3, Para. 2)	Opinions on delivering good taxation service and management regarding overseas Investments of Chinese Enterprises by the state Administration of Taxation (entered into force: 20 March 2007)	State Administration of Taxation
Project bidding	EXIMBANK shall provide project-related bidding guarantee for projects that have passed the risk review and under intended use of special loans for overseas investments (article 7).	Notice on giving credit support to the key overseas investment projects encouraged by the state (entered into force: 27 October 2004)	NDRC, EXIMBANK
Others	Enhance the green level of overseas investment. Encourage and support China's financial institutions, non-financial enterprises and multilateral development agencies, strengthen environmental risk management, improve the level of environmental information disclosure, use green financing tools such as green bonds to raise funds, carry out green supply chain management, and explore the use of environmental pollution liability insurance and other tools for environmental risk management (article 31).	Guiding opinions on building a green financial system (entered into force: 31 August 2016).	PBOC, MOF, NDRC, MEP, banking regulatory commission, securities regulatory commission, and insurance regulatory commission
	Chinese enterprises shall comply with the laws and regulations of countries (regions) where projects are located, pay attention to environmental protection, and perform necessary social responsibilities (article 7). MOFCOM together with the relevant authorities shall establish a bad credit system in respect of overseas investment cooperation (article 11).	Provisions on regulating competitive behaviors in the field of overseas investment cooperation (entered into force: 18 April 2013)	MOFCOM

	The commerce administrations at all levels shall jointly establish a mechanism for collection and release of bad credit records in overseas investment cooperation and foreign trade with the departments of foreign affairs, public security, housing and urban-rural development, customs, inspection and quarantine, taxation and foreign exchange as well as administrations for industry and commerce, within their administrative regions (article 6). The act of damaging local ecological environment shall be included as a bad credit record in overseas investment cooperation (article 4)	Interim measures for bad credit Records in the Fields of foreign investment cooperation and foreign trade (entered into force: 5 August 2013)	MOFCOM, FMPRC, Ministry of Public Security, and six other working departments under the state council

Note: 'Risks' mentioned here include environment-related risks among others
Source: Westlaw (China) database and Pkulaw database

arising from, it.[43] In particular, the credibility of environmental communication should be emphasized, for it affects foreign investor legitimacy directly.[44] In this regard, cooperation and the all-win concept should be emphasized. Cooperation with local stakeholders is helpful for utilizing local resources, specialties, and wisdom, while cooperation with industry leaders and/or opponents could change a disadvantageous position into an advantageous one. Influence from the public on FDI projects is increasingly enhanced by the emergence and development of civil society movements and environmental protection. Chinese enterprises investing directly abroad have to deal carefully with development issues of local residents, communities, and social organizations to establish a community of human destiny. Enterprises could achieve a steadier and more sustainable development by linking their development with that of the local community through mechanisms of information exchange, participation, and benefit sharing.

Regarding any emerged dispute, the nature of the dispute first needs to be identified. Civil disputes can be settled through negotiation, litigation, and arbitration, while administrative disputes can be settled through diplomacy, litigation, and international arbitration. Second, clarify the objectives and interests pursued. In many cases, the objective is not the dispute settlement itself but, rather, the interests that can be achieved from this process. Therefore, whatever mechanism is employed or initiated, the four essential successful disputes resolutions and any of their combinations should be taken into consideration at every stage. Finally, appraise the costs for completing any potential mechanism (not only the direct expenditures in the process but also indirect ones, such as time and interests during a time-wasting process) as well for implementing the results (for example, judgment, award, modified contract, or new contract). Resource constraints must be taken into account when trying to reach a feasible dispute resolution.

5 Conclusion

The BRI aims to promote regional and international harmonious and green development. It is an important move that China has made in participating in international economic governance and promoting sustainable development, which has been brought great opportunities for Chinese enterprises to go abroad. The 'going out' of Chinese enterprises has experienced a relatively extensive development process, where lack of attention to environmental risks has been a major issue. Environmental protection is the fundamental concept and support for building the BRI, and it creates various cooperation opportunities. Under the guidance of ecological civilization and green development, Chinese enterprises should change their operation mindset in direct investment from a domestic one to a foreign-minded one by pursuing the

[43]See Hu and Xu (2013), pp. 21–26.

[44]See Hunter and Bansal (2007), pp. 135–147.

concept of sustainable development. In order to establish a community of human destiny, Chinese enterprises should emphasize an all-win philosophy and approach and, in addition, actively fulfill their social and environmental responsibilities when conducting FDI in other BR countries. Regarding the diversity and differences in environmental standards among BR countries, Chinese enterprises should anticipate and evaluate their environmental responsibilities and comprehensively examine the responsibilities, operation logic, and value orientation of different dispute settlement mechanisms when directly investing abroad. In terms of environmental responsibility, Chinese enterprises face various formal and informal environmental protection requirements from the Chinese government, host countries, and international community. In regard to dispute settlement mechanisms, Chinese enterprises should follow proper environmental standards, examine the legitimacy and rationality of host countries' environmental regulation measures, objectively and scientifically appraise environmental consequence(s) from relevant behaviours, and determine a proper doctrine of liability fixation. In order to tackle environmental responsibility issues in their FDIs, Chinese enterprises should change their operation notion from an unsustainable domestic one to a sustainable foreign-minded one, perform due diligence and prudence, and utilize multiple dispute resolution mechanisms. As market players, Chinese enterprises should balance differentiated interests and objectives in their FDIs, adopt a green development pathway, and promote the pathway towards ecological civilization.

References

Bazillier, R., Hatte, S., & Vauday, J. (2013). *Environmental responsibility and FDI: Do firms relocate their irresponsibilities abroad?* (G-MonD Working Paper no 32), pp. 1–33.

Brammer, S., Jackson, G., & Matten, D. (2012). Corporate social responsibility and institutional theory: New perspectives on private governance. *Socio-Economic Review, 10*(1), 3–28.

Brewer, T. L. (1994). International investment dispute settlement procedures: The evolving regime for foreign direct investment. *Law and Policy in International Business, 26*(1), 633–672.

Dong, B., Gong, J., & Zhao, X. (2012). FDI and environmental regulation: Pollution haven or a race to the top? *Journal of Regulatory Economics, 41*(2), 216–237.

Ghouri, A. (2016). Towards greater integration? Legal and policy directions of Chinese investments in Pakistan on the advent of the Silk Road economic Belt. *The Chinese Journal of Comparative Law, 4*(1), 36–68.

Han, X. (2010). On environmental regulation measures of host country from judgments of the international investment dispute settlement bodies. *Jiangxi Social Sciences, 6*, 22–27 (in Chinese).

Han, X. (2013). Environmental protection issues in China's overseas investment. *International Studies, 157*(5), 103–115 (in Chinese).

Hardin, G. (1968). The tragedy of the commons. *Science, 162*(3859), 1243–1248.

Holmes, O. W. (1991). *The common law* (Rev. ed., p. 1). New York: Dover Publications.

Hopwood, B., Mellor, M., & O'Brien, G. (2005). Sustainable development: Mapping different approaches. *Sustainable Development, 13*(1), 38–52.

Hu, D. (2012). China's governance of exhaustible natural resources under the WTO era. *Energy Procedia, 16*, 656–660.

Hu, D. (2014). On China's framework of energy regulation: A perspective of mixed economy. *Journal of Xi'an Jiaotong University (Social Sciences), 34*(4), 1–8 (in Chinese).

Hu, D., & Xu, S. (2013). Opportunity, challenges and policy choices for China on the development of shale gas. *Energy Policy, 60*, 21–26.

Huang, H. (2015). One Belt One Road strategy: From a perspective of public goods. *World Economics and Politics, 6*, 138–155 (in Chinese).

Hunter, T., & Bansal, P. (2007). How standard is standardized MNC global environmental communication? *Business Ethics, 71*(2), 135–147.

ICSID. (2016). Pac Rim Cayman LLC v Republic of El Salvador, ICSID Case No. ARB/09/12. Retrieved December 31, 2016, from http://www.italaw.com/sites/default/files/case-documents/italaw7640_0.pdf

Kelemen, R. D. (2010). Globalizing European Union environmental policy. *Journal of European Public Policy, 17*(3), 335–349.

Kolstad, I., & Wiig, A. (2012). What determines Chinese outward FDI? *Journal of World Business, 47*(1), 26–34.

Li, F. (2014). China's OFDI and overseas social responsibility strategy. *Journal of International Economic Cooperation, 6*, 35–38 (in Chinese).

Liebowitz, S. J., & Margolis, S. E. (2000). Path dependence. In B. Bouckaert & G. D. Geest (Eds.), *Encyclopedia of law and economics* (Vol. 1, p. 981). Cheltenham: Edward Elgar.

Liu, E. (2015). The structuring of the legal system of environmental protection in the construction of "the Belt and Road" project. *Theory and Modernization, 236*(6), 108–112 (in Chinese).

Liu, H., & Su, J. (2014a). The status and problems of Chinese OFDI. *Journal of International Economic Cooperation, 7*, 37–41 (in Chinese).

Liu, H., & Su, J. (2014b). The status quo of Chinese OFDI and its problems. *Journal of International Economic Cooperation, 7*, 37–41 (in Chinese).

Liu, W. (2014). Scientific understanding of the Belt and Road initiative of China and related research themes. *Progress in Geography, 34*(5), 538–544 (in Chinese).

Liu, Z. (2011). Analyzing and improving the environmental clauses of China's international investment agreements. *Law Science Magazine, 32*(12), 90–93 (in Chinese).

Marconi, D. (2012). Environmental regulation and revealed comparative advantages in Europe: Is China a pollution haven? *Review of International Economics, 20*(3), 616–635.

MOFCOM, National Bureau of Statistics, State Administration of Foreign Exchange. (2016). *2015 Statistical bulletin of China's outward foreign direct investment*. Beijing: China Statistics Press.

MOFCOM-PRC. (2016). *Statistics on China's Non-Financial Direct Investment in other Belt and Road Countries in January–October of 2016* (in Chinese). Retrieved December 31, 2016, from http://www.mofcom.gov.cn/article/tongjiziliao/dgzz/201612/20161202222469.shtml

Moore, S. A. (1996). Defining "successful" environmental dispute resolution: Case studies from public land planning in the United States and Australia. *Environmental Impact Assessment Review, 16*(3), 151–169.

Namballa, V. C. (2014). Global environmental liability: Multinational corporations under scrutiny. *Warwick Research Journal, 1*(2), 181–205.

Nanda, V. P., & Pring, G. R. (2012). *International environmental law and policy for the 21st century* (p. 97). Boston: Martinus Nijhoff.

Nwapi, C. (2014). Jurisdiction by necessity and the regulation of the transnational corporate actor. *Utrecht Journal of International and European Law, 30*(78), 24–43.

Pierson, P. (2000). Increasing returns, path dependence, and the study of politics. *American Political Science Review, 94*(2), 251–267.

Pothmulla, L. (2016). Colombo port city project suspended. In P. Willis (Ed.), *Daily mirror*. London: Trinity Mirror.

Rogers, P. P., Jalal, K. F., & Boyd, J. A. (Eds.). (2012). *An introduction to sustainable development* (p. 46). Earthscan: London.

United Nations Conference on Trade and Development. (2015). *World investment report 2015*. Geneva: United Nations Publication.

Wang, H. (2016). The Belt and Road green development is vibrant. In *Chinese social sciences today*. Beijing: Chinese Academy of Social Sciences, (in Chinese).

Wang, L. (2008). On construction of the structure and system of China's tort liability law: From the perspective of relief law. *China Legal Science, 4*, 3–15 (in Chinese).

Xu, C. (2010). A commentary and critical on the recent international investment disputes arbitration: To introduce the theory of global governance. *The Jurist, 153*(3), 143–153 (in Chinese).

Yang, H., Wu, D., & Wang, S. (2012). The stages and tactics of China's "walking out" strategy. *International Business, 6*, 75–85 (in Chinese).

Zeng, X., & Zhao, H. (2011). On liability principles of environmental tort. *Wuhan University Journal (Philosophy & Social Sciences), 65*(6), 135–139 (in Chinese).

Zhang, X., & Daly, K. (2011). The determinants of China's outward foreign direct investment. *Emerging Markets Review, 12*(4), 389–398.

Zheng, L., & Liu, Z. (2015). Spatial pattern of Chinese outward direct investment in the Belt and Road initiative area. *Progress in Geography, 34*(5), 563–570 (in Chinese).

Some Suggestions for Improving the International Credibility of the Chinese Judiciary: A Focus on the BRI

Yongping Xiao and Meng Yu

1 Introduction

A well-developed international rule of law is required to build the Belt and Road Initiative (BRI). To achieve this requires collaboration among the countries that are members of the BRI by concluding international treaties and coordinating domestic rules to establish an international legal community, which will not be an easy task and which will entail considerable effort. The Chinese judiciary is willing to be among the first to take new measures to safeguard and implement the BRI. Consequently, the Supreme People's Court (SPC) released the Opinions on People's Court's Provision of Judicial Service and Safeguards for the One Belt, One Road Initiative (the Opinions) in July 2015, a judicial document that sets guidelines and rules for Chinese courts to play a role in implementing the BRI.[1]

This article aims to explore approaches to improving the international credibility of the Chinese judiciary under the current legal framework in China from an ideological, systematic, methodical, and cultural perspectives in order to safeguard and implement the BRI and to provide a basis for the rule of law in China to build a

The chapter was published in The Chinese Journal of Comparative Law (2017, Vol. 5, Issue 1) by Oxford University Press.

[1]Opinions on People's Court's Provision of Judicial Service and Safeguards for 'One Belt, One Road' (Zuigao Renmin Fayuan Guanyu Renmin Fayuan Wei Yidaiyilu Jianshe Tigong Sifa Fuwu He Baozhang De Ruogan Yijian) (2015) (PRC).

Y. Xiao (✉)
International Law Institute, Wuhan University, Wuhan, Hubei Province, PR China

Collaborative Innovation Center of Judicial Civilization, China University of Political Science and Law, Wuhan, Hubei Province, PR China

M. Yu
Collabordative Innovation Center of Judicial Civilization, China University of Political Science and Law, Beijing, PR China

W. Shan et al. (eds.), *Normative Readings of the Belt and Road Initiative*,
https://doi.org/10.1007/978-3-319-78018-4_10

community of shared interests, destiny, and responsibility featuring mutual political trust, economic integration, and cultural inclusiveness.

2 Fostering the Judicial Ideology of a Major Country

To be sure, the BRI will remain the core and strategic interest in China for a long time to come. China is committed to peaceful development and welcomes other countries to join its fast-track development and share development opportunities through win–win cooperation. Such diplomatic visions featuring mutual understanding and common development are gaining influence.

How does the Chinese judicial practice reflect or implement these diplomatic visions, to let the international community, especially countries participating in the BRI, understand that the BRI is being proposed with sincerity? First, Chinese courts need to foster the judicial ideology of a major country. This so-called 'major country' is more than a country with some hard power in the economic, political, and military fields but, rather, a country with significant influence in its culture as well as its institutions. In other words, China ought to strengthen its soft power by enhancing the appeal of its culture and institutions—a goal that Chinese judicial practice also strives to achieve.

As a responsible major country, it is necessary for China not only to shoulder economic, political, and cultural responsibility in international relations but also to provide the international community with more public goods. Therefore, when it comes to foreign-related civil procedures, in order to enhance the international credibility of the Chinese judiciary, China needs to weaken the notion of judicial sovereignty and promote a judicial ideology featuring equal protection, win-win cooperation, opening up, and efficiency.

3 Equal Protection

The judicial practice in many countries has shown a trend of applying local law to protect the interests of their own citizens.[2] However, as economic globalization continues to deepen, the bond of common or overall interests among all countries around the world is correlative and interactive. Therefore, when considering the merits of individual cases, Chinese courts should pay more attention to differentiating local interests and overall interests, short-term interests and long-term interests, and the general interests and core interests of the State. In accordance with the equal protection principle, Chinese courts should ensure the equal treatment of all parties in terms of litigation status, application of law, and legal responsibility.

[2]See De Boer (1996), p. 391.

4 Win–Win Cooperation

China advocates building a new model of international relations and international economic order featuring win–win cooperation. In terms of judicial practice, in order to settle disputes in a fair and reasonable way, efficient cooperation among judicial authorities in different countries is also required. Such cooperation includes, but is not limited to, providing legal information, delivery, taking evidence, and recognition and enforcement of judgments and arbitral awards. Only in this way can we promote commercial interaction among countries and lay the basis of rule of law for an opening-up policy.

5 Opening Up and Efficiency

The principle of open development set out by the Communist Party's eighteenth National Congress will upgrade China's open economy. The opening-up policy, which focuses on fostering a fair and win–win environment in all-round opening up with multilateral and regional cooperation, shall also be applied in Chinese judicial practice. That is to say, bearing in mind the concepts of opening up and efficiency, there are certain factors to be considered in individual cases, such as the opening-up needs in different areas, the level of cooperation between China and other countries, and the balance of interests from different aspects.

6 Improving the Judicial System

To achieve the judicial ideology of a major country, a few improvements need to be made regarding China's judicial system.

6.1 *Fully Guaranteeing Foreigners' Litigation Rights*

In international civil procedures, China has been adhering to the national treatment principle.[3] Nevertheless, national treatment does not mean an identical treatment. In China, special provisions are made on certain issues, including the guarantee of litigation fees, judicial succour, agent ad litem, and diplomatic immunity.

[3] Civil Procedure Law of the People's Republic of China (Zhonghua Renmin Gongheguo Minshi Susongfa) (1991, revised in 2012) art 5 (PRC).

6.2 *The Guarantee of Litigation Fees*

In terms of the guarantee of litigation fees, China has experienced a shift from compulsory guarantee for foreign plaintiffs to a waiver of guarantee under reciprocity. Until now, China has reached bilateral agreements using a waiver of guarantee of litigation fees with 18 countries.[4] To better implement the BRI, we suggest that China engage in reaching agreements using the waiver of guarantee of litigation fees with countries participating in the BRI or that China takes the lead in waiving such fees.

6.3 *The Judicial Succor and Litigation Fee Waivers*

In China, based on treaties or reciprocity, a foreign party may apply to the People's Court for judicial succour, including the deferment, reduction, or exemption of litigation fees. Currently, China has reached agreements in judicial succor through treaties of judicial assistance with 14 countries.[5] In addition, China has reached agreements with 24 countries on issues regarding litigation fee waivers.[6] Likewise, China may engage with other countries participating in the BRI in reaching agreements regarding litigation fee waivers or taking the initiative in offering a waiver in individual cases.

6.4 *The Agent ad Litem*

In China, a foreign national may entrust his or her countryman as the agent ad litem or a lawyer of the same nationality as his or her agent ad litem in a non-lawyer capacity.[7] Furthermore, when they need lawyers as agents ad litem to bring an action

---

[4]The 18 countries are: France, Italy, Spain, Bulgaria, Hungary, Morocco, Singapore, Tunisia, South Korea, Poland, Romania, Russia, Turkey, Cuba, Greece, Kyrgyzstan, Tadzhikistan, and Uzbekistan.

[5]The 14 countries are: Italy, Bulgaria, Thailand, Morocco, Tunisia, South Korea, Turkey, Egypt, Greece, Cyprus, Vietnam, Laos, Lithuania, and North Korea.

[6]The 24 countries are: Italy, Bulgaria, Thailand, Poland, Hungary, Morocco, the United Arab Emirates, Mongolia, Romania, Russia, Turkey, Ukraine, Belarus, Kazakhstan, Egypt, Greece, Cyprus, Kyrgyzstan, Tajikistan, Uzbekistan, Vietnam, Laos, Lithuania, and North Korea.

[7]Interpretation of the Supreme People's Court on the Application of the Civil Procedure Law of the People's Republic of China (*Zuigao Renmin Fayuan Guanyu Shiyong Zhonghua Renmin Gongheguo Minshi Susongfa De Jieshi*) (2015) art 528 (PRC) (Interpretation).

or to appear on their behalf, they must appoint lawyers of the People's Republic of China.[8] In addition, China is a State party of the Vienna Convention on Diplomatic Relations (1961) and the Vienna Convention on Consular Relations (1963).[9] In accordance with these conventions and bilateral consular treaties, diplomatic agents and consular officers of a sending state may serve as its nationals' agent ad litem in litigation proceedings, thus protecting the latter's legitimate rights and interests in the receiving state.

To meet the needs of the BRI, Chinese courts could allow and arrange for foreign citizens to sit in on the hearing of cases that are tried publicly. Chinese courts could also invite foreign diplomats and officers in exchanges and cooperation from countries participating in the BRI to sit in on the hearing of such cases so as to address the concerns of the international community.

6.5 *Properly Narrowing the Ambit of Exclusive Jurisdiction*

Pursuant to Articles 33 and 266 of the Civil Procedure Law (CPL), Chinese courts have exclusive jurisdiction over certain disputes, including those arising out of immovable property, the harbouring of operations, and succession.[10] It is noteworthy that under Chinese law:

> actions brought in respect of disputes arising from the performance of contracts for Chinese-foreign equity joint ventures, or Chinese-foreign contractual joint ventures, or Chinese-foreign cooperative exploration and the development of the natural resources in the People's Republic of China shall fall under the jurisdiction of the People's Courts of the People's Republic of China.

This provision is rarely found in other countries' domestic laws or in international treaties.[11] The grounds of this provision, however, were criticized by Chinese scholars as being outdated and improper. In addition, as the scale of China's overseas investments will continue to grow because of the BRI, it is questionable whether there exist solid grounds for Chinese courts to exercise jurisdiction over such investments, if this rule remains.

---

[8]Civil Procedure Law of the People's Republic of China (*Zhonghua Renmin Gongheguo Minshi Susongfa*) (1991, revised in 2012) art 263 (PRC) (Civil Procedure Law).

[9]Vienna Convention on Diplomatic Relations 1961, 500 UNTS 95; Vienna Convention on Consular Relations, 1963, 596 UNTS 261.

[10]Civil Procedure Law (n 8) art 33 (PRC): '[T]he following cases shall be under the exclusive jurisdiction of the people's courts here in specified: (1) a lawsuit brought on a dispute over real estate shall be under the jurisdiction of the people's court of the place where the estate is located; (2) a lawsuit brought on a dispute over harbour operations shall be under the jurisdiction of the people's court of the place where the harbour is located; and (3) a lawsuit brought on a dispute over succession shall be under the jurisdiction of the people's court of the place where the decedent had his domicile upon his death, or where the principal part of his estate is located.'

[11]Civil Procedure Law (n 8) art 266.

It is suggested that China can adopt an alternative that focuses only on two rules. One is that 'the people's court in the location of immovable property has exclusive jurisdiction over disputes relating to the immovable property'. The other is that 'in disputes concerning the validity of the constitution, the nullity or the dissolution of legal persons, the courts where the legal person has its seat' will have exclusive jurisdiction.[12] This is because land, plants, and other immovable property are frequently involved in the three types of contracts prescribed in Article 266: contracts for Chinese-foreign equity joint ventures, Chinese-foreign contractual joint ventures, and Chinese-foreign cooperative exploration and development of natural resources. The first two types of contract are also more likely to be contracts involving Chinese legal persons. Thus, the alternative can, to a large extent, ensure exclusive jurisdiction for Chinese courts and be more consistent with the common practice.[13]

6.6 *Properly Settling Parallel Proceedings*

The CPL does not address the issue of parallel proceedings, yet the Supreme People's Court's 2015 Interpretation on the Application of the Civil Procedure Law (2015 Interpretation of the CPL) does this in Article 533.[14] As for parallel proceedings in divorce cases, to protect Chinese citizens' legitimate rights and interests, a special provision can also be found in Article 15 of the aforesaid interpretation.[15] In July 2015, the SPC's Opinions on the People's Court's Provision of Judicial Service and Safeguards for the BRI stressed in particular the significance of foreign-related civil and commercial proceedings in implementing the BRI. Pursuant to the Opinions, it is essential, through amicable negotiation and judicial

[12] He (2015), p. 129.

[13] He (2007), p. 221.

[14] Interpretation (n 7) art 533: '[W]here both a court of the People's Republic of China and a court of a foreign country have jurisdiction over a case, if one party files a lawsuit to a foreign court, and the other party files a lawsuit to a court of the People's Republic of China, the people's court may accept the lawsuit. After a judgment is rendered on the case, if the foreign court applies to, or the party concerned requests, the people's court to recognise and enforce the judgment/ruling rendered by the foreign court on the case, the people's court shall not allow the application or request, unless otherwise prescribed in the international treaties jointly concluded or acceded to by both the People's Republic of China and the foreign country. Where the judgment/ruling rendered by the foreign court has been recognised by the people's court, the people's court shall not accept the lawsuit, if any, filed thereto by a party concerned against the same disputes.'

[15] Interpretation (n 7) art 15 (PRC): '[W]here a married couple of Chinese citizens has one party living within the Mainland and the other party living abroad, the people's court at the domicile of the party living within the Mainland shall have jurisdiction regardless of which party files divorce to a people's court. Where the party living abroad files divorce to a court in the country of his/her residence, and the party living within the Mainland files divorce to a people's court, the people's court that accepts the divorce case shall have jurisdiction.'

assistance with other countries participating in the BRI to fully respect the right to choice of jurisdiction by agreement between Chinese and foreign parties involved in the BRI, to reduce international jurisdictional conflicts, and to deal appropriately with the issues of parallel proceedings.

We recommend that where concurrent proceedings exist in countries participating in the BRI, a Chinese court may suspend its proceedings under certain circumstances and then, depending on the development of the concurrent proceeding, determine whether to resume jurisdiction or terminate its proceeding.

7 Innovating Judicial Methods

As China promotes the BRI, there are a few innovative improvements that can be made in respect of judicial methods in trying foreign-related civil and commercial cases, as outlined below.

7.1 Actively Applying Forum Non Conveniens

Although Chinese legislation is silent about the principle of forum non conveniens, the early recognition of this principle existed in Chinese judicial practice.[16] Such practice is later recorded in official documents from the year 2000 onwards.[17] The detailed guidance set out in those documents is echoed in the 2015 Interpretation of the CPL, relating to Article 532.[18] The principle of forum non conveniens is self-

[16]By now, there have been quite a few cases where Chinese courts applied the forum non conveniens. These cases include Dahao Chemical Industries, Ltd v Yuyan Paint Co, Ltd et al, Jiangsu High People's Court Su Shang Hai Zhong Zi no 53 (2010); Green Tech Electronics Ltd v Smartech Electronics Co, Shanghai High People's Court, Hu Gao Min Si (Shang) Zhong Zi no 59 (2009).

[17]In 2004, the Supreme People's Court published the Answers to Questions Arising out of Trail Practice of Foreign-Related Commercial or Maritime Cases (2004 Answers). Under the 2004 Answers, it clarifies that forum non conveniens can be used under certain circumstances. In 2005, a more detailed guidance was provided in the Supreme People's Court's Minutes of the Second National Working Conference on the Trial of Foreign-Related Commercial and Maritime Cases.

[18]Interpretation (n 7) art 532 (PRC): '[W]here a foreign-related civil case falls under all of the following circumstances at the same time, a people's court may render a ruling to dismiss the filing of action by the plaintiff, and inform the plaintiff to file a lawsuit to a more convenient foreign court: (1) Where the defendant to the said case raises the request that the case should be governed by a more convenient foreign court, or raises objections on jurisdiction; (2) Where there is no agreement between the parties concerned to select a court of the People's Republic of China as the competent court; (3) Where the said case does not fall under the exclusive jurisdiction of the courts of the People's Republic of China; (4) Where the said case does not involve the national interests of the People's Republic of China and the interests of the citizens, legal persons or other organiations of the People's Republic of China; (5) Where the main facts disputed in the said case did not take place within the territory of the People's Republic of China, and the case is not governed by the laws of

restraint of jurisdiction for local courts. With the spirit of international comity, it works not only to prevent forum shopping but also to conform with the two-convenience principle in China—that is, the principle of being convenient for people and facilitating court proceedings.

Nonetheless, the 2015 Interpretation of the CPL focuses more on the control and limit of the use of forum non conveniens. Very restrictive conditions are imposed, and the court has limited its ability to exercise its discretion. For instance, the forum non conveniens rule is not applied in cases that involve the national interests of the People's Republic of China and the interests of the citizens, legal persons, or other organizations of the People's Republic of China. Another example is that when all conditions are met, a People's Court may render a ruling to dismiss the filing of an action by the plaintiff—that is, to terminate the proceeding immediately instead of suspending it. Our suggestion is to ease the restrictions in applying forum non conveniens in proceedings involving countries participating in the BRI.

7.2 *Actively Confirming Existence of Reciprocity*

In accordance with Article 282 of the CPL and Article 544 of the 2015 Interpretation of the CPL, where there is no international treaty concluded by and between the country of domicile of the foreign court and China, the principle of reciprocity is a prerequisite for recognition and enforcement of foreign judgments, except for divorce judgments. However, it is unclear how the existence of a reciprocal relationship between China and the foreign country can be proven. For years, Chinese courts have adopted the approach of de facto reciprocity, which requires actual precedents demonstrating that the foreign country has recognized and enforced Chinese judgments in the past.[19] However, de facto reciprocity may lead to a vicious circle if both countries have adopted reciprocity as a precondition to the recognition of foreign judgments and both have adopted the approach of reciprocity; in fact, neither country will recognize the other's judgment first and forever. Clearly, such practice does not conform to the BRI and can only establish a factual obstacle to the recognition and enforcement of foreign judgments.

---

the People's Republic of China, posing significant difficulties to the people's court in ascertaining facts and applying laws during the hearing of the case; and (6) Where a foreign court has jurisdiction over the said case, and it is more convenient for the foreign court to hear the case.'

[19]As can be seen in cases including the Application of Gomi Akira (A Japanese Citizen) to Chinese Court for Recognition and Enforcement of Japanese Judicial Decision, Dalian City Intermediate People's Court of Liaoning Province (1994), reprinted in (1996) 1 Supreme People's Court Gazette 29; the Application of Russia National Symphony Orchestra and Art Mont Company for Recognition of a Judgment of the High Court of Justice in England, Intermediate People's Court of Beijing Municipality no 2 (2005); Letter of Reply of the Supreme People's Court on Request for Instructions Re Application of DNT France Power Engine Co, Ltd for Recognition and Enforcement of Australian Court Judgment, Supreme People's Court (2007).

Therefore, the SPC issued its Opinions on the People's Court's Provision of Judicial Service and Safeguards for the BRI, where active reciprocity is encouraged. In accordance with the Opinions, 'in the absence of any treaty of judicial assistance between China and some countries participating in the BRI, Chinese courts may consider rendering judicial assistance first to parties of the said countries, taking into consideration the circumstances, including international judicial cooperation and exchange, and the promised judicial reciprocity to be offered by the said countries. In this way, reciprocity is established and promoted, and the scope of international judicial assistance can be advocated and gradually expanded'.

Nevertheless, the guidance set out in the Opinions is still found wanting when dealing with reciprocity. We suggest that if by examining the foreign law reciprocity is not a precondition to the recognition of foreign judgments in that country, the Chinese court may recognize, first, the existence of the reciprocal relationship, regardless of whether there exists any 'promise' or 'intention of cooperation and exchange'. An inspiring example has been set by the Berlin Superior Court of Justice in Germany 10 years ago in a case where the court recognized a Chinese judgment made by the Intermediate People's Court of Wuxi Municipality in China.[20] Under the framework of the BRI, China can be assured that once the first step is taken the countries participating in the BRI would follow this path to cooperate in reciprocity.

7.3 *Accurately Applying International Treaties and Customs*

The legislature and the judiciary have attached great importance to the application of international treaties and customs. To ensure judicial safeguards for the BRI, when dealing with international treaties and customs, there are two principles to follow: internationality and uniformity.[21] In China, there exits the principle that the application of international treaties is direct and prioritized. Yet it is necessary to note that such a principle has preconditions—that is, that the issue in question falls under an international treaty; for instance, the states of the parties involved in the dispute are contracting states to that international treaty. In other words, normally if China or the country of the foreign party is not a contracting state, then such international treaty cannot prevail. However, there exists an exception. Where the choice of an international treaty falls under all of the following circumstances at the same time, the international treaty chosen by the parties concerned may be applied, even though it is not ratified by China, if: (1) the choice is made explicit; (2) the issue concerned falls under the application scope of that international treaty; (3) the choice does not go against the public policy or violate the mandatory rules of China; and (4) the chosen

[20]Vgl Urteil des Kammergerichts Berlin vom 18.05.2006, Aktenzeichen 20 Sch 13/04. For details see Ma (2007), pp. 150–155.

[21]See Li (1998), pp. 313–320.

international treaty normally refers to international substantive treaty, not including international procedural law or international conflict of laws.[22]

When the application of international customs is involved, more attention needs to be paid to the relationship between international customs and domestic law. First, the law, domestic law, and international treaties concluded or acceded to by the People's Republic of China are applied before international customs.[23] Second, in terms of legal effect, international customs share the same rank as foreign law, which ranks lower than international treaties and higher than national policies. Also, like foreign law, domestic law, and international treaties, an international custom can be applied as the governing law as determined by conflict-of-law rules. Third, pursuant to the party autonomy principle in contracts, the parties concerned may choose substantive practice, such as international commercial custom, as the governing law. In addition, to meet the strategic needs of the BRI, we suggest that where there are neither applicable domestic laws nor bilateral or multilateral treaties, an international treaty with wide-ranging influence, regardless of whether it is ratified by China or not, be applied as an international custom, so that a timely, fair, and reasonable result can be achieved in individual cases.

7.4 Fully Utilizing Model Cases

In the process of promoting the BRI, new legal questions are bound to arise from new needs and circumstances, such as the 'going out' of Chinese enterprises, the protection of maritime interests, the construction of free trade zones, border trade, and regional economic cooperation. Furthermore, the measures adopted during the period of comprehensive reform in China are undoubtedly exerting their influence on the trial of cases involving commercial and maritime matters with a foreign element.[24]

In the trial of such new and emerging foreign-related cases, there is an urgent need to set up a guiding case system so that Chinese judges can be offered specific guidance, conforming with judicial interpretation and meeting the BRI's strategic needs. To start with, the guiding case system needs to collect and compile the most

---

[22]See Han and Xiao (2004), p. 223.

[23]It is noteworthy that when an international custom is applied through party autonomy, its effect is lower than the domestic mandatory rules, but higher than domestic facultative rules. See Han and Xiao (2004), p. 258.

[24]Opinions of the Supreme People's Court on Comprehensively Carrying Forward the Strategy of Producing Fine Works on the Trial of Cases involving Foreign-related Commercial and Maritime Affairs to Provide Effective Judicial Safeguard for Establishing the Open Economic System and Building up a Maritime Power (Zuigao Renmin Fayuan Guanyu Quanmian Tuijin Shewai Shangshi Haishi Shenpan Jingpin Zhanlve Wei Goujian Kaifangxing Jingji Tizhi He Jianshe Haiyang Qiangguo Tiguo Youli Sifa Baozhang De Yijian) (2015) (PRC) (Opinions of the Supreme People's Court).

representative foreign-related cases. After that, the system may publicize judgments of such guiding cases, including those where there is an absence of applicable international treaties, those where the application of law is correct and the reasoning is well grounded, and those that show innovation. Therefore, when dealing with cases involving countries participating in the BRI, we suggest that Chinese courts refer to the guiding cases publicized by the SPC in making their decisions when there are neither international treaties nor domestic law to be applied.

8 Promoting Inclusive Judicial Culture

The inclusiveness of Chinese culture lies in the principles of seeking common ground while shelving differences and drawing on each other's strengths. This inclusive culture is equally important when it comes to promoting the BRI. In regard to the judiciary, the following two aspects need to be focused on.

8.1 Promoting a Diversified Dispute Resolution Mechanism

First, choices made by the parties based on their political, legal, cultural, religious, or any other preference for countries participating in the BRI should be fully respected. In other words, both Chinese and foreign parties are free to choose to settle their disputes through arbitration, mediation, and other alternative dispute resolutions.[25] Second, it is necessary to further develop the judicial review of arbitral awards and to promote the role that international commercial and maritime arbitration can play in the BRI. In terms of the 1958 Convention on the Recognition and Enforcement of Foreign Arbitral Awards, correct comprehension and application of the Convention is a necessity in recognizing and enforcing foreign commercial and maritime arbitral awards.[26] Furthermore, promoting the mutual recognition and enforcement of foreign arbitral awards among those countries participating in the BRI that have not yet ratified the Convention is also encouraged.[27] Third, it is necessary to establish a centralized review system for commercial arbitration cases. Considering that the revised CPL in 2012 has brought about a gradual convergence of the judicial review standards on domestic and foreign-related arbitral awards, it is advisable to allocate to the foreign-related commercial tribunals that have gained substantial experience

[25]See Opinions on People's Court's Provision of Judicial Service and Safeguards for 'One Belt, One Road' (Zuigao Renmin Fayuan Guanyu Renmin Fayuan Wei Yidaiyilu Jianshe Tigong Sifa Fuwu He Baozhang De Ruogan Yijian) (2015) para 11 (PRC) (Opinions on People's Court Provision).

[26]Convention on the Recognition and Enforcement of Foreign Arbitral Awards, 1958, 330 UNTS 38.

[27]See Opinions on People's Court's Provision (n 25) para 8.

over the years all the judicial review cases regarding both domestic and foreign arbitral awards.[28]

8.2 Ascertaining and Correctly Applying Foreign Law

In accordance with Article 10(1) of the Act on the Application of Laws on Foreign-related Civil Relationships (Conflicts Act),[29] it is the court's duty to ascertain the content of foreign law, except where the parties concerned choose that the dispute be governed by foreign laws.[30] The applicable foreign laws may be ascertained in several ways, as prescribed by Articles 17 and 18 of the SPC's Interpretation on the Implementation of the Act on the Application of Laws on Foreign-related Civil Relationships.[31] If foreign laws are unable to be ascertained or contain no relevant provisions, the laws of the PRC shall apply.[32] Furthermore, Article 17 of the Interpretation also provides the circumstances under which foreign laws may be recognized instead of those that cannot be ascertained.[33]

Considering the needs of promoting the BRI, it is crucial to ascertain and apply foreign law to the greatest extent possible. We put forward the following suggestions on the right way to comprehend and apply the Conflicts Act and the Interpretation. First, in regard to Article 10(1) of the Conflicts Act, which stipulates 'parties concerned shall provide laws of the relevant foreign country if they choose to be governed by foreign laws', what this provision indicates is not that judges do not

[28]See Opinions of the Supreme People's Court (n 24) para 25.

[29]Act on the Application of Laws on Foreign-related Civil Relationships of the People's Republic of China (Zhonghua Renmin Gongheguo Shewai Minshi Falv Guanxi Shiyongfa) (2010) art 10 (1) (PRC) (Civil Relationships Act): '[F]oreign laws applicable to foreign-related civil relations shall be ascertained by people's courts, arbitration commissions or administrative organs. Parties concerned shall provide laws of the relevant foreign country if they choose to be governed by foreign laws.'

[30]Han (2014), pp. 153–154.

[31]Interpretation on the Implementation of Act on the Application of Laws on Foreign-related Civil Relationships of the People's Republic of China (Zuigao Renmin Fayuan Guanyu Shiyong Zhonghua Renmin Gongheguo Shewai Minshi Falv Guanxi Shiyongfa Ruogan Wenti de Jieshi Yi), Supreme People's Court (2012) arts 17 and 18 (PRC).

[32]Civil Relationships Act (n 29): 'In the event that foreign laws are unable to be ascertained or contain no relevant provisions, laws of the People's Republic of China shall apply.'

[33]Interpretation (n 7) art 17: 'Where a people's court fails to obtain foreign laws through channels provided by the parties concerned and specified by the international treaty that has already been applicable to the People's Republic of China or reasonable channels provided by domestic and foreign legal experts, etc., such laws may be recognised as foreign laws that cannot be ascertained. Where, in accordance with the provision of the Paragraph 1 of Article 10 of the Law on the Application of Laws to Foreign-Related Civil Relations, the parties concerned should provide the foreign laws but fail to provide such foreign laws without legitimate grounds within the reasonable time limit specified by the people's court, such laws may be recognised as foreign laws that cannot be ascertained.'

have the duty to ascertain foreign law but, rather, that judges bear the minor responsibility while the parties concerned have the main responsibility. Therefore, Article 17(2) of the Interpretation is by no means interpreted as long as the parties concerned fail to provide such foreign laws; such laws are recognized as foreign laws that cannot be ascertained. On the contrary, if judges have the knowledge of, or through more convenient methods, enjoy an access to the content of a foreign law, they are obliged to identify the foreign law ex officio and adjudicate according to such law.

Second, the list of methods in Article 17(1) of the Interpretation is not exclusive, so courts may identify a foreign law through approaches other than the three on the list. For instance, the content of the foreign law may be ascertained through the agreement between, or the admission of, the parties concerned. Since such evidence surely cannot be decisive, courts may, through the best evidence rule, identify foreign law based on more sufficient evidence. Nevertheless, where such agreement constitutes an inseparable part of a contract, courts may identity the content of the foreign law that is based on it, unless the contract is found to be invalid.[34]

Third, it is necessary to explore and develop methods on the proof of foreign law by strengthening ties with academic institutions at home and abroad and setting up research centres and institutions for discerning foreign law. In January 2015, the China Institute for Discerning Foreign Law was established by the SPC, the China University of Political Science and Law, Southwest University of Political Science and Law, and Qianhai Shenzhen-Hong Kong Modern Service Industry Cooperation Zone.[35] We suggest establishing a national centre for discerning foreign law so that more efforts can be made on a long-term basis and legal systems of the countries along the BRI can be focused upon.

9 Conclusion

The BRI aims to promote the connectivity of the Asian, European, and African continents and their adjacent seas, establish and strengthen partnerships among the countries participating in the BRI, and realize diversified, independent, balanced, and sustainable development in these countries. To achieve this goal, it not only requires countries participating in the BRI to jointly build international rules of law that promote the initiative but also requires each country to boost the rule of law at home. As an initiator, China is willing to bear more duties and responsibilities, including building a market environment with fairness and justice guaranteed by the Chinese judiciary.

At this stage, it is crucial to enhance the international credibility of the Chinese judiciary. To this end, we put forward the following suggestions:

[34]See Xiao (2007), p. 228.

[35]See He (2016), p. 12.

It is necessary to foster the judicial ideology of a major country—namely, to weaken the notion of judicial sovereignty and promote a judicial ideology featuring equal protection, win-win cooperation, opening up, and efficiency. It is necessary to improve the judicial system as the basis for enhancing the international credibility of the Chinese judiciary, fully guaranteeing foreigners' litigation rights, properly narrowing the ambit of exclusive jurisdiction, and properly settling parallel proceedings.

It is necessary to innovate judicial methods to guarantee the enhancement of the international credibility of the Chinese judiciary through approaches, including actively applying forum non conveniens, actively confirming the existence of reciprocity, accurately applying international treaties and customs, and fully utilizing guiding cases.

It is necessary to promote an inclusive judicial culture as support for enhancing the international credibility of the Chinese judiciary in various ways, including promoting a diversified resolution mechanism and ascertaining and correctly applying foreign law.

References

De Boer, T. M. (1996). Facultative choice of law: The procedural status of choice of law rules and foreign law. *Hague Academy of International Law, 257*, 225–427.

Han, D. (Ed.). (2014). *International private law* [Guoji Sifa] (3rd ed.). Beijing: Higher Education Press.

Han, D., & Xiao, Y. (Eds.). (2004). *Private international law* [Guojisifa Xue]. Beijing: People's Court Press.

He, Q. (2007). On exclusive jurisdiction of investment contracts in China [Lun Woguo Touzi Hetong Zhuanshu Guanxiaquan]. *Luojia Jurists' Forum* [Luojia Faxue Luntan], *6*, 207–221.

He, Q. (2015). *International civil procedural law from a comparative law perspective* [BiJiaofa Shiye Xia De Guoji Minshi Susongfa]. Beijing: Higher Education Press.

He, R. (2016). On Chinese judiciary's participation in making international economic rues [Lun Zhongguo Sifa Canyu Guoji Jingji Guize De Zhiding]. *Chinese Revolution International Law* [Guojifa Yanjiu], *1*, 3–15.

Li, S. (Ed.). (1998). *Private international law in China and its international unifications* [Zhongguo Yu Guoji Sifa Tongyihua Jincheng]. Wuhan: Wuhan University Press.

Ma, L. (2007). Analysis on the first case to recognise a Chinese civil and commercial judgment in German courts [Xi Deguo Fayuan Chengren Zhongguo Fayuan Minshangshi Panjue Diyian]. *Studies in Law & Business* [Fa Shang Yanjiu], *4*, 150–155.

Xiao, Y. (2007). *Conflict of laws from a jurisprudence perspective* [Falixue Shiye Xia De Chongtufa]. Beijing: Higher Education Press.

China's "Belt and Road Initiative": What's in it for Law Firms and Lawyers?

Tommi Yu

1 One Belt, One Road: Centrepiece of China's Limitless Economic Rise

The Belt and Road Initiative[1] (BRI) is a development strategy, started by the Chinese Government in 2013. In March, 2015 an action plan entitled "Vision and Actions Outlined on Jointly Building Silk Road Economic Belt and 21st-Century Maritime Silk Road" was released by the National Development and Reform Commission (NDRC), the Ministry of Foreign Affairs and the Ministry of Commerce (hereinafter referred to as MOFCOM), outlining its key details. Billed originally as a framework for the promotion of infrastructural projects, the NDRC release has ever since provided a signal for a new, more encompassing and more sophisticated engagement between China and the rest of the world.

Currently the initiative includes not only infrastructure, but also a set of instruments for policy coordination across Asia and beyond, financial integration, trade liberalization, and people-to-people connectivity. According to analysts, China's efforts to implement this initiative will likely have an important effect on the region's economic architecture—patterns of regional trade, investment, infrastructure

The chapter was published in The Chinese Journal of Comparative Law (2017, Vol. 5, Issue 1) by Oxford University Press.

[1]Originally, the Central People's Government announced its initiative to foster closer cooperation between places lying on two ancient economic routes, namely the "Silk Road Economic Belt" and the "21st Century Maritime Silk Road". For practicality and consistency purposes, this chapter will adopt the concise version referred as One Road, One Belt.

T. Yu (✉)
Legal & Risk Control Department, Country Garden Group, Shunde, PR China
e-mail: yut11@mails.tsinghua.edu.cn

W. Shan et al. (eds.), *Normative Readings of the Belt and Road Initiative*,
https://doi.org/10.1007/978-3-319-78018-4_11

development—and in turn have strategic implications[2] for many countries, industries, businesses, and individuals.

China's leadership, in an attempt to offset potential criticism that would unequivocally label BRI as a strategy for global expansion and geopolitical influence, has created the more appealing concept of *youwaizhinei*, or "to bring the outside in." Looking at BRI from the stand point of legal professionals, the BRI is not Chinese, it is something bigger than China itself—it is global and international.[3] Having the potential of turning into one of the largest ever collaborations in trade and infrastructure development, the BRI has two integral components, and it is necessary to understand their geographical dimensions.

"One Belt" refers to the overland dimension of the Silk Road Economic Belt, which starts from Xian and stretches northwest to Central Asia's financial center—Almaty, continuing to Kyrgyzstan, Uzbekistan, Turkmenistan and Iran, extending further northwest to Turkey and Eastern European countries in the Black Sea region, and reaching Moscow, Minsk and Warsaw before arriving to Germany and Netherlands.

"One Road" refers to the Maritime Silk Road beginning in Fuzhou, passing through Quanzhou, Guangzhou, Zhanjiang, Haikou and Beihai, reaching further Vietnam, Malaysia, Indonesia and Singapore, before extending to India and all the way to Kenya on the West African coast, crossing the Horn of Africa and the Red Sea while reaching Greece and shortly after the Mediterranean, where the oversea and overland new silk roads meet.

2 China's Legal Services Industry

Since the gaige kaifang[4] was started under Deng Xiaoping, Chinese economy has grown massively, private enterprise was enabled and has gradually increased ever since. Such changes brought also an increase to foreign business involvement and the demand for legal industry and its services. The demand of these services has reached levels, at which the current number of licensed lawyers in China is nearly a quarter of a million, and the number of law firms across China nears the figure of 19,000, including foreign law firms and offices.[5] With investors being upbeat about China's business climate, the dominant perception from the outside is that law firms in China, big local, or big foreign with domestic presence, or smaller ones, have majority of their work focused on investment related matters.

The narrative here has much more to offer, than just investment related stories and experiences. The reality is, depending on their specialization, work at most Chinese law firms involves dealing with a wide variety of problems that may or may not be in

[2]Kennedy (2015).

[3]Wade (2016).

[4]This is how China's reform and open policies are termed in short.

[5]Zhonghua Quanguo Lushi Xiehui (All China Lawyers Association—ACLA) (2016).

line with perceptions from the outside. No other industry is more aware of the opportunities that come with China having the same rates of stable growth in the coming years, as it had in the past, as well as continuously opening up to the outside world and maintaining massive scale of imports and exports from and to the rest of the world.

As a result of strict requirements with regard to completing legal education and obtaining a license, practicing law in China is formally, well-regulated profession. Due to the character of Chinese economy and involvement with foreign businesses, today's legal professionals in China are generally people with superb abilities to respond to the changing landscapes of legal industry, not only domestically but also internationally. When offering a brief assessment of China's legal industry in the context of BRI, three are the important themes: irrespective of their size, how unimpeded is foreign law firms' access to legal market in China; what are the peculiarities of the legal services industry; and what is the relationship between PRC government and the legal services industry.

For western legal professionals, the size of Chinese economy and its continuous growth, are enticing to an extent that has brought hundreds of foreign law firms to China in the past decade. As a Macfarlanes partner has put it, "you cannot turn your back on China, you have to work out how you can develop the opportunities that this market can offer".[6] And while the bulk of lawyers' work in the past has been with foreign investment flooding into China, experts now observe that "China investment flows have reversed in recent years and there is now a substantial market for foreign legal services assisting Chinese companies in their foreign investments".[7] Certain impediments for foreign law firms do exist as well: foreign law firms and foreign lawyers cannot practice PRC law, and those PRC lawyers who remain employed by foreign law firms do have certain limitations on their right to provide legal advice on domestic law matters. Turning to PRC local firms is necessary on any local law matters. The amount of regulatory approval and efforts associated with that process are also significant, particularly for smaller international law firms. Compared with Western Europe and North America, also client base in China is often cost-driven and immature in its understanding of how western law firms and lawyers work, and charge, which places certain burden and requires more efforts to be invested in potential outreach related to legal services. Earning trust is a time consuming process, during which some law firms may even get frustrated about their incomes from fees.[8]

Some of the peculiarities of the Chinese legal market are stretching lawyers beyond their roles as legal advisers.[9] Lawyers often turn to be involved in assisting clients from China for finding relevant contacts and investment opportunities, from which the legal work will originate. That being said, the reality is also pointing to some of the qualities lawyers shall possess, the supreme among which is often the

[6]Taddia (2013).

[7]Ibid.

[8]The Author (18 April 2016). Personal interview.

[9]The Author (11 August 2016). Personal interview.

linguistic skills. Chinese clients will often opt for someone who might not be the best in the field, but with whom there are no any impediments to communicate or being understood. This makes the Chinese legal market quite demanding, and at the same time rewarding for lawyers who are multilingual, and for law firms that are able to offer a variety of jurisdiction support to clients who will be going along the New Silk Road.

The relationship between PRC government and the legal services industry is one of perennial importance. While representing some distinct traditions in its practice of law, China is unequivocally on a journey that embraces the rule of law and does not grow complacent in improving or seeking innovative ways to ensure legal industry has conditions that permit it to be running smoothly. China's Ministry of Justice has made in recent years steps to further liberalize the legal services industry, particularly with significant achievements in the four free trade zones[10] (FTZs). On August 31, 2016, Beijing passed approval for Chongqing, Zhejiang, Hubei, Henan, Sichuan, Shaanxi, and Liaoning to establish seven new free trade zones, bringing their total number to 11, and potentially extending the liberalization of legal services industry to a new level, anticipating that most of these FTZs would be better suited in the Belt and Road (BR) framework, if such liberalization takes place.

Among the major factors that have driven investments to China, there are factors that potentially could direct investments out of the country as well: capital availability, regulatory environment, competitiveness, political and economic stability, local market and business climate, and the openness to regional and international trade.[11] With export-friendly policies that are taking place, and with intensity of free trade agreements being initiated, prospects that lawyers and law firms face are realistically enticing and huge. And while synergy exists between PRC government on the one side, and legal services industry on the other, it is expectations of lawyers that determine the course which a law firm will take to pull its clients toward a competitive spot on the New Silk Road.

3 Chinese Government and Legal Services Industry in the BR Context

Some governments have entered the BRI, by making political commitments. Within the area of political commitments, lawyers have mostly no role to play. Yet, doing business today and entering emerging and risky markets, some of them more risky than emerging in fact, requires governments and legal industry professionals working in synergy with each other. Realizing the need for such synergy, the master minder of BRI—the Chinese government, has taken several important steps to institutionalize venues and channels for supporting companies, and since few of

[10]There are regional specifics, pertinent to each FTZ, and until the approval by Ministry of Justice from August 31, 2016, the four FTZs were Shanghai, Guangdong, Fujian and Tianjin respectively.

[11]The Author (10 September 2016). Personal interview.

these steps are within the legal realm, they are also with significance not only for businesses, but for lawyers as well. The BRI is centrally featured within the ongoing 13th Five-Year Plan (FYP), which is essentially the set of social and economic development initiatives that map out China's strategies for growth within current five-year period.[12] The FYPs are also important, above everything else, also due to the fact that they guide and direct where investments shall be concentrated at most during that specific period.

On the first day, following the National Day in 2016, All China Lawyers Association (ACLA)'s secretary-general He Yong has informed the public that China will seek partnership with law firms from all the countries along the Silk Road to jointly compile and release books of guidance to reduce risks in cross-border business and investment. The aim would be to help Chinese investors understand legal practices in those countries related to investment, trade, labor, intellectual property, environmental protection and settlement of disputes, and the Ministry of Justice has allocated 1.1 million yuan ($165,100) for compiling the guidebooks.[13]

Ponderous approaches of businesses have made China investments abroad massive, amounting to $870 billion[14] in 2014 and adding 118 billion in 2015. According to MOFCOM, more than 18,500 Chinese enterprises have established 29,700 companies in foreign countries, with total assets of $3 trillion. If one combines the respective data, it would become apparent that with China's worldwide investments and contracts amounting nearly a trillion in 2016, there are lot of opportunities for lawyers. That has also been officially manifested by the Department of Directing Lawyers and Notarization at the Chinese Ministry of Justice, which has the understanding that majority of the Belt and Road countries are developing countries with underdeveloped economies and unsound legal environment[15] which in turn mandates improving professional legal services with the purpose to aid Chinese investments and carefully weigh up potential risks involved.

With the purpose to further develop China's legal services industry and strengthen the rule of law, as well as to cater and protect Chinese companies going abroad, and inadvertently contributing to the opening of China's services economy, in January, 2017 the Ministry of Justice, Ministry of Foreign Affairs, MOFCOM and State Council Legislative Affairs Office have jointly issued "Opinions on the development of foreign-related legal services"[16] (hereinafter referred to as "Opinions"). With five integral parts that prescribe the guiding ideology, basic principles, the main objectives, the main tasks and the main measures for the development of foreign-related legal services industry, the PRC government has clearly termed the

[12]China Daily (2015).

[13]Zhang (2016).

[14]Statistics on Chinese Investment Abroad (2015).

[15]Zhang (2016).

[16]Guanyu fazhan shewai falu fuwu ye de yijian (Opinions on the development of foreign-related legal services) (2017).

BRI and paved the way for other related government-led globalisation strategies and initiatives, as the core of the Opinions.

The Opinions aim by the end of 13th FYP to have established fully functional systems and mechanism for developing foreign-related legal services sector, that will be integral of highly competitive talents, providing foreign-related legal services, and having a thorough knowledge of international rules, world foresight, and own an international vision.[17] In addition, it is aimed that a group of foreign-related legal service institutions that are large in size, powerful in strength and favorable in level of service is established. Accordingly, the Opinions ascertain four tasks, including "providing legal services for significant national development strategies such as the Belt and Road Strategy", as well as six specific measures, such as "improving and perfecting the supportive and security policies". In between the lines of this powerful, joint document it is also laid the expectation for lawyers and law firms to get actively "engaged in due diligence for enterprises' foreign-related commercial deals, conduct evaluations, prevention and control of risks, and assist Chinese enterprises in establishing and improving the mechanisms for prevention of risks arising in overseas investments and financing and for safeguarding rights and interests."[18] In this context it is relevant to explore the expectations of law firms and lawyers as to where do they fit within the new discourse in which the Opinions are another substantially supporting step.

4 Measuring Short-Term and Long-Term Expectations

There are different methods and approaches utilized to measure expectations. Expectations form a great deal of theoretical macroeconomics, financial analyses, and have been part of modern economics intangibility. "Economic expectations are crucial in determining economic activity as they affect economic decisions of consumers, politicians, businesses and economic experts".[19] Among the first to address the subject of expectations, was John Maynard Keynes. In The General Theory, expectations are divided into two categories: short-term and long-term. Although Keynes theorizes over rates of investment and employment, his approach and definitions could serve the purpose and give one of the directions of this chapter, namely to address the short-term and long-term expectations of lawyers with regard to China's BRI.

If we rely on the Keynesian categorization and definitions, short-term expectations shall be understood as "the shortest interval after which the firm is free to revise its decision" (although, short-term expectations may be influenced by long-term expectations). In many occasions Keynes equals "short-term" with the meaning of

[17]Opinions on Developing the Sector of Legal Services for Foreign Affairs Issued (2017).

[18]LexisNexis (2017).

[19]Janzek and Ziherl (2012).

"daily". In the context of BRI, short-term expectations could be re-modelled to expectations that take longer time, they could be daily, but essentially they could be weekly, monthly, or quarterly.

In his own words Keynes defines what are long-term expectations: what an entrepreneur expects to earn in the future if he purchases finished output and uses it in conjunction with his capital equipment.[20] Long-term expectations cannot be checked in short-term intervals and they are liable to sudden revision.[21]

The attempt to measure subjective expectations, especially when the actual unfolding of events has a relatively high degree of sophistication, as within the case of the BRI, has been made by deploying survey methodology and survey design, in the form of short, structured interviews or distributed questionnaires, most practical to the field and environments in which busy legal professionals operate. It would generally pose a difficulty to occupy law firm partner, or another senior legal professional, who would be able to commit longer times for structured interview.

The data in this study covers the period from March until April in 2016, and from September until December of the same year. Questionnaires[22] were answered and responses were received, or one-to-one interviews were conducted with legal professionals from 15 law firms,[23] among which: 3 of the largest foreign law firms with presence in China, 3 of the largest domestic law firms, 3 of the relatively small foreign law firms with presence in China, and 3 small domestic law firms. Geographically, interviews were conducted with 12 law firms from the Mainland and 3 of the largest partnership law firms from Hong Kong SAR. Within the Mainland, interviewees were met at their offices in Beijing, Shanghai, Xian, in addition to Hong Kong. In overall, interviewed were 4 senior partners, 6 partners, and on few instances, responses were given electronically on behalf of the law firm.

While the subject of current chapter is not to study the legal industry in China, it is fair to acknowledge that in some aspects the legal industry in China is fragmented in terms of scales of operations, areas of practice, even background and credentials of lawyers. The design of this study has intentionally brought survey respondents to represent equal number from each of the five categories, that were defined by the author, specifically to aid the absence of bias or inaccurateness when measuring aggregate expectations. The five categories as outlined in the previous paragraph are: i. large foreign law firms with presence in China; ii. large domestic law firms; iii. small foreign law firms with presence in China; iv. small domestic law firms; v. non-mainland law firms.

The assumption, that the best way to understand someone's expectations regarding particular outcome, is by asking that person directly about his expectations, has

[20]Keynes (2008).

[21]Janzek and Ziherl (2012).

[22]Sample of the questions, that have been addressed in the form of questionnaire are included in Appendix 3.

[23]List of Mainland and Hong Kong SAR law firms is included in Appendix 2. List of senior partners, partners, etc. is available upon request by contacting the author.

proven particularly valid for the current study. The survey method has been utilized to measure expectations, by asking a sample of lawyers what they expect within the industry in connection with the Belt and Road Initiative framework, its potential to generate new work and opportunities for these lawyers and their firms, and the prospects for capitalizing on these new opportunities.

5 Expectations on Practice Areas of Demand Within the BR Context

A managing partner of Beijing-based Jun He law firm has stated that export of Chinese capital for M&As in Europe, South America, and countries like Russia and Uzbekistan, among others, will underpin in the "short to medium term" strong domestic consumption,[24] which in turn will be manifested in generating more work for lawyers on investment and trade related matters. Similar are the views of other lawyers in Beijing, Shanghai, and Hong Kong and therefore it would not be far from true to state that the BRI in terms of short term expectations, establishes a blueprint for infrastructure development,[25] while it also catalyzes opportunities for international trade (see Fig. 1). Although the survey related to this study might not take in all diverse voices from law firms, from huge internationals to small boutique offices, its pattern used suggests there are few practice areas, which more or less are rated as practice areas of current or future related demand: international trade; infrastructure development; energy and mining; investment and corporate; finance, banking and capital markets; labor and employment; and dispute resolution.

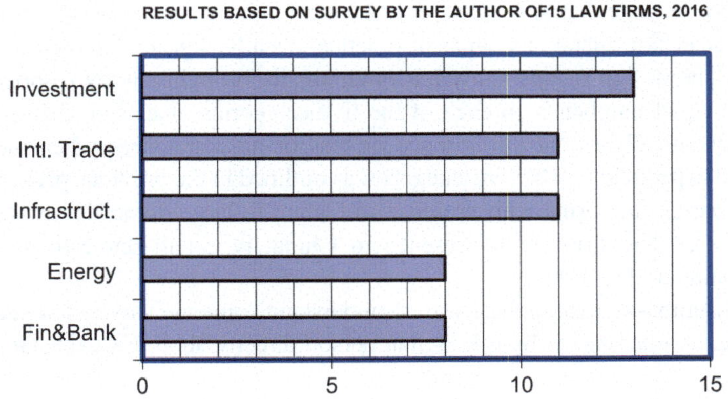

Fig. 1 Practice areas of current BR related demand

[24]Taddia (2013).

[25]The Author (8 April 2016). Personal interview.

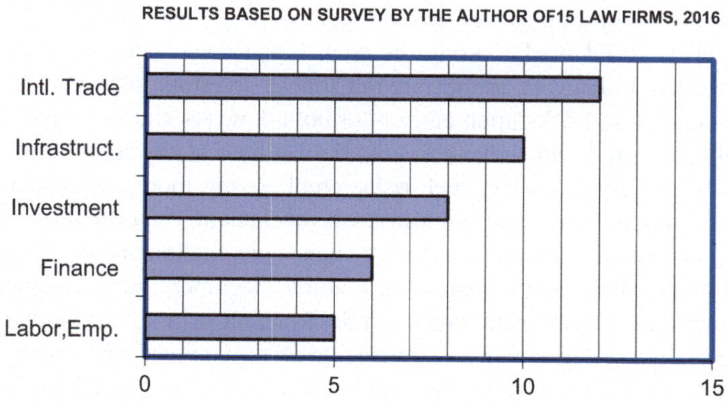

Fig. 2 Practice areas of future expected BR related demand

It is interesting however, to observe that current workload of law firms and practice areas differs in few instances if compared to future expectations of practice areas that would be of demand (see Fig. 2). Nearly all law firms, participating in the survey, regardless of their size and client base, place consensually investment, infrastructure, energy and mining, as well as international trade to be among the top five areas where clients will be and where clients base is to form, or experience further growth. While those practice areas offer a lot of opportunities, for smaller law firms, both Chinese domestic and international ones, of particular concern are the prospects to find multilingual legal professionals who can navigate Chinese businesses across two or more jurisdictions.

The two parallel routes, one maritime and the other overland, link Southeast Asia, Central Asia, Africa and Europe, and thus far they offer unique opportunities for participation in a number of ambitious and investment-intensive infrastructure projects: the China-Kazakhstan rail link, Western Europe- Western China Highway, the new dry ports built by Germany, Poland, and Belarus, or the Bangladesh-China-India-Myanmar economic corridor, the construction of Kra Canal in Thailand, Hambantota deep sea port in Sri Lanka, the Standard Gauge Railway (SGR) project in Nairobi and seaport in Mombasa, Kenya, etc.[26] Short term expectations also suggest that by opening of international economic corridors, the BRI is essentially a bonanza for cross-border and cross-industry ventures, with Chinese businesses and businesses from countries that are located along those corridors, to potentially generate substantial workloads for law firms and lawyers.[27]

The available financing under the $40 billion Silk Road Infrastructure Fund and Asian Infrastructure Investment Bank[28] (AIIB) available funds, and the wave of

[26]Roedl & Partner Law Firm (2016).

[27]The Author (16 November 2016). Personal interview.

[28]Aimed at supporting the building of infrastructure in the Asia-Pacific region, and following its Articles of Agreement entering into force in December, 2015, the Bank has 57 member states and it started operation in January, 2016.

outgoing Chinese investment are sources for keeping legal professionals further interested in the legal market along the New Silk Road. While new markets are equally attractive to lawyers, as they are to Chinese investors, such markets are also prone to volatility and risks upon entry—for both, lawyers and investors.

Several law firms,[29] which have a network of offices at key strategic cities along the BR, offer services to offset such risks, emphasizing more on the multifaceted cooperation opportunities and multifaceted investment opportunities, that may include but not remain limited to sectors such as: construction and civil engineering projects, transportation and logistics, agricultural machinery and equipment, Shipping and maritime, Ocean technology and desalination plants, biotech and pharma, renewable energy, environmental, tourism projects, conventional energy supply, agriculture, fisheries and forestry, textiles, coal and steel, engineering services, IT services and projects, consultancy and financial services, among others.

Based on data obtained through surveying law firms in 2016, there are combination of legal services, tax advisory services, auditing and business process outsourcing services provided by them to clients associated with the BRI that could be summarized as following:

Legal services: corporate law; international procurement law; incorporation of subsidiaries and representative offices; joint ventures; M&A; due diligence; mercantile, distribution and customs law; maritime; transportation and shipping law; investment protection; strategic sectors; foreign investment law and currency law; local employment law; assistance with arbitration proceedings, among others.

Tax advisory services: tax structuring; tax due diligence; tax planning for international group financing; M&A; transfer pricing; taxation of business premises locations; tax advice regarding the set-up of distribution structures and production operations, among others.

Audit services: statutory and voluntary audits of annual financial statements for companies or groups of companies of all legal forms; statutory or voluntary special audits, financial due diligence, company valuations.

Business Process Outsourcing and related services: on-going financial and payroll accounting; preparation of annual financial statements and reporting requirement, in compliance with national and international accounting standards; budget planning and audit; financial analysis, among others.

Law firms' long term expectations suggest that rising disputes due to being unfamiliar with local laws, regulations, culture and customs would be within high likelihood.[30] Affirmative of such expectations is ACLA as well, according to which more Chinese investors have expanded their business in recent years in the Belt and

[29] Among the law firms, contacted for the purpose of this study, Dentons, King & Wood Mallesons, Shearman & Sterling, Yingke law firm, Zhongyin Law Firm, Fangda Law Firm, and Orrick, Herrington & Sutcliffe LLP have increased their presence in countries from Central Asia and Middle East, or are in the process of establishing local partnerships. Compiling a guidebook and listing law firms and law offices along the New Silk Road is currently undertaken by the ACLA, as well as the SME Bureau of Ministry of Industry and Information Technology of the PR China.

[30] Zhang (2016).

Road countries or plan to do so, but many of their investments have failed due to a lack of knowledge about foreign laws and cultural differences.[31]

6 Expectations Related to Law Firms Outreach Activities and Marketing Strategies in Connection with the BRI

China's MOFCOM has been gradually pushing for cooperation between countries involved in the BRI. MOFCOM has been actively encouraging high value-added investments and improving information services and risk-control measures for businesses overseas.[32] Diplomatic efforts aimed at intensifying engagement with Central and South Asia in an effort to accelerate the realization of the New Silk Road, have been central to China's foreign policy as well. It remains very important however, to grasp and understand how the legal industry is gearing up for challenges in connection with the BRI.

Quite interestingly, the BRI has already brought changes to the legal services industry, and many of those changes bear a positive sign. One significant outcome of law firms facing Chinese government's initiative is their internationalization. In 2015, one of the largest Chinese law firms merged with Dentons, while FenXun made a joint venture with Baker & McKenzie. Shanghai-based firm Boss & Young has initiated an international alliance in a bid to seize new opportunities promised by China's BRI.[33] Smaller domestic firms are turning to internationalization by seeking partners from jurisdictions along the New Silk Road, while counterparts even from jurisdictions such as India, Pakistan, and Myanmar are being proactive in seeking partnerships with Chinese law firms.[34]

A multitude of law firms is currently engaged in variety of business development activities, in the opinion of a senior partner from a big international law firm, just as much as any car retailer in China is engaged with marketing its own cars.[35] This diversity is clearly acknowledged within the survey, employed in support of this study, according to which law firms are authentically connecting with potential clients, offering everything from regular reports and information campaigns, to client interface and sponsored ads and academic publications, as well as by actively seeking foreign cooperation (see Fig. 3 on Outreach Activities by Law Firms in Connection with the BRI). At the moment, a number of the larger law firms, including Baker & McKenzie and DLA Piper, have begun producing reports on One Belt One Road and related developments around China's comprehensive infrastructure development activities including the AIIB and the Silk Road initiative.

---

[31] Zhonghua Quanguo Lushi Xiehui (All China Lawyers Association—ACLA) (2016).

[32] Xinhua (2016).

[33] Boss & Young launched OBOR alliance to target Chinese development strategy. See e.g. Kriegler (2015).

[34] The Author (19 April 2016). Personal interview.

[35] The Author (22 November 2016). Personal interview.

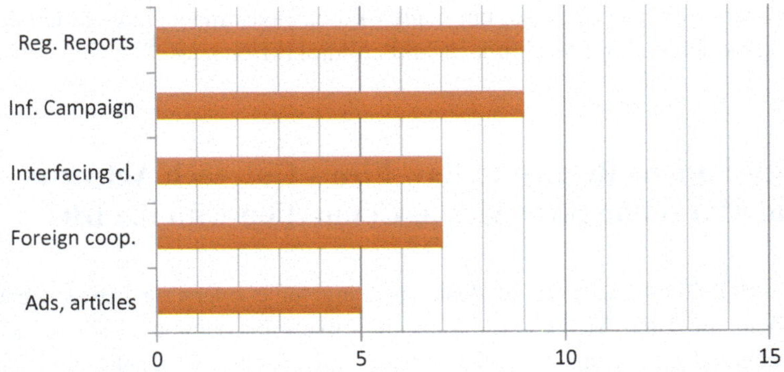

Fig. 3 Outreach activities by law firms in relation to the BRI. Results based on survey by the author of 15 law firms, 2016

Allen & Overy introduced its Peerpoint[36] as a signpost to a happier future for clients and contractors alike.[37] Herbert Smith Freehills recently worked with Baker Botts to help the Chinese Silk Road fund on a project,[38] while Junhe, Linklaters, Sherman & Sterling (in cooperation with a Pakistani firm Kabraji & Talibuddin) worked on substantial Pakistan wind power project financing.[39]

International cooperation is also intensifying, as more law firms in China are seeking for collaboration with legal professionals from other jurisdictions. Involved in one way or another with BR related matters, the Silk Road Fund, or the AIIB, that is the case for majority of Chinese law firms irrespectively of their size, as they pursue careful building of partnerships for the purpose of scaling up effectively provision of legal services to current and prospect future clients. Surveying law firms for the purpose of this chapter suggests, that nearly two thirds of law firms have sought or are planning to seek partnerships abroad, while the rest already possess network of their own local offices located at the key strategic hubs along the length of the Silk Road.[40] The latter group, consisting of predominantly big international law firms with local presence in China, and law firms based in Hong Kong, are better suited to provide not only the typical services law firms provide, but also navigate clients with full range of in-house consultancy services, and address questions regarding any legal, tax or commercial issues, thus potentially turning into a one-stop shop for clients.

[36]Challenging the traditional law firm model, Allen & Overy has launched recently the Peerpoint, which will allow the firm to augment its permanent workforce at times of high demand or when there is a need for particular specialist skills, while offering Peerpoint lawyers greater choice over when, where and how they work and the type of work they do. See Allen & Overy (2013).

[37]Michelmores Law Firm (2016).

[38]Along with the Prolegis law firm, this was a Silk Road Fund's 1.2 billion Russian LNG project, to which both Herbert Smith Freehills and Baker Botts took the lead.

[39]China Law & Practice Ceremony, attended on September 21, 2016 at the Park Hyatt, Beijing.

[40]Roedl & Partner Law Firm (2016).

When it comes to internationalization of legal services, one would generally assume international firms having distinct advantages over Chinese domestic law firms. In the context of creating opportunities and servicing Chinese clients within the BR, such assumption would not be correct. Along with the obvious linguistic and cultural proximities that prescribe a positive relationship between legal practitioners and clients, there are two factors bearing significance for domestic law firms and lawyers that foreign ones do not have. Firstly, Chinese domestic law firms and lawyers are within arm's length for the government to consult with, as domestic lawyers are members of law societies and legal professional associations, which are often tasked with providing advisory or with the expertise of which, governmental authorities put forward policy and legislative reforms. And secondly, particularly for the BR, it is domestic lawyers who are engaged in networks for legal services cooperation, and who provide intellectual support for drafting practical guidelines of how to invest or conduct business in BR jurisdictions, and who also provide trainings to government institutions and civil servants, to Chinese businessmen and investors. Deeply involved from the onset, Chinese domestic law firms and lawyers are indirectly setting standards, and thus, they are in best position to guide decision and policy makers, as well as clients, through the tumultuous times along the New Silk Road.

Compared to large foreign law firms, domestic law firms would often have different approaches for marketing legal services they offer, and for reaching to prospect clients. In September, 2016 Zhonglun Law Firm had 10 of its partners appointed to participate in co-authoring a "National and Regional Investment Law Practice Guide", that was a joint undertaking by the National Law Society, the Ministry of Justice, Ministry of Foreign Affairs, National Development and Reform Commission, and the MOFCOM. Soon after the Zhonglun Law Firm publicised that ten of its partners were in the talent pool of the National Bar Association,[41] that was tasked with drafting, there was increase in clients who opted for firm's legal services in relation to their investment undertakings. Chenyi Law Firm,[42] Duan & Duan Law Firm,[43] Tahota Law,[44] Tianhe Law Firm,[45] HIWAYS Law Firm,[46] and more have followed similar paths of engagement with the objective of reaching to prospect clients by participating in institutional collaborations.

In joint cooperation with the Supreme Court Judges Office and the Beijing Capital Lawyers College, the Jingshi Law Firm has held public lectures that involved judges, prosecutors, lawyers, legal scholars and media representatives to seek what opportunities for lawyers exist in connection with the BR.[47] As a result the law firm gained popularity and although it is not known whether client base has increased,

[41] Zhonglun Law Firm (2017).

[42] Chenyi Law Firm (2016).

[43] Duan & Duan Law Firm (2017).

[44] Tahota Lawyers (2017).

[45] Tianhe Law Firm (2017).

[46] Hiway Law Firm (2017).

[47] Jingshi Law Firm (2017).

one could contemplate that being successful in gathering at one place judges, prosecutors, lawyers, scholars and media is what contributes to law firms' visibility, and visibility of a firm is a major factor when clients make their choices.[48]

As in each country along the BR a client may face a set of distinct risks and challenges, and while the legal profession is not a craft of universal problem solving, there are matters that could not be addressed exclusively with help from lawyers—war conflicts and threats of terrorism, natural cataclysms and climate change, to name but a few. Yet, lawyers have a role to play in assisting clients to understand the multitude of macroeconomic and microeconomic risks, and everything from exchange rate volatilities and debt burdens, to economic and banking sector structures. Naturally, certain decisions lie with the client and some are solely within the discretion of the lawyer. Lawyers are the professionals, who could make the entry for Chinese and foreign enterprises smoother, by assisting such enterprises to understand the complex and varied laws, rules, and regulations shaping the business environment in each country.[49] Developing legal business along the BR is foreseeably not a quick process,[50] yet collaboration with local lawyers and law firms is essential for assisting clients on more rare but equally essential crisis management and exit strategies.

While professional ethics have drastically improved in China, the nature of the BR is such, that poses challenges to professional ethics and lawyers' conduct within the contexts of several developing countries along the New Silk Road, where the judiciary and the rule of law might still be in their infancy. One concern is that some lawyers might possibly go an extra mile for a Chinese client, and indirectly face situations where they are required to play an intermediary between local government officials and Chinese businesses. Lawyers from some jurisdictions might be surprised if they are told their colleagues in other jurisdictions are prepared to make illicit payments to government officials on behalf of businesses, with sole purpose of securing a project or an investment approval.[51] Collaboration within BR framework ensures that Chinese law firms and foreign law firms with presence in China, are able to export their sound anti-corruption practices in jurisdictions in which ethics might have been to some different standards.

Therefore, collaboration between law firms in the context of the BR has an added value to the overall Chinese strategy for exporting best practices to other developing countries. That is to suggest BRI offers opportunities for lawyers and law firms, while it also serves the purpose to extend best practices from where they already take place to jurisdictions within developing countries, which will be positively impacted by them.

---

[48]The Author (6 November 2016). Personal interview.

[49]The World Economic Forum (2016).

[50]The Author (20 April 2016). Personal interview.

[51]The Author (5 June 2016). Personal interview.

7 Expectations for Hong Kong SAR for Capitalizing on Opportunities, Arising Within BR Context

Interestingly, because of how has China been developing in the past two decades, a lot of Hong Kong investors, bankers, lawyers, engineers, construction and project managers, have grown as a generation of professionals, who can easily continue to perform what they have been doing during those years successfully—export their success models and expertise, while bring work that could be serviced by what all Hong Kong industries have to offer. That includes favorable policies on virtually everything from setting up an enterprise's corporate treasure center or their captive insurance company, all the way to receiving tax deductions and certain tax exemptions on profits. Hong Kong banking and financial services, shipping and logistics, the provision of administrative and legal services, all have the potential to meet a demand for talents in finance, tax, law, language and related professional services.

In 2015, Hong Kong's Chief Executive, Leung Chun-ying, has envisioned that Hong Kong should intensify its role as the "super-connector" linking the Chinese mainland and the rest of the world, and grasp the opportunity of the China's BRI to boost its economy.[52] Since 2015, in a series of efforts, Tsang Chun Wah, the Financial Secretary of Hong Kong, led several delegations to visit countries along the BR, starting with destinations within Central and Eastern Europe, and including further stops in the Middle East and Central Asia. Considering that all rival economies in the region are either taking part in the BR, or in multitude of smaller yet alternative economic initiatives, it is more of an imperative rather than a choice for Hong Kong to play a role.[53] As a modern, vibrant, and cosmopolitan center, Hong Kong is integral part of Chinese economy, and has a pivotal role in China's legal services industry as well.

As an international financial center and the legal service hub in Asia, Hong Kong is also an important city along the Maritime Silk Road in BRI, with potentiality acting as an international dispute resolution venue and a debt-issuing platform as a source of financing for the Asian Infrastructure Investment Bank.[54] The legal profession in Hong Kong is well experienced in serving multi-jurisdictional clients in complex cross-border matters, which in turn makes it a perfect place to receive the necessary support for the BR projects.[55] In turn, the New Silk Road initiative provides Hong Kong lawyers with an opportunity to build a lucrative client base, and extend already well developed legal services industry that businesses have enjoyed for decades in such a unique legal ecosystem.

Hong Kong's lawyers are not only adept at the details of both Chinese and Western laws, but also gaining deeper understanding of the legal systems and financing methods of Islamic countries, an important feature for BR's Middle

[52]Xinhua News (2016).

[53]The Author (5 June 2016). Personal interview.

[54]The Author (19 April 2016). Personal interview.

[55]Hung (2016).

Eastern dimension.[56] Furthermore, as Hong Kong's lawyers are bilingual, they are able to accurately analyse the different requirements of the contracting parties, and share their analyses with Chinese customers to help them make accurate judgements.[57] Relying on its current legal status and businesspeople being familiar with its administrative efficiency and order, complete procedural rules, and stringent by-the-book disposal of cases,[58] Hong Kong, courts and institutions can serve as a place for sound and fair dispute resolution.[59]

In 2015, China's Supreme People's Court (SPC) has promulgated an opinion on how the people's court may provide judicial services and protection on the Belt and Road Initiative.[60] The SPC has been clearly in support towards the use of international commercial and maritime arbitration for resolving cross-border disputes arising from the BRI. One way of supporting this objective has been the instruction that all foreign arbitral awards relating to the BR should be promptly recognized and enforced in accordance with the law. SPC has held that also bilateral and multilateral mutual legal assistance should be promoted, and it has been suggested reciprocal recognition and enforcement of judgments among different jurisdictions along the Belt and Road should be encouraged.[61] During the Hong Kong In-House Legal Summit in 2015, the Hong Kong Secretary of Justice announced his expectations towards ample opportunities to open to Hong Kong's legal and dispute resolution professionals under the BRI, emphasizing existing legal system and legal infrastructure as sources for secure and predictable environment, where fair competition for all businesses is taking place.[62]

One may substantiate the claim by Secretary of Justice, by looking at Hong Kong as the home to the Hong Kong International Arbitration Centre ("HKIAC"), one of the leading international arbitration institutions and a major center which employs highly efficient means for dispute resolution in Asia and globally. For reference, according to recently published data, the mean duration of an HKIAC arbitration is 12.25 months and the median duration is 11.60 months. The mean total costs of arbitration are US $65,721.26 and the median total costs of arbitration are US$31,704.04.[63]

So far, nearly all of the China-led AIIB's investments have been in partnership with other international investment funds, such as the Japan-led Asian Development Bank, the World Bank, and the European Bank for Reconstruction.[64] Both, legal and financial industries and professionals in Hong Kong have long assisted and provided advices to businesses and governments, and while AIIB is often seen as the financial hand of the BR, the experience of Hong Kong lawyers and bankers with the rest of

[56]The Author (9 September 2016). Personal interview.

[57]HKTDC Research (2016).

[58]Third party interview with Elsie Leung, Deputy Director of the HKSAR Basic Law Committee.

[59]Ibid.

[60]HKTDC Research (2016).

[61]Department of Justice, Hong Kong SAR (2015).

[62]Ibid.

[63]Hong Kong International Arbitration Centre (2016).

[64]Forbes (2016).

world banking institutions somewhat naturally relates to and demands for their expertise on related transactions. In connection to this, Elsie Leung, Deputy Director of the HKSAR Basic Law Committee has recently stated, it depends on law firms and lawyers to be proactive and seek opportunities,[65] as opportunities do not often come by chances, at least not in the legal services industry.

8 Conclusion and Outlook

The BRI has clearly started to redefine and redesign the economic architecture of regions across three continents. It proves it is not just Chinese or made for China, as in all its nature it is bigger than China, it is global, and it is international and encompassing. While there are many factors that so far have had and will continue to have positive impact for the successful course of the initiative, the legal services industry with law firms and lawyers at hand, is the one that mutually benefits from and is beneficial to the BRI.

It is important to understand the expectations of legal services industry and practitioners, so to better project what expertise shall be developed, how to better serve the changing client base within rapidly changing jurisdictional environments, how to better market legal services and channel legal innovation. The importance of grasping and understanding how the legal industry is gearing up for challenges in connection with the BRI is as crucial, as crucial is every act of Chinese government policy or legislative support for further developing its legal services industry and strengthening the rule of law.

As in each jurisdiction along the BR a client may face a set of distinct risks and challenges, collaboration between law firms in the context of the initiative has an added value for China's export of best practices to other developing countries. Foreign law firms, in the Mainland and in Hong Kong, although some still facing regulatory hurdles in respect of their business and operations, are able to maximize on opportunities that originate from the BRI. An increase of value is also seen by domestic law firms, as multitude of Chinese law firms are now going global, taking on autonomous and independent paths, or alternatively entering into mergers or concluding powerful alliances with larger international firms. This irreversibly changes the legal services industry landscape, and for the better, creates more open, more global, and more competitive legal environment in which there are increasing opportunities for law firms and lawyers.

In terms of expectations, associated with the BRI, clearly there are practice areas of high demand and potential future demand. In short to medium term, those areas include international trade, infrastructure development, energy and mining, investment and corporate, finance, banking and capital markets, labor and employment, and dispute resolution. In longer term, investment, infrastructure, energy and

[65] Hong Kong Trade Development Council (2016).

mining, as well as international trade will remain important, as equally workflow will be linked to maritime, transportation and shipping law, joint ventures, as well as assistance with arbitration proceedings and other forms of dispute resolution, and multidimensional legal consultancy. To this end, the synergy between legal services industry and practitioners on the one side, and government institutions, policies and support on the other, will be the key condition for solidifying and materializing short to medium, and longer term expectations in connection with the BRI.

Acknowledgements The author would like to thank Professor Mingyuan Wang, Director of The Center for Environmental, Natural Resources & Energy Law, Tsinghua University (THCEREL), for the advice, support and guidance throughout this research. The author is much appreciative to his colleagues Roger Jiang and Yueling Liu from the Legal & Risk Control Department of Country Garden Overseas Division, who offered extraordinarily helpful criticism. The author is especially grateful to the Fortum Foundation, Finland for its continuous support and patronage.

Appendix 1

List of all 65 counties (following geographical principle), involved in the BRI:

East Asia: Mongolia, Singapore, Malaysia, Indonesia, Myanmar, Thailand, Laos, Cambodia, Vietnam, Brunei, Philippines
West Asia: Iran, Iraq, Turkey, Syria, Jordan, Lebanon, Israel, Palestine, Saudi Arabia, Yemen, Oman, UAE, Qatar, Kuwait, Bahrain, Greece, Cyprus, Egypt
South Asia: India, Pakistan, Bangladesh, Afghanistan, Sri Lanka, Maldives, Nepal, Bhutan
Middle Asia: Kazakhstan, Uzbekistan, Turkmenistan, Tajikistan, Kyrgyzstan
CIS: Russia, Ukraine, Belarus, Georgia, Azerbaijan, Armenia, Moldova
Mid-East Europe: Poland, Lithuania, Estonia, Latvia, Czech Republic, Slovakia, Hungary, Slovenia, Croatia, Bosnia & Herzegovina, Montenegro, Serbia, Albania, Romania, Bulgaria, Macedonia

Appendix 2

List of Law firms, from which lawyers were interviewed, or questionnaire responses were received:

(Three of the largest foreign law firms with presence in China)

Dentons (For the purpose of the survey, Dentons has been considered as one of the largest foreign law firms with presence in China, although in 2015, Dacheng, one of the largest Chinese law firms merged with Dentons.)
King & Wood Mallesons
Shearman & Sterling

(Three of the largest domestic law firms)

Yingke Law Firm
Zhong Yin Law Firm
Fangda Law Firm

(Three of the relatively small foreign law firms with presence in China)

Sidley Austin LLP
Proskauer Rose LLP
Orrick, Herrington & Sutcliffe LLP

(Three small domestic law firms)

Guantao Law Firm
Hou & Cheng Law Firm
Beijing Ruizhong Law Firm

(Hong Kong SAR based firms)

Latham & Watkins LLP
White & Case
Woo Kwan Lee & Lo

Appendix 3

Excerpt of sample questions, which were part of the survey questionnaire, or asked during in-person interviews with lawyers, for the purpose of current study:

- In your opinion, what exactly is One Belt, One Road?
- Have your legal professionals/colleagues underwent OBOR specific training?
- In your opinion, how a domestic law firm could ensure it has the multijurisdictional capacity to provide clients with the legal services they need in each jurisdiction all along the New Silk Road?
- Funding and financing are among the big challenges, associated with the OBOR. Have you provided/Are you providing legal services to any client of The Asian Infrastructure Investment Bank (AIIB), or in relation to the AIIB?
- Investing in emerging markets carries certain risks. Have you provided/Are you providing legal services to any client who is investing in infrastructure within any of the OBOR countries? (if yes, can you talk about the scale)
- In your opinion, is there a role for your law firm to play within the OBOR Initiative? And what is the scale of projects you aim to be involved at? (addressed exclusively to small international and domestic law firms in China)
- The Silk Road Fund has already came into being. Have you provided/Are you providing legal services to any client of the Fund, or in relation to the Fund? (addressed exclusively to large international and domestic law firms in China)

- Within the context of the OBOR Initiative, what do you think are the advantages that your firm could enjoy, and what do you think the opportunities are for your firm and colleagues?
- Have you conducted any marketing event/info session/client briefing on OBOR Initiative related subject? How often?
- In your opinion, what is the role Hong Kong has to play within the OBOR initiative?
- Is there anything different you do for Chinese clients, that you do not do so often for non-Chinese clients?
- What do you consider was your OBOR related client(s) selection criteria for choosing you as their counsel?
- What are the practice areas, which are/would be of highest demand by clients, with regard to the OBOR Initiative and related projects?

References

Allen & Overy. (2013, November 25). *Allen & Overy launches Peerpoint - a global flexible resourcing business*. Retrieved November 26, 2016, from http://www.allenovery.com/news/en-gb/articles/Pages/Allen--Overy-launches-Peerpoint.aspx

Chenyi Law Firm. (2016). Retrieved February 8, 2017, from http://chenyilaw.com/news/html/?507.html

China Daily. (2015). *What are China's five-year plans?* Retrieved December 18, 2017, from http://www.chinadaily.com.cn/china/2015cpcplenarysession/2015-10/29/content_22311061.htm

Department of Justice, Hong Kong SAR. (2015). *Keynote Speech by Mr Rimsky Yuen, SC, JP, Secretary for Justice at the ALB Hong Kong In-House Legal Summit 2015: Opportunities and challenges for lawyers under the Mainland's "Belt and Road Initiative"*. Retrieved December 18, 2016, from http://www.doj.gov.hk/eng/public/pdf/2015/sj20150922e.pdf

Duan & Duan Law Firm. (2017). Retrieved February 8, 2017, from http://www.duanduan.com/index.php/default/content/10712.html

Forbes. (2016). *The New Silk Road Is Not Chinese, It's International.* Retrieved October 15, 2016, from http://www.forbes.com/sites/wadeshepard/2016/10/14/regardless-of-what-beijing-says-the-new-silk-road-is-not-chinese/#6213706b7289

Guanyu fazhan shewai falu fuwu ye de yijian (Opinions on the development of foreign-related legal services). (2017). *Ministry of Justice of PRC*. Retrieved January 25, 2017, from http://www.moj.gov.cn/index/content/2017-01/09/content_6946567.htm

Hiway Law Firm. (2017). Retrieved February 8, 2017, from http://www.hiwayslaw.com/info/c3cc86e0c36848748855cea95bc387c7

HK can be "super-connector" in China-ASEAN collaboration: HK chief executive. (2016). *Xinhua News*. Retrieved December 12, 2016, from http://news.xinhuanet.com/english/2015-12/14/c_134915077.htm

HKTDC Research. (2016). Retrieved September 19, 2016, from http://beltandroad.hktdc.com/en/market-analyses/details.aspx?ID=475955

Hong Kong International Arbitration Centre. (2016). Retrieved November 19, 2016, from http://hkiac.org/content/costs-duration

Hong Kong Trade Development Council. (2016). Retrieved December 21, 2016, from http://beltandroad.hktdc.com/en/market-analyses/details.aspx?ID=475955

http://www.roedl.com/fileadmin/user_upload/Documents/Publikationen/china-new-silk-road-roedl-partner-brochure-en.pdf. Retrieved December 28, 2016.

Hung, S. (2016). *One Belt, One Road*. The Law Society of Hong Kong. Retrieved December 21, 2016, from http://www.hk-lawyer.org/content/one-belt-one-road

Janzek, T., & Ziherl, P. (2012, August 28–29). *Proceedings of the sixth IFC conference on statistical issues and activities in a changing environment* (Vol. 36, pp. 172–179). Basel.

Kennedy, S. (2015). *Building China's "One Belt, One Road"*. Center for Strategic and International Studies. Retrieved October 20, 2016, from https://www.csis.org/analysis/building-china%E2%80%99s-%E2%80%9Cone-belt-one-road%E2%80%9D

Keynes, J. M. (2008). *The general theory*. New York: BN Publishing.

Kriegler, Y. (2015, June 18). *Boss & Young launched OBOR alliance to target Chinese development strategy*. The Lawyer. Retrieved December 15, 2016, from https://www.thelawyer.com/issues/online-june-2015/boss-young-launches-obor-alliance-to-target-chinese-development-strategy/

Michelmores Law Firm. (2016). *East Meets West: The team at Michelmores on how helping out a Chinese firm is also helping them*. Michelmores Law Firm. Retrieved December 14, 2016, from http://www.michelmores.com/sites/default/files/Briefing_June16_Michelmores.pdf

Mingkang, L. (2016, January 18). *The challenges and opportunities of China's new Silk Road*. The World Economic Forum. Retrieved December 26, 2016, from https://www.weforum.org/agenda/2016/01/the-challenges-and-opportunities-of-china-s-new-silk-road

Opinions on Developing the Sector of Legal Services for Foreign Affairs Issued. (2017). *LexisNexis*. Retrieved January 28, 2017, from https://hk.lexiscn.com/latest_message.php?access=show_detail&id=208189

Roedl & Partner Law Firm. (2016). Retrieved September 9, 2016, from http://www.roedl.com/fileadmin/user_upload/Documents/Publikationen/china-new-silk-road-roedl-partner-brochure-en.pdf

Statistics on Chinese Investment Abroad. (2015). *The Business Insider*. Retrieved December 12, 2016, from http://www.businessinsider.com/statistics-on-chinas-investment-abroad-2015-2

Taddia, M. (2013). *China: A tough market to penetrate*. Via The Law Society Gazette. Retrieved November 18, 2016, from https://www.lawgazette.co.uk/practice/china-a-tough-market-to-penetrate/5038107.article

Tahota Lawyers. (2017). Retrieved February 7, 2017, from http://www.tahota-lawyer.com/cn/news_info.php?id=2142&pid=471&cid=476

Third party interview with Elsie Leung, Deputy Director of the HKSAR Basic Law Committee. Retrieved November 19, 2016, from http://beltandroad.hktdc.com/en/market-analyses/details.aspx?ID=475955

Tianhe Law Firm. (2017). Retrieved February 7, 2017, from http://www.tianhelaw.cn/news_display.asp?Newid=316

Wade, S. (2016). *The New Silk Road Is Not Chinese, It's International*. Available via Forbes. Retrieved November 15, 2016, from http://www.forbes.com/sites/wadeshepard/2016/10/14/regardless-of-what-beijing-says-the-new-silk-road-is-not-chinese/#6213706b7289

Xinhua. (2016). *Interview with Zhou Zhencheng, director of the MOFCOM's Department of Outward Investment and Economic Cooperation*. Retrieved December 15, 2016, from http://www.out-law.com/en/articles/2015/december/new-chinese-policies-to-encourage-firms-to-expand-internationally-/

Yidai yilu Zhong xun lushi jiyu- di si qi zuigao fayuan faguan xilie gongyi jiangzuo zai jingshi lushi shiwu suo chixu juxin (Seeking opportunities for lawyers within the OBOR – The Fourth Supreme Court Judges Series of Public Lectures Held at Jingshi Law Firm). (2017). *Jingshi Law Firm*. Retrieved February 12, 2017, from http://www.jingsh.com/Institute/TrainContent/3

Zhang, Y. (2016). *Legal Links to Sprout on Silk Road*. Available via China Daily. Retrieved December 18, 2017, from http://africa.chinadaily.com.cn/business/2016-10/08/content_26984464.htm

Zhong lun 10 wei hehuo ren ruxuan "yidai yilu" xiangmu kua jing jushi rencai ku bing canyu zhongguo lushi fuwu "yidai yilu" zhanlue jianshe xiangmu (10 Partners of Zhonglun Law Firm have been selected for the One Belt One Road cross-border lawyers talent pool, to provide OBOR strategic legal support). (2017). *Zhonglun Law Firm*. Retrieved January 25, 2017, from http://www.zhonglun.com/Content/2016/09-20/1834290322.html

Zhonghua Quanguo Lushi Xiehui (All China Lawyers Association - ACLA). (2016). Retrieved December 28, 2016, from http://www.acla.org.cn/html/xinwen/20161228/27204.html

Epilogue

Kimmo Nuotio

China is increasingly aware of the role and potential it can have to influence the world development. This has led it to reconsider and develop foreign policies, the Belt and Road Initiative (BRI) being a new flagship of them. The economic tone in China's foreign policy has given it a soft flavor.

China's BRI, which covers both 'the Silk Road Economic Belt' and 'the 21st Century Maritime Silk Road', has in just a few years' time grown to be much more than just an initiative. In addition, it is a work in progress. In a policy paper on the Arctic, the concept of 'the Polar Silk Road' was introduced in January 2018.[1]

As discussed by Anastas Vangeli, in 2017 president Xi Jinping's thought won a formal position since it was included in the Chinese constitution which means that China is firmly set to promote this projects as part of its official policy.[2] Kangle Zhang, in turn, refers to the BRI as part of China's global strategy.[3]

The Initiative comes first and foremost down to trade agreements and huge infrastructure projects[4] made possible by Chinese investment abroad.[5] Even though

[1]China's Arctic Policy. Published by the State Council Information Office of the People's Republic of China. http://english.gov.cn/archive/white_paper/2018/01/26/content_281476026660336.htm.

[2]Vangeli, Anastas, Shared Destiny, Sovereignty, State-led Economics, Connectivity and Flexibility, in this volume.

[3]Zhang, Kangle, A Tale of Ending Poverty: The new financial institutions and China's global strategy, in this volume.

[4]Desheng Hu, Jun Ou and Xueyue discuss the environmental aspects of FDI projects in the article On Environmental Responsibility of Chinese Enterprises for Their FDIs in Countries within the One Belt and One Road Initiative, in this volume. Kangle Zhang discusses the financial aspects of the projects, see the article mentioned in fn 3. Shu Zhang discusses the Investor State Arbitration clause in the article Developing China's Investor-State Arbitration Clause: Discussions in the Context of the "Belt and Road" Initiative, in this volume.

[5]Bath (2016).

K. Nuotio (✉)
University of Helsinki, Helsinki, Finland

W. Shan et al. (eds.), *Normative Readings of the Belt and Road Initiative*,
https://doi.org/10.1007/978-3-319-78018-4_12

the Initiative as such is not aiming to export law, its success will obviously be dependent on legal matters as well.[6] Economic co-operation needs to be legally regulated, and eventual legal disputes will have to be solved. New legal frameworks will have to be created.

The Visions and Actions document,[7] which has a formal status, tells about the level of ambition of the BRI. The Initiative upholds the famous five Principles of Peaceful Coexistence.[8] It is harmonious and inclusive, it respects the paths and modes of development chosen by different countries. It follows market operation as it gives the market the decisive role in resource allocation; it will give a primary role to the enterprises instead of governments.

The cooperation priorities themselves are five: policy coordination, facilities connectivity, unimpeded trade, financial integration and people-to-people bond. Even though much of the Initiative concerns economic development, the underlying tone tells that the true purpose goes much beyond that.

BRI is a fluid and flexible Initiative in the sense that it would be difficult to define it conceptually. Zeng Lingliang has described it as a 'new formula of global governance'. The aim of the Initiative is also to contribute to an awareness of a common destiny of people. The people-to-people bond namely aims at creating support; it 'is a project of transnational public feelings and support of the Initiative'.[9] The role of the cultural level collaboration was extensively discussed above in the article by Guilherme Vasconcelos Vila⍰a.[10]

The current trends in world order and global governance, with the U.S. turning more away from international arrangements, make the BRI both practically and theoretically an interesting approach to societal and economic development. It is an alternative approach, since it does not rely on the Western models (even though, in fact, it of course needs to make use of existing legal tools) and values.[11]

[6]Xiao Yongping and Meng Yu discuss the international credibility of Chinese courts in Some Suggestions for Improving the International Credibility of the Chinese judiciary: A Focus on the OBORI, in this volume. See also Tommy Yu, China's "One Belt, One Road Initiative": What's in it for Law firms and lawyers?, in this volume.

[7]Visions and Actions on Jointly Building Silk Road Economic Belt and 21st Century Maritime Silk Road. 2015/03/28, Issued by the National Development and Reform Commission, Ministry of Foreign Affairs, and Ministry of Commerce of the People's Republic of China, with State Council authorization. Available on-line.

[8]On the five principles, see Chi He, The Belt and Road Initiative as a Global Public Good: Implications for Public International Law, in this volume.

[9]Lingliang (2016), p. 527 and 540.

[10]Vila⍰a, Guilherme Vasconcelos, Strengthening the Cultural and Normative Foundations of the Belt and Road Initiative: The Colombo Plan, Yan Xuetong and Chinese Ancient Thought, in this volume.

[11]Nicholas Morris on developing a sustainable legal system on the basis of traditional Chinese Philosophy, see his Developing A Sustainable Legal System for the Belt and Road Initiative, in this volume.

At least at first sight, the Initiative comes in some sense close to the United Nation's Sustainable Development Goals for the year 2030, adopted in 2015.[12] The Initiative sets goals, but it lets countries, states and peoples to incorporate them and thus find ways to achieve them. The Initiative makes no direct reference to the UN goals, however.

The Initiative is inclusive and open for any country to join. This is also one aspect which renders it different from existing economic or regional forms of collaboration which tend to be predefined in terms of participation and membership.

The BRI has obvious geopolitical connotations. It is a China-driven initiative as China invites States and entire regions to join it. The formulations follow the global governance style and use rather soft tones of popular participation and even give a role to non-state actors, including NGO's, to support the Initiative.

Teemu Ruskola has written about Legal Orientalism, claiming that the Orient has played the role of the "Other" for the US and for the Western legal tradition.[13] For this reason, it has been so difficult to approach Chinese law, since the westerners have continuously looked at the Orient through their Western lenses.

The BRI is a fresh example of how the Orient pushes itself forward. Through BRI the state actors and others seek to create new models of collaboration which would not be built on traditional Western values. The BRI introduces investment to areas that would not otherwise attract them. It is a state-backed and state-steered initiative, meant to mobilize both public and private actors.

The BRI means that China shares its resources with the New Silk Road countries, but this will happen at the cost of becoming bound in a common destiny. Invisible ties evolve which will increase the significance of Chinese interests in faraway regions. But, in the final instance, we all share the destiny of mankind.[14]

The power-balance, or rather power-imbalance, does not have to mean the China should be looked at a new colonizing power. This is, most certainly, the image that China would like to avoid at any cost. But the fact is that interdependencies will follow which will tie entire regions more closely with China's destiny.

President Xi emphasized in a speech given in Astana in 2013 that China does not aim at domination of regions and that it would respect different development paths and domestic and foreign policies pursued independently by every country. At the same time China, both bilaterally and in the Shanghai Cooperation Organization (SCO), seeks partnership to combat terrorism, separatism and extremism as well as drug trafficking and organized transnational crime. This will, says Xi, 'create a favorable environment for promoting economic development and improving the

[12]http://www.un.org/sustainabledevelopment/ Accessed 8 January 2018.

[13]Ruskola (2013).

[14]Understandably, the Polar Silk Road and the policy on Arctic, highlights the shared destiny aspects. See, the document referred to in fn 1.

well-being of the people in this region'.[15] The new institutions, such as the AIIB, are instrumental as well.[16]

The SCO, which originally only consisted of China and the four Central Asian states, seems to be an important vehicle to drive the agenda further. The SCO has broadened its influence, and at the same time China is no longer the only dominant power present. SCO's values do not include democracy, and it is rather an authoritarian organization as regards its organizational structure. The SCO is advocating a multipolar world and it aims at preserving the status quo in the region. The struggle against "the three evils", terrorism, separatism and extremism, is directly linked with the aim to combat all destabilizing factors.[17] The implementation of Silk Road Economic Belt might transform the SCO into one of deep economic collaboration, a Silk Road Union which would be based on association between the SCO and the Eurasian Alliance.[18]

In terms of values, the SCO is very different from the European Union, for instance. But for both, certain evils matter. In the case of the European Union, now conceived also as an Area of Freedom, Security and Justice, issues of terrorism and cross-border organized crime have meant a large scale of measures agreed on the basis of the articles included in the treaty framework. Combatting security threats may often serve common interests. Also BRI will face the issue that increased economic collaboration will create more cross-border criminality.[19]

The creation of the internal market of the European Union has been a project in which the law has played very crucial role. Not just combating international terrorism and cross-border organize crime have been the drivers on the internal security front, but all this has been balanced with an emphasis on human rights, including fair trial, and rule of law; the core values that were set to render this project possible.

Should BRI develop a transnational criminal law for itself, we should be mindful of that transnational criminal law assumes rather than develops rule of law framework.[20] Rule of law does not follow automatically.

For a western observer, the crucial issue is, in fact, will it be possible to achieve real development in societies by means of increased trade and investment only, without concerns about the quality of rule of law, or even with a conscious disregard of the rights of the individual.

The Western view has been that by improving the rule of law, the economic prosperity can be increased since this attracts investment and also increases fairness in the distribution of the economic benefits. Anti-corruption measures are important

[15]Xi (2014), p. 317.

[16]On the financial aspect of AIIB, see Kangle Zhang, above fn 3, in this volume. On the environmental clause of the AIIB, see Brombal, Daniele, Planning for a Sustainable OBOR: An appraisal of the AIIB environmental and social safeguards, in this volume.

[17]Kembayev (2016), pp. 691–699.

[18]Ibid., p. 699.

[19]Sprick (2016).

[20]Boister (2012), p. 278.

since the market lives out of trust to the predictability of legal rules, and corruption tends to bend them.

The Belt and Road (BR) concept seems to work the other way round. Investment in infrastructures, such as roads and bridges, introduces new connections which again lead to increased economic activities. The BR repeats in some sense the old Silk Road spirit of trusting in connections. Linking markets with each other is expected to lead to positive outcomes even when the traditional human rights and rule of law will be set aside. Connectivity has been said to be the most revolutionary force of the twenty-first century.[21]

This is not to say that the rule of law matters would have disappeared, rather the contrary. Improving the Chinese legal system towards a 'rule of law with Chinese characteristics' has been one of the core ambitions of China under Xi Jinping. The Chinese discussion concerning what is the Chinese concept of rule of law is vivid, and the nuances are many. China is aiming at building a rule of law system, which will require profound changes, but it seems equally clear, that the Chinese concept of rule of law will continue be different form its Western counterparts.[22] The scholarly debates, however, flourish and cover a variety of approaches.[23]

The BRI does of course not mean that the Chinese concept of rule of law would become immediately significant for BR participating states, since the (equally Chinese) principle of harmonious co-existence leaves the legal and political systems of those countries out of the legitimate scope of influence of China. The main concern and interest is, surely, to protect the (Chinese) investment legally, and to ensure other BR objectives.

I believe it will continue to be important to discuss the significance of BRI for the development of legal culture or cultures, even if many of things are not yet in place. A Non-Western regional legal development seems to be underway, one that places priorities in another order than the West would have done.

This is not necessarily a bad thing. Regional legal cooperation works like this. And there will always be many roads for the legal development to take. But the risk seems obvious that a project of introducing investment and facilitating growth in regions which do not have a good record in governance so far may end up creating less added value than expected to the less well-off people.

An indirect effect of BR, when it really gets running, will be the increased significance of knowing China, of knowing about China's political and legal developments. Chinese law will become a natural point of reference for all concerned. The people-to-people policies of China will further contribute to this by increasing the individual level contacts and mobility, also including academic exchange.

The times of a Western view at the Orient are long gone. The Orient presents itself against its own premises and on its own right. Law is a public good and legal

[21]Khanna (2016).

[22]See, e.g., Lin (2017).

[23]Seppänen (2014).

developments deserve to be looked at with a critical eye, both from inside and outside. Globalisation and common destiny binds us all together.

We already mentioned about the SCO and the rather authoritarian view about states. Also, as regards the BR, the people-to-people bond seems not to mean any concession as regards democratic participation or introducing of human rights. The emphasis on economic cooperation with a conscious abandonment of human rights may even hide a policy to downgrade the international human rights law since it is being looked at as a Western idea which should therefore be rejected.[24]

It might, in any case, still be important for the BR participating countries to continue working on issues of public law and legal reform and development beyond or parallel to the project of BR. Good and transparent administration, for instance, is almost inevitable for reaching the goal of better services for the people, not to mention environmental protection. Ending poverty requires impartial and rule-based government. Otherwise the benefits of trade and investment risk ending up in the hands of the local elites.[25]

Promoting economic development entails a promise. Nothing prevents the individual participating countries still to complement the BR with other development projects which would help them solve such internal problems which hinder economic as well as societal development, including the strengthening of the rule of law and the protection of the rights of the individual.

It might only be logical that, as the BRI does not aim to intervene in national politics of other countries, that the participating countries will themselves take responsibility of adjusting to the new models of global governance for the benefit of their people. Labor rights standards might, to give an example, deserve attention.

The construction of the legal frameworks for cooperation under the BRI will require that the Chinese courts will be better served in terms of knowledge about foreign role. Xiao and Yu suggest that China should establish a national centre for discerning foreign law.[26] Increasing trust will require opening up, and recognition and enforcement of foreign judgements.

Soft power is fluid, and sometimes it may be difficult to see where it comes from. Anu Bradford has presented the rather interesting argument that the European Union has global power since it is a regulator which is able to introduce legal standards that simply become global standards by the force of global markets. The EU has the advantage of being a market large enough as well as having a regulatory capacity and the willingness to use it. As a results the EU regulations gain significance much beyond European borders. This is the so-called Brussels Effect.[27] Bradford discusses a.o. regulation of the use of chemicals, setting standards of environmental protection, and food safety regulation as examples.

[24]See the discussion in Ahl (2016).

[25]See the discussion by Kangle Zhang, in this volume.

[26]See, above, the article mentioned in fn 6, in this volume.

[27]Bradford (2012).

Should we accept that thesis, we might say that the BRI will not easily be able to do away with this part of soft European power. But with increased growth of Chinese and Asian markets, the Brussels Effect might be challenged, in the long run: 'It will be a while before China could replace the EU as a source of de facto global standards.'[28] And why should BRI of China seek to do away this soft power, if the system works well?

It is much too early to judge the potential of BRI in terms of transnational legal development. It seems also clear that the BRI consciously seeks new avenues of legal development rather than replicates existing ones. If the BRI develops structures and patterns and communications that deserve to be called transnational law, something qualitatively new will come into being.

Even though European Union law, or US Law, for that matter, will not be models in this work and even though the values informing this legal development will be different, the theoretical tools for analyzing transnational law developed in the West may still be helpful in terms of making sense this new type of transnational law.[29] Together with new lines of legal communications across boundaries of legal orders, new things emerge.

References

Ahl, B. (2016, August 25). China's new global presence and its position towards public international law: Obeying, using or shaping? In L. Wolff & X. Chao (Eds.), *Legal dimensions of China's Belt and Road initiative* (pp. 481–505). Hong Kong: Wolters Kluwer. Retrieved from SSRN: https://ssrn.com/abstract=2830199

Bath, V. (2016, November). 'One Belt, One Road' and Chinese investment. In C. Xi, & L.-C. Wolff (Eds.), *Legal dimensions of China's Belt and Road initiative*. Hong Kong: Wolters Kluwer. Sydney Law School Research Paper No. 16/98. Retrieved from SSRN: https://ssrn.com/abstract=2866169

Boister, N. (2012). *An introduction to transnational criminal law*. Oxford: OUP.

Bradford, A. (2012). The Brussels effect. *Northwestern University Law Review, 107*(1), 1–67.

China's Arctic Policy. The State Council Information Office of the People's Republic of China. http://english.gov.cn/archive/white_paper/2018/01/26/content_281476026660336.htm

Kembayev, Z. (2016). Letter to the editors: Towards a silk road union? *Chinese Journal of International Law, 15*(3), 691–699.

Khanna, P. (2016). *Connectography: Mapping the future of global civilization*. New York: Random House.

Lin, L. (2017). *Building the rule of law in China*. Kidlington: Social Science Academic Press/ Chandos Publishing.

Lingliang, Z. (2016). Conceptual analysis of China's Belt and Road initiative: A Road towards a regional community of common destiny. *Chinese Journal of International Law, 15*, 517–541.

Maduro, M., Tuori, K., & Sankari, S. (Eds.). (2014). *Transnational law. Rethinking European law and legal thinking*. Cambridge: Cambridge University Press.

[28]*Ibid.*, p. 49.

[29]See, for instance, various chapters in the book Transnational Law. Maduro et al. (2014).

Ruskola, T. (2013). *Legal orientalism: China, The United States, and modern law*. Cambridge, MA: Harvard University Press.

Seppänen, S. (2014). Ideological renewal and Nostalgia in China's 'Avant-Garde' legal scholarship. *Washington University Global Studies Law Review, 13*(1). Retrieved from SSRN: https://ssrn.com/abstract=2653090

Sprick, D. (2016, July 12). One Belt, One Road: Many Routes for transnational crime and its suppression in China. In L. Wolff & X. Chao (Eds.), *Legal dimensions of China's Belt and Road initiative*. Hong Kong: Wolters Kluwer. Retrieved from SSRN: https://ssrn.com/abstract=2924453 or https://doi.org/10.2139/ssrn.2924453

Visions and Actions on Jointly Building Silk Road Economic Belt and 21st Century Maritime Silk Road. (2015, March 28). The National Development and Reform Commission, Ministry of Foreign Affairs, and Ministry of Commerce of the People's Republic of China, with State Council authorization. Available on-line.

Xi, J. (2014). *The governance of China*. Beijing: Foreign Languages Press.

The manufacturer's authorised representative in the EU is Springer Nature Customer Service Centre GmbH, Europaplatz 3, 69115 Heidelberg, Germany. If you have any concerns regarding our products, please contact ProductSafety@springernature.com

Printed and bound by CPI Group (UK) Ltd, Croydon, CR0 4YY
05/10/2026
02228138-0009